INTERNET DENIAL OF SERV

The Radia Perlman Series in Computer Networking and Security

Radia Perlman, Series Editor

INTERNET DENIAL OF SERVICE

Attack and Defense Mechanisms

Jelena Mirkovic

Sven Dietrich

David Dittrich

Peter Reiher

PRENTICE
HALL
PTR   Prentice Hall Professional Technical Reference

Upper Saddle River, NJ • Boston • Indianapolis • San Francisco • New York
Toronto • Montreal • London • Munich • Paris • Madrid • Capetown
Sydney • Tokyo • Singapore • Mexico City

The publisher offers excellent discounts on this book when ordered in quantity for bulk purchases or special sales, which may include electronic versions and/or custom covers and content particular to your business, training goals, marketing focus, and branding interests. For more information, please contact:

U. S. Corporate and Government Sales
(800) 382-3419
corpsales@pearsontechgroup.com

For sales outside the U. S., please contact:

International Sales
international@pearsoned.com

Visit us on the Web: www.phptr.com

Library of Congress Cataloging-in-Publication Data:

Internet denial of service : attack and defense mechanisms / Jelena Mirkovic, Sven Dietrich,
    David Dittrich, and Peter Reiher.
        p. cm.
    Includes bibliographical references and index.
    ISBN 0-13-147573-8 (pbk. : alk. paper)
    1. Computer networks—Security measures.   2. Internet—Security measures.   3. Computer crimes—
Prevention.   I. Mirkovic, Jelena.
    TK5105.59.I5455 2004
    005.8—dc22   2004020335

ISBN 0-13-147573-8
Text printed in the United States on recycled paper at Courier in Stoughton, Massachusetts.
First printing, December 2004

Contents

Foreword

Society is getting to be more and more dependent on the reliability of the Internet. Businesses are relying on the Internet as their link to their customers. Customers are being encouraged to do most of their business in the Internet.

It is not enough to protect your communication from eavesdroppers, or to protect your own system from being infected with viruses. Traditionally, the security community has focused its attention on unauthorized disclosure or modification of information, and perhaps theft of services. Denial of service was largely ignored as being unlikely to occur because the attacker would not gain anything from such an attack.

Clearly this is not the case today. Denial of service can be a devastating attack. It can put merchants out of business and can cause major and very visible disruption to our world. It can be (and is) used against specific companies for which the attacker has a grudge or has been paid to attack; or it can be used by terrorists to cause major disruption to critical infrastructure.

As widely publicized denial-of-service attacks occur, the subject is finally getting needed attention. Not so long ago, it was assumed that the amount of damage any attacker could do was limited by the speed of that attacker's Internet connection. If that were true, it wouldn't be too hard to find the attacker's machine, filter out its packets, disconnect it from the Internet, and prosecute the machine's owner (presumably the attacker). Unfortunately, attacks grew more sophisticated. Instead of attacking directly from the attacker's own machine, an attacker breaks into a lot of machines, and causes them to attack. The attacks are now coming from many machines owned by innocent, if careless, owners.

Why is it so easy to break into machines? Unfortunately, there is little incentive for vendors to provide secure software, and little incentive for owners of machines to keep up with patches and turn security on in their machine. Vendors are in business to make money. Time to market, fancy features (which are likely to introduce vulnerabilities), and price are more important differentiators than security. A vendor that provides a low-frills product that goes to market later due to stringent testing will lose in the marketplace. If manufacturers were routinely sued for security bugs in their products, perhaps security would feature more prominently in the economic equation.

It is tempting to blame the users. Why don't they install patches promptly? Why don't they turn off dangerous features such as cookies? However, it is completely unfair to blame the users. Users are getting less and less sophisticated. When computers were used primarily by university computer science students, it was reasonable to make them arcanely difficult to manage. Today just about everyone is using computers, and is expected to manage their own systems. And when there are features that can be exploited by attackers (such as ActiveX), users can't simply turn these features off, because many Web sites wind up using these features. Not because they need to, but because the features are there. If users say no to anything, they get strange error messages and all sorts of things stop working.

Fighting denial of service is going to be a constant spy vs. spy game. The good guys (the defenders) will try to defend against all the known attacks, and the bad guys (the attackers) will try to disguise their attacks to stay under the radar. It is good that the good guys have been awakened to the need to be ever vigilant, and to get ahead of the game through research.

This book is timely and written by an ideal author team. It is crucial to understand the world as currently deployed, and it is also crucial to look to the future. This author team provides expertise along the whole range. David Dittrich, of the University of Washington's Information School and the Center for Information Assurance and Cybersecurity, is one of the foremost frontline DDoS fighters today, and indeed, an "I'm feeling lucky" Google search for DDoS brings up the DDoS page that he maintains.

Jelena Mirkovic did her Ph.D. work at UCLA, with advisor Peter Reiher, on innovative approaches to DDoS defense. Their work produced the first source-end DDoS defense system, which helps network administrators ensure that poorly secured machines in their network cannot be misused to attack others. They also worked on developing taxonomies of DDoS attacks and defenses, and defining methods for measuring the success of defenses. Jelena continues her fight against DDoS as an assistant professor at the University of Delaware.

Sven Dietrich is a researcher at the CERT Coordination Center. He is part of the research group that investigates the survivability of networked systems. The CERT Coordination Center is the first organization of its kind, and has helped to start similar organizations around the world. It is likely to be the first place to hear about attacks, and to marshal the resources necessary to provide defenses. Sven also works closely with Carnegie Mellon CyLab—a cybersecurity research and education center. Following their meeting at the CERT DSIT Workshop, Sven teamed up with David Dittrich and others in producing analyses of several early DDoS tools.

—Radia Perlman

Acknowledgments

The authors wish to thank Radia Perlman from Sun Microsystem Laboratories, and Mary Franz and her colleagues at Prentice Hall for their support and assistance in producing this book. Radia and Mary were instrumental in encouraging us to write the book and getting Prentice Hall to commit to its publication.

The authors also wish to thank distinguished researchers and practitioners in the network security community who reviewed this book: Steven M. Bellovin from AT&T Labs, Angelos D. Keromytis from Columbia University, Giovanni Vigna from the University of California at Santa Barbara, Cat Okita from Earthworks, Kevin Fu from MIT, Warwick Ford from Wyltan, Inc., Harlan Carvey, and Howard Lipson from the CERT Coordination Center. Their reviews have been instrumental to us in improving the technical content and the readability of this book.

The authors would like to thank the CERT Coordination Center, for permitting us to reproduce some of their copyrighted figures and other material in this book. We also thank the companies that have granted us the permission to use their products' copyrighted material in preparation of Appendix B. These are: Mazu Networks, Arbor Networks, WebScreen Technologies, Captus Networks, CS3, Riverhead Networks (now part of Cisco Systems), and Lancope.

David Dittrich

I wish to thank the following people: my parents, Carol and William Dittrich (I wish he were still here to read this), for raising me to consider how I can best contribute to the good of society; my cousin Dan and uncle Richard Kegel, for being early inspirations to me to explore computing; my extended family and friends (especially Ali Ritter) for putting up with me working through two plus years' holidays analyzing DDoS malware; my coworkers at the University of Washington who have assisted or inspired me to find better ways to deal with an ever-growing number of compromised computers (e.g., Corey Satten; Aaron Racine; my former assistant director Oren Sreebny and his wonderful Client Services group; Sandy Moy, Mike Hornung, Eliot Lim, Alexander Howard, and Daniel Schwalbe, who continue to deal with compromised hosts on campus; Terry Gray and his Network Engineering and Network Operations crews; and the many others in C&C and MCIS who deal with computer security incident response); Lance Spitzner and all of the members of the Honeynet Project and Research Alliance for sharing my curiosity about how computer attack tools function and how to detect and counter them; Kirk Bailey and members of the Agora, who form connections with others in government and industry to deal with issues like DDoS, incident response, forensics, identity theft, and online privacy; Ivan Orton, John Christiansen, Alisha Ritter, James Vasquez, Jennifer Granick, Richard Salgado, Dario Forte, Steve Schroeder, Ken Himma, Marc Lampson, and the many participants at the 3rd Agora Active Defense Workshop for their guidance through the varied and complex landscape of the Law; Dean Michael Eisenberg, David Notkin, Harry Bruce, Alpha Delap, Ed Lazowska, and all in the Information School and Center for Information Assurance and Cybersecurity for supporting and encouraging me to publish, develop research, teach, and consult in this fascinating field; the staff of the CERT Coordination Center and attendees at the Distributed Intruder Tools Workshop with whom I have maintained contact and worked over the years; to the many former and current members of the federal government, military, and intelligence community, who share a desire to protect our critical cyberinfrastructure from attack, and who have involved me in this effort over the years in ways that make me and my family proud.

Sven Dietrich

Sven Dietrich would like to thank the following for their dedication, integrity, and support: Aghadi Shraim, Karen Petraska, Frank Ottens, Bill Farrell, Andy Schain, and Neil Long. Without their help the early DDoS analysis work could not have been completed.

Sven would also like to thank Howard Lipson, Eric Hayes, Sheila Rosenthal, Tom Longstaff, John McHugh, Nancy Mead, Carrie Gates, Mike Collins, Sarah Strauss, Mindi McDowell, David Biber, Jason Rafail, Chad Dougherty, Art Manion, Allen Householder, and many others from the CERT Coordination Center and the Software Engineering Institute for their support, scrutiny, and contributions. Sven is grateful for the environment at CERT Research that allowed him to continue and extend his

DDoS research, both in the context of the Survivable Systems Engineering Team and the Carnegie Mellon CyLab, and to eventually write this book.

Finally, Sven would like to thank his friends and family for their patience and support during the writing of this book.

Jelena Mirkovic

Jelena Mirkovic and Peter Reiher are very grateful to the Defense Advanced Research Project Agency (DARPA) for supporting their research in DDoS defense, through the Fault Tolerant Networking (FTN) program led by Dr. Douglas Maughan, program manager. The FTN program funded a large number of cybersecurity research projects, with an aim of improving Internet robustness in face of attacks. Many of these projects were focused on DDoS defenses, and they greatly affected the DDoS research community by both advancing the knowledge of the threat and by proposing innovative defense measures (some of which evolved into full-fledged commercial products). Dr. Maughan stepped outside the conventional funding paradigm, which fosters individual projects developed in isolation and with no relation to one another, by encouraging partnerships between projects. This enabled both combinations of defense approaches and their independent evaluation, and resulted in a higher quality of research.

Jelena is very grateful to the Computer and Information Sciences Department at the University of Delaware, for supporting her DDoS research and her book-writing efforts. Friendly and supporting colleagues, bright students, and helpful and capable staff make this department an enjoyable and inspiring place to work.

Jelena would like to extend profound thanks to the faculty, students, and staff associated with the University of Utah Emulab testbed, a shared testbed resource that enables researchers to acquire multiple machines, load them with their code, and test to their hearts' content. The people at Emulab did a superb job creating and maintaining this facility; they were very forthcoming in meeting the special needs of various projects she has worked on, and they heroically coped with occasional mishaps in these projects (such as escaped scans, overloaded disks, and excessive traffic that brought down the NFS server) without revoking her account. Testing DDoS defenses in a (as much as possible) realistic setting requires multiple machines—usually many more than an average university lab can acquire. Those machines must further be recombined into various topologies, and doing this in an ordinary lab environment is painful and includes a lot of cable reconnecting, manual reconfiguration, and anguish when packets just don't flow. In Emulab, the act of acquiring a hundred machines, organizing them in a desired topology and installing the code one needs to run takes about 10 minutes. Imagine how this advances research! Jelena has used Emulab resources and found them invaluable both in her Ph.D. work, her current research at the University of Delaware, and in teaching network security classes.

Jelena is especially grateful to her husband, Nikola, and numerous friends and family members, who lent her their patience, advice, and energy in the challenging process of writing this book.

Peter Reiher

Peter Reiher would like to thank several students who have worked on research projects related to distributed denial of service problems with him. These students have been instrumental in helping him develop a better understanding of the problems caused by DDoS attacks and the advantages and disadvantages of various possible solutions to those problems. These students include (in addition to Jelena Mirkovic) Gregory Prier, Max Robinson, Matthew Schnaider, B. Scott Michel, and Jun Li. Peter would also like to thank Dr. Gerald Popek and Dr. Geoff Kuenning for their contributions to his research group's work on distributed denial of service attacks.

Peter would also like to thank Raj Yavatkar and the Intel Corporation for support they've provided to allow him to pursue the use of programmable routers for combating DDoS attacks. This support helped develop ideas and approaches to DDoS defense discussed in this book.

Peter would also like to thank his wife, Cathleen, for her understanding, support, and patience through the long process of producing this book.

About the Authors

Jelena Mirkovic received her B.Sc. in Electrical and Computer Engineering from the University of Belgrade, Serbia, and Montenegro in 1998, and her M.S. and Ph.D. from UCLA in 2000 and 2003. She is currently an assistant professor in the Computer and Information Sciences Department, University of Delaware.

Jelena developed an interest in networking and security research during her graduate studies, and became involved in projects working on new defenses against IP spoofing and distributed denial of service attacks. Her Ph.D. work led to the first source-end DDoS defense system, called D-WARD, that prevents participation of poorly managed networks in DDoS attacks. She further worked to improve the understanding of the DDoS threat and the solution space by developing a taxonomy of DDoS attacks and of DDoS defense mechanisms. She is currently working on developing benchmarks and common evaluation methodology for testing DDoS defenses.

Since her graduation, Jelena's research interests have grown to include other network security problems such as Internet worms, intrusions, and routing attacks, but DDoS remains her "first research love" and the main focus of her investigations.

Sven Dietrich is a member of the technical staff for the CERT Coordination Center, part of the Software Engineering Institute at Carnegie Mellon University in Pittsburgh, Pennsylvania. He also has an appointment at the Carnegie Mellon CyLab, a university-wide cybersecurity research and education initiative. Prior to joining Carnegie Mellon University, Sven worked as a Senior Security Architect at the NASA Goddard Space Flight Center from 1997 to 2001, where he observed and analyzed the first distributed denial-of-service attacks against the University of Minnesota in 1999. He taught Mathematics and Computer Science as an adjunct faculty member at Adelphi University, his alma mater, from 1991 to 1997.

His research interests include survivability, computer and network security, anonymity, cryptographic protocols, and cryptography. His previous work has included a formal analysis of the secure sockets layer protocol (SSL), intrusion detection, analysis of distributed denial-of-service tools, and the security of IP communications in space. For his work on the latter he received a National Resource Group Achievement Award from the NASA Goddard Space Flight Center in 2000. His publications include *Analyzing Distributed Denial of Service Tools: The Shaft Case* (with N. Long and D. Dittrich) and *The "mstream" Distributed Denial of Service Tool* (with D. Dittrich, G. Weaver, and N. Long), as well as articles on Active Network Defense, DDoS tool analysis, and survivability. He has given invited talks and presentations on DDoS at conference venues such as USENIX, ACSAC, the IEEE Symposium on Security and Privacy, and HAL 2001, and at NASA-wide briefings, and has participated in DDoS panels at HAL 2001 and SANS Network Security 2002. He also teaches computer and network security at both the national and international level, including giving tutorials and guest lectures on DDoS.

He received a D.A. in Mathematics in 1997, a M.S. in Mathematics in 1991, and a B.S. in Computer Science and Mathematics in 1989, all from Adelphi University in Garden City, New York, and an International Baccalaureate from the International School of Geneva, Switzerland, in 1985. He is a member and former president of the New York Xi chapter of Pi Mu Epsilon, the National Mathematics Honor Society.

Sven discovered his interest in computers working on Apple][+/e computers and a Commodore 64 in the early 1980s, in networks during his dealings with X.25 packet-switched networks, such as TELENET and TYMNET, and networked PC- and Unix-based bulletin board systems in the mid- to late-1980s. His curiosity about denial of service was piqued in the early 1990s on Internet Relay Chat networks, and by witnessing an intruder flood his alma mater's Internet connection in the mid-1990s. Early on he was fascinated by the book *Hackers for Moscow* (Rowohlt Verlag, 1989) describing the hackers' view of Clifford Stoll's *Cuckoo's Egg* (a book he has not read to this day). His passion remains the beauty of mathematics.

David Dittrich began his computing career in 1979 with a "family owned" (read "his personal") Apple][+, which he used to maintain a local credit union's membership mailing list. He wrote his own terminal emulator (in assembly, dove-tailed using jump instructions into the slack space between subroutines in the published

Apple DOS assembly listing so as not to take up any added space on the only disk drive, a 720KB floppy disk!). This allowed him to be the primary user of one of the two modems owned by Western Washington University to do his Computer Science homework from at home while drinking beer and listening to the likes of Pink Floyd, Led Zeppelin, and Steely Dan (while the other students had to sit in straight-back chairs at VT100 terminals in the main terminal room). Dave's background in programming and system administration on several platforms and operating systems was honed first at WWU, then the Boeing Company, and finally when he moved in 1990 to the University of Washington. His role as the main Unix workstation support contact for the entire UW campus led him to become an expert in dealing with Unix computer intrusions and malware of all types. Dave has been a prolific self-publisher of white papers, FAQs, and malware tool analyses, all intended to make his (and everyone else's) life easier in dealing with computer intrusions. Dave is most widely known for his research into Distributed Denial of Service attack tools, starting with an invited talk at the November 1999 CERT Distributed System Intruder Tools Workshop and leading to invited talks and panels on DDoS at SANS, the USENIX Security Symposium, JASON summer workshop, DDoS BoF sessions at RSA 2000 and NANOG, and HAL 2001 in the Netherlands. Dave received one of SANS' Security Technology Leadership Awards in 2000 for his work in understanding DDoS tools.

Besides DDoS, Dave is also active in other areas of host and network forensics, honeynets, and information assurance. He has taught Unix Forensic Analysis at the Black Hat Briefings and both taught in and cochaired SANS' first forensic track at SANS FIRE '01. As one of the founding members of the Honeynet Project, he led the "Forensic Challenge" (the first ever forensic analysis challenge based on a published "in the wild" compromised Linux system), and now leads the development of the next-generation distributed Honeywall CD-ROM.

Dave has contributed to the books *Know Your Enemy,* by the Honeynet Project (Addison-Wesley, 2001), *The Hacker's Challenge,* edited by Mike Schiffman (McGraw Hill, 2001), and two articles in the *Handbook of Information Security,* edited by Hossein Bidgoli (John Wiley & Sons, 2005). His Web page and papers are referenced in dozens of popular Linux, system administration, and computer security books. He has also spoken around the world at conferences such as the Black Hat Briefings, CanSecWest, SANS, Korea's OlymFair, and Austalia's AusCERT; and at several workshops, classes, professional organizations, and government agencies. He has been interviewed in print, radio, and television from the campus level to international media outlets.

His home page can be found at `http://staff.washington.edu/dittrich/`

Peter Reiher received his B.S. in Electrical Engineering from the University of Notre Dame in 1979. He received an M.S. and a Ph.D. in Computer Science from UCLA in 1983 and 1987, respectively.

Dr. Reiher spent five years working at JPL, where he served as the principal designer for the Time Warp Operating System. He then returned to UCLA, where he is now an adjunct associate professor in the Computer Science Department. He has worked on a variety of research topics, including distributed operating systems, parallel discrete event simulation, optimistically replicated file systems and databases, mobile computing, active networks, and various issues in file system design. In recent years, much of his research has centered around network security topics, particularly combatting IP spoofing and defending against distributed denial of service attacks. The SAVE system to combat IP spoofing, the D-WARD DDoS defense system, and the DefCOM DDoS defense system all originated in his research group at UCLA.

## CHAPTER 1

Introduction

It is Monday night and you are still in the office, when you suddenly become aware of the whirring of the disks and network lights blinking on the Web server. It seems like your company's Web site is quite well visited tonight, which is good because you are in e-business, selling products over the Internet, and more visits mean more earnings. You decide to check it out too, but the Web page will not load. Something is wrong.

A few minutes later, network operations confirm your worst fears. Your company's Web site is under a denial-of-service attack. It is receiving so many requests for a Web page that it cannot serve them all—50 times your regular load. Just like *you* cannot access the Web site, *none of your customers can.* Your business has come to a halt.

You all work hard through the night trying to devise filtering rules to weed out bogus Web page requests from the real ones. Unfortunately, the traffic you are receiving is very diverse and you cannot find a common feature that would make the attack packets stand out. You next try to identify the sources that send you a lot of traffic and blacklist them in your firewall. But there seem to be hundreds of thousands of them and they keep changing. You spend the next day bringing up backup servers and watching them overload as your earnings settle around zero. You contact the FBI and they explain that they are willing to help you, but it will take them a few days to get started. They also inform you that many perpetrators of denial-of-service attacks are never caught, since they do not leave enough traces behind them.

All you are left with are questions: Why are you being attacked? Is it for competitive advantage? Is an ex-employee trying to get back at you? Is this a very upset customer? How long can your business be offline and remain viable? How did you get into this situation, and how will you get out of it? Or is this just a bug in your own Web applications, swamping your servers accidentally?

This is a book about *Denial-of-Service attacks*, or *DoS* for short. These attacks aim at crippling applications, servers, and whole networks, disrupting legitimate users' communication. They are performed intentionally, easy to perpetrate, and very, very hard to handle. The popular form of these attacks, *Distributed Denial-of-Service (DDoS) attacks,* employs dozens, hundreds, or even well over 100,000 compromised computers, to perform a coordinated and widely distributed attack. It is immensely hard to defend yourself against a coordinated action by so many machines.

This book describes DoS and DDoS attacks and helps you understand this new threat. It also teaches you how to prepare for these attacks, preventing them when possible, dealing with them when they do occur, and learning how to live with them, how to quickly recover and how to take legal action against the attackers.

1.1 DoS and DDoS

The goal of a DoS attack is to disrupt some legitimate activity, such as browsing Web pages, listening to an online radio, transferring money from your bank account, or even docking ships communicating with a naval port. This *denial-of-service effect* is achieved by sending messages to the target that interfere with its operation, and make it hang, crash, reboot, or do useless work.

One way to interfere with a legitimate operation is to exploit a vulnerability present on the target machine or inside the target application. The attacker sends a few messages crafted in a specific manner that take advantage of the given vulnerability. Another way is to send a vast number of messages that consume some key resource at the target such as bandwidth, CPU time, memory, etc. The target application, machine, or network spends all of its critical resources on handling the attack traffic and cannot attend to its legitimate clients.

Of course, to generate such a vast number of messages the attacker must control a very powerful machine—with a sufficiently fast processor and a lot of available network bandwidth. For the attack to be successful, it has to overload the target's resources. This means that an attacker's machine must be able to generate more traffic than a target, or its network infrastructure, can handle.

Now let us assume that an attacker would like to launch a DoS attack on example.com by bombarding it with numerous messages. Also assuming that example.com has abundant resources, it is then difficult for the attacker to generate a sufficient number of messages *from a single machine* to overload those resources. However, suppose he gains control over 100,000 machines and engages them in generating messages to example.com simultaneously. Each of the attacking machines now may be only moderately provisioned (e.g., have a slow processor and be on a modem link) but together they form a formidable attack network and, with proper use, will be able to overload a well-provisioned victim. This is a distributed denial-of-service—DDoS.

Both DoS and DDoS are a huge threat to the operation of Internet sites, but the DDoS problem is more complex and harder to solve. First, it uses a very large number of machines. This yields a powerful weapon. Any target, regardless of how well-provisioned it is, can be taken offline. Gathering and engaging a large army of machines has become trivially simple, because many automated tools for DDoS can be found on hacker Web pages and in chat rooms. Such tools do not require sophistication to be used and can inflict very effective damage. A large number of machines gives another advantage to an attacker. Even if the target were able to identify attacking machines (and there are effective ways of hiding this information), what action can be taken against a network of 100,000 hosts? The second characteristic of some DDoS attacks that increases their complexity is the use of seemingly legitimate traffic. Resources are consumed by a large number of legitimate-looking messages; when comparing the attack message with a legitimate one, there are frequently no telltale features to distinguish them. Since the attack misuses a legitimate activity, it is extremely hard to respond to the attack without also disturbing this legitimate activity.

Take a tangible example from the real world. (While not a perfect analogy to Internet DDoS, it does share some important characteristics that might help you understand why DDoS attacks are hard to handle.) Imagine that you are an important politician and that a group of people that oppose your views recruit all their friends and relatives around the world to send you hate letters. Soon you will be getting so many letters each day that your mailbox will overflow and some letters will be dropped in the street and blown away. If your supporters send you donations through the mail, their letters will either be lost or stuffed in the mailbox among the copious hate mail. To find these donations, you will have to open and sort all the mail received, wasting lots of time. If the mail you receive daily is greater than what you can process during one day, some letters will be lost or ignored. Presumably, hate letters are much more numerous than those carrying donations, so unless you can quickly and surely tell which envelopes contain donations and which contain hate mail, you stand a good chance of losing most of the donations. Your opponents have just performed a real-world distributed denial of service attack on you, depriving you of support that may be crucial to your campaign.

What could you do to defend yourself? Well, you could buy a bigger mailbox, but your opponents can simply increase the number of letters they send, or recruit more helpers. You must still identify the donations in the even larger pool of letters. You could hire more people to go through letters—a costly solution since you have to pay them from diminishing donations. If your opponents can recruit more helpers for free, they can make your processing costs as high as they like. You could also try to make the job of processing mail easier by asking your supporters to use specially colored envelopes. Your processing staff can then simply discard all envelopes that are not of the specified color, without opening them. Of course, as soon as your opponents learn of this tactic they will purchase the same colored envelopes and you are back where you started. You could try to contact post offices around the country asking them to keep an eye on people sending loads of letters to you. This will only work if your opponents are not widely spread and must therefore send many letters each day from the same post office. Further, it depends on cooperation that post offices may be unwilling or unable to provide. Their job is delivering letters, not monitoring or filtering out letters people do not want to get. If many of those sending hate mail (and some sending donations) are in different countries, your chances of getting post office cooperation are even smaller. You could also try to use the postmark on the letters to track where they were sent from, then pay special attention to post offices that your supporters use or to post offices that handle suspiciously large amounts of your mail. This means that you will have to keep a list of all postmarks you have seen and classify each letter according to its postmark, to look for anomalous amounts of mail carrying a certain postmark. If your opponents are numerous and well spread all over the world this tactic will fail. Further, postmarks are fairly nonspecific locators, so you are likely to lose some donations while discarding the hate letters coming to you from a specific postmark.

As stated before, the analogy is not perfect, but there are important similarities. In particular, solutions similar to those above, as well as numerous other approaches specific to the Internet world, have been proposed to deal with DDoS. Like the solutions listed above that try to solve the postal problem, the Internet DDoS solutions often have limitations or do not work well in the real world. This book will survey those approaches, presenting their good and bad sides, and provide pointers for further reference. It will also talk about ways to secure and strengthen your network so it cannot be easily taken offline, steps to take once you are under attack (or an unwitting source of the attack), and what law enforcement can do to help you with a DDoS problem.

1.2   Why Should We Care?

Why does it matter if someone can take a Web server or a router offline? It matters because the Internet is now becoming a critical resource whose disruption has financial implications, or even dire consequences on human safety. An increasing number of critical services are using the Internet for daily operation. A DDoS attack may not just mean missing out on the latest sports scores or weather. It may mean losing a bid on an item you want to buy or losing your customers for a day or two while you are under attack. It may mean, as it did for the port of Houston, Texas, that the Web server providing the weather and scheduling information is unavailable and no ships can dock [MK03]. Lately, a disturbing extortion trend has appeared—online businesses are threatened by DDoS if they do not pay for "protection." Such a threat is frequently backed up by a small demonstration that denies the business service for a few hours [Sha].

How likely are you to be a DDoS target? A study evaluated Internet DDoS activity in 2001, looking at a small sample of traffic observable from its network [MVS01]. The authors were able to detect approximately 4,000 attacks per week (for a three-week period), against a variety of targets ranging from large companies such as Amazon and Hotmail to small Internet Service Providers (ISPs) and dial-up connections. The method they used was not able to notice all attacks that happened during that period, so 4,000 is an underestimate. Further, since DDoS activity has increased and evolved since then, today's figure is likely to be much bigger. In the 2004 FBI report on cybercrime, nearly a fifth of the respondents who suffered financial loss from an attack had experienced a DoS attack. The total reported costs of DoS attacks were over $26 million. Denial of service was the top source of financial loss due to cybercrime in 2004. It is safe to conclude that the likelihood of being a DDoS target is not negligible.

But DDoS affects not only the target of the attack traffic. Legitimate users of the target's services are affected, too. In January 2001, a DDoS attack on Microsoft prevented about 98% of legitimate users from getting to any of Microsoft's servers. In October 2002, there was an attack on all 13 root Domain Name System (DNS) servers. DNS service is crucial for Web browsers and for many other applications, and those 13 servers keep important data for the whole Internet. Since DNS information is heavily cached and the attack lasted only an hour, there was no large disruption of Internet activity. However, 9 of these 13 servers were seriously affected. Had the attack lasted longer, the Internet could conceivably have experienced severe disruption. The aforementioned attack that disabled the port of Houston, Texas, was actually directed at a South African chat room user, with the port's computers being misused for the attack [Reg]. DDoS affects all of us directly or indirectly and is a threat that should be taken seriously.

1.3   What Is This Book?

This is the first book that is written exclusively about the DoS problem. There have been a number of important shorter treatments of the DDoS problem and solution approaches ([CER99, HMP+01]), but this book greatly expands on and updates these seminal works. It is intended to speak to both technical and nontechnical audiences, informing them about this problem and presenting and discussing potential solutions. Whether you are a CTO of a company, a network administrator, or a computer science student, we are sure you will find the information in this book informative and helpful and will want to learn more about DoS and DDoS. We have provided references to further reading, conferences, and journals that publish papers from this field and organizations that deal with the DoS problem specifically for this purpose. Since the DDoS field is very dynamic both in new threats and new defenses, we will gather and publish current information to accompany the book on a Web page: http://staff.washington.edu/dittrich/misc/ddos/book/. Following is an overview of all the useful things you will find inside this book.

- A thorough explanation of DoS and DDoS—why these attacks occur, how frequently they are conducted and in what manner, and how they affect the victim.

- Examples of some DoS and DDoS attack types that have been seen to date and a discussion of trends, in an effort to give the reader a good overview of the field.

- An extensive overview of the defensive methods and tools that exist now or are in research and development stages.

- Examples of the true fragility of services that depend on the current Internet infrastructure that will provide decision makers (or those who advise them) with a better context for making risk assessments and judgments about what services to place in the Internet, how to protect them, and what the consequences might be if they are attacked.

- Descriptions of how DDoS attack tools function, how to respond to DDoS attacks, and how to collect and analyze evidence in ways that support both DDoS defense and the needs of law enforcement, should you choose to pursue criminal prosecution or civil litigation.

1.4 Who Is This Book For?

The book is meant for readers with a good background in general computer networking and some knowledge of general network security issues, but little specialized knowledge of DDoS attacks.

- It is primarily aimed at computer system (end host) and network administrators, those who are responsible for keeping computers and networks functioning in the face of failure (whether natural or human-induced). There should be sufficient depth and detail for technical readers, with many citations to provide the added detail this audience demands.

- It is also aimed at those in management and policy positions who need to understand how to manage businesses and other organizations that rely on the Internet functioning in an operational sense. There should be enough general and easy-to-digest information to bring the picture of DDoS into view for those who have never encountered this subject before, allowing them to see how they may be affected by this problem in the future or how to deal with it now if they are affected.

- This book will be useful to those with political and legal responsibilities, helping them understand how the technical and legal worlds intersect in the Internet. The concepts of *cybercrime* and *cyberwarfare* involve the potential use of denial of service as a weapon to disrupt or degrade critical infrastructures. Many services, such as computers designed for medical imaging, were not designed to be used in a hostile network environment. They use Common Off-The-Shelf (COTS) commercial operating systems as delivered by the vendor, and often without securing them or updating the software. These computers are vulnerable to potential denial of service or complete compromise. As more and more critical applications migrate to the Internet, the risk of potential loss of income or even loss of life grows. This book will provide political and legal representatives with the background necessary to make sound decisions on public policy and law enforcement. Understanding the risks and making appropriate investments in protective measures or new security research can help prevent this risky future.

- Finally, the book is meant for anyone who has heard rumors about DDoS and would like to understand more about the phenomenon (e.g., students, teachers, corporate employees, home business owners, journalists). These people will gain detailed knowledge of the problem and of the current defense approaches. Some of them may be intrigued enough to join the search for solutions!

1.5   What Can This Book Help You Do?

This book will help you understand the problem of DDoS. It will help you in evaluating current defenses and in choosing the right ones for you. It will help you protect your network, minimizing damages and quickly recovering if you do get attacked.

We wrote this book because—surprisingly, considering DDoS has existed as a problem since 1999—there are currently no books that focus exclusively on DDoS. Existing network security books either ignore the topic or devote at most a chapter to it. These works provide enough information for computer practitioners who merely need to be familiar with the concept, but not nearly enough for a network administrator or CTO who needs to protect her network from such attacks and must be prepared to recover from them. There are many academic papers on the subject, but their view is limited to their particular research topic. There are also white papers from companies offering products to ameliorate DDoS attacks, but they are primarily interested in demonstrating the effectiveness and other advantages of their particular product.

1.6   Outline of the Remaining Chapters

Since the book is intended for a variety of readers, we divided its content into chapters with different difficulty levels (denoted in italics next to chapter names in the overview below). Chapters marked *nontechnical* are intended for readers who do not have extensive knowledge of networking and security and who are seeking a gradual introduction to DDoS. These readers may wish to read only the nontechnical chapters. Chapters marked *technical* are for those readers who are familiar with networking operations, such as system administrators, and who are looking for a quick reference to specific DDoS issues or for a fast technical overview of the problems and potential solutions. These readers may wish to read only the technical chapters. There is also a chapter that bears a *nontechnical/technical* mark. This chapter has a blend of material that contains both technical and nontechnical items. Both of the above groups should read this chapter. Finally, readers who are specifically seeking to learn about DDoS in order to work in this field in the future, such as students and teachers, will find it useful to read the book from cover to cover, as nontechnical chapters set the stage for technical ones.

- **Chapter 2: Understanding Denial of Service.** *(Nontechnical/technical level)* This chapter explains the DDoS phenomenon and illustrates the scope and seriousness of the problem.

- **Chapter 3: History of DoS and DDoS.** *(Nontechnical level)* This chapter recounts how and when DoS attacks came about, how they evolved into DDoS attacks, what is behind the DDoS problem, and what aspects of Internet design and management are especially related to this problem.

- **Chapter 4: How Attacks Are Waged.** *(Technical level)* This chapter gives a detailed description of the "modus operandi" of a DDoS attack and discusses different DDoS variants.

- **Chapter 5: An Overview of DDoS Defenses.** *(Nontechnical level)* This chapter discusses the challenges that DDoS defense is facing. It also discusses different approaches to design a DoS or DDoS defense, and presents some key ideas, found both in research and commercial solutions. These ideas are building blocks of current defenses.

- **Chapter 6: Detailed Defense Approaches.** *(Technical level)* This chapter explains practical approaches to strengthen your network and make it resist and recover from DDoS attacks. It discusses how to analyze DDoS incidents and gather detailed information that will help respond to the attack and, later, take legal action against perpetrators.

- **Chapter 7: Survey of Research Defense Approaches.** *(Technical level)* This chapter gives an overview of many research approaches to DoS and DDoS defense.

- **Chapter 8: Legal Issues.** *(Nontechnical level)* This chapter speaks about laws that are applicable to DoS and DDoS, and steps you can take to bring legal action against attackers.

- **Chapter 9: Conclusions.** *(Nontechnical level)* This chapter offers a prognosis for DDoS defense and conclusions, along with useful pointers to Web pages, mailing lists, conferences, and journals that publish DDoS-related information.

- **Appendix A: Glossary.** *(Technical level)* This appendix contains a glossary of technical terms used throughout the book, with detailed explanation and organized as an easy reference.

- **Appendix B: Survey of Commercial Defense Approaches.** *(Technical level)* This appendix offers a survey of several commercial DDoS solutions to inform the reader of design decisions implemented in these solutions, and functionalities that can be found in the market.

- **Appendix C: DDoS Data.** *(Technical level)* This appendix offers a survey of available quantitative studies of the DDoS phenomenon, detailing the frequency and type of observed attacks, how they are performed, and the damages incurred.

## CHAPTER 2

Understanding Denial of Service

A denial-of-service attack is different in goal, form, and effect than most of the attacks that are launched at networks and computers. Most attackers involved in cybercrime seek to break into a system, extract its secrets, or fool it into providing a service that they should not be allowed to use. Attackers commonly try to steal credit card numbers or proprietary information, gain control of machines to install their software or save their data, deface Web pages, or alter important content on victim machines. Frequently, compromised machines are valued by attackers as resources that can be turned to whatever purpose they currently deem important.

In DDoS attacks, breaking into a large number of computers and gaining malicious control of them is just the first step. The attacker then moves on to the DoS attack itself, which has a different goal—to prevent victim machines or networks from offering service to their legitimate users. No data is stolen, nothing is altered on the victim machines, and no unauthorized access occurs. The victim simply stops offering service to normal clients because it is preoccupied with handling the attack traffic. While no unauthorized access to the victim of the DDoS flood occurs, a large number of other hosts have previously been compromised and controlled by the attacker, who uses them as attack weapons. In most cases, this is *unauthorized access,* by the legal definition of that term.

While the denial-of-service effect on the victim may sound relatively benign, especially when one considers that it usually lasts only as long as the attack is active, for many network users it can be devastating. Use of Internet services has become an important part of our daily lives. The Internet is increasingly being used to conduct business and even to provide some critical services. Following are some examples of the damaging effects of DoS attacks.

- Sites that offer services to users through online orders make money only when users can access those services. For example, a large book-selling site cannot sell books to its customers if they cannot browse the site's Web pages and order products online. A DoS attack on such sites means a severe loss of revenue for as long as the attack lasts. Prolonged or frequent attacks also inflict long-lasting damage to a site's reputation—customers who were unable to access the desired service are likely to take their business to the competition. Sites whose reputations were damaged may have trouble attracting new customers or investor funding in the future.

- Large news sites and search engines are paid by marketers to present their advertisements to the public. The revenue depends on the number of users that view the site's Web page. A DoS attack on such a site means a direct loss of revenue from the marketers, and may have the long-lasting effect of driving the customers to more easily accessible sites. Loss of popularity translates to a direct loss of advertisers' business.

- Some sites offer a critical free service to Internet users. For example, the Internet's Domain Name System (DNS) provides the necessary information to translate human-readable Web addresses (such as www.example.com) into Internet Protocol (IP) addresses (such as 192.0.34.166). All Web browsers and numerous other applications depend on DNS to be able to fetch information requested by the users. If DNS servers are under a DoS attack and cannot respond due to overload, many sites may become unreachable because their addresses cannot be resolved, even though those sites are online and fully capable of handling traffic. This makes DNS a part of the critical infrastructure, and other equally important pieces of the Internet's infrastructure are also vulnerable.

- Numerous businesses have come to depend on the Internet for critical daily activities. A DoS attack may interrupt an important videoconference meeting or a large customer order. It may prevent a company from sending out an important document for a rapidly approaching deadline or interfere with its bid for a large contract.

- The Internet is increasingly being used to facilitate management of public services, such as water, power, and sewage, and to deliver critical information for important activities, such as weather and traffic reports for docking ships. A DoS attack that disrupts these critical services will directly affect even people whose activities are not related to computers or the Internet. It may even endanger human lives.

- A vast number of people use the Internet on a daily basis for entertainment or for communicating with friends and family. While a DoS attack that disrupts these activities may not cause them any serious damage, it is certainly an unpleasant experience that they wish to avoid. If such disruptions occur frequently, people are likely to stop using the Internet for these purposes, in favor of more reliable technologies.

2.1   The Ulterior Motive

Why do attackers seek to deny service? This act, very disruptive in nature, is not always an end in and of itself. What could be the ultimate goal then?

Some of the early DoS attacks were largely proofs of concept or simple pranks played by hackers. The ultimate goal was to prove that something could be done, such as taking a large, popular Web site offline. Such a major achievement brings an attacker recognition in the underground community.

Frequently, attackers would also fight each other for supremacy via denial of service. Internet chat channels were and still are a sought-after resource by the attackers. They are used to coordinate multiple attacking machines and to trade code and illegal information with other attackers. The user who created the channel controls the access to it, and is called a *moderator, operator,* or *owner.* The easy way to take over the channel (and along with it all the attack machines that are controlled via this channel) and to dominate all the communications is to perform a DoS attack on its current moderator. When a moderator's machine goes offline, another user can take over the channel. Besides supremacy, attackers also sought revenge through denial of service. A hacker whose machines were knocked offline by DoS would "return the favor" by attacking the perpetrator. People who dared to speak ill of hackers in public have also felt DoS revenge.

Another frequent motive of DoS attacks is self-described as being political. Individuals or groups who disagree with views or actions of a certain organization (an online media site, a corporation, or a government) have been known to launch DoS attacks against computers and networks owned by this organization.

If the target of the attack is a company, a conceivable motive can be a competitor's wish to gain an edge in the market. So far, no attacks have been proved to have this motive. However, there is a major lack of data on perpetrators and motives of DoS attacks. The vast majority of attacks are not reported, let alone investigated. Of those that do undergo detailed investigation, only a few contain enough evidence to establish the motive. It is thus quite possible that some companies may resort to such illegal means of driving the competition out of the market.

Recently, a number of attacks have appeared as part of extortion attempts [ZDn04]. The attackers threaten an online business with a denial of service, and a payment is requested for "protection." Sites that refuse the payment are being "persuaded" by small-scale attacks.

2.2   Meet the Attackers

Who are the likely perpetrators of DDoS attacks? We have evidence from studies that thousands of attacks occur on a regular basis, yet very few attackers have been caught and prosecuted. This is partly due to the inability of victims to meet the minimum damage limits necessary to prosecute, or because the victim doesn't feel prosecution is worthwhile or fears negative publicity. Another factor is the ease of performing a DoS attack without leaving many traces for investigators to follow. It is impossible to judge the profile of perpetrators from such a small sample of provable crimes. Still, from the lack of sophistication in many attacks, it is safe to assume that a very large percentage seem to be perpetrated by inexperienced hackers, so-called *script kiddies*. These hackers download crude attack tools from the Internet and use them unaltered. While such attacks can still severely cripple the victim, sufficient traces sometimes exist for investigators to be able to understand much about the attacker. Such crude attacks also frequently generate an easily recognizable traffic pattern that can be controlled by simple filters.

Another type of a DoS perpetrator is a sophisticated hacker who uses several means to obscure her identity and create subtle variations in traffic patterns to bypass defenses. While these attacks are less common than the simple ones, they are particularly vicious and hard to handle. Sophisticated hackers may act on their own accord (when attacking for supremacy in their peer circle or for revenge) or may be hired by an underground movement or a criminal organization.

The most dangerous potential attacker is the nation-state actor that has significant resources and skill available to write his own tools, using sophisticated command and control techniques, and taking advantage of intelligence resources that are hard to come by. Such an attacker could create very subtle effects that are difficult to even notice using common methods or tools. Besides, the monitoring tools may potentially have vulnerabilities themselves that can be exploited to hide the presence of the attack. To date, no DDoS attacks can be confidently ascribed to such nation-state actors, but they are inherently better at covering their tracks. If no such attacks have occurred yet, they may well occur in the future.

2.3 Behind the Scenes

How do DoS attacks work? As mentioned in Chapter 1, there are two main approaches to denying a service: exploiting a vulnerability present on the target or sending a vast number of seemingly legitimate messages. The first kind of an attack is usually called a *vulnerability attack*, while the second is called a *flooding attack*.

Vulnerability attacks work by sending a few specifically crafted messages to the target application that possesses a vulnerability. This vulnerability is usually a software bug in the implementation or a bug in a default configuration of a given service. Malicious messages by the attacker represent an unexpected input that the application programmer did not foresee. The messages cause the target application to go into an infinite loop; to severely slow down, crash, freeze, or reboot a machine; or to consume a vast amount of memory and deny service to legitimate users. This process is called *exploiting a vulnerability*, and the malicious messages are called the *exploit*. In some cases, vulnerabilities of this kind can be exploited in the operating system, a common piece of middleware, or in a network protocol, as well as in application programs.[1] While it is impossible to detect all vulnerabilities, it can also be quite hard to find new exploits. This means that each vulnerability that is detected and patched is a large gain and a sure step ahead for the defenders.

Flooding attacks work by sending a vast number of messages whose processing consumes some key resource at the target. For instance, complex messages may require lengthy processing that takes up CPU cycles, large messages take up bandwidth, and messages that initiate communication with new clients take up memory. Once the key resource is tied up by the attack, legitimate users cannot receive service. The crucial

---

[1] For example, some implementations of the 802.11 wireless access protocol have a vulnerability that allows an attack to deny service selectively to one user in the wireless network or promiscuously to all of them. In effect, the attacker can send a packet to the wireless access point that claims to be from another user and that indicates that the user is finished and essentially wants to "hang up" [BS03]. The wireless access point then no longer recognizes communications from the targeted user. That user can reestablish communications with the access point, but the attacker can shut it down again in the same way.

feature of flooding attacks is that their strength lies in the volume, rather than in content. This has two major implications:

1. The attackers can send a variety of packets. The attack traffic can be made arbitrarily similar to the legitimate traffic, which greatly hinders defense.
2. The flow of traffic must be so large as to consume the target's resources. The attacker usually has to engage more than one machine to send out the attack traffic. Flooding attacks are therefore commonly DDoS attacks.

The simplest form of a DDoS attack is merely to send a very large quantity of messages, divided into packets, to a service on the victim machine. Unless something between the attacking machines and the victim drops those request packets, the victim will spend resources attempting to receive and properly handle them. If there are enough of these packets, all of the machine's resources will be spent trying to handle packets that have no value.

Another DDoS option is to attack the victim's network interface. If the network card in the victim's machine can handle only 10 Mbps of traffic, then an attacker needs to merely generate 10 or more Mbps of any deliverable IP packets and send them to the victim. Again assuming that no other entity drops those packets before they reach the victim's interface, they will easily exhaust its network resources and also create a sizable congestion on the path to the victim. If there are a few legitimate packets in addition to the large flood of attack packets, they are unlikely to receive service.

The attacker can also target the local network that attaches the victim to the Internet. If the attacker knows that the victim is attached to a 1-Gbps network segment, then she can send enough packets to the victim or other nodes on the segment to overwhelm it. Most networks become unusable as the traffic offered to them approaches their rated capacity, so little or no legitimate traffic will get through to the victim. In this form of DDoS attack, all of the other nodes on the network segment will similarly suffer. This example illustrates a curious property of DDoS: The damage is inflicted not only on the victim, but also on its legitimate users (who cannot get the service) and anyone else who shares the critical resource. For instance, the attacker may target a network that has the same ISP as you. If the amount of attack traffic is sufficiently high, your services may also be denied.

The above attacks are all based on large volumes of traffic. The attacker can sometimes perpetrate an effective flooding attack with much smaller volumes. If the victim has some service running that requires more time to process a remote request than it takes to generate that request, or that ties up a scarce resource on the server, the attacker can make use of this asymmetry. Even short or infrequent bursts of malicious traffic will effectively tie up the critical resource. A common example is the TCP SYN flood attack, described in detail in Chapter 4. The attacker floods the victim with TCP SYN packets, which are usually used to initiate new communication. The victim reserves some memory in a limited-size buffer for each new communication request, while the attacker can send out those requests without any memory cost. This asymmetry helps the attacker disable any new communication during the attack, while sending very few TCP SYN packets.

This discussion illustrates the fact that the line between vulnerability and flooding attacks is thin, and many attacks may well fall into both the vulnerability and flooding categories.

2.3.1 Recruiting and Controlling Attacking Machines

DDoS attacks require engagement of multiple machines, which will be sending the attack traffic to the victim. Those machines do not belong to the attacker. They are usually poorly secured systems at universities, companies, and homes—even at government institutions. The attacker breaks into them, takes full control, and misuses them for the attack. Therefore, the attacking machines are frequently called *zombies*, *daemons*, *slaves*, or *agents*. In this book we use the term *agents*.

How does the attacker gain control over machines that belong to others? The agents are usually poorly secured machines—they do not have recent patches and software updates, they are not protected by a firewall or other security devices, or their users have easily guessed passwords. The attacker takes advantage of these well-known holes to break in. Unpatched and old software has well-known vulnerabilities with already-written exploits. These belong to a specific kind of vulnerabilities—once exploited, they allow the attacker unlimited access to the system, as if he had an administrator's account. Accounts with easily guessed passwords, such as combinations of users' names or dictionary words, allow another easy way into the machine. There are several password-guessing tools that will quickly reveal if any of the accounts on a system have weak passwords.[2] For example, *Phatbot* will attempt to connect and log in to Windows hosts using a set of several dozen very commonly chosen passwords. Even if these programs find accounts that do not have administrator privileges, this access can still be misused

---

[2] A weak password is one that is easily guessed, by either a human guesser or an automated program that tries many possible passwords, such as all very short passwords, all the words in the dictionary, or the most commonly used men's and women's names.

for a DDoS attack or, by exploiting other vulnerabilities, can elevate privileges to the administrator level.

Once the attacker has gained control of the host, she installs the DDoS attack agent and makes sure that all traces of the intrusion are well hidden and that the code runs even after the machine is rebooted.

DDoS attacks frequently involve hundreds or thousands of agents. It would be tedious and time consuming if the attacker had to manually break into each of them. Instead, there are automated tools that discover potential agent machines, break into them, and install the attack code upon a single command from an attacker, and report success back to her. Such tools can easily be downloaded from the Web or acquired from Internet chat channels. In addition to recruiting the collection of agents, automated tools also facilitate the control of this network by keeping track of the agents and providing easy ways of delivering commands to all of them at once. The attacker needs only to issue a single command and have all agents start the flood to the given victim.

2.3.2   Hiding

The attacker further hides her identity by deploying several layers of indirection between her machine and the agents. She uses one or several machines that deliver her commands to the agents. These machines are called *handlers* or *masters*. In this book we use the term *handlers*. Figure 2.1 illustrates this handler/agent architecture.

Another layer of indirection consists of the attacker's logging on to several machines *in sequence*, before accessing the handlers. These intermediary machines between the attacker's machine and the handlers are called the *stepping stones*, and are illustrated in Figure 2.2.

Both handlers and stepping stones are used to hinder investigation attempts. If authorities located and examined an agent machine, all its communication would point to one of the handlers. Further examination of the handler would point to a stepping stone, and from there to another stepping stone. If stepping stones are selected from different countries and continents (and they usually are), it becomes very difficult to follow the trail back to the attacker's machine and unveil her identity.

Another means of obscuring the attack is through the use of *IP spoofing*. Each packet in the Internet carries some control information preceding the data—an *IP header*. One field in the IP header specifies the address of the sender—the *source IP* field. This information is filled in by the machine that sends the packet (an action similar to putting a return address on a letter), and is used by the destination, or the routers on the path to the destination, to send replies back to the source. Attackers

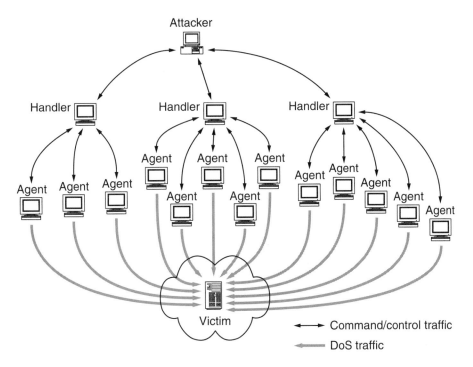

Figure 2.1 Handler/agent architecture

commonly forge this field to achieve impunity for the attacks and hinder the discovery of agent machines. IP spoofing also greatly complicates some DDoS defense approaches that rely on a source address for differentiation between legitimate clients and attackers. With IP spoofing, an attacker easily assumes the identity of a legitimate client or even several of them.

2.3.3 Misusing Legitimate Services

IP spoofing creates an opportunity for fooling noncompromised and otherwise perfectly secure machines into participating in a DDoS attack. The attacker chooses a publicly available service or protocol, such as the Domain Name System (DNS), Web, or ping, and sends service requests to many such servers, forging the source address of the victim. Servers then reply back to the victim, and this flood of replies creates denial of service. This type of attack is called a *reflection attack*, and the servers participating in it are called *reflectors*. Of special interest to the attacker are services that can generate lengthy

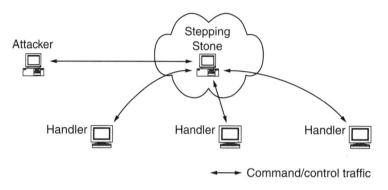

Figure 2.2   Illustration of a site hosting a stepping stone

or numerous replies for a few short requests. This is called *amplification*, and it enables the attacker to create a DoS effect with a few small packets.

2.4   Distribution Effects

Denial of service is possible without using distributed techniques, but it poses a challenge for an attacker. For example, imagine that a DoS attack based on pure flooding originates at a single machine with a 10-Mbps link and is directed toward a victim machine that has a 100-Mbps link. In an attempt to overwhelm the victim's link, the attacker will flood his own network and deny service to himself. To successfully disrupt the victim's communication, the attacker must compromise an agent machine that has more network resources than the victim. Locating and breaking into such a machine may prove difficult, especially if the target of the attack is a well-provisioned site.

However, consider what happens if the same attack is performed in a distributed manner, say, by a hundred machines. Each machine now sends 1 Mbps toward the victim. Assuming all hundred machines have 10-Mbps links, none of them generates enough traffic to cause serious harm to its own local network. But the Internet delivers all attack traffic to the victim, overwhelming its link. Thus, the victim's service is denied, while the attackers are still fully operational.

Distribution brings a number of benefits to the attacker:

- A typical server machine has more computing, memory, and bandwidth resources than a typical client machine. An attacker with control of only one client machine would thus have difficulty overwhelming the server's resources without first overwhelming his own. By using distributed techniques, the attacker can multiply the resources on the attacking end, allowing him to deny service to more powerful machines at the target end.

- To stop a simple DoS attack from a single agent, a defender needs to identify that agent and take some action that prevents it from sending such a large volume of traffic. In many cases, the attack from a machine can be stopped only if the machine's human administrator, or network operator, takes action. If there are 10, 100, or 1,000 agents participating in the attack, however, stopping any single one of them may provide little benefit to the victim. Only by stopping most or all of them can the DoS effect be alleviated. Getting thousands of people to take some action to stop an attack from their machine is an overwhelming challenge.[3]

- If the attacker chooses agents that are spread widely throughout the Internet, attempts to stop the attack are more difficult, since the only point at which all of the attack traffic merges is close to the victim. This point is called the *aggregation point*. Other nodes in the network might experience no telltale signs of the attack and might have difficulty distinguishing the attack traffic from legitimate traffic. Thus, they cannot help defend against the attack.

- In a DoS attack executed from a single agent, the victim might be able to recover by obtaining more resources. For example, an overwhelmed Web server might be able to recruit other local servers to help handle the extra load. Regardless of how powerful a single agent might be, the defender can add more capacity until he outstrips the attacker's ability to generate load. This approach is less effective in defending against DDoS attacks. If the defender doubles his resources to handle twice as many requests, the attacker merely needs to double the number of agents— often an easy task.

Another aspect makes both DoS and DDoS attacks hard to handle: Defenses that work well against many other kinds of attacks are not necessarily effective against denial of service. For years, system administrators have been advised to install a firewall and keep its configuration up to date, to close unnecessary ports on all machines, to stay current with patches of operating systems and other important software, and to run intrusion detection systems to discover any attacks that have managed to penetrate the outer bastions of defense. Unfortunately, these security measures often will not

---

[3] Alternatively, defenders might attempt to locate a handler machine and command agents to stop flooding. This is a challenging task, too, since the attacker may have multiple handlers or use a legitimate service (e.g., IRC) instead of a handler, and the agent commands may be encrypted or password-protected.

help against denial of service. The attack can consist of traffic that the firewall finds acceptable, probably because it bears a close resemblance to legitimate traffic. Since the DoS attack merely needs to exhaust resources, it can work on any port left open, including those that must be open for a node to do its normal business. Attackers can perform DoS attacks on machines that have no vulnerabilities (by the standard definition of that term), so patches to close vulnerabilities may not help. Also, intrusion detection systems are of limited value in dealing with DoS, since, unlike break-ins and thefts, DoS attacks rarely hide themselves. After all, their whole purpose is to interrupt normal business, an event that will usually be noticed.

2.5   DDoS: Hype or Reality?

The issues described in the previous section make DDoS attacks a frightening possibility. Yet researchers in computer and network security are aware of many frightening possibilities that never come to pass. Are security researchers merely alarming the public with claims of the dangers of DDoS?

Unfortunately, DDoS attacks are not speculation or fiction. They occur on a daily basis, directed against a wide range of sites. Chapter 3 details, in timeline fashion, a large number of representative attacks. The details of these attacks will be left to that chapter, while some specifics will be mentioned in this chapter. In addition to several well-known occurrences of DDoS attacks that were widely reported in the press, there are scientific studies of the frequency of these attacks that demonstrate the reality of the problem (see Appendix C for a summary of these studies).

2.5.1   How Common Are DDoS Attacks?

There are some forms of cyberattacks that receive a lot of publicity because they generate a few high-profile incidents, even though these types of attacks do not actually occur that often. Unless these incidents are particularly disastrous, the overall impact of the attacks is more related to publicity than large amounts of damage done to many businesses or individuals.

DDoS attacks do not fit that category. A number of recent studies have demonstrated that DDoS attacks are extremely common in today's networks. Given that they are usually quite effective and perpetrators are rarely caught, there is reason to believe they will become even more popular in the future.

Measuring the frequency of any form of attack in the Internet is difficult. Victims do not always realize that they are under attack. Even if they do, they often fail to report the attack to any authority. A number of organizations use survey techniques to gain some insight into the prevalence of different kinds of cyberattacks and the amount of damage they do. One example is the FBI's annual report on cybercrime, based on information provided by nearly 500 organizations. In the 2004 report, nearly a fifth of the respondents who suffered financial loss from an attack had experienced a DoS attack. The total reported costs of DoS attacks to these companies was over $26 million. Denial of service was the top source of financial loss due to cybercrime! These surveys are often criticized because their methodology is unavoidably subject to certain limitations, but relatively little better data exists.

The methods used in these surveys do not differentiate between distributed and nondistributed DoS attacks, since the technology for making the distinction is in its infancy. In the meantime, researchers have used a variety of techniques to estimate data on the frequency of DDoS attacks and their other characteristics.

For example, Farnam Jahanian of the University of Michigan has been able to observe network activities in the MichNet ISP. This network provider offers ISP service to government and nonprofit organizations in the state of Michigan, including most educational institutions in that state. Over the course of time, Jahanian's team has gathered data suggesting that DDoS attacks are quite common and are increasingly sophisticated. Jahanian's full results have not yet been published; however, a presentation covering some of his results can be found at `http://www.arbor.net/downloads/nanogSlides4 .pdf`.

A number of researchers have investigated various technical means to deduce information about the prevalence and character of DDoS attacks in the Internet [DLD00]. CAIDA (the Cooperative Association for Internet Data Analysis), for example, used a technique called *backscatter*. Full details of this technique and CAIDA's results can be found in Appendix C. Their results suggest that during a three-week observation period in 2001 there were around 4,000 DDoS attacks per week on Internet nodes.

For reasons covered in Appendix C, CAIDA's numbers are certainly an underestimate. Jahanian's results can be interpreted to suggest that the CAIDA figure of 4,000 attacks per week would be more realistically set at 12,000 attacks per week, even leaving aside some classes of DDoS attacks. Further, other data suggests that DDoS attacks have become more common since 2001.

If DDoS attacks are so common, why do we not hear more about them? Evidence gathered by CAIDA and Jahanian suggests that most DDoS attacks are launched against fairly small targets (home machines, for example) for short durations. Some have speculated that many of the incidents represent hackers attacking each other, though too little evidence exists to come to any strong conclusion on this point. Short durations can cause a DDoS attack to appear to be no more than another network glitch. When a user clicks on a link and receives no response for a minute or two, he is more likely to conclude that the server is busy or that there are general network congestion problems, rather than that he (or, more likely, the server) is suffering a DDoS attack. Thus, in many cases DDoS attacks may pass unnoticed.

If many DDoS attacks are not even noticed, how seriously should we regard the problem? First, there is a significant and growing number of high-profile incidents of serious, persistent, powerful DDoS attacks clearly meant to deny service to important sites. Second, remember that the small, short attacks are typically small and short because that was what the attacker wanted to do, rather than what he could do. A DDoS agent network can continue its attack for hours, or perhaps even indefinitely. And attackers can easily gather huge agent armies. The techniques are already well known and of proven effectiveness. All that remains is a sufficient motive for them to be widely used for destructive purposes.

2.5.2   The Magnitude of DDoS Attacks

Another potentially measurable dimension of a DDoS attack is its size. The size of an attack can be measured in the traffic it generates or in the number of sites participating in the attack. It can also be measured in its duration, a characteristic that some DDoS studies have addressed.

The built-in statistics capabilities of the Shaft attack tool [DLD00] allowed researchers to estimate the magnitude of a given attack in late 1999, at 4.5 Mbps emanating from a single DDoS agent in a network of about 100 agents (see also Figure 4.11 in Chapter 4). Also, MultiRouter Traffic Grapher (MRTG) measurements [Oet] from an actual attack in May 2001 collected close to the target location provide a lower estimate for the inbound attack traffic volume of about 25 Mbps (see Figure 4.13 in Chapter 4). The lower estimate is due to the measurement equipment collapsing intermittently under the heavy load.

DDoS attacks that have taken out large network links in the past, such as an attack on Australian Uecomm, have involved volumes of up to 600,000 pps [Gra]. In attacks on the DNS root servers in 2002, each server received 100,000 to 200,000 pps [Nar]. In some cases, such as the Al-Jazeera attack in 2003, the attackers added attack volume as the defenders added capacity to handle traffic. This shows that attackers can easily increase the attack strength when necessary, so the measured attack magnitudes have more to do with what the attacker feels is required than with the maximum amount that he can generate. In fact, many attacks may have specifically used a set of moderate-sized discrete attack networks so as to not expose all of them at one time. More recent attackers have learned that it is wasteful to use all of their resources at one time and instead ramp up an attack slowly to maximize how long the attack can be maintained in the face of attrition of the agents.

The backscatter approach used by CAIDA can also estimate the volume of attacks. (Again, for details on how this can be done, see Appendix C.) Taking into account certain limitations of the approach that might lead to underestimates, half of the attacks they observed caused volumes of 350 pps or more. Depending on the target's capabilities, the type of packet, and the target's defenses, this volume is often enough to deny service. The largest volumes CAIDA deduced were hundreds of thousands of packets per second. For example, in the TCP SYN flood attacks against SCO in December 2003, CAIDA estimated that SCO's servers received as many as 50,000 pps at one point and dealt with a total of over 700 million attack packets over a 32-hour period. They estimated this peak rate of 50,000 pps yielded "approximately 20 Mbits/second of Internet traffic in each direction, comparable to half the capacity of a DS3 line (roughly 45 MBits/second.)" [MVS01].

In terms of the number of machines involved in an attack, statistics are harder to come by. It is clear from evidence gathered by the University of Minnesota, which suffered one of the first DDoS attacks in 1999, that DDoS attack networks could be assembled from well over 2,200 systems using only partially automated agent recruitment methods. This minimum number is known because that attack did not use IP spoofing. In attacks in which some form of IP spoofing is used, merely counting the number of IP addresses observed during a particular DDoS attack will grossly overestimate the number of nodes involved.

Another approach is to deduce the number of machines from the observed volume. The largest attack rate observed by CAIDA was estimated to be 679,000 pps. How many packets a machine can generate per second depends on several factors, including its CPU speed and network connectivity. For machines with 10-Mbps links to the Internet, generating 20,000 pps is probably near their maximum capability. So if we assume the largest attack observed by CAIDA was performed by a group of such machines, there had to be at least 30 or 40 of them. For the DNS server attack mentioned above, there had to be at least 90 of them. Many machines have substantially lower speed Internet connections, and if these machines are used as agents, many more of them would be required to achieve these rates. For example, if all agents used 56 Kbps links to connect to the Internet, CAIDA's largest observed attack would have involved at least 5,800 agents. The actual number of agents used in this attack is probably between these ballpark figures. Reflected attacks, where attacking hosts send out forged attack packets that are reflected off a very large number of legitimate servers around the world, greatly amplify the attack. One such attack against futuresite.register.com involved a very small number of attacking hosts, but was still able to generate 60 to 90 million bits per second flooding the victim.

One might wonder where the DDoS agents come from. Most experts believe that very few attackers use their own machines to launch DDoS attacks, since doing so would increase their risk of being caught. Instead, they compromise other machines remotely and use them to launch the attack. If compromising a remote machine were a difficult process requiring extensive human intelligence and attention, this factor would limit the seriousness of the DDoS threat. However, experience has shown that automated techniques are highly effective at compromising remote sites, which can then be used to launch DDoS attacks.

Just to give an idea of how easy it is to compromise a large number of hosts, here are some figures:

- Microsoft announced that their MSBlast cleanup tool was downloaded and used to successfully clean up 9.5 million hosts from August 2003 to April 2004, an average of approximately 1 million compromised computers per month (see `http://zdnet.com.com/2100-1105-5201807.html?tag=nl`).

- Microsoft announced in May 2004 that they had cleaned up 2 million *Sasser* infected hosts (see `http://www.securityfocus.com/news/8573`).

- The same news story reports Symantec had identified a bot network of 400,000 hosts.

- A network administrator in the Netherlands has identified between 1 million and 2 million unique IP addresses associated with *Phatbot* infections. *Phatbot* has features to harvest MyDoom- and Bagel-infected hosts, among other infection vectors (see `http://www.ladlass.com/archives/001938.html`).

Probably the most common method of recruiting agents is to run an automated program that scans a large IP address range attempting to find machines that are susceptible to well-known methods of compromise. These programs, called automated infection toolkits, or auto-rooters (after the name of the system administrator account on Unix systems, *root*, also the hacker verb meaning "to compromise or gain elevated privileges on"), are generally quite successful in finding large numbers of vulnerable machines, particularly if they are updated to include newly discovered vulnerabilities that are less likely to have been patched.

The ultimate in automation is an Internet worm—a program that looks for vulnerable machines and infects them with a copy of its code. Worms propagate extremely rapidly. Some worms have used their armies of infected machines specifically to perform DDoS attacks. The worm can even carry the code to perpetrate the DDoS attack. For example, Code Red was designed to perform a DDoS attack from all the nodes it compromised on a particular IP address. Code Red succeeded in infecting over 250,000 machines, by some estimates. Code Red II infected as many as 500,000 machines. Estimates for the number of machines infected by the *W32/Blaster* and *W32/Sobig*.F worms run from the tens of thousands to a few hundreds of thousands, and some reports refer to these numbers as "small." Sasser infected at least 2 million hosts, judging by Microsoft's report (`http://www.securityfocus.com/news/8573`). Thus, it is quite realistic to envision DDoS attacks originating from hundreds of thousands, even millions of points in the Internet.

2.6   How Vulnerable Are You to DDoS?

If you accept that DDoS attacks are a real threat to some Internet sites, the next question likely to come to mind is: How vulnerable is my site? The simple answer is that if your site is connected to the Internet, you are a potential target of a DDoS attack. A DDoS attack can target any IP address and, if the attack is strong enough, it is likely to be successful. Large and small businesses, ISPs, government organizations that rely on networking, and even private individuals are among those who may be damaged by a DDoS attack. The more use you have for the Internet in your enterprise, the greater the damage you will suffer if a DDoS attack takes it offline for an extended period.

Even if your machine sits behind a NAT box,[4] a firewall, or some other form of protection that prevents arbitrary traffic from being directly routed to it, you may still be vulnerable to the more sophisticated DDoS attacks. A sophisticated attacker can replay or spoof traffic that should go to your node or indirectly subject you to denial of service by overloading the NAT box, firewall, router, or network link.

---

[4] A Network Address Translation (NAT) box is a firewall-like host acting as a gateway to a network. All packets leaving the network pass through the NAT box and have their source addresses replaced by the address of this box. A reverse transformation is applied to destination addresses of incoming packets— the address of the NAT box is replaced with the appropriate address of a machine inside the network. The NAT technique enables a network to hide its internal structure—the only address that external users ever see is that of the NAT box.

Further, as we previously discussed, careful system and network administration will not necessarily save you from an attack. While some fixes will prevent vulnerability attacks, your site will still be susceptible to large flooding attacks.

Heavy provisioning, in the form of ample server and network capacity, can protect you from many flooding DDoS attacks, but cannot guarantee your immunity. Any realistic amount of capacity you provide can be overcome if an attacker recruits enough machines to press his attack against you. Reflect on how heavily you would have to provision yourself to withstand a DDoS attack by the million-plus *Phatbot* network reported earlier.

Nonetheless, there are things you can do to decrease your vulnerability to DDoS attacks and make you a less attractive target. Heavy provisioning helps, since it rules out casual attacks by hackers who have only one or two dozen agent machines at their disposal. Closing vulnerabilities also helps, since it fends off vulnerability attacks. If keeping a low profile on the network is an option for your organization, doing so requires the attacker to find some obscure information before he can launch his attack. There are practical steps to take to strengthen your network and also efficient attack responses that alleviate the DoS effect. We will discuss these in more detail in Chapter 6. Chapter 7 looks at research approaches that may lead to new DDoS defense tools in the future. A number of commercial products have successfully defended against many forms of DDoS attack; we will discuss some of them in Appendix B.

Generally, the evidence suggests that practically all DDoS attacks that occur are not nearly as bad as catastrophic worst-case-scenario thinking suggests they could be. Even some of the high-profile attacks on major Internet sites were not that difficult to handle once the defenders were aware of the nature of the attack and had a little time to respond to it. If you depend on continual Internet availability of your resources, you are almost certainly in danger from DDoS attacks; but with a little knowledge, forethought, and vigilance you can prevent DDoS attacks on your site from becoming disasters.

Even if you are not particularly dismayed by the prospect of being a DDoS victim, another element of DDoS attacks might cause you trouble. To perpetrate a strong DDoS attack, the attacker typically compromises a large number of machines. If your machine is among them, at best you are unwillingly sharing your resources with a criminal who definitely doesn't have your best interests at heart. At worst, you may find yourself partially liable for some of the damages done by his attack, or your vital data may be stolen or damaged by the attacker who has taken over your machine. The value attackers obtain by performing DDoS attacks on others has made such criminals more motivated to compromise ever larger armies of agent machines, meaning that your machine has become more likely to be taken over by an outside party.

## CHAPTER 3

History of DoS and DDoS

In this chapter we will discuss the origins of Internet denial of service, based on the historical aspects of the Internet and its design principles, as well as the events that led to major DDoS attacks on Internet sites and beyond, up to today. We describe the motivations of both the Internet designers and the attackers.

3.1 Motivation

It is human nature that when groups of people get together, there is bound to be disagreement and conflict. This conflict can take many forms: glaring at someone who is crowding you in line to get them to back off, cutting someone off in traffic, using the favorite national hand gesture that shows the utmost contempt possible for them. Or even worse acts: slashing someone's tires, pouring sugar in their gas tank to make their car fail, or throwing a bundle of money into a public square or street causing a riot and obstructing passage. As it happens, all of these are examples of physical-world forms of DoS, denial of transportation, in these last examples.

As the Internet gained popularity as a virtual meeting place, it also became a place of conflict. Usenet newsgroups that bring together people with like interests degrade into flame-filled series of tirade after tirade among arguing members. Or someone who feels wronged goes "trolling" [Wik]—making inflammatory statements, calling someone names, asking a blatantly off-topic question—anything to purposely cause flame wars and degrade conversation in a newsgroup or e-mail list. Someone who trolls can cause dozens, even hundreds, of useless e-mail messages saying, "Stop this!," "You're just an idiot and should leave this group," "Can't someone ban this jerk from our newsgroup?", etc. In some cases, it gets so bad that people unsubscribe and leave the group permanently. The degradation of discourse is another form of DoS—some kind of interference that prevents a computer user from doing something that he or she would otherwise have been able to do had there been no interference, but one that often cannot be maintained very long.

Articles like Suler and Phillips' "The Bad Boys of Cyberspace" [SP98] and a study titled "The Experience of Bad Behavior in Online Social Spaces: A Survey of Online Users," by Davis [JPD] show that people can sometimes behave quite differently, often in very antisocial ways, when interacting in the Internet as opposed to when they interact with people face to face. They may misinterpret things because they lack nonverbal cues or because they lack detail or context. They may be quicker to anger than if speaking to someone face to face, and because they cannot see the person they are speaking to, they may react more strongly. Anonymity may give them a sense of invisibility, and they may consider the icons that represent other users as being unreal and disassociated from another person.

This point is important. Some people consider online chat rooms to be just like real rooms, and they can form a picture in their mind that gives these other participants *identity*. Other people in the same chat room will only see the words on the screen, and they will themselves feel invisible and invincible because they sit in the comfort of their own room and can turn off the computer whenever they want. The other world (and everyone in it) then ceases to exist, just like the TV world vanishes when the set is turned off. Unlike the physical world, where two people having a conflict are often standing toe to toe, in the Internet the conflict takes place with an intermediary network that is effectively a black box to the parties involved. There is only a keyboard and monitor in front of each person, and their respective moral and ethical frameworks to guide them in how they act. This disassociation and lack of physical proximity encourages people to participate in illegal activities in the Internet, such as hacking, denial of service, or collecting copyrighted material. They do not feel that in reality they are doing any serious harm.

Typical end users do not care about the intrinsics of network communications in the Internet. Instead, they are merely interested in the benefits the Internet provides them with, such as e-commerce or Internet banking. However, those who have that detailed knowledge of network specifics and can abuse it to exclude and effectively deny the services to others feel greatly empowered. That is the point at which DoS programs enter the scene.

Over the years, DoS attacks in the Internet have predominantly been associated with communication mechanisms such as newsgroups, chat rooms, online games, etc. These are *asynchronous* communication mechanisms, meaning that there is no direct and immediate acknowledgment of receipt, and no real-time dialogue. E-mail gets delivered when it gets delivered, and messages can come in out of order and get mixed in with all the rest. Asynchronous communication mechanisms in the Internet, such as Usenet newsgroups or e-mail lists, can be attacked by trolling or by flooding with bogus messages, but these attack mechanisms do not have a direct effect and can fairly easily be dealt with by filtering. Since these communication mechanisms are asynchronous, there is a delay and thus the attacker does not get instant gratification.

DoS attacks that cause servers to crash or fill networks with useless traffic, on the other hand, *do* provide immediate satisfaction. They directly affect a system and, if combined with a threat immediately beforehand, increase the potency and satisfaction for the attacker. They work best on synchronous means of communication, like real-time chat or Web activity that involves a sustained series of interactions between a browser and a Web server.

For example, if Jane wants to hurt NotARealSiteForPuppies.com, to really scare them, she might first send them a threatening e-mail that states, "You people are scum! I am going to take your site down for three hours, and then I'm going after your little dog, too!" She waits until she gets a reply saying this is being reported to the ISP of the account that sent the message (most likely a stolen account), and then she immediately begins the promised attack. She then checks to see if the Web page comes up, and sees that the browser reports, "Timeout connecting to server." Mission accomplished!

Synchronous communication mechanisms like online games [Gam] and Internet Relay Chat (IRC [vLL]), as opposed to Usenet newsgroups and mailing lists, are more often subjected to DoS attacks because of this direct effect. Not only can you directly affect an individual user, causing them to get knocked off of IRC channels, but you can also disrupt an entire IRC network. It is important to understand these attacks (even if you don't use or have anything to do with IRC) because the tools and techniques are just as effective against a Web server, or a corporation's external Domain Name System (DNS) or mail servers.

Early attacks on the IRC network were known to a few security experts, such as co-author Sven Dietrich, in the early 1990s. DoS attacks, which in one instance took the form of a TCP RST flood, caused IRC servers to "split" (i.e., to lose track of who owns a channel). A remote user, being the only one left in that channel, would then "own" one or more chat channels, since the legitimate owner was split from the local network. When the networks would join again, legitimate and illegitimate owners would have a face-off, which could lead to further retribution. Larger-scale attacks were also used to remove unwelcome users from chat channels, as an effective method of kicking them off forcefully. These problems were known to some IRC operators at Boston University at the time.

Over the years, IRC has been one of the main motivators for development and use of DoS and DDoS tools, as well as being its major target. This relationship between IRC and DDoS attacks shares some similarities to the development of the HIV/AIDS crisis in the 1980s.[1] When HIV/AIDS was first discovered, many considered it a problem for only gays or Haitians or intravenous drug users. As long as you were not in that group, why should you worry about HIV/AIDS? Research into treatments and cures did not start early enough, and as a result HIV/AIDS spread across the world, to the point where today, the world's largest country, China, has cases in all levels of society throughout the entire country.

Similarly, DoS and DDoS were originally seen as an IRC-related problem, affecting only IRC servers and IRC users. Some sites even banned IRC servers on their campus, or moved IRC servers outside of the main network to a *DMZ* (DeMilitarized Zone) "free fire zone" that wouldn't impact the main network, all with the belief that this would "solve" the problem of DoS. (In fact, it just pushed it away, allowing it to continue to develop and outpace defense capabilities.) The same issue involved in DDoS—a large flood of packets—in 2003 began to occur as a result of worms, taking down many of the largest networks in the world, which had nearly five years to understand the problem and prepare for it but chose not to.

In this same time, the attack tools themselves have grown in power, capabilities, ability to spread, and sophistication to the point where they are today being used in sophisticated attacks with financial motivations by organized criminal gangs. How did all this happen?

We begin our quest for answers by examining the assumptions and principles on which the Internet was built.

---

[1] We are certainly not trying to say that DDoS has caused even a minute fraction of the harm that HIV/AIDS has. That is ridiculous. What is common are the lack of recognition of the problem by the general populace and media, the lack of response by some because it was believed to be "somebody else's problem," and a slow increase to the point where the problem becomes well entrenched and widespread. It was Machiavelli who said, "When trouble is sensed well in advance it can easily be remedied; if you wait for it to show itself any medicine will be too late because the disease will have become incurable. . . . Political disorders can be quickly healed if they are seen well in advance (and only a prudent ruler has such foresight); when, for lack of a diagnosis, they are allowed to grow in such a way that everyone can recognize them, remedies are too late."

3.2 Design Principles of the Internet

The predecessor to today's Internet, called *ARPANET* (Advanced Research Project Agency Network), was born in the late 1960s when computers were not present in every home and office.[2] Rather, they existed in universities and research institutions, and were used by experienced and knowledgeable staff for scientific calculations. Computer security was viewed as purely host security, not network security, as most hosts were not networked yet. As those calculations became more advanced and computers started gaining a significant presence in research activities, people realized that interconnecting research networks and enabling them to talk to each other in a common language would advance scientific progress. As it turned out, the Internet advanced more than the field of science—it transformed and revolutionized all aspects of human life, and introduced a few new problems along the way.

3.2.1 Packet-Switched Networks

The key idea in the design of the Internet was the idea of the *packet-switched network* [Kle61, Bar64]. The birth of the Internet happened in the middle of the Cold War, when the threat of global war was hanging over the world. Network communications were already crucial for many critical operations in the national defense, and were performed over dedicated lines through a *circuit-switched network*. This was an expensive and vulnerable design. Government agencies had to pay to set up the network infrastructure everywhere they had critical nodes, then set up communication channels for every pair of nodes that wanted to talk to each other. During this communication, the route from the sender to the receiver was fixed. The intermediate network reserved resources for the communication that could not be shared by information from other source-destination pairs. These resources could only be freed once the communication ended. Thus, if the sender and the receiver talked infrequently but in high-volume bursts, they would tie down a considerable amount of resources that would lie unutilized most of the time.

The bigger problem was the vulnerability of the communication to intermediate node failures. The dedicated communication line was as reliable as the weakest of the intermediate nodes comprising it. Single node or link failure led to the teardown of the whole communication line. If another line was available, a new channel

---

[2] For a historical overview of the ARPANET, see the University of Texas timeline at `http://www.cs.utexas.edu/users/chris/think/ARPANET/Timeline/`

between the sender and the receiver had to be set up from the start. Nodes in circuit-switched networks had only a few lines available, which were high-quality leased lines dedicated to point-to-point connectivity between computers. These were not only very expensive, but made the network topology extremely vulnerable to physical node and link failures and consequently could not provide reliable communications in case of targeted physical attack. A report [Bar64] not only discussed this in detail, but also offered simulation results that showed that adding more nodes and links to a circuit-switched network only marginally improves the situation.

The packet-switched network emerged as a new paradigm of network design. This network consists of numerous low-cost, unreliable nodes and links that connect senders and receivers. The low cost of network resources facilitates building a much larger and more tightly connected network than in the circuit-switched case, providing redundancy of paths. The reliability of communication over the unreliable fabric is achieved through link and node redundancy and robust transport protocols. Instead of having dedicated channels between the sender and the receiver, network resources are shared among many communication pairs. The senders and receivers communicate through packets, with each packet carrying the origin and the destination address, and some control information in its header. Intermediate nodes queue and interleave packets from many communications and send them out as fast as possible on the best available path to their destination. If the current path becomes unavailable due to node or link failure, a new route is quickly discovered by the intermediate nodes and subsequent packets are sent on this new route. To use the communication resource more efficiently, links may have variable data rates. To compensate for the occasional discrepancy in the incoming and outgoing link rates, and to accommodate traffic bursts, intermediate nodes use *store-and-forward switching*—they store packets in a buffer until the link leading to the destination becomes available. Experiments have shown that store-and-forward switching can achieve a significant advantage with very little storage at the intermediate nodes [Bar64].

The packet-switched network paradigm revolutionized communication. All of its design principles greatly improved transmission speed and reliability and decreased communication cost, leading to the Internet we know today—cheap, fast, and extremely reliable. However, they also created a fertile ground for misuse by malicious participants. Let's take a closer look at the design principles of the packet-switched network.

- **There are no dedicated resources between the sender and the receiver**. This idea allowed a manifold increase in network throughput by multiplexing packets from many different communications. Instead of providing a dedicated channel with the peak bandwidth for each communication, packet-switched links can support numerous communications by taking advantage of the fact that peaks do not occur in all of them at once. A downside of this design is that there is no resource guarantee, and this is exactly why aggressive DDoS attack traffic can take over resources from legitimate users. Much research has been done in fair resource sharing and resource reservation at the intermediate nodes, to offer service guarantees to legitimate traffic in the presence of malicious users. While resource reservation and fair sharing ensure balanced use among legitimate users, they do not solve the DDoS problem. Resource reservation protocols are sparsely deployed and thus cannot make a large impact on DDoS traffic. Resource-sharing approaches assign a fair share of a resource to each user (e.g., bandwidth, CPU time, disk space). In the Internet context, the problem of establishing user identity is escalated due to IP spoofing. An attacker can thus fake as many identities as he wants and monopolize resources in spite of the fair sharing mechanism. Even if these problems were solved, an attacker could effectively slow service to legitimate users to an unacceptable rate by compromising enough machines and using their "fair shares" of the resources.

- **Packets can travel on any route between the sender and the receiver.** Packet-switched network design facilitates the development of dynamic routing algorithms that quickly discover an alternative route if the primary one fails. This greatly enhances communication robustness as packets in flight can take a different route to the receiver from the one that was valid when they were sent. The route change and selection process are performed by the intermediate nodes directly affected by the route failure, and are transparent to the other participants, including the sender and the receiver. This facilitates fast packet forwarding and low routing message overhead, but has a side effect that no single network node knows the complete route between the packet origin and its destination.

  To illustrate this, let us observe the network in Figure 3.1. Assume that the path from A to B leads over one node, C, and that a node D is somewhere on the other side of the Internet. If D ever sees a packet from A to B, it cannot infer if the source address (A) is fake, or if C somehow failed and the packet is trying to follow an alternative path. Therefore, D will happily forward the packet to B. This example illustrates why it is difficult to detect and filter spoofed packets.[3] IP spoofing is one of the centerpieces of the DDoS problem. It is not necessary

---

[3] Packets that have a fake source IP address

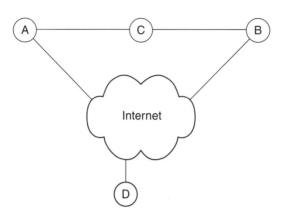

Figure 3.1   Routing in a packet-switched network

for many DDoS attacks, but it significantly aggravates the problem and challenges many DDoS defense approaches.

- **Different links have different data rates.** This is a logical design principle, as some links will naturally be more heavily used than others. The Internet's usage patterns caused it to evolve a specific topology, resembling a spider with many legs. Nodes in the Internet core (the body of the spider) are heavily interconnected, while edge nodes (on the spider's legs) usually have one or two paths connecting them to the core. Core links provide sufficient bandwidth to accommodate heavy traffic from many different sources to many destinations, while the links closer to the edges need only support the end network traffic and need less bandwidth. A side effect of this design is that the traffic from the high-bandwidth core link can overwhelm the low-bandwidth edge link if many sources attempt to talk to the same destination simultaneously, which is exactly what happens during DDoS attacks.

3.2.2   Best-Effort Service Model and End-to-End Paradigm

The main purpose of the Internet is to move packets from source to destination quickly and at a low cost. In this endeavor, all packets are treated as equal and no service guarantees are given. This is the *best-effort service model*, one of the key principles of the Internet design. Since routers need only focus on traffic forwarding, their design is simple and highly specialized for this function.

It was understood early on that the Internet would likely be used for a variety of services, some of which were unpredictable. In order to keep the interconnection network scalable and to support all the services a user may need now and in the future, the Internet creators decided to make it simple. The *end-to-end paradigm* states that application-specific requirements, such as reliable delivery (i.e., assurance that no packet loss occurred), packet reorder detection, error detection and correction, quality-of-service requirements, encryption, and similar services, should not be supported by the interconnection network but by the higher-level transport protocols deployed at the end hosts—the sender and the receiver. Thus, when a new application emerges, only the interested end hosts need to deploy the necessary services, while the interconnection network remains simple and invariant. The Internet Protocol (IP) manages basic packet manipulation, and is supported by all routers and end hosts in the Internet. End hosts additionally deploy a myriad of other higher-level protocols to get specific service guarantees: Transport Control Protocol (TCP) for reliable packet delivery; User Datagram Protocol (UDP) for simple traffic streaming; Real Time Protocol (RTP), Real Time Control Protocol (RTCP), and Real Time Streaming Protocol (RTSP) for streaming media traffic; and Internet Control Message Protocol (ICMP) for control messages. Even higher-level services are built on these, such as file transfer, Web browsing, instant messaging, e-mail, and videoconferencing.

The end-to-end argument is frequently understood as justification not to add new functionalities to the interconnection network. Following this reasoning, DDoS defenses located in the interconnection network would not be acceptable. However, the end-to-end argument, as originally stated, did not claim that the interior of the network should never again be augmented with any functionality, nor that all future changes in network behavior had to be implemented only on the ends. The crux of this argument was that only services that were required for all or most traffic belonged in the center of the network. Services that were specific to particular kinds of traffic were better placed at the edge of the network.

Another component of the end-to-end argument was that security functions (which include access control and response functions to mitigate attacks) were the responsibility of the edge devices (i.e., end hosts) and not something the network should do. This argument assumes that owners of end hosts:

- Have the resources, including time, skills, and tools, to ensure the security of every end host
- Will be able to notice malicious activity themselves and take response actions quickly

It also assumes that compromised hosts will themselves not become a threat to the availability of the network to other hosts.

These assumptions have increasingly proven to be incorrect, and network stability became a serious problem in 2003 and 2004 due to rampant worms and bot networks.

(The *mstream* DDoS program, for example, caused routers to crash as a result of the way it spoofed source addresses, as did the Slammer worm.)

Taking that into account, there is a good case for putting DDoS defense mechanisms in the core of the network, since DDoS attacks can leverage any sort of packet whatsoever, and pure flooding attacks cannot be handled at an edge once they achieve a volume greater than the edge connection's bandwidth. DDoS defense mechanisms that add general defenses against attacks using any kind of traffic are not out of bounds by the definitions of the end-to-end argument, and should be considered, provided they can be demonstrated to be safe, effective, and cheap—the latter especially—for ordinary traffic when no attack is going on. It is not clear that any of the currently proposed DDoS defense mechanisms requiring core deployment meet those requirements yet, and obviously any serious candidate for such deployment must do so before it should even be considered for actual insertion into the routers making up the core of the Internet. However, both proponents and critics of core DDoS defenses should remember that the authors of the original end-to-end argument put it forward as a useful design principle, not absolute truth.

Critiques of DDoS defense solutions based solely on violation of the end-to-end argument miss the point. On the other hand, critiques of particular components of DDoS defense solutions on the basis that they could be performed as well or better on the edges are proper uses of the end-to-end argument.

These two above-mentioned ideas, the *best-effort service model* and the *end-to-end paradigm*, essentially define the same design principle: *The core network should be kept simple; all the complexity should be pushed to the edge nodes*. Thanks to this simplicity and division of functionalities between the core and the edges, the Internet easily met challenges of scale, the introduction of new applications and protocols, and a manifold increase in traffic while remaining a robust and cheap medium with ever-increasing bandwidth and speed. A downside of this simple design becomes evident when one of the parties in the end-to-end model is malicious and acts to damage the other party. Since the interconnection network is simple, intermediate nodes do not have the functionality necessary to step in and police the violator's traffic.

This is exactly what happens in DDoS attacks, IP spoofing, and congestion incidents. The problem first became evident in October 1986 when the Internet suffered a series of congestion collapses [Nag84]. End hosts were simply sending more traffic than could be supported by the interconnection network. The problem was quickly addressed by the design and deployment of several TCP congestion control mechanisms [Flo00]. These mechanisms augment end-host TCP implementations to detect packet drops as a sign of congestion and respond to them by rapidly reducing the sending rate.

However, it soon became clear that end-to-end flow management cannot ensure a fair allocation of resources in the presence of aggressive flows. In other words, those users who would not deploy congestion control were able to easily steal bandwidth from well-behaved congestion-responsive flows. As congestion builds up and congestion-responsive flows reduce their sending rate, more bandwidth becomes available for the aggressive flows that keep on pounding.

This problem was finally handled by violating the end-to-end paradigm and enlisting the help of intermediate routers to monitor and police bandwidth allocation among flows to ensure fairness. There are two major mechanisms deployed in today's routers for congestion avoidance purposes—*active queue management* and *fair scheduling* algorithms [BCC+98]. A similar approach may be needed to completely address the DDoS problem. We discuss this further in Section 5.5.3.

3.2.3 Internet Evolution

The Internet has experienced immense growth in size and popularity since its creation. The number of Internet hosts has been growing exponentially and currently (in 2004) there are over 170 million computers online. Thanks to its cheap and fast message delivery, the Internet has become extremely popular and its use has spread from scientific institutions into companies, government, public works, schools, homes, banks, and many other places.

This immense growth has also brought on several issues that affect Internet security.

- **Scale.** In the early days of the ARPANET, there was a maximum of 64 hosts allowed in the network, and if a new host needed to be added to the network, another had to leave. In 1971, there were 23 hosts and 15 connection hosts (nowadays called routers). In August 1981, when these restrictions no longer applied (NCP, with 6-bit address fields allowing only 64 hosts, was being phased out—it was being replaced by TCP, which was specified in 1974 and initially deployed in 1975), there were only 213 hosts online. By 1983, there were more than 1,000, by 1987 more than 10,000, and by 1989 (when the ARPANET was shut down) more than 100,000 hosts. In January 2003, there were more than 170 million Internet hosts. It is quite feasible to manage several hundred hosts, but it is impossible to manage 170 million of them. Poorly managed machines tend to be easy to compromise. Consequently, in spite of continuing efforts to secure online machines, the pool of vulnerable (easily compromised) hosts does not get any smaller. This means that attackers can easily enlist hundreds or thousands of agents for DDoS attacks, and will be able to obtain even more in the future.

- **User profile**. A common ARPANET user in the 1970s was a scientist who had a fair knowledge of computers and accessed a small, fairly constant set of machines at remote sites that typically ran a well-known and static set of software. A large number of today's Internet users are home users who need Internet access for Web browsing, game downloads, e-mail, and chat. Those users usually lack knowledge to properly secure and administer their machines. Moreover, they commonly download binary files (e.g., games) from unknown Internet sites or receive them in e-mail. A very effective way for the attacker to spread his malicious code is to disguise it to look like a useful application (a *Trojan horse*), and post it online or send it in an e-mail. The unwitting user executes the code and his machine gets compromised and recruited into the agent army. An ever-growing percentage of the Internet users are home users whose machines are constantly online and poorly secured, representing an easy recruiting pool for an attacker assembling a DDoS agent army.

- **Popularity**. Today, Internet use is no longer limited to universities and research institutions, but permeates many aspects of everyday life. Since connectivity plays an important role in many businesses and infrastructure functions, it is an attractive target for the attackers. Internet attacks inflict great financial damage and affect many daily activities.

The evolution of the Internet from a wide-area research network into the global communication backbone exposed security flaws inherent in the Internet design and made the task of correcting them both pressing and extremely challenging.

3.2.4   Internet Management

The way the Internet is managed creates additional challenges for DDoS defense. The Internet is not a hierarchy but a community of numerous networks, interconnected to provide global access to their customers. As early as the days of NSFnet,[4] there existed little islands of self-managed networks as part of the noncommercial network. Each of the Internet networks is managed locally and run according to policies defined by its owners. There is no central authority. Thanks to this management approach, the Internet has remained a free medium where any opinion can be heard. On the other hand, there is no way to enforce global deployment of any particular security mechanism or policy. Many promising DDoS defense solutions need to be deployed at

---

[4] NSFnet, founded in 1986, was the National Science Foundation offspring from the ARPANET, meant to connect educational and research institutions.

numerous points in the Internet to be effective, as illustrated in Chapter 5. IP spoofing is another problem that will likely need a distributed solution. The distributed nature of these threats will make it very difficult for single-node solutions to counteract them. However, the impossibility of enforcing global deployment makes highly distributed solutions unattractive. See Chapter 5 for a detailed discussion of defense solutions and their deployment patterns.

Due to privacy and business concerns, network service providers typically do not wish to provide information on cross-network traffic behavior and may be reluctant to cooperate in tracing attacks (see [Lip02] for further discussion of Internet tracing challenges and possible solutions, as well as the legal issues in Chapter 8). Furthermore, there is no automated support for tracing attacks across several networks. Each request needs to be authorized and put into effect by a human at each network. This introduces large delays. Since many DDoS attacks are shorter than a few hours, they will likely end before agent machines can be located.

3.3   DoS and DDoS Evolution

There are many security problems in today's Internet. E-mail viruses lurk to infect machines and spread further, computer worms—sometimes silently—swarm the Internet, competitors and your neighbor's kids attempt to break into company machines and networks and steal industrial secrets, DDoS attacks knock down online services. The list goes on and on. None of these problems have been completely solved so far, but many have been significantly lessened through practical technological solutions. Firewalls have greatly helped reduce the danger from the intrusions by blocking all but necessary incoming traffic. Antivirus programs prevent the execution of known worms and viruses on the protected machine, thus defeating infection and stopping the spread. Applications and operating systems check for software updates and patch themselves automatically, greatly reducing the number of vulnerabilities that can be exploited to compromise a host machine.

However, the DoS problem remains largely unhandled, in spite of great academic and commercial efforts to solve it. Sophisticated firewalls, the latest antivirus software, automatic updates, and a myriad of other security solutions improve the situation only slightly, defending the victim from only the crudest attacks. It is, however, strikingly easy to generate a successful DDoS attack that bypasses these defenses and takes the victim down for as long as the attacker wants. And there is often nothing a victim can do about it.

How did these tools develop, and how are they being used? We will now look at a combined history of the development of network-based DoS and DDoS attack tools, in relation to the attacks waged with them.

3.3.1   History of Network-Based Denial of Service

The developmental progression of DoS and DDoS tools and associated attacks can give great insight into likely trends for the future, as well as allowing an organization to gauge the kinds of defenses they need to consider based on what is realistic to expect from various attackers, from less skilled up to advanced attackers.

These are only some representative tools and attacks, not necessarily all of the significant attacks. For more stories, see `http://staff.washington.edu/dittrich/misc/ddos/`.

The Late 1980s

The CERT Coordination Center (CERT/CC, which was originally founded by DARPA as the Computer Emergency Response Team) at Carnegie Mellon University's Software Engineering Institute was established in 1988 in response to the so-called Morris worm, which brought the Internet to its knees.[5] The CERT Coordination Center has a long-established expertise in handling and responding to incidents in the Internet, analyzing and reporting vulnerabilities within systems, as well as research in computer and network security, and networked system survivability. Figure 3.2 presents a CERT Coordination Center–created summary of the trends in attacker tools over the last few years.

The Early 1990s

After the story of the Morris worm incident died out, the Internet continued to grow through the early 1990s into a fun place, with lots of free information and services. More and more sites were added, and Robert Metcalf stated his now famous law: *The usefulness, or utility, of a network equals the square of the number of users.* But as we saw earlier in Section 3.1, some percentage of these new users will not be nice, friendly users.

In the mid-1990s, remote DoS attack programs appeared and started to cause problems. In order to use these programs, one needed an account on a big computer, on a fast network, to have maximum impact. This led to rampant account theft at

---

[5] The Morris worm, written by and named after Robert Morris, Jr., was a self-propagating program that spread from computer system to computer system via its network connections [Spa86].

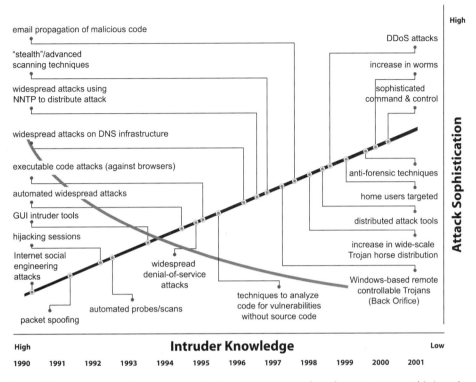

Figure 3.2 Over time, attacks on networked computer systems have become more sophisticated, but the knowledge attackers need has decreased. Intruder tools have become more sophisticated and easy to use. Thus, more people can become "successful intruders" even though they have less technical knowledge. (Reprinted with permission of the CERT Coordination Center.)

universities in order for attackers to have use of stolen accounts to run DoS programs—as they were easy to identify and shut down, they were often considered "throwaway" accounts—which drove a market for installing sniffers.[6] These accounts would be traded for pirated software, access to hard-to-reach networks, stolen computers, credit card numbers, cash, etc. At the time, flat thick-wire and thin-wire Ethernet networks were popular, as was the use of *telnet* and *ftp* (both of which suffered from a clear-text password problem). The result of this architectural model, combined with vulnerable

---

[6] A Network sniffer is a program that can observe communication on a shared network looking for interesting information (e.g., user passwords). Ethernet is one example of a shared network. A sniffer installed on one computer connected to an Ethernet can observe communication of all other computers connected to this same Ethernet.

network services, were networks that were easy prey to attackers running network sniffers.

1996

In 1996, a vulnerability in the TCP/IP stack was discovered that allowed a flood of packets with only the SYN bit set (known as a SYN flood; see Chapter 4 for detailed description). This became a popular and effective tool to use to make servers unavailable, even with moderate bandwidth available to an attacker (which was a good thing for attackers, as modems at this time were very slow). Small groups used these tools at first, and they circulated in closed groups for a time.

1997

Large DoS attacks on IRC networks began to occur in late 1996 and early 1997. In one attack, vulnerabilities in Windows systems were exploited by an attacker who took out large numbers of IRC users directly by crashing their systems [Val]. DoS programs with names like *teardrop*, *boink*, and *bonk* allowed an attacker to crash unpatched Windows systems at will. In another attack, a Romanian hacker took out portions of IRC network Undernet's server network with a SYN flood [KC]. SYN flood attacks on IRC networks are still prevalent today. A noteworthy event in 1997 was the complete shutdown of the Internet due to (nonmalicious) false route advertisement by a single router [Bon97]

For the most part, these DoS vulnerabilities are simple bugs that were fixed in subsequent releases of the affected operating systems. For example, there were a series of bugs in the way the Microsoft Windows TCP/IP stack handled fragmented packets. One bug in Windows' TCP/IP stack didn't handle fragmented packets whose offset and length did not match properly, such that they overlapped. The TCP/IP stack code authors expected packets to be properly fragmented and didn't properly check start/end/offset conditions. Specially crafted overlapping packets would cause the stack to allocate a huge amount of memory and hang or crash the system.[7] As these bugs were fixed, attackers had to develop new means of performing DoS attacks to up the ante and increase the disruption capability past the point where it can be stopped by simple patches.

---

[7] Most of these simple attacks no longer affect consumer PC operating systems although they are still an issue for new memory-constrained "Internet-ready" cell phones and Personal Digital Assistants (PDAs) that have more primitive TCP/IP stacks similar to those in Windows PCs of the early 1990s. Proof-of-concept malware [Lab04] has been written for Symbian-based cell phones.

Another effective technique that appeared around 1997 was a form of reflected, amplified DoS attack, called a *Smurf attack*. Smurf attacks allowed for amplification from a single source. By bouncing packets off a misconfigured network, attackers could amplify the number of packets destined for a victim by a factor of up to 200 or so for a so-called Class C or /24 network, or by a factor of several thousands for a moderately populated Class B or /16 network. The attacker would simply craft packets with the return address of the intended victim, and send those packets to the broadcast address of a network. These packets would effectively reach all available and responsive hosts on that particular network and elicit a response from them, Since the return address of the requests was forged, or spoofed, the response would be sent to the victim.[8]

Attackers next decided to explore another avenue for crashing machines. Instead of exploiting a vulnerability, they just sent *a lot* of packets to the target. If the target was on a relatively slow dial-up connection (say, 14.4Kbps), but the attacker was using a stolen university computer on a 1Mbps connection, she could trivially overwhelm the dial-up connection and the computer would be *lagged*, or slowed down to the point of being useless (each keystroke typed could take 10 seconds or more to be received and echoed).

1998

As the bandwidth between attacker and target became more equal, and more network operators learned to deal with simple Smurf attacks, the ability to send enough traffic at the target to lag it became harder and harder to achieve. The next step was to add the ability to control a large number of remotely located computers—someone else's computers—and to direct them all to send massive amounts of useless traffic across the network and flood the victim (or victims). Attackers began organizing themselves into coordinated groups, performing an attack in concert on a victim. The added packets, whether in sheer numbers or by overlapping attack types, obtained the desired effect.

Prototypes of DDoS tools (most notably *fapi,* see [CER99]) were developed in mid-1998, serving as examples of how to create client/server DDoS networks. Rather than relying on a single source, attackers could now take advantage of all the hosts they can compromise to attack with. These early programs had many limitations and didn't see widespread use, but did prove that coordination of computers in an attack was possible.

---

[8] The defense against the Smurf attack is to simply turn off the directed incoming broadcast capability in routers, which was allowed by default at the time. Still, many networks did not take this step, for whatever reasons, and thus remain potential sources of Smurf attacks.

Vulnerability-based attacks did not simply go away, and in fact continued to be possible due to a constant stream of newly discovered bugs. Successful DoS attacks using the relatively simple fragmented packet vulnerability targeting tens to hundreds of thousands of vulnerable hosts have been waged in the past. For example, the attacks in 1998, took advantage of fragmented packet vulnerabilities but added scripts to prepare the list of vulnerable hosts in advance and then rapidly fired exploit packets at those systems. This attacker prepared the list by probing potential victims for the correct operating system (by a technique called OS fingerprinting, which can be defeated by packet normalization [SMJ00]) and for the existence of the vulnerability, and creating a list of those that "pass the test." The University of Washington network was one of the victims of the attack. In computer labs across campus, some with hundreds of PCs being busily used by students doing their homework, the sound of keystrokes turned to dead silence as *every screen* in the lab went blue, only to be replaced seconds later with the chatter of "Hey, did your computer just crash too?" A large civilian U.S.-based space agency was a similar victim of these attacks during the same time period. Users at many locations were subjected to immediate patching, since subsequent controlled tests clearly turned unpatched systems' screens (and their respective users) blue.

The next step to counter the patching issue, which made it harder for an attacker to predict which DoS attack would be effective, was to combine multiple DoS exploits into one tool, using Unix shell scripts. This increased the speed at which an effective DoS attack could be waged. One such tool, named *rape,* (according to the code, written in 1998) integrates the following DoS attacks into a single shell script:

```
echo "Editted for use with www.ttol.base.org"
echo "rapeing $IP. using weapons:"
echo  "latierra            "
echo -n "teardrop v2         "
echo -n "newtear            "
echo -n "boink              "
echo -n "bonk               "
echo -n "frag               "
echo -n "fucked             "
echo -n "troll icmp         "
echo -n "troll udp          "
echo -n "nestea2             "
echo -n "fusion2            "
echo -n "peace keeper       "
echo -n "arnudp             "
echo -n "nos                "
```

```
echo -n "nuclear        "
echo -n "ssping         "
echo -n "pingodeth      "
echo -n "smurf          "
echo -n "smurf4         "
echo -n "land           "
echo -n "jolt           "
echo -n "pepsi          "
```

A tool like this has the advantage of allowing an attacker to give a single IP address and have multiple attacks be launched (increasing the probability of a successful attack), but it also means having to have a complete set of precompiled versions of each individual exploit packaged up in a Unix "tar" format archive for convenient transfer to a stolen account from which to launch the attack.

To still allow multiple DoS exploits to be used, but with a single precompiled program that is easier to store, transfer, and use quickly, programs like *targa.c* by Mixter were developed (this same strategy was used again in 2003 by *Agobot/Phatbot*). *Targa* combines all of the following exploits in a single C source program:

```
/* targa.c - copyright by Mixter <mixter@gmx.net>
   version 1.0 - released 6/24/98 - interface to 8
   multi-platform remote denial of service exploits
 */
 .
 .
 .
/* bonk by route|daemon9 & klepto
 * jolt by Jeff W. Roberson (modified by Mixter for overdrop effect)
 * land by m3lt
 * nestea by humble & ttol
 * newtear by route|daemon9
 * syndrop by PineKoan
 * teardrop by route|daemon9
 * winnuke by _eci */
```

Even combined DoS tools like *targa* still only allowed one attacker to DoS one IP address at a time, and they required the use of stolen accounts on systems with maximum bandwidth (predominantly university systems). To increase the effectiveness of these attacks, groups of attackers, using IRC channels or telephone "voice bridges" for communication, could coordinate attacks, each person attacking a different system using a different stolen account. This same coordination was being seen in probing for vulnerabilities, and in system compromise and control using multiple backdoors and "root kits."

The years 1998 and 1999 saw a significant increase in the ability to attack computer systems, which came as a direct result of programming and engineering efforts, the same ones that were bringing the Internet to the world: automation, increases in network bandwidth, client/server communications, and global chat networks.

1999

In 1999, two major developments grew slowly out of the computer underground and began to take shape as everyday attack methods: *distributed computing* (in the forms of distributed sniffing, distributed scanning, and distributed denial of service), and a *rebirth of the worm* (the worm simply being the integration and automation of all aspects of intrusion: reconnaissance scanning, target identification, compromise, embedding, and attacker control). In fact, many worms today (e.g., Nimda, Code Red, Deloder, Lion, and Blaster) either implement a DDoS attack or bundle in DDoS tools.

The summer of 1999 saw the first large-scale use of new DoS tools: *trinoo* [Ditf], *Tribe Flood Network* (*TFN*) [Dith], and *Stacheldraht* [Ditg]. These were all simple client/server style programs—handlers and agents, as mentioned earlier—that performed only DDoS-related functions of command and control, various types of DoS attacks, and automatic update in some cases. They required other programs to propagate them and build attack networks, and the most successful groups using these tools also used automation for scanning, target identification, exploitation, and installation of the DDoS payload. The targets of nearly all the attacks in 1999 were IRC clients and IRC servers.

One prominent attack against the IRC server at the University of Minnesota and a dozen or more IRC clients scattered around the globe was large enough to keep the University's network unusable for almost three full days. This attack used the trinoo DDoS tool, which generated a flood of UDP packets with a 2-byte payload and did not use IP spoofing. The University of Minnesota counted 2,500 attacking hosts, but the logs were not able to keep up with the flood, so that count was an underestimate.[9] These hosts were used in several DDoS networks of 100 to 400 hosts each, in rolling attacks that activated and deactivated groups of hosts. This made locating the agents,

---

[9] Again, e-mail correspondence sent privately to two DDoS researchers from individuals claiming involvement in these attacks stated the real number was more likely 4,000 to 5,000 hosts total.

identification, and cleanup take several hours to a couple of days. The latency in cleanup contributed to the attack's duration.

The change to using distributed tools was inevitable. The growth of network bandwidth that came about through the development of Internet2 [Con] (officially launched in 2000) made simple point-to-point tools less effective against well-provisioned networks, and attacks that used single hosts for flooding were easy to filter out and easy to track back to their source and stop. Scripting of vulnerability scans (which are also made faster because of the same bandwidth increase) and scripting of attacks made it much easier to compromise hundreds, thousands, even tens of thousands of hosts in just a few hours. If you control thousands of computers, why not program them to work in a coordinated manner for leverage? It wasn't a large leap to automate the installation of attack tools, back doors, sniffers—whatever the attackers wanted to add.

Private communications with some of the authors of the early DDoS tools[10] indicated the motivation for this automation was for a smaller group of attackers to counter attacks wielded at it by a large group (using the classic DoS tools described above, and manual coordination). The smaller group could not wield the same number of manual tools and thus resorted to automation. In almost all cases, these were first coding efforts, and even with bugs they were quite effective at waging large-scale attacks. The counterattacks were strikingly effective, and the smaller group was able to retake all their channels and strike back at the larger group.

Similar attacks, although on a slightly smaller scale, continued through the late fall of 1999, this time using newer tools that spoofed source addresses, making identification of attackers even harder. Nearly all of these attacks were directed at IRC networks and clients, and there was very little news coverage of them. *Tribe Flood Network* (or *TFN*), *Stacheldraht*, and then *Tribe Flood Network 2000* (*TFN2K*) saw popular use, while *Shaft* showed up in more limited attacks.

In November of 1999, CERT Coordination Center sponsored (for the first time ever) a workshop to discuss and develop a response to a situation they saw as a significant problem of the day, in this case Distributed System Intruder Tools (including distributed scanners, distributed sniffers, and distributed denial of service tools.) The product of the workshop was a report [CER99], which covered the issue from multiple perspectives (those of managers, system administrators, Internet service providers, and incident response teams). This report is still one of the best places to start in

---

[10] This information was relayed to David Dittrich in 2000, after the initial DDoS analyses of *trinoo*, *TFN*, and *Stacheldraht* were published.

understanding DDoS, and what to do about it in the immediate time frame (<30 days), medium term (30–180 days) and long term (>180 days). Ironically, only days after this workshop, a new tool was discovered that was from a different strain of evolution, yet obeyed the same attack principles as *trinoo*, *TFN*, and *Stacheldraht* [Ditf, Dith, Ditg]. The *Shaft* [DLD00] tool, as discussed in Chapter 4, was wreaking havoc with only small numbers of agents across Europe, the United States, and the Pacific Rim, and caught the attention of some analysts.

This next generation of tools included features such as encryption of communications (to harden the DDoS tools against counterattack and detection), multiplicity of attack methods, integrated chat functions, and reporting of packet flood rates. This latter function is used by the attacker to make it easier to determine the yield of the DDoS attack network, and hence when it is large enough to obtain the desired goal and when (due to attrition) it needs to be reinforced. (The attackers, at this point, knew more about how much bandwidth they were using than many network operators knew was being consumed. Refer to the discussion of *Shaft* in Chapter 4 for more on this statistics feature, and the OODA Loop in Chapter 4 to understand how this affects the attacker/defender balance of power.) As more and more groups learned of the power of DDoS to engage in successful warfare against IRC sites, more DDoS tools were developed.

As Y2K Eve approached, many security professionals feared that widespread DDoS attacks would disrupt the telecommunications infrastructure, making it look like Y2K failures were occurring and panicking the public [SSSW]. Thankfully, these attacks never happened. That did not mean that attack incidence slowed down, however.

2000

On January 18, 2000, a local ISP in Seattle, Washington, named Oz.net was attacked [Ric]. This appeared to be a Smurf attack (or possibly an ICMP Echo reply flood with a program like *Stacheldraht*). The unique element of this attack was that it was directed against not only the servers at Oz.net, but also at their routers, the routers of their upstream provider Semaphore, and the routers of the upstream's provider, UUNet. It was estimated that the slowdown in network traffic affected some 70% of the region surrounding Seattle.

Within weeks of this attack, in February 2000, a number of DDoS attacks were successfully perpetrated against several well-provisioned and carefully run sites—many of the major "brand names" of the Internet. They included the online auction company eBay (with 10 million customers), the Internet portal Yahoo (36 million visitors in December 1999), online brokerage E*Trade, online retailer Buy.com (1.3 million customers), online bookselling pioneer Amazon.com, Web portal Excite.com, and the widely consulted news site CNN [Har]. Many of these sites were used to high, fluctuating traffic volume, so they were heavily provisioned to provide for those fluctuations. They were also frequent targets of other types of cyberattacks, so they kept their security software up to date and maintained a staff of network administration professionals to deal with any problems that arose. If anyone in the Internet should have been immune to DDoS problems, these were the sites. (A detailed timeline of some of the lesser known events surrounding the first public awareness of DDoS, leading up to the first major DDoS attacks on e-commerce sites, is provided in the side bar at the end of this chapter.)

However, the attacks against all of them were quite successful, despite being rather unsophisticated. For example, the attack against Yahoo in February 2000 prevented users from having steady connectivity to that site for three hours. As a result, Yahoo, which relies on advertising for much of its revenue, lost potentially an estimated $500,000 because its users were unable to access Yahoo's Web pages and the advertisements they carried [Kes]. The attack method used was not sophisticated, and thus Yahoo was eventually able to filter out the attack traffic from its legitimate traffic, but a significant amount of money was lost in the process. Even the FBI's own Web site was taken out of service for three hours in February of 2000 by a DDoS attack [CNN].

2001

In January 2001, a reflection DDoS attack (described in Section 2.3.3) [Pax01] on futuresite.register.com [el] used false DNS requests sent to many DNS servers throughout the world to generate its traffic. The attacker sent many requests under the identity of the victim for a particularly large DNS record to a large number of DNS servers. These servers obediently sent the actually undesired information to the victim. The amount of traffic inbound to the victim's IP address was reported to be 60 to 90 Mbps, with one site reporting seeing approximately 220 DNS requests per minute per DNS server.

This attack lasted about a week, and could not be filtered easily at the victim network because simple methods of doing so would have disabled all DNS lookup for the victim's customers. Because the attack was reflected off many DNS servers, it was hard to characterize which ones were producing only attack traffic that should be filtered out.

Arguably, the DNS servers responding to this query really shouldn't have done so, since it would not ordinarily be their business to answer DNS queries on random records from sites not even in their domain. That they did so could be considered a bug in the way DNS functions, a misconfiguration of DNS servers, or perhaps both, but it certainly underscores the complexity of Internet protocols and protocol implementations and inherent design issues that can lead to DoS vulnerabilities.

The number and scope of DDoS attacks continued to increase, but most people (at least those who didn't use IRC) were not aware of them. In 2001 David Moore, Geoffrey Voelker, and Stephan Savage published a paper titled, "Inferring Internet Denial-of-Service Activity" [MVS01]. This work investigates Internet-wide DDoS activity and is described in detail in Appendix C. The technique for measuring DDoS activity underestimates the attack frequency, because it cannot detect all occurring attacks. But even with these limitations, the authors were able to detect approximately 4,000 attacks per week for the three-week period they analyzed. Similar techniques for attack detection and evaluation were already in use among network operators and network security analysts in 1999 and 2000. What many operators flagged as "RST scans" were known to insiders as "echoes" of DDoS attacks [DLD00].

Microsoft's prominent position in the industry has made it a frequent target of attacks, including DDoS attacks. Some DDoS attacks on Microsoft have failed, in part because Microsoft heavily provisions its networks to deal with the immense load generated when they release an important new product or when an upgrade becomes available. But some of the attacks succeeded, often by cleverly finding some resource other than pure bandwidth for the attack to exhaust. For example, in January 2001 someone launched a DDoS attack on one of Microsoft's routers, preventing it from routing normal traffic at the required speeds [Del]. This attack would have had relatively little overall effect on Microsoft's Internet presence were it not for the fact that all of the DNS servers for Microsoft's online properties were located behind the router under attack. While practically all of Microsoft's network was up and available for use, many users could not get to it because their requests to translate Microsoft Web site names into IP addresses were dropped by the overloaded router. This attack was so successful that the fraction of Web requests that Microsoft was able to handle dropped to 2%.

2002

Perhaps inspired by this success, in October 2002 an attacker went a step further and tried to perform a DDoS attack on the complete set of the Internet's DNS root servers. DNS is a critical service for many Internet users and many measures have been taken to make it robust and highly available. DNS data is replicated at 13 root servers, that are themselves well provisioned and maintained, and it is heavily cached in nonroot servers throughout the Internet. An attacker attempted to deny service to all 13 of these root servers using a very simple form of DDoS attack. At various points during the attack, 9 of the 13 root servers were unable to respond to DNS requests, and only 4 remained fully operational throughout the attack. The attack lasted only one hour, after which the agents stopped. Thanks to the robust design of the DNS and the attack's short duration, there was no serious impact in the Internet as a whole. A longer, stronger attack, however, might have been extremely harmful.

2003

It wasn't until 2003 that a major shift in attack motivations and methodologies began to show up. This shift coincided with several rapid and widespread worm events, which have now become intertwined with DDoS.

First, spammers began to use distributed networks in the same ways as DDoS attackers to set up distributed spam networks [KP]. As antispam sites tried to counter these "spambots," the spammers' hired guns retaliated by attacking several antispam sites [AJ]. Using standard DDoS tools, and even worms like *W32/Sobig* [JL], they waged constant attacks against those who they perceived were threatening their very lucrative business.

Second, other financial crimes began to involve the use of DDoS. In some cases, online retailers with daily gross sales on the order of tens of thousands of dollars a day (as opposed to larger sites like the ones attacked in February 2000) were also attacked, using a form of DDoS involving seemingly normal Web requests. These attacks were just large enough to bring the Web server to a crawl, yet not large enough to disrupt the networks of the upstream providers. Similarly to the reflected DNS attacks described earlier, it was difficult (if not impossible) to filter out the malicious Web requests, as they appeared to be legitimate. Similar attacks were waged against online gambling sites and pornography sites. Again, in some cases extortion attempts were made for sums in the tens of thousands of dollars to stop the attacks (a new form of protection racketeering) [CN].

DDoS had finally become a component of widespread financial crimes and high-dollar e-commerce, and the trend is likely to only increase in the near future. DDoS continued to also be used as in prior years, including for political reasons.

During the Iraq War in 2003, a DDoS attack was launched on the Qatar-based Al-Jazeera news organization, which broadcast pictures of captured American soldiers. Al-Jazeera attempted to outprovision the attackers by purchasing more bandwidth, but they merely ratcheted up the attack. The Web site was largely unreachable for two days, following which someone hijacked their DNS name, redirecting requests to another Web site that promoted the American cause.

In May 2003, then several more times in December, SCO's Web site experienced DDoS attacks that took it offline for prolonged periods of time. Statements by SCO management indicated the belief that the attacks were in response to SCO's legal battle over Linux source code and statements criticizing the Open Source community's role in these lawsuits [Lem].

In mid-2003, Clickbank (an electronic banking service) and Spamcop (a company that filters e-mail to remove spam) were subjected to powerful DDoS attacks [Zor]. The attacks seemingly involved thousands of attack machines. After some days, the companies were able to install sophisticated filtering software that dropped the DDoS attack traffic before it reached a bottleneck point.

2004

Financially motivated attacks continue, along with speculation that worm attacks in 2004 were used to install Trojan software on hundreds of thousands of hosts, creating massive bot networks. Two popular programs—*Agobot*, and its successor *Phatbot* [LTIG]—have been implicated in distributed spam delivery and DDoS; in some cases networks of these bots are even being sold on the black market [Leya]. *Phatbot* is described in more detail in Chapter 4.

Agobot and *Phatbot* both share many of the features that were predicted in 2000 by Michal Zalewski [Zal] in his write-up on features of a "super-worm." This paper was written in response to the hype surrounding the "I Love You" virus. Zalewski lists such features as portability (*Phatbot* runs on both Windows and Linux), polymorphism, self-update, anti-debugging, and usability (*Phatbot* comes with usage documentation and online help commands). Since *Phatbot* preys on previously infected hosts, other parts of Zalewski's predictions are also possible (via programming how *Phatbot* executes) and thus *Phatbot* is one of the most advanced forms of automation seen to date in the category of DDoS (or *blended threat*, actually) tools.

Like all histories, this history of DDoS attacks does not represent a final state, but is merely the prelude to the future. In the next chapter, we will provide more details on exactly how today's attacks are perpetrated, which will then set the stage for discussing what you must do to counter them. Remember, however, that the history we've just covered suggests, more than anything else, continued and rapid change for the future. Early analyses of DDoS attack tools like *trinoo, Tribe Flood Network, Stacheldraht,* and *Shaft* all made predictions about future development trends based on past history, but attackers proved more nimble in integrating new attack methods into existing tools than those predictions suggested. We should expect both the number and sophistication of attack tools to grow steadily, and perhaps more rapidly than anyone predicts. Therefore, the tools attackers will use in upcoming years and the methods used to defend against them will progress from the current states we describe in the upcoming chapters, requiring defenders to keep up to date on new trends and defense methods.

Early DDoS Attack Tool Time Line

There was a flurry of media attention paid to the potential for DoS attacks to be used around the time of Y2K Eve. These attacks were expected to mimic anticipated Y2K bug failures and potentially attract much public attention and invoke panic. This potential generated, rightly from a protective role, a lot of attention from within the government and organizations that support the government. Many stories covering the possibility of a DoS attack were published in the media. The media attention continued at a low level after Y2K, then picked up sharply after the first major DDoS attacks against e-commerce sites in February 2000. Many of the authors of then-published stories could not benefit from behind-the-scenes activity or information that was unpublished at the time. This created an impression that DDoS is a phenomenon that was largely neglected by incident responders. Later, some articles took very critical positions against federal government agencies, mostly due to the reporters not knowing all of the events leading up to February 2000. Those articles can be obtained following links at `http://security.royans.net/info/articles/feb_attack.shtml` and `http://staff.washington.edu/dittrich/misc/ddos/`.

The time line below follows a talk given at the Usenix Security Symposium in 2000 on DDoS attacks (see `http://www.computerworld.com/news/2000/story/0,11280,48796,00.html` and `http://staff.washington.edu/dittrich/talks/sec2000/`) and provides more information about early DoS/DDoS incidents.

- **May/June, 1998.** First primitive DDoS tools developed in the underground— small networks, only mildly worse than coordinated point-to-point DoS attacks. These tools did not see widespread use at the time, but classic point-to-point DoS attacks continued to cause problems, as well as increasing "Smurf" amplification attacks (see Section 2.3.3).

- **July 22, 1999.** The CERT Coordination Center released Incident Note 99-04 mentioning widespread intrusions on Solaris RPC services. (See `http://www.cert.org/incident_notes/IN-99-04.html`.)

- **August 5, 1999.** First evidence seen at sites around the Internet of programs being installed on Solaris systems in what appeared to be "mass" intrusions using massive autorooters and using multiple attack vectors. (This was a precursor to some of today's worms and blended threats, such as *Phatbot*.) It was not clear at first how these incidents were related.

- **August 17, 1999.** Attack on the University of Minnesota reported to University of Washington (among many others) network operations and security teams. The University of Minnesota reported as many source networks as it could identify (but *netflow* records were overwhelming their storage capacity, so some records were dropped).

- **September 2, 1999.** Contents of a stolen account used to cache files were recovered. Over the next month, a detailed analysis of the files was performed. An initial draft analysis of trinoo was circulated privately at first.

- **October 21, 1999.** Final drafts of *trinoo* and *TFN* analyses were finished. (See http://packetstormsecurity.nl/distributed/trinoo.analysis and http://packetstormsecurity.nl/distributed/tfn.analysis.)

- **November 2–4, 1999.** The Distributed Systems Intruder Tools (DSIT) workshop, organized by the CERT Coordination Center, was held near the Carnegie Mellon University campus in Pittsburgh. It was agreed by attendees that it was important not to panic people, but instead provide meaningful steps to deal with this new threat. All attendees agreed to keep information about DDoS programs private until the attendees finished a report on how to respond, and not to release other information provided to them without permission of the sources.

- **November 18, 1999.** The CERT Coordination Center released Incident Note 99-07 "Distributed Denial of Service Tools," mentioning DDoS tools. (See http://www.cert.org/incident_notes/IN-99-07.html.)

- **November 29, 1999.** *SANS NewsBytes*, Vol. 1, Num. 35, mentioned *trinoo/TFN* in the context of widespread Solaris intrusion reports they were getting that were consistent with the CERT Coordination Center IN-99-07 and involving ICMP Echo Reply packets.

- **Late November/Early December, 1999.** Evidence of another DDoS agent (*Shaft*) was found in Europe. (An analysis by Sven Dietrich, Neil Long, and David Dittrich wasn't published until March 13, 2000.
  See http://www.adelphi.edu/~spock/shaft_analysis.txt.)

- **December 4, 1999** Massive attack using *Shaft* is detected. (Data acquired during this attack was analyzed in early 2000 and presented by Sven Dietrich in a paper at the USENIX LISA 2000 conference.
  See http://www.adelphi.edu/~spock/lisa2000-shaft.pdf.)

- **December 7, 1999**. ISS released an advisory on *trinoo/TFN* after first non-technical mention of DDoS tools in a *USA Today* article. The CERT Coordination Center released final report of the DSIT workshop. David Dittrich sent his analyses of *trinoo* and *TFN* to the BUGTRAQ e-mail list.
  (See `http://www.usatoday.com/life/cyber/tech/review/crg681.htm`,
  `http://www.cert.org/reports/dsit_workshop-final.html`,
  `http://packetstormsecurity.nl/distributed/trinoo.analysis`, and
  `http://packetstormsecurity.nl/distributed/tfn.analysis`.)

- **Remainder of December 1999 and into January 2000**. Many conference calls were held within a group of government, academic, and private industry participants who worked cooperatively and constructively in helping develop responses to the DDoS threat. Fears of Y2K-related attacks helped drive the urgency. (See `http://news.com.com/2100-1001-234678.html` and `http://staff.washington.edu/dittrich/misc/corrections/cnet.html`.)

- **December 8, 1999**. According to a *USA Today* article, NIPC sent a note briefing FBI director Louis Freeh on DDoS tools.
  (See `http://www.usatoday.com/life/cyber/tech/cth523.htm`.)

- **December 17, 1999**. According to a *USA Today* article, NIPC director Michael Vatis briefed Attorney General Janet Reno as part of an overview of preparations being made for Y2K.
  (See `http://www.usatoday.com/life/cyber/tech/cth523.htm`.)

- **December 27, 1999**. As final work on the analysis of *Stacheldraht* was being performed by David Dittrich, with help from Sven Dietrich, Neil Long, and others, Dittrich scanned the University of Washington network with *gag* (the scanner included in the *Stacheldraht* analysis). Three active agents were found and traced to a handler in the southern United States. The ISP and its upstream provider were able to use the Stacheldraht analysis to identify over 100 agents in this network and take it down.

- **December 28, 1999**. The CERT Coordination Center releases Advisory CA-1999-17 "Denial-of-Service Tools" (covers TFN2K and MacOS 9 DoS exploit).
  (See `http://www.cert.org/advisories/CA-1999-17.html`.)

- **December 30, 1999.** Analysis of *Stacheldraht* posted to the BUGTRAQ e-mail list. NIPC issued a press release on DDoS programs and released "Distributed Denial of Service Attack Information (*trinoo/ Tribe Flood Network*)," including a tool for scanning local file systems/memory for DDoS programs. (See `http://packetstormsecurity.nl/distributed/stacheldraht.analysis`, `http://www.fbi.gov/pressrm/pressrel/pressrel99/prtrinoo.htm`, and `http://www.fbi.gov/nipc/trinoo.htm`.)

- **January 3, 2000.** The CERT Coordination Center and FedCIRC jointly published Advisory 2000–01 "Denial-of-Service Developments," discussing Stacheldraht and NIPC scanning tool. (See `http://www.cert.org/advisories/CA-2000-01.html`.)

- **January 4, 2000.** SANS asked its membership to use published DDoS detection tools to determine how widely DDoS attack tools are being used. Reports of successful searches started coming in within hours. Several DDoS networks were discovered and taken down.

- **January 5, 2000.** Sun released bulletin #00193, "Distributed Denial-of-Service Tools."
  (See `http://packetstorm.securify.com/advisories/sms/sms.193.ddos`.)

- **January 14, 2000.** Attack on OZ.net in Seattle affected Semaphore and UUNET customers (affecting as much as 70% of Puget Sound Internet users, and possibly other sites in the United States—no national press attention until January 18). This attack targeted the network infrastructure, as well as end servers.

- **January 17, 2000.** ICSA.net organized Birds of a Feather (BoF) session on DDoS attacks at the RSA 2000 conference in San Jose.

- **February 7, 2000.** A talk was given by Steve Bellovin on DDoS attacks, and another ICSA.net DDoS BoF was organized at a NANOG [Ope] meeting in San Jose. Coincidentally (although not necessarily related), the first attacks on e-commerce sites began.

- **February 10, 2000.** Jason Barlow and Woody Thrower of AXENT Security Team published analysis of TFN2K.

- **February 8–12, 2000.** Attacks on e-commerce sites continued. Popular media began to widely publish reports on these DDoS attacks. To this day, most stories incorrectly refer to this as the beginning of DDoS.

While the government was criticized heavily in some early media reports, the following points are considered important in understanding these stories.

- Technical details of the developing DDoS tools did not start circulating, even privately, until October 1999.

- The CERT Coordination Center released IN-99-07 mentioning DDoS tools on November 18, 1999, and published CA-1999-17 on December 28, 1999. Any sites paying attention to the CERT Coordination Center Incident Notes and Advisories learned of trinoo, TFN, and TFN2K in November and December 1999.

- Anyone reading BUGTRAQ learned of trinoo and TFN on December 7, 1999, and Stacheldraht on December 30, 1999.

- NIPC's advisory and tool came out just after the technical analyses were published, but because all three commonly used DDoS tools were discussed publicly by late December 1999, it seems overly critical to say the government "failed to warn" e-commerce sites before February 7, 2000. The e-commerce sites could have learned about the possible attacks from the CERT Coordination Center Incident Note, the DSIT Workshop Report, SANS publications, and postings to BUGTRAQ in November and December 1999.

- Several news stories mentioned all of these information sources in December 1999 through February 2000.

- Various agencies widely spread the analyses of DDoS tools as necessary, so the problem was known and being handled privately long before any media stories were published.

CHAPTER 4

How Attacks Are Waged

A DDoS attack has to be carefully prepared by the attacker. She first recruits the agent army. This is done by looking for vulnerable machines, then breaking into them, and installing her attack code. The attacker next establishes communication channels between machines, so that they can be controlled and engaged in a coordinated manner. This is done using either a handler/agent architecture or an IRC-based command and control channel. Once the DDoS network is built, it can be used to attack as many times as desired against various targets.

4.1 Recruitment of the Agent Network

Depending on the type of denial of service planned, the attacker needs to find a sufficiently large number of vulnerable machines to use for attacking. This can be done manually, semi-automatically, or in a completely automated manner. In the cases of two well-known DDoS tools, trinoo [Ditf] and Shaft [DLD00], only the installation process was automated, while discovery and compromise of vulnerable machines were performed manually. Nowadays, attackers use scripts that automate the entire process, or even use scanning to identify already compromised machines to take over (e.g., Slammer-, MyDoom-, or Bagle-infected hosts). It has been speculated that some worms may be used explicitly to create a fertile harvesting ground for building bot networks that are later used for various malicious purposes, including DDoS attacks. If the owners didn't notice the worm infection, they will likely not notice the bot that harvests them!

4.1.1   Finding Vulnerable Machines

The attacker needs to find machines that she can compromise. To maximize the yield, she will want to recruit machines that have good connectivity and ample resources and are poorly maintained. Unfortunately, many of these exist within the pool of millions of Internet hosts.

In the early days of DDoS, hosts with high-availability connections were found only in universities and scientific and government institutions. They further tended to have fairly lax security and no firewalls, so they were easily compromised by an attacker. The recent popularity of cable modem and digital subscriber line (DSL) high-speed Internet for business and home use has brought high-availability connections into almost every home and office. This has vastly enlarged the pool of lightly administered and well-provisioned hosts that are frequently continuously connected and running—ideal targets for DDoS recruitment. The change in the structure of potential DDoS agents was followed by a change in DDoS tools. The early tools ran mostly on Unix-based hosts, whereas recent DDoS code mostly runs on Windows-based systems. In some cases, such as the *Kaiten* and *Knight* bots, the same original Unix source code was simply recompiled using the Cygwin portable library.

The process of looking for vulnerable machines is called *scanning*. Figure 4.1 depicts the simple scanning process. The attacker sends a few packets to the chosen target to see whether it is alive and vulnerable. If so, the attacker will attempt to break into the machine.

Scanning was initially a manual process performed by the attacker using crude tools. Over time, scanning tools improved and scanning functions were integrated and made automatic. Two examples of this are "blended threats" and worms.

Blended threats are individual programs or groups of programs that provide many services, in this case command and control using an *IRC bot* and vulnerability scanning.

A *bot* (derived from "robot") is a client program that runs in the background on a compromised host, and watches for certain strings to show up in an IRC channel. These strings represent encoded commands that the bot program executes, such as inviting someone into an IRC channel, giving the user channel operator permissions, scanning a block of addresses (netblock), or performing a DoS attack. Netblock scans are initiated in certain bots, such as *Power* [Dita], by specifying the first few octets of the network address (e.g., 192.168 may mean to scan everything from 192.168.0.0 to 192.168.255.255). Once bots get a list of vulnerable hosts, they inform the attacker using the botnet (a network of bots that all synchronize through communication in an IRC channel). The attacker retrieves the file and adds it to her list of vulnerable

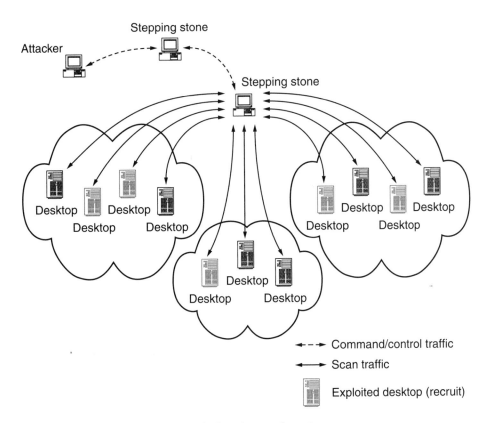

Figure 4.1   Recruitment of agent army

hosts. Some programs automatically add these vulnerable hosts to the vulnerable host list, thereby constantly reconstituting the attack network. Network blocks for scanning are sometimes chosen randomly by attackers. Other times they are chosen explicitly for a reason (e.g., netblocks owned by DSL providers and universities are far more "target-rich environments" than those owned by large businesses and are less risky than a military site).

The scanning can be performed with separate programs that are simply "plugged in" to the blended threat kit, or (as is the case with *Phatbot*), built into the program as a module. An IRC bot scanning is depicted in Figure 4.2.

Another program that employs scanning to identify vulnerable hosts is an Internet worm. Internet worms are automated programs that propagate from one vulnerable host to another, in a manner similar to biological viruses (e.g., the flu). A worm

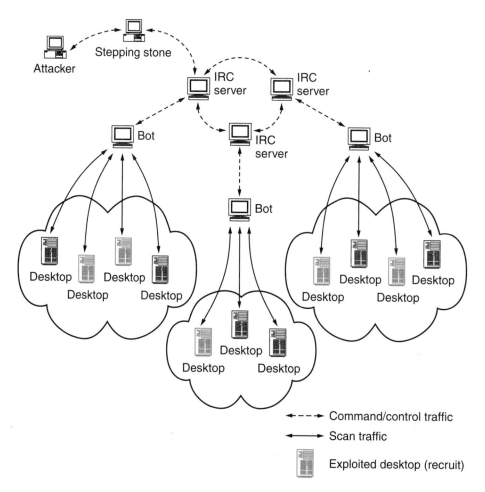

Figure 4.2 Sophisticated scanning for recruitment

has three distinct primary functions: (1) scanning, to look for vulnerable machines; (2) exploitation, which compromises machines and establishes remote control; and (3) a payload (code they execute upon compromise to achieve some attack function). Since the worm is designed to propagate, once it *infects* a machine, the scan/infect cycle repeats on both the infected and infecting machines. The payload can be simply a copy of the worm (in memory or written to the file system), or it may be a complete set of programs loaded into the file system. Internet worms are an increasingly popular method of recruiting DDoS agents, so the worm payload frequently includes DDoS attack code. Figure 4.3 illustrates worm propagation.

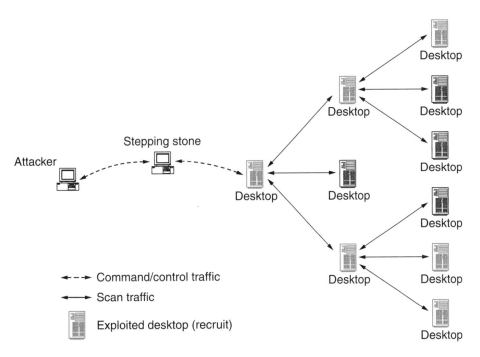

Figure 4.3   Worm scanning for recruitment

Worms choose the addresses to scan using several methods.

- **Completely randomly**. Randomly choose all 32 bits of the IP address (if using IPv4) for targets, effectively scanning the entire Internet indiscriminately.

- **Within a randomly selected address range**. Randomly choose only the first 8 or 16 bits of the IP address, then iterate from .0.0 through .255.255 in that address range. This tends to scan single networks, or groups of networks, at a time.

- **Using a hitlist**. Take a small list of network blocks that are "target rich" and preferentially scan them, while ignoring any address range that appears to be empty or highly secured. This speeds things up tremendously, as well as minimizing time wasted scanning large unused address ranges.

- **Using information found on the infected machine**. Upon infecting a machine, the worm examines the machine's log files that detail communication activity, looking for addresses to scan. For instance, a Web browser log contains addresses of recently visited Web sites, and a file known_hosts contains addresses of destinations contacted through the SSH (Secure Shell) protocol.

Worms spread extremely fast because of their parallel propagation pattern. Assume that a single copy successfully infects five machines in one second. In the next second, all six copies (the original one and five new copies) will try to propagate further. As the worm spreads, the number of infected machines and number of worm copies swarming over the Internet grow exponentially. Frequently, this huge amount of scanning/attacking traffic clogs edge networks and creates a DoS effect for many users. Some worms carry DDoS payloads as well, allowing the attacker who controls the compromised machines to carry out more intentional and targeted attacks after the worm has finished spreading. Since history suggests that worms are often not completely cleaned up (for example, Code Red–infected hosts still exist in the Internet, years after Code Red first appeared), some infected machines might continue serving as DDoS agents indefinitely.

4.1.2   Breaking into Vulnerable Machines

The attacker needs to exploit a vulnerability in the machines that she is intending to recruit in order to gain access to them. You will find this referred to as "owning" the machine. The vast majority of vulnerabilities provide an attacker with administrative access to the system, and she can add/delete/change files or system settings at will.

Exploits typically follow a vulnerability exploitation cycle.

1. A new vulnerability has been discovered in attacker circles and is being exploited in a limited fashion.
2. The vulnerability makes it outside of this circle and gets exploited at a wider scale.
3. Automated tools appear, and nonexperts (*script kiddies*) are running the tools.
4. A patch for the vulnerability appears and gets applied.
5. Exploits for a given vulnerability decline.

Once one or more vulnerabilities have been identified, the attacker incorporates the exploits for those vulnerabilities into his DDoS toolkit. Some DDoS tools actually take advantage of several vulnerabilities to propagate their code to as many machines as possible. These are often referred to as *propagation vectors*.

Frequently, the attackers patch the vulnerability they exploited to break into the machine. This is done to prevent other attackers from gaining access in the same manner and seizing control of the agent machine. To facilitate his future access to the compromised machine, the attacker will start a program that listens for incoming connection attempts on a specific port. This program is called a *backdoor*. Access through the backdoor is sometimes protected by a strong password, and in other cases is wide open and will respond to any connection request.

One vulnerability that is not mitigated by patching, which some blended threats take advantage of, is weak passwords. Some exploits contain a list of common passwords. They try these passwords in a brute-force or iterative manner, one after another. This sometimes exceeds system limits for failed logins and causes a lockout condition (a safe fallback for the system, but disruptive to legitimate users who cannot get in to the system). All too many times, these exploits succeed in finding a weak login/password combination and gain unauthorized access to the system. Users often think that leaving no password on the Administrator account is reasonable, or that "password" or some other simple word is sufficient to protect the account. They are mistaken.

4.1.3   Malware Propagation Methods

The attacker needs to decide on a propagation model for installing his malware. A simple model is the *central repository*, or *cache*, approach: The attacker places the malware in a file repository (e.g., an FTP server) or a Web site, and each compromised host downloads the code from this repository. One advantage of the caching model for the defender is that such central repositories can be easily identified and removed. Attackers installing *trinoo* [Ditf] and *Shaft* [DLD00] agents used such centralized approaches in the early days. In 2001, W32/Leaves [CER01c] used a variant of reconfigurable sites for its cache, as did the *W32/SoBig* mass-mailing worm in 2003. Figure 4.4 illustrates propagation with central repository.

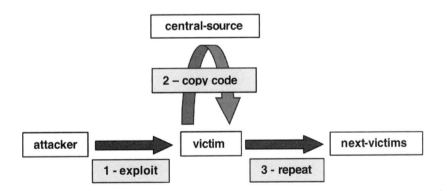

Figure 4.4   Propagation with central repository. (Reprinted from [HWLT01] with permission of the CERT Coordination Center.)

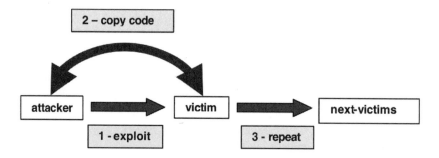

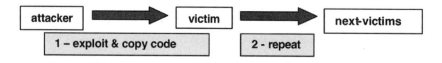

Figure 4.5 Propagation with back chaining. (Reprinted from [HWLT01] with permission of the CERT Coordination Center.)

Figure 4.6 Autonomous propagation. (Reprinted from [HWLT01] with permission of the CERT Coordination Center.)

Another model is the *back-chaining*, or *pull*, approach, wherein the attacker *carries* his tools from an initially compromised host to subsequent machines that this host compromises. Figure 4.5 illustrates propagation with back-chaining.

Finally, the *autonomous*, *push*, or *forward propagation* approach combines propagation and exploit into one process. The difference between this approach and back chaining is that the exploit itself contains the malware to be propagated to the new site, rather than performing a copy of that malware after compromising the site. The worm carries a DDoS tool as a payload, and plants it on each infected machine. Recent worms have incorporated exploit and attack code, protected by a weak encryption using linear feedback shift registers. The encryption is used to defeat the detection of well-known exploit code sequences (e.g., the buffer overflow "sled," a long series of NOOP commands [Sko02]) by antivirus or personal firewall software. Once on the machine, the code self-decrypts and resumes its propagation. Figure 4.6 illustrates autonomous propagation.

All of the preceding propagation methods are described in more detail in [HWLT01].

Other complexities of attack tools and toolkits include such features as anti-forensics and encryption. Methods of analyzing DDoS tools are described in Chapter 6.

4.2 Controlling the DDoS Agent Network

When the agent army has been recruited in sufficiently large numbers, the attacker communicates with the agents using special "many-to-many" communication tools. The purpose of this communication is twofold.

1. The attacker commands the beginning/end and specifics of the attack.
2. The attacker gathers statistics on agent behavior.

Note here that "sufficiently large" depends on the frame of reference: Early tools like *trinoo, Tribe Flood Network (TFN)*, and *Shaft* dealt with hundreds and low thousands of agents, but nowadays it is not uncommon to see sets of agents (or botnets) of tens of thousands being traded on IRC. *Phatbot* networks as large as 400,000 hosts have reportedly been witnessed (http://www.securityfocus.com/news/8573).

4.2.1 Direct Commands

Some DDoS tools like *trinoo* [Dith] build a handler/agent network, where the attacker controls the network by issuing commands to the handler, which in turn relays commands (sometimes using a different command set) to the agents. Commands may consist of unencrypted (clear) text, obfuscated or encrypted text, or numeric (binary) byte sequences. Analysis of the command and control traffic between handlers and agents can give insight into the capabilities of the tools without having access to the malware executable or its source code, as demonstrated with *Shaft* [DLD00].

In order for some handlers and agents, such as *trinoo, Stacheldraht,* and *Shaft* to function, the handler must learn the addresses of the agents and "remember" this across reboots or program restarts. The early DDoS tools have hardcoded the IP address of a handler, and agents would report to this handler upon recruitment. Usually the agent list is kept in a file that the handler maintains in order to keep state information about the DDoS network. In some cases, there is no authentication of the handler (in fact any computer can send commands to some DDoS agents, and they will respond). The early analyses of *trinoo, TFN, Stacheldraht, Shaft,* and *mstream* all showed ways in which handlers and agents could be detected or controlled. Early DDoS attacks were waged between underground groups fighting for supremacy and ownership of IRC channels. Attackers would sometimes act to take over another's DDoS network if access to it was

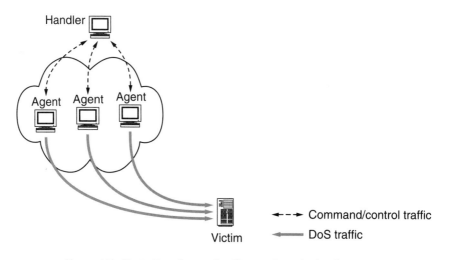

Figure 4.7   Illustration of control traffic seen from site hosting agents

not somehow protected.[1] For instance, an attacker who captures a plaintext message sent to another's agent can control this same agent by modifying the necessary message fields and resending it. Or the defender can issue a command that stops the attack. Some DDoS tools that used a handler/agent architecture protected remote access to the handler using passwords, and some tried to protect the handler/agent communication through passwords or encryption using shared secrets. The first handlers even encrypted (using RC4 and Blowfish ciphers; see [MvOV96] for an excellent reference on applied cryptography) their list of agents to avoid disclosure of the identity of the agents, if the handler was examined by investigators. By replaying the commands the list of agents could be exposed, or the file could sometimes be decrypted using keys obtained from forensic analysis or reverse engineering of the handler. Other tools like *Stacheldraht* [Ditg] allowed encryption of the command channel between the attacker and the handler, but not between handlers and agents. Over time, these handlers became traceable and were, in most cases, removable.

Figures 4.7 and 4.8 illustrate the control and attack traffic visible from the site hosting an agent and from the site hosting a handler, respectively.

---

[1] The analyses of *trinoo* [Ditf], *TFN* [Dith], and *Stacheldraht* [Ditg] all showed weaknesses that could be used to take over a DDoS network. IRC-based botnets can also be taken over with the right information.

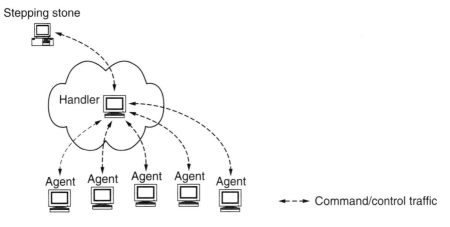

Figure 4.8   Illustration of control traffic seen from site hosting a handler

4.2.2   Indirect Commands

Direct communication had a few downsides for the attackers. Because the handlers needed to store agents' identities and, frequently, an agent machine would store the identity of the handler, once investigators captured one machine the whole DDoS network could be identified. Further, direct communication patterns were generating anomalous events on network monitors (imagine a Web server that suddenly initiates communication with a foreign machine on an obscure port), which network operators were quick to spot. Investigating captured messages, they could identify the foreign peer's address. Operators were able to detect agent or handler processes even when no messages were actively flowing, by monitoring open ports on their machines. For direct communication, both agents and handlers had to be "ready" to receive messages all the time. This readiness was manifested by the attack process' opening a port and listening on it. Operators were able to spot this by looking at the list of currently open ports; unidentified listening processes were promptly investigated. Finally, the attacker needed to write his own code for command and control.

A drawback to the original handler/agent design that caused a limitation in the size of DDoS networks was the number of open file handles required for TCP connections between the handler and agents. Many versions of Unix have limits to the number of open file descriptors each process can have, as well as limits for the kernel itself. Even if these limits could be increased, some DDoS tools would simply stop being able to add new agents after reaching 1024, a typical limit on the number of open file handles for many operating systems.

Since many of the authors of DDoS tools were developing them to fight battles on IRC, and since they were already programming bots for other purposes, they began to extend existing code for IRC bots to implement DDoS functions and scanning. An early example of this was the *Kaiten* bot, programmed originally for Unix systems. Another example coded for the Windows operating environment is the *Power* bot. Rather than running a separate program that listens for incoming connections on an attacker-specified port, both the DDoS agents (the bots) and the attacker connect to an IRC server like any other IRC client. Since most sites would allow IRC as a communications channel for users, the DDoS communication does not create anomalous events. The role of the handler is played by a simple channel on an IRC server, often protected with a password. There is typically a default channel hard-coded into the bot, where it connects initially to learn where the current control channel is really located. The bot then jumps to the control channel. Channel hopping, even across IRC networks, can be implemented this way. Once in the current control channel, the bots are ready to respond to attacker commands to scan, DDoS someone, update themselves, shut down, etc.

The advantage to the attacker of communicating via IRC is manifold. The server is already there and is being maintained by others. The channel is not easily discovered within thousands of other chat channels (although it might be unusual for a channel full of real humans to suddenly have 10,000 "people" in it in a few minutes). Even when discovered, the channel can be removed only through cooperation of the server's administrators. This cooperation may be difficult to obtain in the case of foreign servers. Due to the distributed nature of IRC, not all clients have to access the same IRC server to get to the "handler channel," but merely have to access a server within the same IRC network or alliance. Most tools appearing after *Trinity* (discussed in [DLD00]) take advantage of this alternate communication mechanism.

As a means of hardening IRC-based communications, attackers regularly compromise hosts and turn them into rogue IRC servers, often using nonstandard ports (instead of the typical 6667/tcp that regular IRC servers use.) Another mechanism, made trivial by *Phatbot*, is to turn some of the bots into TCP proxies on nonstandard ports, which in turn connect to the real IRC servers on standard ports. Either way, another form of stepping stone in the command and control channel easily defeats many incident responders trying to identify and disable botnets.

The attacker's communication with agents via IRC is illustrated in Figure 4.9.

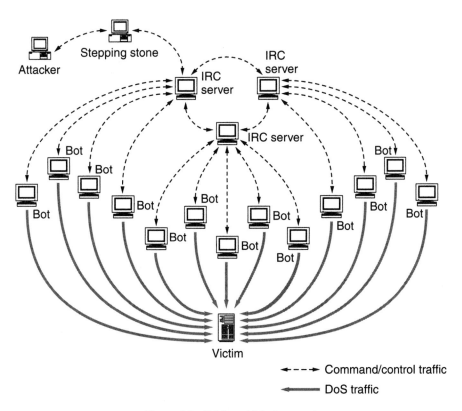

Figure 4.9 IRC-based DDoS network

4.2.3 Malware Update

Like everyone else, attackers need to update the code for their tools. DDoS attackers essentially wanted a software update mechanism analogous to the software update function available in many common desktop operating systems, though without the actual machine owner's controlling the update process, of course. Using the same mechanism to perform updates as was used for initial recruitment—scanning for machines with attack code and planting new code—is noisy and not always effective, since some attack tools patch the vulnerability they used to gain entrance to ensure that no one else can take over their agents. The attacker then cannot break in the same way as before. Many existing tools and bots distribute updates by sending a command to their agents that tells each agent to download a newer version of the code from some source, such as a Web server.

With the increased use of peer-to-peer networks, attackers are already looking at using peer-to-peer mechanisms for malicious activity. The Linux *Slapper* worm, for example, used a peer-to-peer mechanism that it claimed could handle millions of peers. More recently, *Phatbot* has adopted peer-to-peer communication using the "WASTE" protocol, linking to other peers by using Gnutella caching servers to appear to be a Gnutella client (see `http://www.lurhq.com/phatbot.html`). Using this mechanism, attackers can organize their agents into peer-to-peer networks to propagate new code versions or even to control the attack. Robustness and reliability of peer-to-peer communication can make such DDoS networks even more threatening and harder to dismantle than today.

4.2.4   Unwitting Agent Scenario

There is also a class of DDoS attacks that engage computers with vulnerabilities whose exploitation does not necessarily require installing any malicious software on the machine but, instead, allows the attacker to control these hosts to make them generate the attack traffic. The attacker assembles a list of vulnerable systems and, at the time of the attack, has agents iterate through this list sending exploit commands to initiate the traffic flow. The generated traffic appears to be legitimate. For example, the attacker can misuse a vulnerability present in a Web server to cause it to run the `PING.EXE` program.[2] Some researchers have called these *unwitting agents*.

The distinction between an "unwitting agent" and other DDoS attack scenarios is subtle. Rather than a remotely executable vulnerability being used to install malicious software, the vulnerability is used to execute legitimate software already on the system. A more complete description can be found in a talk by David Dittrich (see `http://staff.washington.edu/dittrich/talks/first/`).

Although attacks generated by unwitting agents, like the Web server vulnerability used to run `PING.EXE`, are similar in some respects to reflection attacks, they are not identical. In most reflection attacks, the attacker misuses a perfectly legitimate service, generating legitimate requests with a fake source address. In unwitting agent attacks, the

---

[2] *Ping* was designed to allow a user to determine if a remote computer is available, and its primary purpose is for troubleshooting connectivity problems. Firewalls may, however, prevent the ICMP packets that ping relies on from getting to the remote system. Sending a ping request corresponds to saying, "Are you there?" and waiting for the reply, "I am here."

misused service possesses a remotely exploitable vulnerability that enables the attacker to initiate attack traffic. Patching this vulnerability will immunize unwitting agents from misuse, while defense against reflection attacks is far more complex and difficult.

Unwitting agents cannot be identified by remote port-scanning tools (e.g., *RID* [Bru] or *Zombie Zapper* [Tea]), nor can they be found by running file system scanners such as NIPC's *find_ddos* or antivirus software. This is because there is no malicious software or obscure open ports, just a remotely exploitable vulnerability. The vulnerable machines may be identified by monitoring network traffic, looking for DDoS attack traffic. They can also be discovered by doing typical vulnerability scans with programs such as *Nessus* (http://www.nessus.org).

An example of an unwitting agent attack is the ICMP Echo Request (ping) flood leveled on www.whitehouse.gov on May 4, 2001. The attack misused a Microsoft IIS server vulnerability to trigger a *ping* application on unwitting agents and start the flood. It was reported that hundreds of systems worldwide were flooding. The systems were identified to be running Windows 2000 and NT, and some administrators found PING.EXE running on their systems, targeting the IP address of www.whitehouse.gov. Since *ping* is a legitimate application, antivirus software cannot help in detecting or disabling this attack. A message to the UNISOG mailing list shown in the sidebar provides some more technical information about the attack.

The *Power* bot used the identical mechanism to do some of its flooding. The recruited bots would use scanning techniques described earlier to identify unwitting agents. When an attack was initiated the bots would send exploit code to the agent's vulnerable Web server to start the flood. The exploit details are given in the sidebar on page 76.

4.2.5 Attack Phase

Some attacks are prescheduled—hard-coded in the propagated code. However, most attacks occur when an attacker disseminates a command from his handlers to the agents. During the attack, the control traffic has mostly subsided. Depending on the type of attack tool used, the attacker may or may not be able to stop the ongoing attack. The duration of the attack is either specified in the attacker's command or controlled by default variable settings (e.g., 10 minutes of flooding). It could very well be that the attacker has moved on by the time the flooding has started. However, it is likely that the attacker is observing the ongoing attack, looking for its effects on test targets. Some

UNISOG E-mail Message

```
Date: Fri, 04 May 2001 14:26:29 -0700
From: Computer Security Officer <security@stanford.edu>
To: unisog@sans.org
Subject: [unisog] DDoS against www.whitehouse.gov
```

The attack exploited vulnerable IIS5 servers on Win2K and WinNT
systems.
Immediately prior to the attack we see an incoming port 80 connection
from IP address 202.102.14.137 (CHINANET Jiangsu province network) to
each of the systems that subsequently began pinging 198.137.240.92.
The argus log looks in part like this.

```
Fri 05/04 05:18:21     tcp  202.102.14.137.41406 <->  128.12.177.11.80 EST
Fri 05/04 05:18:21     tcp  202.102.14.137.41495 <->  128.12.157.89.80 EST
Fri 05/04 05:18:22  F  icmp  128.12.157.89      -> 198.137.240.92 ECO
Fri 05/04 05:18:22  F  icmp  128.12.177.11      -> 198.137.240.92 ECO
```

Each of the systems reviewed so far had two ping processes running.
One of the hosts had the following in its IIS log file.

```
12:21:36 202.102.14.137 GET /scripts/../../winnt/system32/ping.exe 200
12:29:29 202.102.14.137 GET /scripts/../../winnt/system32/ping.exe 200
```

While I am surprised that such a simple exploit could work, it looks
like it may be exactly what happened.

The attack was targeted at less than 2% of the total residence
network population so it was probably mapped out earlier. ZDNet
has a story running that indicated that we were not the only one
used in this way.

We are issuing an alert to our dorm network users to update their
systems with the relevant security patches. We've been working so
hard at cleaning up the Linux boxes that we've tended to ignore the
Windows boxes. Not any more.

Stephen

Excerpt from "Power Bot" Analysis

The HTTP GET request exploiting the Web server vulnerability (as seen by the *ngrep* utility from `http://www.packetfactory.net/Projects/Ngrep/`) and the corresponding flood traffic generated by the request:

```
T 2001/06/08 02:20:09.406262 10.0.90.35:2585 -> 192.168.64.225:80 [AP]
  GET /scripts/..%c1%9c../winnt/system32/cmd.exe?/c+ping.exe+"-v"+igmp+"
  -t"+"-l"+30000+10.2.88.84+"-n"+9999+"-w"+10..

I 2001/06/08 02:20:09.430676 192.168.64.225 -> 10.2.88.84 8:0 7303@0:1480
  ...c....abcdefghijklmnopqrstuvwabcdefghijklmnopqrstuvwabcdefghijklmnop
  qrstuvwabcdefghijklmnopqrstuvwabcdefghijklmnopqrstuvwabcdefghijklmnopq
  rstuvwabcdefghijklmnopqrstuvwabcdefghijklmnopqrstuvwabcdefghijklmnopqr
  stuvwabcdefghijklmnopqrstuvwabcdefghijklmnopqrstuvwabcdefghijklmnopqrs
  tuvwabcdefghijklmnopqrstuvwabcdefghijklmnopqrstuvwabcdefghijklmnopqrst
  uvwabcdefghijklmnopqrstuvwabcdefghijklmnopqrstuvwabcdefghijklmnopqrstu
  vwabcdefghijklmnopqrstuvwabcdefghijklmnopqrstuvwabcdefghijklmnopqrstuv
  wabcdefghijklmnopqrstuvwabcdefghijklmnopqrstuvwabcdefghijklmnopqrstuvw
  abcdefghijklmnopqrstuvwabcdefghijklmnopqrstuvwabcdefghijklmnopqrstuvwa
  bcdefghijklmnopqrstuvwabcdefghijklmnopqrstuvwabcdefghijklmnopqrstuvwab
  ..........
```

The exploit is contained in the embedded Unicode characters `%c1%9c`, which trick the server into performing a directory traversal and executing a command shell `/winnt/system32/cmd.exe`.

tools, like *Shaft* [DLD00], have the ability to provide feedback on flood statistics. Figure 4.10 shows the initial compromise and test runs of the *Shaft* tool. The attacker is testing several attack types, such as ICMP, TCP SYN, and UDP floods, which we will discuss in section 4.3, prior to the real full-fledged attack aimed at multiple targets shown in Figure 4.11.

During the attack phase, levels of network activity can be above normal, depending on the type of attack. In a flooding attack, the majority of it is felt at the aggregation point, that is, the target. This is illustrated in Figure 4.12.

In another example, you can observe unusual levels of traffic in Figure 4.13, as seen from the victim's perspective. The quick fluctuations between 12:00 and 18:00 represent a full-scale attack, whereas the somewhat tamed flood between 00:00 and 12:00 reflects a repeated attack, only this time mitigated by a defense mechanism. The

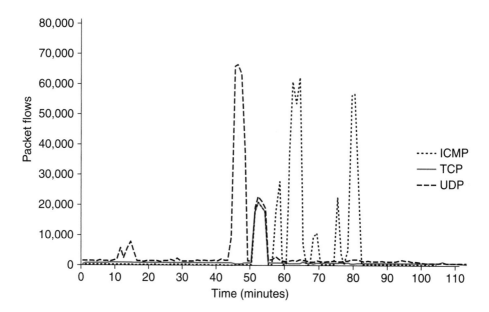

Figure 4.10 Illustration of test runs of the Shaft tool

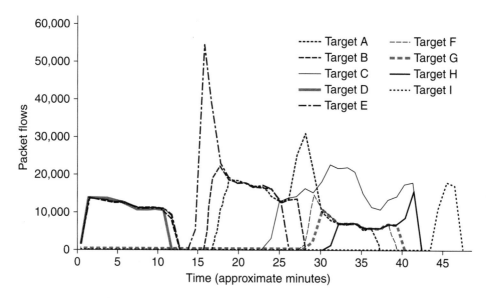

Figure 4.11 Illustration of full-scale attack with the Shaft tool

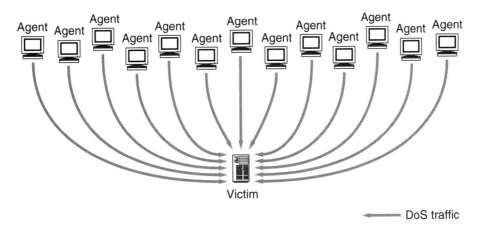

Figure 4.12   Floods from the perspective of the victim

aforementioned fluctuations are not due to variations in the attack, but solely to the measuring equipment collapsing under the load.

From a different perspective, the same attack viewed from an upstream provider a few hops into the Internet in Figure 4.14 barely shows an impact of traffic levels. (The box on the right side of Figure 4.14 indicates the attack timeframe shown in Figure 4.13.) It is important to realize that what affects the target or victim can have little impact on an upstream provider, thus not creating any anomalous observations.

4.3   Semantic Levels of DDoS Attacks

There are several methods of causing a denial of service. Creating a DoS effect is all about breaking things or making them fail. There are many ways to make something fail, and often multiple vulnerabilities will exist in a system and an attacker will try to exploit (or target) several of them until she gets the desired result: The target goes offline.

4.3.1   Exploiting a Vulnerability

As mentioned in Chapter 2, vulnerability attacks involve sending a few well-crafted packets that take advantage of an existing vulnerability in the target machine. For example, there is a bug in Windows 95 and NT, and some Linux kernels, in handling improperly fragmented packets. Generally, when a packet is too large for a given network, it is divided into two (or more) smaller packets, and each of them is marked

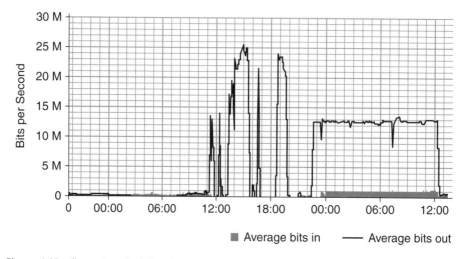

Figure 4.13   Illustration of a full-scale attack as seen by a victim. Average bits out denote the traffic received by the victim.

as fragmented. The mark indicates the order of the first and the last byte in the packet, with regard to the original. At the receiver, chunks are reassembled into the original packet before processing. The fragment marks must fit properly to facilitate reassembly. The vulnerability in the above kernels causes the machine to become unstable when improperly fragmented packets are received, causing it to hang, crash, or reboot. This vulnerability can be exploited by sending two malformed UDP packets to the victim. There were several variations of this exploit—fragments that indicate a small overlap, a negative offset that overlaps the second packet before the start of the header in the first packet, and so on. These were known as the *bonk*, *boink*, *teardrop*, and *newtear* exploits [CER98b].

Vulnerability attacks are particularly bad because they can crash or hang a machine with just one or two carefully chosen packets. However, once the vulnerability is patched, the original attack becomes completely ineffective.

4.3.2   Attacking a Protocol

An ideal example of protocol attacks is a TCP SYN flood attack. We first explain this attack and then indicate general features of protocol attacks.

A TCP session starts with negotiation of session parameters between a client and a server. The client sends a TCP SYN packet to the server, requesting some service. In the SYN packet header, the client provides his *initial sequence number*, a unique

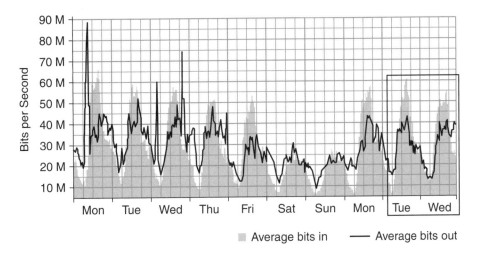

Figure 4.14   Illustration of a full-scale attack seen further upstream. Average bits in denote the traffic
sent to the victim.

per-connection number that will be used to keep count of data sent to the server
(so the server can recognize and handle missing, misordered, or repeated data). Upon
SYN packet receipt, the server allocates a transmission control block (TCB), storing
information about the client. It then replies with a SYN-ACK, informing the client
that its service request will be granted, acknowledging the client's sequence number
and sending information about the server's initial sequence number. The client, upon
receipt of the SYN-ACK packet, allocates a transmission control block. The client then
replies with an ACK to the server, which completes the opening of the connection. This
message exchange is called a *three-way handshake* and is depicted in Figure 4.15.

The potential for abuse lies in the early allocation of the server's resources. When
the server allocates his TCB and replies with a SYN-ACK, the connection is said to be
half-open. The server's allocated resources will be tied up until the client sends an ACK
packet, closes the connection (by sending an RST packet) or until a timeout expires
and the server closes the connection, releasing the buffer space. During a TCP SYN
flooding attack, the attacker generates a multitude of half-open connections by using
IP source spoofing. These requests quickly exhaust the server's TCB memory, and the
server can accept no more incoming connection requests. Established TCP connections
usually experience no degradation in service, though, as they naturally complete and
are closed, the TCB records spaces they were using will be exhausted by the attack,
not replaced by other legitimate connections. In rare cases, the server machine crashes,

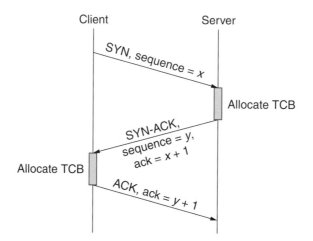

Figure 4.15   Opening of TCP connection: three-way handshake

exhausts its memory, or is otherwise rendered inoperative. In order to keep buffer space occupied for the desired time, the attacker needs to generate a steady stream of SYN packets toward the victim (to reserve again those resources that have been freed by timeouts or completion of normal TCP sessions).

The TCP SYN flooding attack is described in detail in [CER96, SKK+97]. This is an especially vicious attack, as servers expect to see large numbers of legitimate SYN packets and cannot easily distinguish the legitimate from the attack traffic. No simple filtering rule can handle the TCP SYN flooding attack because legitimate traffic will suffer collateral damage. Several solutions for TCP SYN flooding have been proposed, and their detailed description is given in [SKK+97].

In order to perform a successful TCP SYN flooding attack, the attacker needs to locate an open TCP port at the victim. Then he generates a relatively small volume packet stream—as few as ten packets per minute [SKK+97] can effectively tie up the victim's resources. Another version of the TCP SYN flooding attack, *random port TCP SYN flooding*, is much less common. In it, the attacker generates a large volume of TCP SYN packets targeting random ports at the victim, with the goal of overwhelming the victim's network resources, rather than filling his buffer space.

Protocol attacks are often difficult to fix—if the fix requires changing the protocol, both the sender and receiver must use the new version of the protocol. Changing commonly used Internet protocols for any reason has proven difficult. In a few cases, clever use of the existing protocol can solve the problem. For example, TCP SYN cookies (described in Chapters 5 and 6) deal with the SYN flood attack without changing the protocol specification, only how the server's stack processes the connections.

Simple Nomad of the RAZOR team at BindView came up with an attack that targets the same resource as a SYN flood, connection state record, but in a novel manner. Instead of creating lots of half-open connections, the attacker actually completes the three-way handshake and creates many established connection state records in the kernel's TCB table. The trick that enables the attacker to quickly set up a lot of established connections without using up the agent's TCB memory lies in the attack programming using custom packets rather than the TCP API [Wright]. The agent machine never allocates a TCB. Instead, it listens promiscuously on the Ethernet card and responds to TCP packets based on header flags alone. The agent infers from the victim's replies the TCP header information that the victim expects to see in future packets. For instance, if the victim has sent a SYN-ACK packet with SEQ number 1232 and ACK number 540, the agent infers that it should next send an ACK packet with SEQ 540 and ACK 1233. While the server uses TCBs, the attacker does not. This attack can even forge the source address to make it look like packets are coming from a nonexistent host on the local network. Since the attacker is listening to communications on the local network in promiscuous mode, he will be able to hear and reply to the victim's packets, even though they are sent to the spoofed address.

The attacker leaves established TCP connections idle but responds to keep-alive packets so that the connections do not time out and free up kernel resources. He can even rate limit the connection establishment to avoid SYN flooding protections within the stack [CER00]. This attack is called the *Naptha attack* [Bin00], and TCP SYN cookies are an ineffective defense against it.

To generalize, protocol attacks target an asymmetry inherent in certain protocols. This asymmetry enables the attacker to create a large amount of work and consume substantial resources at the server, while sparing its own resources. Generally, the only fix that works against protocol attacks is creating a protocol patch that balances the asymmetry in the server's favor.

4.3.3   Attacking Middleware

Attacks can be made on algorithms, such as hash functions that would normally perform its operations in linear time for each subsequent entry. By injecting values that force worst-case conditions to exist [CW03], such as all values hashing into the same bucket, the attacker can cause the application to perform their functions in exponential time for each subsequent entry [MvOV96].

As long as the attacker can freely send data that is processed using the vulnerable hash function, she can cause the CPU utilization of the server to exceed capacity and degrade what would normally be a subsecond operation into one that takes several minutes to complete. It does not take a very large number of requests to overwhelm some applications this way and render them unusable by legitimate users.

The victim can immunize the host from this kind of attacks by changing (or even removing) the middleware to remove the vulnerability. Doing so may not always be easy, and if the attacker has truly found a previously unknown vulnerability, even detecting what he has done to cause the slowdown may be a challenge. Also, the middleware may not be changeable by the victim himself, who may need to wait for an update from the author or manufacturer of the middleware. Further, if the middleware is vital to the victim's proper operation, disabling or removing it may prove to be as damaging as the attack itself.

Note that a node under a successful middleware attack might not appear to be in any trouble at all, except that those of its services that rely on the middleware are slow. The number of packets it receives might be unexceptional, other unrelated services on the node might be behaving properly, and there might be few telltale signs of an ongoing DoS attack, beyond services not working. Further, many DDoS defense mechanisms that aim to defend against flooding might be unable to help with this kind of attack.

4.3.4   Attacking an Application

The attacker may target a specific application and send packets to reach the limit of service requests this application can handle. For example, Web servers take a certain amount of time to serve normal Web page requests, and thus there will exist some finite number of maximum requests per second that they can sustain. If we assume that the Web server can process 1,000 requests per second to retrieve the files that make up a company's home page, then at most 1,000 customers' requests can be processed concurrently. For the sake of argument, let's say the normal load a Web server sees daily is 100 requests per second (one tenth of capacity).

But what if an attacker controls 10,000 hosts, and can force each one of them to make one request every 10 seconds to the Web server? That is an average of 1,000 requests per second, and added to the normal traffic results in 110% of the server's capacity. Now a large portion of the legitimate requests will not make it through because the server is saturated.

As with middleware attacks, an application attack might not cripple the entire host or appear as a vast quantity of packets. So, again, many defenses are not able to help defend against this kind of attack.

4.3.5 Attacking a Resource

The attacker may target a specific resource such as CPU cycles or router switching capacity. In January 2001, Microsoft suffered an outage that was reported to have been caused by a network configuration error, as described in Chapter 3. This outage disrupted a large number of Microsoft properties. When news of this attack came out, it was discovered that *all* of Microsoft's DNS servers were on the same network segment, served by the same router. Attackers then targeted the routing infrastructure in front of these servers and brought down all of Microsoft's online services.

Microsoft quickly moved to disperse its name servers geographically and to provide redundant routing paths to the servers to make it more difficult for someone to take them all out of service at once. Removing bottlenecks and increasing capacity can address resource attacks, though, again, an attacker may respond with a stronger attack. For companies with fewer resources than Microsoft, overprovisioning and geographically dispersing services may not be a financially viable option.

Attacking Infrastructure Resources

Infrastructure resources are particularly attractive targets because attacks on them can have effects on large segments of the Internet population. Routing is a key Internet infrastructure service that could be (and, indeed, sometimes has been) targeted by DoS attacks. Briefly, this infrastructure maintains the information required to deliver packets to their destinations, and thus is critical for Internet operation. At a high level, the service operates by exchanging information about paths through the Internet among routers, which build tables that help decide where to send packets. As a packet enters a router, the table is consulted to determine where to send the packet next.

This infrastructure can be attacked in many ways to cause denial of service [Gre02] [ZPW+02] [MV02] [Jou00]. In addition to flooding routers, the protocols used to exchange information have various potential vulnerabilities that could be exploited to deny service. These are not only bugs in the implementations of the protocols, but also characteristics of how the protocols were designed that could be misused by an attacker. For example, there are various methods by which an attacker could try to fill up a router's tables with unimportant entries, perhaps leaving no room for critical entries or making the router run much slower. A router could be instructed by an attacker to send packets to the wrong place, preventing their delivery.[3] Or the routing infrastructure could be made unstable by forcing extremely frequent changes in its routing information. There are a number of fairly effective approaches to countering these attacks [Tho] [Ope], and research is ongoing into even better methods of protecting this critical infrastructure [KLS00].

4.3.6　Pure Flooding

Given a sufficiently large number of agents, it is possible to simply send any type of packets as fast as possible from each machine and consume all available network bandwidth at the victim. This is a *bandwidth consumption attack*. The victim cannot defend against this attack on her own, since the legitimate packets get dropped on the upstream link, between the ISP and the victim network. Thus, frequently the victim requests help from its ISP to filter out offending traffic.

It is not unusual that the victim's ISP is also affected by the attack (at least on the "customer attach router" connecting the victim to the ISP's network) and may have to filter on their upstream routers and even get their upstream provider or peers to also filter traffic coming into their network. In some cases, the attack traffic is very easy to identify and filter out (e.g., large-packet UDP traffic to unused ports, packets with an IP protocol value of 255). In other cases, it may be very difficult to identify specific packet header fields that could be used for filtering (e.g., reflected DNS queries, which could look like responses to a legitimate DNS query from clients within your network, or a flood of widely dispersed legitimate-looking HTTP requests). If this happens, filtering will simply save both the victim's and the ISP's resources, but the victim's customer traffic will be brought down to zero, achieving a DoS effect.

4.4　Attack Toolkits

While some attackers are sophisticated enough to create their own attack code, far more commonly they use code written by others. Such code is typically built into a general, easily used package called an *attack toolkit*. It is very common today for attackers to bundle a large number of programs into a single archive file, often with scripts that automate its installation. This is a blended threat, as discussed in Section 4.4.2.

---

[3] One cannot exclude that a router can be compromised either through an existing vulnerability or through a weak or default password.

4.4.1 Some Popular DDoS Programs

While there are numerous scripts that are used for scanning, compromise and infection of vulnerable machines, there are only a handful of DDoS attack tools that have been used to carry out the actual attacks. A detailed overview of these tools, along with a timeline of their appearance, is given in [HWLT01]. DDoS attack tools mostly differ in the communication mechanism deployed between handlers and agents, and in the customizations they provide for attack traffic generation. The following paragraphs provide a brief overview of these popular tools. The reader should bear in mind that features discussed in this overview are those that have been observed in instances of attack code detected on some infected machines. Many variations may (and will) exist that have not yet been discovered and analyzed.

Trinoo [Ditf] uses a handler/agent architecture, wherein an attacker sends commands to the handler via TCP and handlers and agents communicate via UDP. Both handler and agents are password protected to try to prevent them from being taken over by another attacker. *Trinoo* generates UDP packets of a given size to random ports on one or multiple target addresses, during a specified attack interval.

Tribe Flood Network (TFN) [Dith] uses a different type of handler/agent architecture. Commands are sent from the handler to all of the agents from the command line. The attacker does not "log in" to the handler as with *trinoo* or *Stacheldraht*. Agents can wage a UDP flood, TCP SYN flood, ICMP Echo flood, and Smurf attacks at specified or random victim ports. The attacker runs commands from the handler using any of a number of connection methods (e.g., remote shell bound to a TCP port, UDP-based client/server remote shells, ICMP-based client/server shells such as LOKI [rou97], SSH terminal sessions, or normal telnet TCP terminal sessions). Remote control of *TFN* agents is accomplished via ICMP Echo Reply packets. All commands sent from handler to agents through ICMP packets are coded, not cleartext, which hinders detection.

Stacheldraht [Ditg] (German for "barbed wire") combines features of *trinoo* and *TFN* tools and adds encrypted communication between the attacker and the handlers. *Stacheldraht* uses TCP for encrypted communication between the attacker and the handlers, and TCP or ICMP for communication between handler and agents. Another added feature is the ability to perform automatic updates of agent code. Available attacks are UDP flood, TCP SYN flood, ICMP Echo flood, and Smurf attacks.

Shaft [DLD00] is a DDoS tool that shares a combination of features similar to those in *trinoo, TFN,* and *Stacheldraht*. Added features are the ability to switch handler and agent ports on the fly (thus hindering detection of the tool by intrusion detection systems), a "ticket" mechanism to link transactions, and a particular interest in packet statistics. *Shaft* uses UDP for communication between handlers and agents. Remote control is achieved via a simple telnet connection from the attacker to the handler. *Shaft* uses "tickets" for keeping track of its individual agents. Each command sent to the agent contains a password and a ticket. Both passwords and ticket numbers have to match for the agent to execute the request. Simple letter shifting (a Caesar cipher) is used to obscure passwords in sent commands. Agents can generate a UDP flood, TCP SYN flood, ICMP flood, or all three attack types. The flooding occurs in bursts of 100 packets per host (this number is hard-coded), with the source port and source address randomized. Handlers can issue a special command to agents to obtain statistics on malicious traffic generated by each agent. It is suspected that this is used to calculate the yield of a DDoS network.

Tribe Flood Network 2000 (TFN2K) [CERb] is an improved version of the *TFN* attack tool. It includes several features designed specifically to make *TFN2K* traffic difficult to recognize and filter; to remotely execute commands; to obfuscate the true source of the traffic, to transport *TFN2K* traffic over multiple transport protocols including UDP, TCP, and ICMP, and to send "decoy" packets to confuse attempts to locate other nodes in a *TFN2K* network. *TFN2K* obfuscates the true traffic source by spoofing source addresses. Attackers can choose between random spoofing and spoofing within a specified range of addresses. In addition to flooding, *TFN2K* can also perform some vulnerability attacks by sending malformed or invalid packets, as described in [CER98a, CERa].

Mstream [CER01b, DWDL] generates a flood of TCP packets with the ACK bit set. Handlers can be controlled remotely by one or more attackers using a password-protected interactive login. The communications between attacker and handlers, and a handler and agents, are configurable at compile time and have varied significantly from incident to incident. Source addresses in attack packets are spoofed at random. The TCP ACK attack exhausts network resources and will likely cause a TCP RST to be sent to the spoofed source address (potentially also creating outgoing bandwidth consumption at the victim).

Trinity is the first DDoS tool that is controlled via IRC. Upon compromise and infection by *Trinity*, each machine joins a specified IRC channel and waits for commands. Use of a legitimate IRC service for communication between attacker and agents replaces the classic independent handler and elevates the level of the threat, as explained in Section 4.2.2. *Trinity* is capable of launching several types of flooding attacks on a victim site, including UDP, IP fragment, TCP SYN, TCP RST, TCP ACK, and other floods.

From late 1999 through 2001, the *Stacheldraht* and *TFN2K* attack tools were the most popular. The *Stacheldraht* agent was bundled into versions of the *t0rnkit* rootkit and a variant of the 2001 *Ramen* worm. The *1i0n* worm included the *TFN2K* agent code.

On the Windows side, a large number of *blended threat* rootkit bundles include the *knight.c* or *kaiten.c* DDoS bots. *TFN2K* was coded specifically to compile on Windows NT, and versions of the *trinoo* agent have also been seen on Windows systems. In fact, *knight.c* was originally coded for Unix systems, but can be compiled with the Cygwin development libraries. Using this method, nearly any Unix DDoS program could reasonably be ported to Windows, and in fact some Windows blended threat bundles are delivered in Unix *tar*-formatted archives that are unpacked with the Cygwin-compiled version of GNU tar [Dev].

Agobot and its descendant **Phatbot** saw very widespread use in 2003 and 2004. This blended threat is packed into a single program that some have called a "Swiss army knife" of attack tools. *Phatbot* implements two types of SYN floods, a UDP flood, an ICMP flood, the *Targa* flood (random IP protocol, fragmentation and fragment offset values, and spoofed source address), the *wonk* flood (one SYN packet, followed by 1,023 ACK packets) floods, and a recursive HTTP GET flood or a single HTTP GET flood with a built-in delay in hours (either set by the user or randomly chosen). The latter, when distributed across a network of tens or hundreds of thousands of hosts, would look like a normal pattern of HTTP traffic that would be very difficult to detect and block by some defense mechanisms.

4.4.2   Blended Threat Toolkits

Blended threats typically include some or all of the following components, which can vary due to operating system, degree of automation (for example, worms), author, etc.

- **A Windows network service program**. A tool commonly found in Windows blended threats is a program called *Firedaemon*. *Firedaemon* is responsible for registering programs to be run as servers, so they can listen on network sockets for incoming connections. *Firedaemon* would typically control the FTP server, IRC bounce program, and/or backdoor shell.

- **Scanners**. Various network scanners are included to help the attacker reconnoiter the local network and find other hosts to attack. These may be simple SYN scanners like *synscan*, TCP banner grabbers like *mscan*, or more full-featured scanners like *nmap* (http://www.nmap.org).

- **Single-threaded DoS programs.** While these programs may seem old-fashioned, a simple UDP or SYN flooder such as *synk4* can still be effective against some systems. The attacker must log in to the host and run these commands from the command line, or use an IRC bot that is capable of running external commands, such as the *Power* bot.

- **An FTP server.** Installing an FTP server, such as *Serv-U* FTP daemon, allows an attacker (or software/media pirate who doubles as DDoS attacker) to upload files to the compromised host. These files are then served up by the next category of programs, the *Warez* bot.

- **An IRC file service (Warez) bot.** Pirated media files (music and video) and software programs are known as *Warez*. Bots that serve Warez are known as—you guessed it—*Warez* bots. Bots and IRC clients are able to transfer files using a feature of IRC called the *Direct Client-to-Client* (*DCC*) protocol.

  One of the most popular Warez bots is called the *iroffer* bot. Large bot networks using the *iroffer* form *XDCC* Warez bot nets (a peer-to-peer DCC network) and rely on *Serv-U* FTP daemons for uploading gigabytes of pirated movies.[4]

- **An IRC DDoS bot or DDoS agent.** As mentioned earlier, standard DDoS tools like *Stacheldraht* or *TFN*, or IRC bots like *GTbot* or *knight*, are typically found in blended threats. These programs may be managed by *Firedaemon* on Windows hosts, or *inetd* or *cron* on Unix hosts.

- **Local exploit programs.** Since these kits are used for convenience, they often include some method of performing privilege escalation on the system, in the event they are loaded into a normal user account that was compromised through password sniffing. This allows the attacker to gain full administrative rights, at which point all the programs can then be installed completely on the compromised host.

- **Remote exploit programs.** Going along with the scanner program will often be a set of remote exploits that can be used to extend the attacker's reach into your network, or use your host as a stepping stone to go attack another site. Scripts that automate the scanning and remote exploitation are often used, making the process as simple as running a single command and giving just the first one, two, or three octets of a network address.

---

[4] For a description of this activity, see http://www.cs.rochester.edu/~bukys/host/tonikgin /EduHacking.html.

- **System log cleaners**. Once the intruder has gained access to the system, she often wants to wipe out any evidence that she ever connected to the host. There are log cleaners for standard text log files (e.g., Unix *syslog* or Apache log files), or for binary log files (e.g., Windows Event Logs or Unix *wtmp* and *lastlog* files).

- **Trojan Horse operating system program replacements**. To provide backdoors to regain access to the system, or to make the system "lie" about the presence of the attackers running programs, network connections, and files/directories, attackers often replace some of the operating system's external commands. On Unix systems, the candidate programs for replacement would typically be *ls* and *find* (replaced to hide files), *ps* and *top* (replaced to hide processes), *netstat* (replaced to hide network connections), and *ifconfig* (replaced to hide the fact the network interface is in promiscuous mode for sniffing).

- **Sniffers**. Installing a sniffer allows the attacker to steal more login account names and passwords, extending his reach into your network. Most sniffers look for commonly used protocols that put passwords in cleartext form on the network, such as *telnet*, *ftp*, and the *IMAP* and *POP* e-mail protocols. Some sniffers allow logging of the sniffed data to an "unlinked" (or removed) file that will not show up in directory listings, possibly encrypted, or even located on a remote host (*Phantom sniffer*).

As described earlier, *Phatbot* implements a large percentage of these functions in a single program, including its own propagation.

4.4.3   Implications

Security sites such as `PacketStormSecurity.org` have assembled large numbers of malicious programs. Some of the tools are clearly written for reuse and allow easy adaptation for a specific purpose, and others are clearly crippled so that script kiddies cannot easily apply them.

Hacker Web sites offer readily downloadable DDoS toolkits. This code can frequently be used without modification or real understanding, just by specifying a command to start recruiting agents and then, at the time of the attack, specifying another command with the target address and type of the attack. As a result, those who wish to use existing tools, or craft their own, have a ready supply of code with which to work. They must still learn how to recruit an attack network, to keep it from being

stolen by others, how to target their victims, and how to get around any defenses. With
dedication and time, or money to buy these skills, this is not a significant obstacle.

4.5   What Is IP Spoofing?

One tactic used in malicious attacks, particularly in DDoS, is IP spoofing. In normal IP
communications, the header field contains the source IP address and the destination
address as set by the default network socket operations. IP spoofing occurs when a
malicious program creates its own packets and does not set the true source IP address
in the packet's header. It is easy to craft individual packets with full control over the IP
header and send them out over the network if one has sufficient privileges within the
operating system. This is referred to as *raw socket access*.

A natural question to ask is why does this capability exist in the TCP/IP stack?
There are perfectly legitimate reasons to craft packets by hand and transmit them on
the network, rather than only use functions provided by a given TCP/IP stack's API;
for example, in mobile IP environments, where a roaming host must use a "home" IP
address in a foreign network [Per02], virtual private networks that set the host IP to an
address local to the organization's network, etc. Regardless of the advisability of allowing
use of raw sockets in the TCP/IP API, current operating systems lacking mandatory access control [Bell] and other advanced security features will have ways of getting around
such limitations. Removal of raw sockets from the Windows API was proposed in 2001,
and researchers showed many examples of programmers getting around the lack of raw
sockets in earlier versions of Windows (e.g., the l0pht implemented a workaround for a
lack of raw sockets in Windows 9x in *l0phtcrack* 3; PCAUSA provides a raw sockets implementation for Windows 9x—see `http://www.pcausa.com/`; WinPcap implements
a means of sending raw packets—see `http://netgroup-serv.polito.it/winpcap/`).
With the release of Windows XP Service Pack 2 in August 2004, Microsoft removed
the raw sockets API, which broke applications like the public domain *nmap* port scanner. In just a few days, a workaround was produced restoring the ability of *nmap*
to craft custom packets. See `http://seclists.org/lists/nmap-hackers/2004/Jul-`
`Sep/0003.html`. We must also live with the fact that even if the ability to spoof addresses
did not exist in the first place, DDoS would still not only be possible, but be just as
damaging. There are simply too many ways to perform viable denial of service attacks.

There are several levels of spoofing.

- **Fully random IP addresses.** The host generates IP addresses that are taken at
  random from the entire IPv4 space, 0.0.0.0–255.255.255.255. This strategy will

sometimes generate invalid IPv4 addresses, such as addresses from 192.168.0.0 range, that are reserved for private networks, and may also generate nonroutable IP addresses, multicast addresses, broadcast addresses, and invalid addresses (e.g., 0.2.45.6). Some of these exotic addresses cause significant problems in their own right for routing hardware, which must process spoofed packets, and in some cases they crash or lock up the router. However, most randomly generated addresses will be valid and routable. If the attacker cares little about whether a particular packet is delivered, she can send large numbers of randomly spoofed packets and expect that most of them will be delivered.

A frequently proposed defense against random spoofing is to use a form of ingress and egress filtering [FS00]. (See Sidebar "Ingress/Egress Filtering" for a complete description of these sometime confusing terms and how they apply to the problem of IP spoofing.) This technique compares the packet's source address with the range of IP addresses assigned to its source or destination network, depending on the location of the filtering router, and drops nonmatching ones that appear to be randomly spoofed.

While ingress/egress filtering has the potential to greatly limit the ability of attackers to generate spoofed packets, it has to be widely deployed to really impact the DDoS threat. An edge network performing ingress/egress filtering is mostly scrutinizing its own traffic to protect others, but itself gains little benefit. This may be the reason why this type of filtering is still not widely deployed.

- **Subnet spoofing**. If a host resides in, say, the 192.168.1.0/24 network, then it is relatively easy to spoof a neighbor from the same network. For example, 192.168.1.2 can easily spoof 192.168.1.45 or any other address in 192.168.1.0/24 range unless the network administrators have put in protective measures that prevent an assigned Ethernet hardware address (MAC address) being associated with any but the administratively assigned IP address. This is an expensive fix from an administration point of view.

  If the host is part of a larger network (for example, a /16 network that contains 65,536 addresses), then it could spoof addresses from the larger domain, assuming the protective measures outlined in the previous point have not been implemented.

  Packets spoofed at the subnet level can be filtered by ingress/egress filtering only at the subnet level, since their source address is, by definition, from an assigned address range for a given network. Even with such filtering at the subnet level, spoofing can still make it difficult to identify the flooding host.

Ingress/Egress Filtering

The terms *ingress* and *egress* mean, respectively, the acts of entering and exiting. In an interconnected network of networks, such as the Internet, what leaves (egresses) one network will enter (ingress) another. It is extremely important to clearly define the location where the filtering is done with respect to the network whose traffic is being filtered, to avoid confusion.

If there was one "Big I" Internet, and we all connected our hosts directly to "The Internet," life would be simple and we could just say "ingress means entering the Internet" and "egress means leaving the Internet," and everything would be clear. There would be only one perspective. But there is no "Internet" to which we all connect, and to make matters worse there are tier 1 and tier 2 network providers, as well as leaf networks (e.g., university and enterprise networks).

To see how a confusion can occur, take the example given in RFC 2827 [FS00]. It discusses ingress filtering in terms of an attacker's packets coming in to an edge router of ISP D. This is illustrated by the following figure.

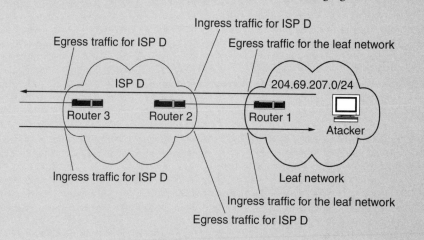

Ingress/egress filtering example from RFC 2827

The authors of the RFC describe an attacker residing within the 204.69.207. 0/24 address space, which is provided Internet connectivity by ISP D. (This is shown in the above figure.) They describe an input traffic filter being applied on the ingress (input) link of Router 2, which provides connectivity to the attacker's network. This restricts traffic to allow only packets originating from source addresses within the 204.69.207.0/24 prefix, prohibiting the attacker from spoofing addresses of any other network besides 204.69.207.0/24.

The authors of this RFC only discuss ISP D doing filtering of traffic coming *in* to their edge router from their customer, shown in the figure on page 94 as Router 2. So in their example, ISP D does *ingress* filtering to avoid an attacker using "invalid" source addresses that appear to come from networks other than the customer's address range.

This RFC does not consider this same filtering also being done by the customer through the router the customer owns, Router 1. (This customer is known as an edge network, an end customer of a network service provider, or simply a leaf network.) If outbound packets are filtered on Router 1 to prevent source addresses from networks other than 204.69.207.0/24 leaving this leaf network, the customer would be doing *egress* filtering.

It would be very confusing to always say "ingress means packets going to the ISP" and explain that customer 204.69.207.0/24 does ingress filtering to block packets leaving its network, especially if the description is taken across more than one network (e.g., moving to the left in the figure on page 94.)

Another possible source of confusion in the use of these terms is that the filtering to be performed could be on any criteria, not just on source addresses. While discussion of these terms often focuses on the issue of mitigating IP spoofing, the filtering could be on protocol type, port number, or any other criteria of importance.

Within the context of handling IP spoofing, there are two important reasons for making the ingress/egress distinction, and they have to do with filtering being done for the same reason at two locations (perhaps simultaneously), the customer network's egress router and the ingress router of an ISP that connects to the customer's network.

1. It can be argued that egress filtering of traffic leaving a leaf network is less expensive, CPU-wise, than the equivalent ingress filtering for that same traffic coming into a tier 2 network provider (and it is even worse if you go up one level to tier 1, or backbone providers, which is *not* the place to do ingress filtering to stop spoofed packets coming in from their peers.)* Given this argument, egress filtering on leaf networks to stop attackers from spoofing off-network hosts is more desirable.

---

* see http://www.netsys.com/firewalls/firewalls-2001-06/msg00385.html

2. Spoofing can happen in either direction. Attackers outside your network can send packets inbound to your network pretending to be hosts *on* your network, and attackers inside your network can send packets outbound from your network pretending to be from hosts *outside* your network. This means that leaf networks *should do both ingress and egress filtering* to protect their network as well as other networks. Even if your ISP says it will filter packets coming into your network to prevent spoofing, you may want to do redundant filtering of those same packets to make *sure* that spoofing cannot take place. After all, don't things fail sometimes?

In this book, we will be careful to use *ingress filtering* to mean *filtering the traffic coming into your network* and *egress filtering* to mean *filtering the traffic leaving your network*. We will be explicit when talking about filtering being done by an ISP or tier 1 provider versus filtering being done by a leaf network. Where the filters are applied and why really does matter.

- **Spoofing the victim's addresses.** This is the reflection attack scenario. The host forges the source address in service request packets (for example, a SYN packet for a TCP connection) to invoke a flood of service replies to be sent to the victim. If there is no filtering of packets as they leave the source network or at the entry point to the upstream ISP's router, these forged packets allow a reflection DoS attack.

4.5.1 Why Is IP Spoofing Defense Challenging?

There is nothing to prevent someone from spoofing IP addresses, since all that is required is privileged access to the network socket. One must put up filters and restrictions at the edge of every network to allow only packets with source addresses from that network to leave. For example, a network 192.168.1.0/24 (a /24 network containing 254 host addresses) should allow only address packets carrying a source from the range 192.168.1.1–192.168.1.254 to leave the network. Note the clear omission of the broadcast addresses 192.168.1.0 and 192.168.1.255 which are used in conjunction with spoofing in a Smurf attack. If any network does not put this form of filtering in place on its router, machines in that network can spoof any IP address.

There are sometimes good reasons not to turn this form of filtering on in your network. It requires a little extra network administration, and may temporarily shut off your Internet access if you make configuration mistakes. If you do turn anti-spoofing egress filtering on, it may break mobile IP support. It may be worth considering for other security implications, but you must realize that you are contributing to other networks' security, not your own. You would need expensive solutions to prevent spoofed traffic from reaching you. Some ideas are discussed in Chapter 7.

There are research results suggesting that it may be possible to detect many spoofed packets in the core of the Internet [PL01, LMW+01, FS00]. However, these approaches are immature, they require deployment in core Internet routers, and there is no reason to believe any of them will be adopted in the foreseeable future.

4.5.2   Why DDoS Attacks Use IP Spoofing

IP spoofing is not necessary for a successful DDoS attack, since the attacker can exhaust the victim's resources with a sufficiently large packet flood, regardless of the validity of source addresses. However, some DDoS attacks do use IP spoofing for several reasons.

- **Hiding the location of agent machines**. In single-point DoS attacks, spoofing was used to hide the location of the attacking host. In such attacks, network operators find it hard to block the source of the attack and/or remove the offending host from the network, or even clean it. In DDoS attacks, the agents are the path to the handler, which provides an additional layer of indirection to the attacker. Hiding agents means hiding a quick path to the attacker.

- **Reflector attacks**. Reflector attacks require spoofing to be accomplished. The agents must be able to spoof the victim's addresses in service requests directed at legitimate servers, to invoke replies that flood the victim.

- **Bypassing DDoS defenses**. Some DDoS defenses build a list of legitimate clients that are accessing the network. During the attack, these clients are given preferential treatment. Other defenses attempt to share resources fairly among all current clients, each source IP address being assigned its fair share. In both of these scenarios, IP spoofing defeats the separation of clients based on their IP addresses, and enables the attack packets to assume the IP addresses of legitimate clients. Of course this only applies to UDP-based attacks, as one cannot typically spoof source addresses on TCP connection–based services in order to bypass DDoS mitigation defenses.

4.5.3   Spoofing Is Irrelevant at 10,000+ Hosts

Looking at the history of DDoS attacks, one quickly realizes that given the sheer number of agents in a DDoS network, spoofing is not really necessary in a flooding attack, as described in Section 4.3.6. Agent networks of 10,000 hosts or more are not uncommon and are easily traded on IRC networks, where some malicious attackers use them as "currency." As shown in Section 2.5.2, botnets of 400,000 hosts are not impossible to obtain. At this size, preventing all spoofing could somewhat help certain DDoS defense approaches deal with certain forms of DDoS attacks. This alone would not eliminate the problem of DDoS.

4.6   DDoS Attack Trends

There is a constant arms race between the attackers and the defenders. As soon as there are effective defenses against a certain type of attack, the attackers change tactics finding a way to bypass these defenses. Due to improved security practices such as ingress/egress filtering, attackers have improved their tools, adding the option of specifying the spoofing level or spoofing netmask. A large number of attacks nowadays use subnet spoofing, as discussed in Section 4.5, bypassing anti-spoofing ingress/egress filters.

The defenses that detect command and control traffic based on network signatures of known DDoS tools have led the attackers to start encrypting this traffic. As an added benefit, this encryption prevents the DDoS networks from being easily taken over by competing attacker groups, as well as from being easily discovered and dismantled.

New techniques in anti-analysis and anti-forensics make discovery of the mission of the tool difficult. Obfuscation of the running code by encryption exists in both the Windows and Unix worlds. Code obfuscators like *burneye, Shiva,* and *burneye2* are under scrutiny by security analysts.

The trend of making DDoS tools and attack strategies more advanced in response to advanced defenses will likely continue. This was predicted in the original *trinoo* analysis [Ditf], and the trend has continued unabated. There are a variety of potential DDoS scenarios that would be very difficult for defense mechanisms to handle, yet painfully simple for attackers to perpetrate. Some of these were detailed in a CERT Coordination Center publication on DDoS attack trends [HWLT01].

To prevail, the defenders must always keep in mind that they have intelligent and agile adversaries. They themselves need to be intelligent and agile in response. While it is unlikely that we will ever design a perfect defense which handles all possible DDoS attacks, making determined progress in handling simple scenarios will discourage all but the most sophisticated attackers, and dramatically reduce the incidence of attacks.

In defending against an advanced attacker, one needs to get into the mindset of the attacker and pay close attention to DDoS attack tool capabilities and features. Attackers often must test their attack method in advance, or probe your network for weaknesses. They may also need to test to see if their attack has succeeded. Evidence of this can be found in logs, or collected during an attack as you adjust your defenses. This is known as "network situational awareness."

When facing an advanced DDoS attack, one would be wise to study Boyd's OODA Loop (which stands for Observe, Orient, Decide, and Act) [Boy]. While a complex concept, the essential aspects are employing methods of observing what is happening on your network and hosts, using a body of knowledge of DDoS attack tools and behavior such as what is provided in this book, knowing the available set of actions that can be taken to counter an attack (and the results you expect to obtain by taking those actions), and finally acting to counter the attack. Once action is taken, you immediately go back to observation to determine if you obtained the expected results, and if not, go through the process again to choose another course of action.

Boyd goes on to suggest taking two actions, one conventional and the other nonconventional, to attempt to confuse your attacker and either slow them down, or force them to expose themselves through their actions. (For example, DDoS attackers may expose themselves as they test your Web site again and again to see if it has gone down and stayed down. If you increase logging prior to making a defensive move, and do additional analysis during and after, you may be able to detect these probes and gain information on your attacker.) In other words, a simple defense may only stop simple attacks; a sophisticated attack may call for a sophisticated defense.

CHAPTER 5

An Overview of DDoS Defenses

How can we defend against the difficult problems raised by distributed denial-of-service attacks? As discussed in Chapter 4, there are two classes of victims of DDoS attacks: the owners of machines that have been compromised to serve as DDoS agents and the final targets of DDoS attacks. Defending against the former attack is the same as defending against any other attempt to compromise your machine. We will concentrate in this chapter on the issue of defending the final target of the DDoS attack—the machine or network that the attacker wishes to deny service to.

We will begin by discussing the aspects of DDoS attacks that make defending against them difficult. We will then discuss the types of challenges a DDoS defense solution must overcome, and then cover basic concepts of defense: prevention versus detection and reaction, the basic goals to be achieved by a defense system, and where to locate the defenses in the network.

In spite of several years of intense research, these attacks still inflict a large amount of damage to Internet users. Why are these attacks possible? Can we identify some feature in the Internet design or in its core protocols, such as TCP and IP, that facilitates DoS attacks? Can we then remove or modify this feature to resolve the problem? Like all histories, the history of DDoS attacks discussed in Chapter 3 does not represent a final state, but is merely the prelude to the future. We have presented publically known details on exactly how today's attacks are perpetrated, which has set the stage for discussing what you must do to counter them. Remember, however, that the current DDoS attack trends suggest, more than anything else, continued and rapid change for the future. Early analyses of DDoS attack tools like *trinoo, TFN, Stacheldraht,* and *Shaft* all made predictions about future development trends based on past history. Attackers continued in the directions identified, as well as going in new directions (e.g., using IRC for command and control, and integration of several other malicious functions). We should expect both the number and sophistication of attack tools to grow steadily. Therefore, the tools attackers will use in upcoming years and the methods used to defend against them will progress from the current states we describe in this book, requiring defenders to keep up to date on new trends and defense methods.

Another big problem in the arms race between the attackers and the defenders is the imbalance of the effort needed to take another step. Developing DDoS solutions is costly and they usually work for a small range of attacks. The attacker needs only to change a few lines of code, or gather more agents (hardly any effort at all) to bypass or overwhelm the existing defenses. The defenders, on the other hand, spend an immense amount of time and resources to augment their systems for handling new attacks. It seems like an unfair competition. But does it have to be so, or is there something we have overlooked that could restore the balance?

5.1   Why DDoS Is a Hard Problem

The victim of a vulnerability attack (see Chapter 2) usually crashes, deadlocks, or has some key resource tied up. Vulnerability attacks need only a few packets to be effective, and therefore can be launched from one or very few agents. In a flooding attack, the resource is tied up as long as the attack packets keep coming in, and is reclaimed when the attack is aborted. Flooding attacks thus need a constant flow of the attack packets into the victim network to be effective.

Vulnerability attacks target protocol or implementation bugs in the victim's systems. They base their success on much the same premise as intrusion attempts and worms do, relying on the presence of protocol and implementation bugs in the victim's software that can be exploited for the attacker's purpose. While intruders and worm writers simply want to break into the machine, the aim of the vulnerability attack is to crash it or otherwise cripple it. Future security mechanisms for defending against intrusions and worms and better software writing standards are likely to help address DDoS vulnerability attacks. In the meantime, patching and updating server machines and filtering malformed packets offer a significant immunity to known vulnerability attacks. A resourceful attacker could still bypass these defenses by detecting new vulnerabilities in the latest software releases and crafting new types of packets to exploit them. This is a subtle attack that requires a lot of skill and effort on the part of the attacker, and is not very common. There are much easier ways to deny service.

Flooding attacks target a specific resource and simply generate a lot of packets that consume it. Naturally, if the attack packets stood out in any way (e.g., they had a specific value in one of the header fields), defense mechanisms could easily filter them out. Since a flooding attack does not need any specific packets, attackers create a varied mixture of traffic that blends with the legitimate users' traffic. They also use IP spoofing to create a greater variety of packet sources and hide agent identities. The victim perceives the flooding attack as a sudden flood of requests for service from numerous (potentially legitimate) users, and attempts to serve all of them, ultimately exhausting its resources and dropping any surplus traffic it cannot handle. As there are many more attack packets than the legitimate ones, legitimate traffic stands a very low chance of obtaining a share of the resource, and a good portion of it gets dropped. But the legitimate traffic does not lose only because of the high attack volume. It is usually congestion-responsive traffic— it perceives packet drops as a sign of congestion and reduces its sending rate. This decreases the chance of obtaining resources even further, resulting in more legitimate drops. The following characteristics of DDoS flooding attacks make these attacks very effective for the attacker's purpose and extremely challenging for the defense:

- **Simplicity**. There are many DDoS tools that can be easily downloaded or otherwise obtained and set into action. They make agent recruitment and activation automatic, and can be used by inexperienced users. These tools are exceedingly simple, and some of them have been around for years. Still, they generate effective attacks with little or no tweaking.

- **Traffic variety**. The similarity of the attack traffic to legitimate traffic makes separation and filtering extremely hard. Unlike other security threats that need specially crafted packets (e.g., intrusions, worms, viruses), flooding attacks need only a high traffic volume and can vary packet contents and header values at will.

- **IP spoofing**. IP spoofing makes the attack traffic appear as if it comes from numerous legitimate clients. This defeats many resource-sharing approaches that identify a client by his IP address. If IP spoofing were eliminated, agents could potentially be distinguished from the legitimate clients by their aggressive sending patterns, and their traffic could be filtered. In the presence of IP spoofing, the victim sees a lot of service initiation requests from numerous seemingly legitimate users. While the victim could easily tell those packets apart from ongoing communications with the legitimate users, it cannot discern new legitimate requests for service from the attack ones. Thus, the victim cannot serve any new users during the attack. If the attack is long, the damage to victim's business is obvious.

- **High-volume traffic.** The high volume of the attack traffic at the victim not only overwhelms the targeted resource, but makes traffic profiling hard. At such high packet rates, the defense mechanism can do only simple per-packet processing. The main challenge of DDoS defense is to discern the legitimate from the attack traffic, at high packet speeds.

- **Numerous agent machines.** The strength of a DDoS attack lies in the numerous agent machines distributed all over the Internet. With so many agents, the attacker can take on even the largest networks, and she can vary her attack by deploying subsets of agents at a time or sending very few packets from each agent machine. Varying attack strategies defeat many defense mechanisms that attempt to trace back the attack to its source. Even in the cases when the attacker does not vary the attacking machines, the mere number of agents involved makes traceback an unattractive solution. What if we knew the identities of 10,000 machines that are attacking our network? This would hardly get us any closer to stopping the attack. The situation would clearly be simplified if the attacker were not able to recruit so many agents. As mentioned above, the general increase of Internet hosts and, more recently, the high percentage of novice Internet users suggest that the pool of potential agents will only increase in the future. Furthermore, the distributed Internet management model makes it unlikely that any security mechanism will be widely deployed. Thus, even if we found ways to secure machines permanently and make them impervious to the attacker's intrusion attempts, it would take many years until these mechanisms would be sufficiently deployed to impact the DDoS threat.[1]

- **Weak spots in the Internet topology.** The current Internet hub-and-spoke topology has a handful of highly connected and very well provisioned spots that relay traffic for the rest of the Internet. These hubs are highly provisioned to handle heavy traffic in the first place, but if these few spots were taken down by an attacker or heavily congested, the Internet would grind to a halt. Amassing a large number of agent machines and generating heavy traffic passing through those hot spots would have a devastating effect on global connectivity. For further discussion of this threat, see [GOM03] or [AJB00, Bar02].

---

[1] One could contemplate a self-spreading patching or updating mechanism, as done before by some independent party [Hex01] in response to the CodeRed worm threat [CER01a], but that is legally and ethically questionable and more challenging than it might at first appear.

Let's face it: A flooding DDoS attack seems like a perfect crime in the Internet realm. Means (attack tools) and accomplices (agent machines) are abundant and easily obtainable. A sufficient attack volume is likely to bring the strongest victim to its knees and the right mixture of the attack traffic, along with IP spoofing, will defeat attack filtering attempts. Since numerous businesses rely heavily on online access, taking that away is sure to inflict considerable damage to the victim. Finally, IP spoofing, numerous agent machines and lack of automated tracing mechanisms across the networks guarantee little to no risk to perpetrators of being caught.

The seriousness of the DDoS problem and the increased frequency, sophistication and strength of attacks have led to the advent of numerous defense mechanisms. Yet, although a great effort has been invested in research and development, the problem is hardly dented, let alone solved. Why is this so?

5.2   DDoS Defense Challenges

The challenges in designing DDoS defense systems fall roughly into two categories: technical challenges and social challenges. Technical challenges encompass problems associated with the current Internet protocols and characteristics of the DDoS threat. Social challenges, on the other hand, largely pertain to the manner in which a successful technical solution will be introduced to Internet users, and accepted and widely deployed by these users.

The main problem that permeates both technical and social issues is the problem of large scale. DDoS is a distributed threat that requires a myriad of overlapping "solutions" to various aspects of the DDoS problem, which must be spread across the Internet because attacking machines may be spread all over the Internet. Clearly, attack streams can only be controlled if there is a point of defense between the agents and the victims. One approach is to place one defense system close to the victim so that it monitors and controls all of the incoming traffic. This approach has many deficiencies, the main one being that the system must be able to efficiently handle and process huge traffic volumes. The other approach is to divide this workload by deploying distributed defenses. Defense systems must then be deployed in a widespread manner to ensure effective action for any combination of agent and victim machines. As widespread deployment cannot be guaranteed, the technical challenge lies in designing effective defenses that can provide reasonable performance even if they are sparsely deployed. The social challenge lies in designing an economic model of a defense system in a manner that motivates large-scale deployment in the Internet.

5.2.1   Technical Challenges

The distributed nature of DDoS attacks, similarity of the attack packets to the legitimate ones, and the use of IP spoofing represent the main technical challenges to designing effective DDoS defense systems, as discussed in Section 5.1. In addition to that, the advance of DDoS defense research has historically been hindered by the lack of attack information and absence of standardized evaluation and testing approaches. The following list summarizes and discusses technical challenges for DDoS defense.

- **Need for a distributed response at many points in the Internet.** There are many possible DDoS attacks, very few of which can be handled only by the victim. Thus, it is necessary to have a distributed, possibly coordinated, response system. It is also crucial that the response be deployed at many points in the Internet to cover diverse choices of agents and victims. Since the Internet is administered in a distributed manner, wide deployment of any defense system (or even various systems that could cooperate) cannot be enforced or guaranteed. This discourages many researchers from even considering distributed solutions.

- **Lack of detailed attack information**. It is widely believed that reporting occurrences of attacks damages the business reputation of the victim network. Therefore, very limited information exists about various attacks, and incidents are reported only to government organizations under obligation to keep them secret. It is difficult to design imaginative solutions to the problem if one cannot become familiar with it. Note that the attack information should not be confused with attack tool information, which is publicly available at many Internet sites. Attack information would include the attack type, time and duration of the attack, number of agents involved (if this information is known), attempted response and its effectiveness, and damages suffered. Appendix C summarizes the limited amount of publicly available attack information.

- **Lack of defense system benchmarks**. Many vendors make bold claims that their solution completely handles the DDoS problem. There is currently no standardized approach for testing DDoS defense systems that would enable their comparison and characterization. This has two detrimental influences on DDoS research: (1) Since there is no attack benchmark, defense designers are allowed to present those tests that are most advantageous to their system; and (2) researchers cannot compare actual performance of their solutions to existing defenses; instead, they can only comment on design issues.

- **Difficulty of large-scale testing.** DDoS defenses need to be tested in a realistic environment. This is currently impossible due to the lack of large-scale test beds, safe ways to perform live distributed experiments across the Internet, or detailed and realistic simulation tools that can support several thousand nodes. Claims about defense system performance are thus made based on small-scale experiments or simulations and are not credible.

  This situation, however, is likely to change soon. The National Science Foundation and the Department of Homeland Security are currently funding a development of a large-scale test bed and have sponsored research efforts to design benchmarking suites and measurement methodology for security systems evaluation [USC]. We expect that this will greatly improve quality of research in DDoS defense field. Some test beds are in use right now by DDoS researchers (e.g. PlanetLab [BBC+04] and Emulab/Netbed [WLS+02]).

5.2.2   Social Challenges

Many DDoS defense systems require certain deployment patterns to be effective. Those patterns fall into several categories.

- **Complete deployment.** A given system is deployed at each host, router, or network in the Internet.

- **Contiguous deployment.** A given system is deployed at hosts (or routers) that are directly connected.

- **Large-scale, widespread deployment.** The majority of hosts (or routers) in the Internet deploy a given system.

- **Complete deployment at specified points in the Internet.** There is a set of carefully selected deployment points. All points must deploy the proposed defense to achieve the desired security.

- **Modification of widely deployed Internet protocols,** such as TCP, IP or HTTP.

- **All (legitimate) clients of the protected target deploy defenses.**

None of the preceding deployment patterns are practical in the general case of protecting a generic end network from DDoS attacks (although some may work well to protect an important server or application that communicates with a selected set of clients). The Internet is extremely large and is managed in a distributed manner. No solution, no matter how effective, can be deployed simultaneously in hundreds of millions of disparate places. However, there have been quite a few cases of an Internet product (a protocol, an application, or a system) that has become so popular after release that it was very widely deployed within a short time. Examples include Kazaa, the SSH (Secure Shell) protocol, Internet Explorer, and Windows OS. The following factors determine a product's chances for wide deployment:

- **Good performance.** A product must meet the needs of customers. The performance requirement is not stringent, and any product that improves the current state is good enough.

- **Good economic model.** Each customer must gain direct economic benefit, or at least reduce the risk of economic loss, by deploying the product. Alternately, the customer must be able to charge others for improved services resulting from deployment.

- **Incremental benefit.** As the degree of deployment increases, customers might experience increased benefits. However, a product must offer considerable benefit to its customers even under sparse partial deployment.

Development of better patch management solutions, better end-host integrity and configuration management solutions, and better host-based incident response and forensic analysis solutions will help solve the first phase of DDoS problems—the ability to recruit a large agent network. Building a DDoS defense system that is itself distributed, with good performance at sparse deployment, with a solid economic model and an incremental benefit to its customers, is likely to ensure its wide deployment and make an impact on second-phase DDoS threat—defending the target from an ongoing attack.

In the remainder of this chapter we discuss basic DDoS defense approaches at a high level. In Chapter 6, we get very detailed and describe what steps you should take today to make your computer, network, or company less vulnerable to DDoS attacks, and what to do if you are the target of such an attack. In Chapter 7, we provide deeper technical details of actual research implementations of various defense approaches. This chapter is intended to familiarize you with the basics and to outline the options at a high conceptual level.

5.3   Prevention versus Protection and Reaction

As with handling other computer security threats, there are two basic styles of protecting the target of a DDoS attack: We can try to prevent the attacks from happening at all, or we can try to detect and then react effectively when they do occur.

5.3.1 Preventive Measures

Prevention is clearly desirable, when it can be done. A simple and effective way to make it impossible to perform a DDoS attack on any Internet site would be the best solution, but it does not appear practical. However, there is still value in preventive measures that make some simple DDoS attacks impossible, or that make many DDoS attacks more difficult. Reasonably effective preventive defenses deter attackers: If their attack is unlikely to succeed, they may choose not to launch it, or at least choose a more vulnerable victim. (Remember, however, that if the attacker is highly motivated to hit you in particular, making the attack a bit more difficult might not deter her.)

There are two ways to prevent DDoS attacks: (1) We can prevent attackers from launching an attack, and (2) we can improve our system's capacity, resiliency, and ability to adjust to increased load so that an ongoing attack fails to prevent our system from continuing to offer service to its legitimate clients.

Measures intended to make DDoS attacks impossible include making it hard for attackers to compromise enough machines to launch effective DDoS attacks, charging for network usage (so that sending enough packets to perform an effective DDoS attack becomes economically infeasible), or limiting the number of packets forwarded from any source to any particular destination during a particular period of time. Such measures are not necessarily easy to implement, and some of them go against the original spirit of the Internet, but they do illustrate ways in which the basis of the DoS effect could be undermined, at least in principle.

Hardening the typical node to make it less likely to become a DDoS agent is clearly worthwhile. Past experience and common sense suggest, however, that this approach can never be completely effective. Even if the typical user's or administrator's vigilance and care increase significantly, there will always be machines that are not running the most recently patched version of their software, or that have left open ports that permit attackers to compromise them. Nonetheless, any improvement in this area will provide definite benefits in defending against DDoS attacks, and many other security threats such as intrusions and worms. More effective ways to prevent the compromise of machines would be extremely valuable. Similarly, methods that might limit the degree of damage that an attacker can cause from a site after compromising it might help, provided that the damage limitation included preventing the compromised site from sending vast numbers of packets.

Hardening a node or an entire installation to protect it from swelling the ranks of a DDoS army is no different from hardening them to protect from other network threats. Essentially, this is a question of computer and network hygiene. Entire books are written on this subject, and many of the necessary steps depend very much on the particular operating system and other software the user is running. If the reader does not already have access to such a book, many good ones can be found on the shelves of a typical bookstore that stocks computer books. So other than reiterating the vital importance of making it hard for an attacker to take control of your node, for complete details we refer the reader to resources specific to the kinds of machines, operating systems, and applications deployed.

While perfectly secure systems are a fantasy, not a feature of the next release of your favorite operating system, there are known things that can be done to improve the security of systems under development. More widespread use of these techniques will improve the security of our operating systems and applications, thus making our machines less likely to be compromised. Again, these are beyond the scope of this book and are subjects worthy of their own extended treatment. Possible avenues toward building more secure systems that might help us all avoid becoming unwilling draftees in a DDoS army in the future include the following:

- Better programmer education will lead to a generally higher level of application and operating system security. There are well-known methods to avoid common security bugs like buffer overflows, yet such problems are commonplace. A better-educated programmer workforce might reduce the frequency of such problems.

- Improvements in software development and testing tools will make it easier for programmers to write code that does not have obvious security flaws, and for testers to find security problems early in the development process.

- Improvements in operating system security, both from a code quality point of view and from better designed security models for the system, will help. In addition to making systems harder to break into, these improvements might make it harder for an attacker to make complete use of a system shortly after she manages to run any piece of code on it, by compartmentalizing privileges or by having a higher awareness of proper and improper system operations.

- Automated tools for program verification will improve in their ability to find problems in code, allowing software developers to make stronger statements about the security of their code. This would allow consumers to choose to purchase more secure products, based on more than the word and reputation of the vendor. Similarly, development of better security metrics and benchmarks for security could give consumers more information about the risks they take when using a particular piece of software.

Beyond hardening nodes against compromise, prevention measures may be difficult to bring to bear against the DDoS problem. Many other types of prevention measures have the unfortunate characteristic of fundamentally changing the model of the Internet's operation. Charging for packet sending or always throttling or metering packet flows might succeed in preventing many DDoS attacks, but they might also stifle innovative uses of the Internet. Anything based on charging for packets opens the Internet to new forms of attacks based on emptying people's bank accounts by falsely sending packets under their identities. From a practical point of view, these types of prevention measures are unrealistic because they would require wholesale changes in the existing base of installed user machines, routers, firewalls, proxies, and other Internet equipment. Unless they can provide significant benefit to some segments of the Internet with more realistic partial deployment, they are unlikely to see real use.

Immunity to some forms of DDoS attack can potentially be achieved in a number of ways. For example, a server can be so heavily provisioned that it can withstand any amount of traffic that the backbone network could possibly deliver to it. Or the server and its router might accept packets from only a small number of trusted sites that will not participate in a DDoS attack. Of course, when designing a solution based on immunity, one must remember that the entire path to your installation must be made immune. It does little good to make it challenging to overload your server if it is trivial to flood your upstream ISP connection.

Some sites have largely protected themselves from the DDoS threat by these kinds of immunity measures, so they are not merely theoretical. For example, during the DDoS attacks on the DNS root servers in October 2002, all of the DNS servers were able to keep up with the DNS requests that reached them, since they all were sufficiently provisioned with processing power and memory [Nar]. Some of them, however, did not have enough incoming bandwidth to carry both the attack traffic and the legitimate requests. Those servers thus did not see all of the DNS requests that were sent to them. Other root servers were able to keep up with both the DDoS traffic (which consisted of a randomized mixture of ICMP packets, TCP SYN requests, fragmented TCP packets, and UDP packets) and the legitimate requests because these sites had ample incoming bandwidth, had mirrored their content at multiple locations, or had hardware-switched load balancing that prevented individual links from being overloaded. A number of DDoS attacks on large sites have failed because they targeted companies' sites that have high-bandwidth provisions to handle the normal periodic business demand for download of new software products, patches, and upgrades.

The major flaw to the immunity methods as an overall solution to the DDoS problem is that known immunity methods are either very expensive or greatly limit the functionality of a network node, often in ways that are incompatible with the node's mission. For example, limiting the nodes that can communicate with a small business's Web site limits its customer base and makes it impossible for new customers to browse through its wares. Further, many immunity mechanisms protect only against certain classes of attacks or against attacks up to a particular volume. An immunity mechanism that rejects all UDP packets does not protect against attacks based on floods of HTTP requests, for example, and investing in immunity by buying bandwidth equal to that of your ISP's own links will be a poor investment if the attacker generates more traffic than the ISP can accept. If attackers switch to a different type of DDoS attack or recruit vastly larger numbers of agents, the supposed immunity might suddenly vanish.

5.3.2   Reactive Measures

If one cannot prevent an attack, one must react to it. In many cases, reactive measures are better than preventive ones. While there are many DDoS attacks on an Internet-wide basis, many nodes will never experience a DDoS attack, or will be attacked only rarely. If attacks are rare and the costs of preventing them are high, it may be better to invest less in prevention and more in reaction. A good reactive defense might incur little or no cost except in the rare cases where it is actually engaged.

Reaction does not mean no preparation. Your reaction may require you to contact other parties to enlist their assistance or to refer the matter to legal authorities. If you know who to contact, what they can do for you, and what kind of information they will need to do it, your reaction will be faster and more effective. If your reaction includes locally deployed technical mechanisms that expect advice or confirmation from your system administrators, understanding how to interact with them and the likely implications of following (or not following) their recommendations will undoubtedly pay off when an attack hits. Certainly, with the current state of DDoS defense mechanisms, your preparation should include some ability to analyze what's going on in your network. As discussed in Chapter 6, many sites have assumed a DDoS attack when actually there was a different problem, and their responses have thus been slow, expensive, and ineffective. Being well prepared to detect and react to DDoS attacks will prove far more helpful than anything you can buy or install.

Unlike preventive measures, reactive measures require attack detection. No reaction can take place until a problem is noticed and understood. Thus, the effectiveness of reactive measures to DDoS attacks depends not only on how well they reduce the DoS effect once they are deployed, but also on the accuracy of the system that determines which defenses are required to deal with a particular attack, when to invoke them, and where to deploy them. False positives, signals that DDoS attacks are occurring when actually they are not, may be an issue for the detection mechanism, especially if some undesirable costs or inconveniences are incurred when the reactive defense is deployed. At the extreme, if the detection mechanism falsely indicates that the reactive defense needs to be employed all the time, a supposedly reactive mechanism effectively becomes a preventive one, probably at a higher cost than having designed it to prevent attacks in the first place.

Reactive defenses should take effect as quickly as possible once the detection mechanism requests them. Taking effect does not mean merely being turned on, but reaching the point where they effectively stop (or, at least, reduce) the DoS effect. Presuming that there is some cost to engaging the reactive defense, this defense should be turned off as soon as the DoS attack is over. On the other hand, the defense must not be turned off so quickly that an attacker can achieve the DoS effect by stopping his attack and resuming it after a brief while, repeating the cycle as necessary.

Regardless of the form of defense chosen, the designers and users of the defenses must keep their real aim in mind. Any DoS attack, including distributed DoS attacks, aims to cripple the normal operation of its target. The attack's goal is not really to deliver vast numbers of attack packets to the target, but to prevent the target from servicing most or all of its legitimate traffic. Thus, defenses must not only stop the attack traffic, but must let legitimate traffic through. If one does not care about handling legitimate traffic, a wonderful preventive defense is to pull out the network cable from one's computer. Certainly, attackers will not be able to flood your computer with attack packets, but neither can your legitimate customers reach you. A defensive mechanism that, in effect, "pulls the network cable" for both good and bad traffic is usually no better than the attack itself. However, in cases in which restoring internal network operations is more important than allowing continued connectivity to the Internet, pulling the cable, either literally or figuratively, may be the lesser of two evils.

5.4 DDoS Defense Goals

Whether our DDoS defense strategy is preventive, reactive, or a combination of both, there are some basic goals we want it to achieve.

- **Effectiveness.** A good DDoS defense should actually defend. It should provide either effective prevention that really makes attacks impossible or effective reaction ensuring that the DoS effect goes away. In the case of reactive mechanisms, the response should be sufficiently quick to ensure that the target does not suffer seriously from the attack.

- **Completeness.** A good DDoS defense should handle all possible attacks. If that degree of perfection is impossible, it should at least handle a large number of them. A mechanism that is capable of handling an attack based on TCP SYN flooding, but cannot offer any assistance if a ping flood arrives, is clearly less valuable than a defense that can handle both styles of attack. Thus, a preventive measure like TCP SYN cookies helps but is not sufficient unless coupled with other defense mechanisms. Completeness is also required in detection and reaction. If our detection mechanism does not recognize a particular pattern of incoming packets as an attack, presumably it will not invoke any response and the attack will succeed.

  While completeness is an obvious goal, it is extremely hard to achieve, since attackers are likely to develop new types of attacks specifically designed to bypass existing defenses. Defensive mechanisms that target the fundamental basis of DoS attacks are somewhat more likely to achieve completeness than those targeted at characteristics of particular attacks, even if those are popular attacks. For example, a mechanism that validates which packets are legitimate with high accuracy and concentrates on delivering only as many such packets as the target can handle is more likely to be complete than a mechanism that filters out packets based on knowledge of how a particular popular DDoS toolkit chooses its spoofed source addresses. However, it is often easier to counter a particular attack than to close basic vulnerabilities in networks and operating systems. Virus detection programs have shown that fairly complete defenses can be built by combining a large number of very specific defenses. A similar approach might solve the practical DDoS problem, even if it did not theoretically handle all possible DDoS attacks.

- **Provide service to all legitimate traffic.** As mentioned earlier, the core goal of DDoS defense is not to stop DDoS attack packets, but to ensure that the legitimate users can continue to perform their normal activities despite the presence of a DDoS attack. Clearly, a good defense mechanism must achieve that goal.

  Some legitimate traffic may be flowing from sites that are also sending attack traffic. Other legitimate traffic is destined for nodes on the same network as the target node. There may be legitimate traffic that is neither coming from an attack machine nor being delivered to the target's network, but perhaps shares some portion of its path through the Internet with some of the attack traffic. And some legitimate traffic may share other characteristics with the attack traffic, such as application protocol or destination port, potentially making it difficult to distinguish between them. None of these legitimate traffic categories should be disturbed by the DDoS defense mechanism. Legitimate traffic dropped by a DDoS defense mechanism has suffered *collateral damage*. (Collateral damage is also used to refer to cases where a third party who is not actually the target of the attack suffers damage from the attack.) Since DDoS attackers often strive to conceal their attack traffic in the legitimate traffic stream, it is common for legitimate traffic to closely resemble the attack packets, so the problem of collateral damage is real and serious.

Consider a DDoS defense mechanism that detects that a DDoS attack stream is coming from a local machine and then shuts down all outgoing traffic from that machine. Assuming high accuracy and sufficient deployment, such a mechanism would indeed stop the DDoS attack, but it would also stop much legitimate traffic. As mentioned early in this chapter, many machines that send DDoS attack streams are themselves victims of the true perpetrators of the attacks. It would be undesirable to shut down their perfectly legitimate activities simply because they have been taken over by a malicious adversary.[2]

If a DDoS defense mechanism develops some form of signature by which it distinguishes attack packets from nonattack packets, then unfortunate legitimate packets that happen to share that signature are likely to suffer at the hands of the DDoS defense mechanism. For example, a Web server might be flooded by HTTP request packets. If a DDoS defense mechanism decides that all HTTP request packets are attack packets, using that as the signature to determine which packets to drop, not only will the packets attacking the Web server be dropped, but so will all of the server's legitimate traffic.

Many proposed DDoS defenses inflict significant collateral damage in some situations. While all collateral damage is bad, damage done to true third parties, who are neither at the sending nor receiving end of the attack, is probably the worst form of collateral damage. Any defense mechanism that deploys filtering, rate limiting, or other technologies that impede normal packet handling in the core of the network must be carefully designed to avoid all such third-party collateral damage.

---

[2] Some might argue that those who do not maintain their machines well and thus allow them to be taken over by attackers deserve these consequences. However, a defense based on degrading the service of huge numbers of careless, but otherwise legitimate, users is unlikely to be embraced by the broader community. Clearly, a defense that harms such users' legitimate activities is less desirable than a defense that does not.

- **Low false-positive rates.** Good DDoS defense mechanisms should target only true DDoS attacks. Preventive mechanisms should not have the effect of hurting other forms of network traffic. Reactive mechanisms should be activated only when a DDoS attack is actually under way. False positives may cause collateral damage in many cases, but there are other undesirable properties of high false-positive rates. For example, when a reactive system detects and responds to a DDoS attack, it might signal the system administrator of the targeted system that it is taking action. If most such signals prove to be false, the system administrator will start to ignore them, and might even choose to turn the defense mechanism off. Also, reactive mechanisms are likely to have costs of some sort. Perhaps they use some fraction of a system's processing power, perhaps they induce some delay on all packets, or, in the longer term, perhaps a sufficiently frequent occurrence of reactions demands investment in a more powerful piece of defensive equipment. If these costs are frequently paid when no attack is under way, then the costs of running the defense system may outweigh the benefits achieved in those rare cases when an attack actually occurs.

- **Low deployment and operational costs.** DDoS defenses are meant to allow systems to continue operations during DDoS attacks, which, despite being very harmful, occur relatively rarely. The costs associated with the defense system must be commensurate with the benefits provided by it. For commercial solutions, there is an obvious economic cost of buying the hardware and software required to run it. Usually, there are also significant system administration costs with setting up new security equipment or software. Depending on the character of the DDoS defense mechanism, it may require frequent ongoing administration. For example, a mechanism based on detecting signatures of particular attacks will need to receive updates as new attacks are characterized, requiring either manual or automated actions.

  Other operational costs relate to overheads imposed by the defense system. A system that performs stateful inspection of all incoming packets may delay each packet, for example. Or a system that throttles data streams from suspicious sources may slow down any legitimate interactions with those sources. Unless such costs are extremely low or extremely rarely paid, they must be balanced against the benefits of achieving some degree of protection against DDoS attacks.

  You must further remember that part of the cost you will need to pay to protect yourself against DDoS attacks will not be in delays or CPU cycles, nor even in money spent to purchase a piece of hardware or software. Nothing beats preparation, and preparation takes time. You need to spend time carefully analyzing your network, developing an emergency plan, training your employees to recognize and deal with a DDoS attack, contacting and negotiating with your ISP and other parties who may need to help you in the case of an attack, and taking many other steps to be ready. The cost of any proposed DDoS solution must take these elements into account.

5.5 DDoS Defense Locations

The DDoS threat can be countered at different locations in the network. A DDoS attack consists of several streams of attack packets originating at different source networks. Each stream flows out of a machine; through a server or router into the Internet; across one or more core Internet routers; into the router, server, or firewall machine that controls access to the target machine's network; and finally to the target itself. Defense mechanisms can be placed at some or all of these locations. Each possible location has its strengths and weaknesses, which we discuss in this section.

Figure 5.1 shows a highly simplified network with several user machines at different locations, border routers that attach local area networks to the overall network, and a few core routers. This figure will be used to illustrate various defensive locations. In this and later figures, the node at the right marked T is the target of the DDoS attack, and nodes A1, A2, and A3 are sources of attack streams.

5.5.1 Near the Target

The most obvious location for a DDoS defense system is near the target (the area surrounded by a dashed rectangle in Figure 5.2). Defenses could be located on the target's own machine, or at a router, firewall, gateway, proxy, or other machine that is very close to the target. Most existing defense mechanisms that protect against other network threats tend to be located near the target, for very good reasons. Many of those reasons are equally applicable to DDoS defense. Nodes near the target are in good positions to know when an attack is ongoing. They might be able to directly observe the attack, but even if they cannot, they are quite close to the target and often have a trust relationship with that target. The target can often tell them when it is under attack. Also, the target is the single node in the network that receives the most complete information about the characteristics of the attack, since all of the attack packets are observed there. Mechanisms located elsewhere will see only a partial picture and might need to take action based on incomplete knowledge.

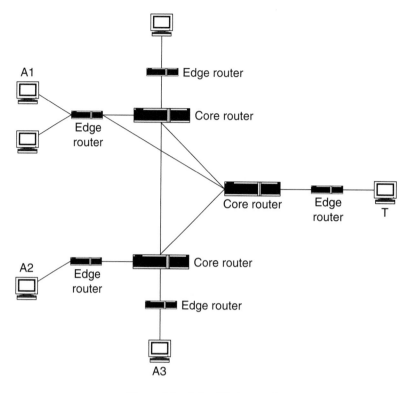

Figure 5.1 A simplified network

Another advantage of locating a defense near the target is deployment motivation. Those who are particularly worried about the danger of DDoS attacks will pay the price of deploying such a defense mechanism, while those who are unaware or do not care about the threat need not pay. Further, the benefit of deploying the mechanism accrues directly to the entity that paid for it. Historically, mechanisms with these characteristics (such as firewalls and intrusion detection systems) have proved to be more widely accepted than mechanisms that require wide deployment for the common good (such as ingress/egress filtering of spoofed IP packets).

A further advantage of deployment near the target is maximum control by the entity receiving protection. If the defense mechanism proves to be flawed, perhaps generating large numbers of false positives, the target machine that suffers from those flaws can turn off or adjust the defense mechanism fairly easily. Similarly, different users who choose different trade-offs between the price they pay for defense and the amount of protection they receive can independently implement those choices when the defense mechanisms

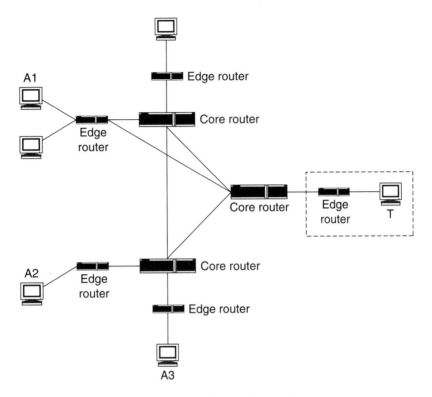

Figure 5.2   Deployment near the attack's target

are close to them and under their control. (Note that this advantage assumes a rather knowledgeable and careful user. It is far more common for users to install a piece of software or hardware using whatever defaults it specifies, and then never touch it again unless problems arise.)

But there are also serious disadvantages to defense mechanisms located close to the target. A major disadvantage is that a DDoS attack, by definition, overwhelms the target with its volume. Unless the defense mechanism can handle this load more cheaply than the target, or is much better provisioned than the target, it is in danger of being similarly overloaded. Instead of spending a great deal of money to heavily provision a defense box whose only benefit is to help out during DDoS attacks, one might be better off spending the same money to increase the power of the target machine itself. In some cases where the defense mechanism is just a little bit upstream of the potential target, we may gain advantages by sharing the defense mechanism among many different potential targets, somewhat lessening this problem, since several entities can pool the resources they are willing to devote to DDoS defense on a more powerful mechanism.

A less obvious problem with this location is that the target may be in a poor position to perform actions that require complex analysis and differentiation of legitimate and attack packets. The defense mechanism in this location is, as noted above, itself in danger of being overwhelmed. Unless it is very heavily provisioned, it will need to perform rather limited per-packet analysis to differentiate good packets from attack traffic. Such mechanisms are thus at risk of throwing away the good packets with the bad.

A further potential disadvantage is that, unless the solution is totally automated and completely effective, some human being at the target will have to help in the analysis and defense deployment. If you do not have a person on your staff capable of doing that, you will have to enlist the assistance of others who are not at your site, which limits the advantages of the defense being purely local. Further, if the flood is large and the necessary countermeasures are not obvious, many of your local resources could well be overwhelmed, not least of which are the human resources you need to adjust your defenses to the attack. This problem may not be too serious for very large sites that maintain many highly trained system and network administrators, but it could be critical for a small site that has few or no trained computer professionals on its regular staff.

A final disadvantage is that deployment near each potential target benefits only that target. Every edge network that needs protection must independently deploy its own defense, gaining little benefit from any defense deployed by other edge networks. The overall cost of protecting all nodes in the Internet using this pattern of deployment might prove higher than the costs of deploying mechanisms at other locations that provide protection to wider groups of nodes.

5.5.2   Near the Attacker

Figure 5.3 illustrates the option of deploying a defense mechanism near attack sources. Such a defense could be statically deployed at most or all locations from which attacks could possibly originate or could be dynamically created at locations close to where streams belonging to a particular ongoing attack actually are occurring. The multiple dotted rectangles in Figure 5.3 suggest one important characteristic of locating the defense near the attacker. An effective defense close to the attacker must actually be located close to all or most of the attackers. If the attack is coming from A1 and A2, but the defense is deployed only at A3, it will not be able to stop this attack. Even if it

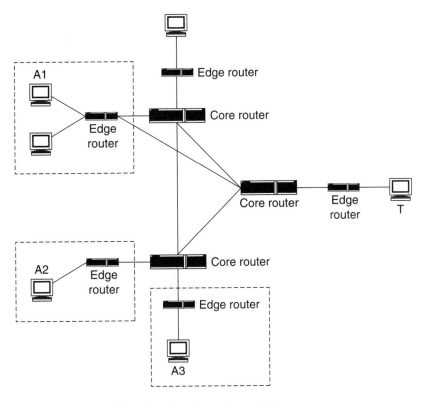

Figure 5.3   Deployment near attack sources

is deployed also at A2, the attack streams coming out of A1 will not be affected by the defense.

One advantage of this deployment location is that DDoS attack streams are not highly aggregated close to the source, unlike close to the attack's target. They are of a much lower volume, allowing more processing to be devoted to detecting and characterizing them than is possible close to the target. This low volume and lack of aggregation may also prove helpful in separating the packets participating in an attack from those that are innocent traffic.

There are also disadvantages. Typically, a host that originates a DDoS attack stream suffers little direct adverse effect from doing so.[3] Its attack stream is a tiny fraction of

---

[3] There are some notable exceptions. For example, the *mstream* DDoS tool forged its source addresses using full randomization of all 32 bits in the address, which meant invalid addresses, network addresses,

the huge flood that will swamp the target, and thus will rarely cause problems to its own network. A DDoS defense system located close to a source might have trouble determining that there is an attack going on. Even if it does know that an attack is being sent out of its network, the defense mechanism must determine which of its packets belong to attack streams. Existing research has shown that some legitimate traffic can be differentiated from attack traffic at this point, but it is not clear that all traffic can be confidently characterized as legitimate or harmful.

The second disadvantage is deployment motivation. A DDoS defense node close to a source will provide its benefits to other nodes and networks, not to the node where the attack originates or to its local network. Thus, there are few direct economic advantages to deploying a DDoS defense node of this kind, leading to a variant on the tragedy of the commons.[4] While everyone might be better off if all participants deployed an effective DDoS defense system at the exit point of their own network, nobody benefits much from his own deployment of such a system. The benefits derive from the overall deployment by everyone, with no incremental benefit accruing to the individual who must perform each deployment.

If there were advantages to deploying a source-end defense system, then this problem might be overcome. Proponents of these kinds of solutions have thus devoted some effort to finding such advantages. One possible advantage is that a target-end defense might form a trust relationship with the source-end network that polices its own traffic. During an attack, this trust relationship may bring privileged status to this source-end network, delivering its packets despite the DDoS attack. Another possible advantage is that one might avoid legal liability by preventing DDoS flows from originating in one's network, though it is unclear if existing law would impose any such liability. Finally, there is the advantage that accrues from being known as a good network citizen. However, these motivations have not been sufficient to ensure widespread deployment of other defense mechanisms with a similar character. For example, egress filtering at the exit router of the originator's local network can detect most packets with spoofed IP source addresses before they get outside that network (see Chapter 4 for

---

multicast addresses, etc., would all go through the router. If the router had to process each of these packets due to egress-filtering Access Control Lists (ACLs), it could be overwhelmed or even crash. A single host running mstream could take out a multi-interface router.

[4] *The tragedy of the commons* is a phrase referring to a problem of shared resources. Increased use of the resource by any sharing member hurts all members equally. Yet the benefit to a member that uses more of the resource outweighs, to him, the damage from the overall increased use. As a result, all sharing members choose to maximize their use of the resource, resulting in its inevitable depletion [Har68].

details on ingress and egress filtering). However, despite the feature's being available on popular routing platforms and recommendations from knowledgeable sources to enable it, many installers do not turn it on.[5] DDoS defense mechanisms designed to operate close to potential sources would need to overcome similar reluctance.

The reluctance will be even greater if the defense mechanism does not have superb discrimination. If the defense's ability to separate attack traffic from good traffic is poor, it will harm many legitimate packets. Assuming that the mechanism either drops or delays packets that it classifies as part of the attack, anyone who chooses to deploy the mechanism will suddenly see some of her legitimate traffic being harmed. Perhaps the defense mechanism will even start dropping good packets when no attack stream is actually coming out of the local network. If so, it would be quickly turned off and discarded.

A final disadvantage is the deployment scale required for this approach to be effective. If attack streams emanate from 10,000 sources to converge on one poor victim, this style of defense mechanism would need to be deployed close to a significant fraction of those 10,000 sources to do much good. A DDoS defense mechanism that is only applied to 5 to 10% of the attack packets will very likely do no good. The attacker would merely need to recruit 5 to 10% more machines to perform his attack, not a very challenging task. Unless the defense mechanism in question is located near a large fraction of all possible sites, it would not have enough coverage to be effective.

5.5.3   In the Middle

Deployments in the middle of the network generally refer to defenses living at core Internet routers (depicted in Figure 5.4). As a rule, such defenses are deployed at more than one core router, as the figure suggests. However, deployment "in the middle" might also refer to routers and other network nodes that are close to the target but not part of the target's network, such as an ISP. At some point, "middle" blends into "edges," and the deployment location is really near the target or near the attacker, having the characteristics of those locations. For true core deployments, there are obvious advantages and disadvantages.

---

[5] The reasons that this filtering feature is not turned on more widely are not clear. Some possible reasons include potentially bad interactions with mobile IP, the extra maintenance costs of keeping the information up to date, possible lack of flexibility in handling network traffic, the need to act as a transit domain for some other network, and, perhaps, ignorance. Given that the feature provides little or no local benefit, it is no surprise that installers do not bother turning it on.

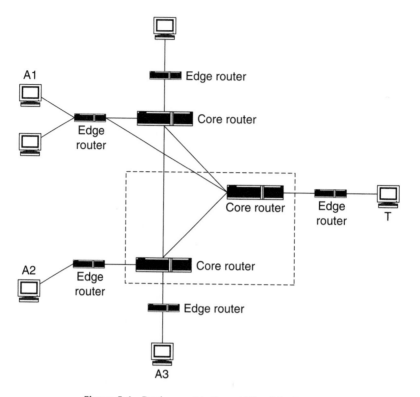

Figure 5.4 Deployment in the middle of the Internet

The vast bulk of the Internet's traffic goes through a relatively small number of core Autonomous Systems (ASs), each of which deploys a large, but not immense, number of routers to carry that traffic. Thus, any defense located at a reasonably large number of well-chosen ASs can get excellent coverage. To the degree that the defense is effective, it can provide its benefit to practically every node attached to the Internet. In Figure 5.4, if the defense is located at the two routers shown, all traffic coming from the three attack sources will pass through it. Further, even if there were a different victim (say T1, located in the same network as A3), the same two deployment points would offer protection to that victim against all attack traffic except that originating in its own network. (Core defenses inherently cannot protect against attacks that do not traverse the core; most attacks do, however.) If core defenses were effective, accurate, cheap, and easy to deploy, they could thus completely solve the problem of DDoS attacks.

These caveats suggest the disadvantages of deploying DDoS defense in the middle of the network. First, routers at core ASs are very busy machines. They cannot devote any substantial resources to handling or analyzing individual packets. Thus, a core defense mechanism cannot perform any but the most cursory per-packet inspection, and cannot perform any serious packet-level analysis to determine the presence, characteristics, or origins of a DDoS attack, even assuming we had analysis methods that could do so.

The basic problem in DDoS defense is, again, separating the huge volume of DDoS traffic from the relatively tiny volume of legitimate traffic. DDoS defenses at core routers cannot afford to devote many resources to making such differentiation decisions. They must have simple, cheap rules for dealing with the vast majority of the packets they see.

A second problem arises because core routers could inflict massive collateral damage if they are not exceptionally accurate in discriminating DDoS traffic from legitimate traffic. If they make mistakes at a rate that might be acceptable for a victim-side deployment, they could easily drop a huge amount of legitimate traffic. Those running core routers consider dropping legitimate traffic as extremely undesirable. Combined with their lack of resources to perform careful examination of packets, we thus would require the core defense to provide high accuracy with little analysis, a very challenging task.

Another problem with this deployment location is that core routers are unlikely to notice DDoS attacks. They themselves are unlikely to be overwhelmed, and they cannot afford to keep statistics on packets coming through on a per-destination basis. Perhaps they can afford to look for DDoS attacks by a statistical method that examines a tiny fraction of the total packets, looking for suspiciously high numbers of packets to a single destination, but one node's overwhelming DDoS attack is another node's ordinary daily business. There is ongoing research on using measurements of entropy in packet traffic to detect DDoS attacks in the core. However, proven methods applied at core routers are not likely to pinpoint all DDoS attacks without generating unacceptable levels of false positives.

Deployment incentives are also problematic for core-located DDoS defense mechanisms. By and large, the routers comprising the Internet backbone are not likely targets of DDoS attacks. They are heavily provisioned, are designed to perform well under high load, and are not easy to send packets to directly. Attackers are likely to need to deduce which network paths pass through such a router if they want to target it, which is not always easy. Thus, the companies running these machines would probably not receive direct benefit from deploying DDoS defenses. They would receive indirect benefit, since they typically try to minimize the time a packet travels through their system (and quickly dropping a packet because it is part of a DDoS flow certainly minimizes that time), and because their business ultimately depends on the usability of the Internet as a whole. On the other hand, their equipment is expensive and must operate correctly even under conditions of heavy strain, so they are generally little inclined to install unproven hardware and software. A very compelling case for the need for a particular defense mechanism, its correctness, and the acceptability of its performance would be required before there would be any hope of deployment in the core.

If a core router defense performs badly, many users would be affected. Yet, unlike defenses located in their own domains (whether source-side or victim-side), users would have no power to turn the defense mechanisms off or adjust them. Those running the Internet backbone cannot afford to field calls from every ISP or, worse, every user who is having her legitimate packets dropped by a core-deployed DDoS defense mechanism.

A final point against this form of defensive deployment is based on the respected end-to-end argument, which states that network functionality should be deployed at the endpoints of a network connection, not at nodes in the middle, unless it cannot be achieved at the endpoints or is so ubiquitously required by all traffic that it clearly belongs in the middle. While the end-to-end argument should not be regarded as the final deciding word in any discussion of network functionality, its careful application is arguably an important factor in the success of the Internet. Core-deployed DDoS defense mechanisms tend to run counter to the end-to-end argument, unless one can make a strong case for the impossibility of achieving similar results at the endpoints.

5.5.4   Multiple Deployment Locations

Some researchers have argued that an inherently distributed problem like DDoS requires a distributed solution. In the most trivial sense, we must have distributed solutions, unless someone comes up with a scheme that protects all potential targets against all possible attacks by deploying something at only one machine in the Internet. Most commercial solutions are, in this trivial sense, distributed, since each network that wants protection deploys its own solution. There are actually nontrivial distributed system problems related to this kind of deployment for other cyberdefenses, as exemplified by the issue of updating virus protection databases. Similarly, updating all target-side deployments to inform them of a new DDoS toolkit's signatures would be such a distributed system problem even for this trivial form of distribution.

Some source end solutions operate purely autonomously to control a single network's traffic, and these are distributed in the same trivial sense. All other types of defense schemes suggested to date are distributed in a less trivial sense. Some of those require defense deployment at the source and at the victim, with the defense systems communicating during an attack. Others require deployment at multiple core routers, which may also cooperate among themselves. Some require defense nodes scattered at the edge networks to cooperate. All these schemes will be discussed in more detail in Chapter 7.

There's a simple argument for why distributed solutions are necessary. Source-side nondistributed deployments just will not happen at a high enough rate to solve the problem. Target-side deployments cannot handle high-volume flooding attacks. There is no single location in the network core where one can capture all attacks, since not all packets pass any single point in the Internet. What is left? A solution that is deployed in more than one place, or multiple cooperating solutions at different places. Hence, a distributed solution.

Perhaps each instance of such a solution can work independently, rendering its distributed nature nearly trivial. However, this seems unlikely, since the common characteristic of the flooding attacks that force distributed solutions is that you cannot observe all the traffic except at a point where there is too much of it to do anything with. Unless each instance can independently, based on its own local information, reach a conclusion on the character of the attack that is generally the same as the conclusion reached by other instances, independent defense points might not engage their defenses against enough attack traffic. Most likely, some information exchange between instances will be required to reach a common agreement on the presence and character of attacks and the nature of the response, leading to true distributed characteristics.

With a good design, a distributed defense could exploit the strong points of each defense location while minimizing its weaknesses. For example, locations at aggregation points near the target are in a good position to recognize attacks. Locations near the attackers are well positioned to differentiate between good and bad packets. Locations in the center of the network can achieve high defensive coverage with relatively few deployment points. One approach to solving the DDoS problem is stitching together a defensive network spanning these locations. One such distributed deployment is shown in Figure 5.5. This approach must avoid the pitfall of accumulating the weaknesses of the various defensive locations, in addition to their strengths. For example, if locations near potential attackers are reluctant to deploy defensive mechanisms because they see no direct benefit and core router owners hesitate because they are unwilling to take the risk of damaging many users' traffic, a defense mechanism requiring deployments in both locations might be even less likely to be installed than one requiring deployment in only one of these locations.

Generally speaking, a defensive scheme that deploys cooperating mechanisms at multiple locations requires handling the many well-known difficulties of properly designing a distributed system. Distributed systems, while potentially powerful, are

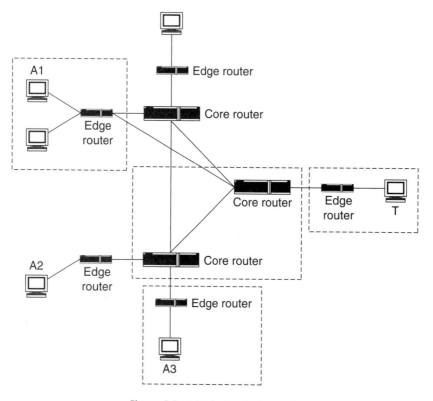

Figure 5.5   Distributed deployment

notorious for being bug-ridden and prone to unpredicted performance problems. Given that a distributed DDoS defense scheme is likely to be a tempting target for attackers, it must carefully resolve all distributed system problems that may create weak points in the defense system. These problems include standard distributed system issues (such as synchronization of various participants and behavior in the face of partial failures) and security concerns of distributed systems (such as handling misbehavior by some supposedly legitimate participants).

5.6   Defense Approaches

Given the basic dichotomy between prevention and reaction, the goals of DDoS defense, and the three types of locations where defenses can be located, we will now discuss the basic options on how to defend against DDoS attacks that have been investigated, to date. The discussion here is at a high level, with few examples of actual systems that have been built or actions that you can take, since the purpose of this material is to lay out for you the entire range of options. Doing so will then make it easier for you to understand and evaluate the more detailed defense information presented in subsequent chapters.

Some DDoS defenses concentrate on protecting you against DDoS. They try to ensure that your network and system never suffer the DDoS effect. Other defenses concentrate on detecting attacks when they occur and responding to them to reduce the DDoS effect on your site. We will discuss each in turn.

Most of these approaches are not mutually exclusive, and one can build a more effective overall defense by combining several of them. Using a layered approach that combines several types of defenses, at several different locations, can be more flexible and harder for an attacker to completely bypass. This layering includes host-level tuning and adequate resources, close-proximity network-level defenses, as well as border- or perimeter-level network defenses.

5.6.1 Protection

Some protection approaches focus on eliminating the possibility of the attack. These *attack prevention* approaches introduce changes into Internet protocols, applications and hosts, to strengthen them against DDoS attempts. They patch existing vulnerabilities, correct bad protocol design, manage resource usage, and reduce the incidence of intrusions and exploits. Some approaches also advocate limiting computer versatility and disallowing certain functions within the network stack (see, for example, [BR00, BR01]). These approaches aspire to make the machines that deploy them impervious to DDoS attempts. Attack prevention completely eliminates some vulnerability attacks, impedes the attacker's attempts to gain a large agent army, and generally pushes the bar for the attacker higher, making her work harder to achieve a DoS effect. However, while necessary for improving Internet security, prevention does not eliminate the DDoS threat.

Other protection approaches focus on enduring the attack without creating the DoS effect. These *endurance approaches* increase and redistribute a victim's resources, enabling it to serve both legitimate and malicious requests during the attack, thus canceling the DoS effect. The increase is achieved either statically, by purchasing more resources, or dynamically, by acquiring resources at the sign of a possible attack from a set of distributed public servers and replicating the target service. Endurance approaches can significantly enhance a target's resistance to DDoS—the attacker must now work exceptionally hard to deny the service. However, the effectiveness of endurance approaches is limited to cases in which increased resources are greater than the attack volume. Since an attacker can potentially gather hundreds of thousands of agent machines, endurance is not likely to offer a complete solution to the DDoS problem, particularly for individuals and small businesses that cannot afford to purchase the quantities of network resources required to withstand a large attack.

Hygiene   Hygiene approaches try to close as many opportunities for DDoS attacks in your computers and networks as possible, on the generally sound theory that the best way to enhance security is to keep your network simple, well organized, and well maintained.

Fixing Host Vulnerabilities   Vulnerability DDoS attacks target a software bug or an error in protocol or application design to deny service. Thus, the first step in maintaining network hygiene is keeping software packages patched and up to date. In addition, applications can also be run in a contained environment (for instance, see Provos' Systrace [Pro03]), and closely observed to detect anomalous behavior or excess resource consumption.

Even when all software patches are applied as soon as they are available, it is impossible to guarantee the absence of bugs in software. To protect critical applications from denial of service, they can be duplicated on several servers, each running a different operating system and/or application version akin to biodiversity. This, however, greatly increases administrative requirements.

As described in Chapters 2 and 4, another major vulnerability that requires attention is more social than technical: weak or no passwords for remotely accessible services, such as Windows remote access for file services. Even a fully patched host behind a good firewall can be compromised if arbitrary IP addresses are allowed to connect to a system with a weak password on such a service. Malware, such as *Phatbot,* automates the identification and compromise of hosts that are vulnerable due to such password problems. Any good book on computer security or network administration should give you guidance on checking for and improving the quality of passwords on your system.

Fixing Network Organization   Well-organized networks have no bottlenecks or hot spots that can become an easy target for a DDoS attack. A good way to organize a network is to spread critical applications across several servers, located in different subnetworks. The attacker then has to overwhelm all the servers to achieve denial of service. Providing path redundancy among network points creates a robust topology that cannot be easily disconnected. Network organization should be as simple as possible to facilitate easy understanding and management. (Note, however, that path redundancy and simplicity are not necessarily compatible goals, since multiple paths are inherently more complex than single paths. One must make a trade-off on these issues.)

A good network organization not only repels many attack attempts, it also increases robustness and minimizes the damage when attacks do occur. Since critical services are replicated throughout the network, machines affected by the attack can be quarantined and replaced by the healthy ones without service loss.

Filtering Dangerous Packets   Most vulnerability attacks send specifically crafted packets to exploit a vulnerability on the target. Defenses against such attacks at least require inspection of packet headers, and often even deeper into the data portion of packets, in order to recognize the malicious traffic. However, data inspection cannot be done with most firewalls and routers. At the same time, filtering requires the use of an inline device. When there are features of packets that can be recognized with these devices, there are often reasons against such use. For example, a lot of rapid changes to firewall rules and router ACLs is often frowned upon for stability reasons (e.g., what if an accident leaves your firewall wide open?) Some types of Intrusion Prevention Systems (IPS), which act like an IDS in recognition of packets by signature and then filter or alter them in transit, could be used, but may be problematic and/or costly on very high bandwidth networks.

Source Validation

Source validation approaches verify the user's identity prior to granting his service request. In some cases, these approaches are intended merely to combat IP spoofing. While the attacker can still exhaust the server's resources by deploying a huge number of agents, this form of source validation prevents him from using IP spoofing, thus simplifying DDoS defense.

More ambitious source validation approaches seek to ensure that a human user (rather than DDoS agent software) is at the other end of a network connection, typically by performing so-called *Reverse Turing tests*.[6] The most commonly used type of Reverse

---

[6] The original Turing test was passed when an artificial intelligence program could fool people into thinking it was human. The Reverse Turing test can only be passed by a human.

Turing test displays a slightly blurred or distorted picture and asks the user to type in the depicted symbols (see [vABHL03] for more details). This task is trivial for humans, yet very hard for computers. These approaches work well for Web-based queries, but could be hard to deploy for nongraphical terminals. Besides, imagine that you had to decipher some picture *every time* you needed to access an online service. Wouldn't that be annoying? Further, this approach cannot work when the communications in question are not supposed to be handled directly by a human. If your server responds directly to any kind of request that is not typically generated by a person, Reverse Turing tests do not solve your problem. Pings, e-mail transfers between mail servers, time synchronization protocols, routing protocol updates, and DNS lookups are a few examples of computer-to-computer interactions that could not be protected by Reverse Turing tests.

Finally, some approaches verify the user's legitimacy. In basic systems, this verification can be no more than checking the user's IP address against a list of legitimate addresses. To achieve higher assurance, some systems require that the user present a certificate, issued by some well-known authority, that grants him access to the service, preferably for a limited time only. Since certificate verification is a cryptographic activity, it consumes a fair amount of the server's resources and opens the possibility for another type of DDoS attack. In this attack, the attacker generates many bogus certificates and forces the server to spend resources verifying them.

Note that any agent machine that is capable of proving its legitimacy to the target will pass these tests. If nothing more is done by the target machine, once the test is passed an agent machine can perpetrate the DDoS attack at will. So an attacker who can recruit sufficient legitimate clients of his target as agents can defeat such systems. If you run an Internet business selling to the general public, you may have a huge number of clients who are able to prove their legitimacy, making the attacker's recruitment problem not very challenging.

This difficulty can perhaps be addressed by requiring a bit more from machines that want to communicate with your site, using a technique called *proof of work*.

Proof of Work

Some protocols are asymmetric—they consume more resources on the server side than on the side of the client. Those protocols can be misused for denial of service. The attacker generates many service requests and ties up the server's resources. If the protocol is such that the resources are released after a certain time, the attacker simply repeats the attack to keep the server's resources constantly occupied.

One approach to protect against attacks on such asymmetric protocols is to redesign the protocols to delay commitment of the server's resources. The protocol is balanced by introducing another asymmetric step, this time in the server's favor, before committing the server's resources. The server requires a *proof of work* from the client.

The asymmetric step should ensure that the client has spent sufficient resources for the communication before the server spends its own resources. A commonly used approach is to send a client some puzzle to solve (e.g., [JB99, CER96]). The puzzle is such that solving it takes a fair amount of time and resources, while verifying the correctness of the answer is fast and cheap. Such puzzles are called *one-way functions* or *trapdoor functions* [MvOV96]. For example, a server could easily generate a large number and ask the client to factor it. Factoring of large numbers is a hard problem and it takes a lot of time. Once the client provides the answer, it is easy to multiply all the factors and see that they produce the number from the puzzle. After verifying the answer, the server can send another puzzle or grant the service request. Of course, the client machine runs software that automatically performs the work requested of it, so the human user is never explicitly aware of the need to solve the puzzle.

The use of proof-of-work techniques ensures that the client has to spend a lot more resources than the server before his request is granted. The amount of work required must not be sufficiently onerous for legitimate clients to mind or even usually notice, but it must be sufficient to slow down DDoS agents very heavily, making it difficult or perhaps impossible for them to send enough messages to the target to cause a DDoS effect.

At best, proof-of-work techniques make attacks using spoofed source addresses against handshake protocols less effective from small- to moderate-sized attack networks. (The exact efficiency of these techniques is not clear.) DDoS attacks are still feasible if the attacker uses much larger attack networks. Beyond simple flooding, there are two possible ways to use spoofed packets to perform an attack against a proof-of-work system. One way is for the agents to generate a lot of requests, then let the server send out puzzles to many fake addresses, thus exhausting its resources. Since puzzle generation consumes very few resources, the attacker would have to amass many agents to make this attack effective. The other way is for agents to generate a lot of false solutions to puzzles with spoofed source addresses (with or without previously sending in spoofed requests). Since the server spends some resources to verify the reply, this could be a way to tie up the server's resources and deny service. However, puzzle verification is also cheap for the server, and the attacker needs a huge number of agents to make this attack effective. (Keep in mind that some of today's attackers do, indeed, already have a huge number of agents.) The only "economical" way to deny service is for agents to act like legitimate clients, sending valid service requests and providing correct solutions for puzzles, to lead the server to commit his resources. Spoofing cannot be used in this attack, since the agent machine must receive the puzzles from the target to solve them. If the requests are spoofed, the puzzle will be delivered to another machine and the agent will not be able to provide the desired answer.

Elimination of IP spoofing facilitates use of other DDoS defenses that may help in the latter case. Thus, proof-of-work techniques would best be combined with other defensive techniques.

There are several requirements to make the proof-of-work approach practical and effective. First, it would be good if the approach were transparent to the clients and deployed only by the server. Popular services have no way to ensure that their vast client population simultaneously upgrades the software. For these services, a proof-of-work solution will be practical only if it can be unilaterally deployed. For instance, imagine a protocol that goes as follows:

1. Client sends a request to the server.
2. Server allocates some resources and sends a reply back to the client.
3. Client allocates some resources and sends a reply back to the server.
4. Server grants the request.

This protocol can be balanced unilaterally by modifying steps 2 and 4. In step 2, the server does not allocate any resources. Instead, he embeds some information from the request in the reply he sends to the client. When the client replies, the server recreates the original request information in step 4 and allocates resources. The proof of work on the client side consists not in solving some puzzle, but in allocating resources, just like the original protocol prescribes. For this solution to work, the client must repeat the embedded information in his reply, so that the server can use it in step 4.

Consider the TCP protocol as an example. TCP performs a three-way handshake at connection establishment. In its original form, this was an asymmetric protocol that required the server to commit resources early in the protocol. The server allocates resources (transmission control blocks from a fixed length table) upon receipt of a connection request (SYN packet). If the client never completes the connection, the server's resources remain allocated for a fairly long time. TCP SYN attacks, described in Chapter 4, allowed attackers to use this characteristic to perform a DoS attack with a relatively low volume of requests.

The TCP SYN cookie approach [Ber] modifies this protocol behavior to require the client to commit his resources first. The server encodes the information that would normally be stored in the transmission control block in the server's initial sequence number value. The server then sends this value in the connection reply packet (SYN-ACK) to the client and does not preserve any state. If the client completes the connection (and allocates its own transmission control block locally), the server retrieves encoded information from client's connection-completion packet and only then allocates a transmission control block. If the client never completes the connection, the server never allocates resources for this connection.

The second requirement for proof-of-work solutions is that the required work has to be equally hard for all clients, regardless of their hardware. Otherwise, an attacker who has compromised a powerful machine might be able to solve puzzles very quickly, thus generating enough requests to overwhelm the server despite solving all the puzzles. This requirement is hard to meet in the case of protocols that send out puzzles, because puzzle solving is computationally intensive and much easier for faster processors. Unless the amount of work is reasonable for even the least powerful legitimate client, a proof-of-work solution causes performance degradations even when no attack is ongoing. Some recent research [LC04] suggests that proofs hard enough to cause problems for attackers are so hard that many legitimate clients are hurt.

The third requirement states that theft or replay of answers must be prevented. In other words, a client himself must do the work. He cannot save and reuse old answers, and he cannot steal somebody else's answer. Puzzle-generation techniques usually meet these requirements by generating time-dependent puzzles, and making them depend on the client identity.

Ultimately, proof-of-work systems cannot themselves defend against attacks that purely flood network bandwidth. Until the server machine establishes that the incoming message has not provided the required proof of work for a particular source, messages use up network resources. Similarly, putative (but false) proofs of work use up resources until their deception is discovered. Lastly, these techniques only work on protocols involving session setup (not UDP services, for example).

Resource Allocation

Denial of service is essentially based on one or more attack machines seizing an unfair share of the resources of the target. One class of DDoS protection approaches based on resource allocation (or fair resource sharing) approaches seeks to prevent DoS attacks by assigning a fair share of resources to each client. Since the attacker needs to steal resources from the legitimate users to deny service, resource allocation defeats this goal.

A major challenge for resource allocation approaches is establishing the user's identity with confidence. If the attacker can fake his identity, he can exploit a resource allocation scheme to deny service. One attack method would be for the attacker to fake a legitimate user's identity, and take over this user's resources. Another attack method is to use IP spoofing to create a myriad of seemingly legitimate users. Since there are not enough resources to grant each user's request, some clients will have to be rejected. Because fake users are much more numerous than the legitimate ones, they are likely to grab more resource slots, denying the service.

The common approach for establishing the user's identity is to couple resource allocation with source validation schemes. Another approach is to combine resource allocation with a proof of work. Once the client submits the correct proof of work, the server is assured not only of the client's identity but also of his commitment to this communication. Resource allocation can then make sure that no client can monopolize the service.

Bear in mind that the attacker can still perform a successful attack, in spite of a strong resource allocation scheme. Just like with proof-of-work or source validation approaches, a large number of attack agents can overload the system if they behave like the legitimate users. However, resource allocation significantly raises the bar for the attacker. He needs *a lot* more agents than before that can only send with a limited rate, and they must abstain from IP spoofing to pass the identity test. This makes the game much more balanced for the defenders than before.

However, unless resource allocation schemes are enforced throughout the entire Internet, the attacker can still attempt to flood the point at which resource allocations are first checked. Most such schemes are located near the target, often at its firewall or close to its connection to the Internet. At that point, the function that determines the owner of each message and performs accounting can reject incoming messages that go beyond their owners' allocations, protecting downstream entities from flooding. But it cannot prevent itself from being flooded. A resource allocation defense point that can only handle 100 Mbps of incoming traffic can be overwhelmed by an attacker who sends 101 Mbps of traffic to it, even if he has not been allocated any downstream resources at all.

A further disadvantage of this approach is that it requires users to divulge their identities in verifiable ways, so that their resource usage can be properly accounted for. Many users are understandably reluctant to provide these kinds of identity assurances when not absolutely necessary. A DDoS solution that requires complete abandonment of all anonymous or pseudonymous interactions [DMS04] in the Internet has a serious downside. Some researchers are examining the use of temporary pseudonyms or other identity-obscuring techniques that might help solve this problem, but it is unclear if they would simultaneously prevent an attacker from obtaining as many of these pseudonyms as he needs to perpetrate his attack.

Hiding

None of the above approaches protect the server from bandwidth overload attacks that clog incoming links with random packets, creating congestion and pushing out the legitimate traffic. Hiding addresses this problem. Hiding obscures the server's or the service's location. As the attacker does not know how to access the server, he cannot attack it anymore. The server is usually hidden behind an "outer wall of guards." Client requests first hit this wall, and then clients are challenged to prove their legitimacy. Any source validation or proof-of-work approach can be used to validate the client. The legitimacy test has to be sufficiently reliable to weed out attack agent machines. It also has to be distributed, so that the agents cannot crash the outer-wall guards by sending too many service requests. Legitimate clients' requests are then relayed to the server via an overlay network. In some approaches, a validated client may be able to send his requests more directly, without going through the legitimacy test for every message or connection. In the extreme, trusted and preferred clients are given a permanent "passkey" that allows them to take a fast path to the service without ever providing further proof of legitimacy. There are clear risks to that extreme. An example hiding approach is SOS [KMR02], discussed in more detail in Chapter 7.

A poor man's hiding scheme actually prevented one DDoS attack. The Code Red worm carried, among its other cargo, code intended to perform a DDoS attack on the White House's Web site. However, the worm contained a hard-coded IP address for the victim's Web site. When the worm was captured and analyzed, this IP address was identified and the target was protected simply by changing its IP address. By sending out routing updates that caused packets sent to the old address to be dropped, the attack packets would not even be delivered to the White House's router. Had the worm instead used a DNS name to identify its victim, a DNS name resolution lookup would have occured. This would mean both worms and legitimate clients would be directed to any new IP address (thus making a change of the DNS host name to IP address mapping an ineffective solution.)[7] This approach is not generally going to help you against a reasonably intelligent DDoS attacker, but it illustrates the basic idea.

Hiding approaches show a definite promise, but incur high cost to set up the overlay network and distribute guard machines all over the Internet. Further, client software is likely to need modification for various legitimacy tests. All this extra cost makes hiding impractical for protection of public and widely accessed services, but well suited for

---

[7] On the other hand, if DDoS agents do DNS lookups for a particular victim IP address, they can be discovered by watching for these queries on local name servers. They may then be individually blocked at the site's border using filtering methods.

protection of corporate or military servers. A major disadvantage of hiding schemes is that they rely on the secrecy of the protected server's IP address. If this secret is divulged, attackers can bypass the protection by sending packets directly to that address, and the scheme can become effective again only by changing the target's address.

Some hiding solutions have been altered to provide defense benefits even when the protected target's address is not a secret. More details can be found in Chapter 7, but, briefly, the target's router is configured to allow messages to be delivered to the target only if they originate from certain hosts in a special overlay network. Legitimate users must prove themselves to the overlay network, while attackers trying to work through that network are filtered out. Whether this scheme can provide effective protection is uncertain at this time. At the least, flooding attacks on the router near the target will be effective if they can overcome that router's incoming bandwidth.

Overprovisioning

Overprovisioning ensures that excess resources that can accommodate both the attack and the legitimate traffic are available, thus avoiding denial of service. Unlike previous approaches that deal with attack prevention, overprovisioning strengthens the victim to withstand the attack.

The most common approach is purchasing abundant incoming bandwidth and deploying a pool of servers behind a load balancer. The servers may share the load equally at all times, or they may be divided into the primary and backup servers, with backup machines being activated when primary ones cannot handle the load. Overprovisioning not only helps withstand DDoS attacks, but also accommodates spikes in the legitimate traffic due to sudden popularity of the service, so-called *flash crowds*. For more information on flash crowds and their similarity to DDoS attacks see [JKR02] and the discussion in Chapter 7.

Another approach is to purchase content distribution services from an organization that owns numerous Web and database servers located all over the Internet. Critical services are then replicated over these distributed servers. Client requests are redirected to the dedicated content distribution server, which sends them off to the closest or the least loaded server with the replicated service for processing. The content distribution service may dynamically increase its replication degree of a user's content if enough requests are generated, possibly keeping ahead of even rapidly increasing volumes of DDoS requests.

After the attack on the DNS root servers in October 2002, many networks operating these services set up extra mirror sites for their service at geographically distributed locations. For example, ISC, which runs the DNS root server designated as the F server, expanded its mirroring to 20 sites on five continents, as of this writing, with plans to expand even further. The fairly static nature of the information stored at DNS root servers makes them excellent candidates for this defense technique.

Overprovisioning is by far the most widely used approach for DDoS defense. It raises the bar for the attacker, who must generate a sufficiently strong attack to overwhelm abundant resources. However, overprovisioning does not work equally well for all services. For instance, content distribution is easily implemented for static Web pages, but can be quite tricky for pages with dynamic content or those that offer access to a centralized database. Further, the cost of overprovisioning may be prohibitive for small systems. If a system does not usually experience high traffic volume, it needs modest resources for daily business. Purchasing just a bit more will not help fend off many DDoS attacks, while purchasing a lot more resources is wasteful, as they rarely get used. Finally, while it is more difficult to perpetrate a successful attack against a well-provisioned network, it is not impossible. The attacker simply needs to collect more agents—possibly a trivial task with today's automated tools for malicious code propagation. With known attack networks numbering 400,000 or more, and some evidence suggesting the existence of million-node armies (see http://www.ladlass.com/archives/001938.html), one might question whether it is sufficient to prepare for DDoS attacks by overprovisioning.

5.6.2   Attack Detection

If protection approaches cannot make DDoS attacks impossible, then the defender must detect such attacks before he can respond to them. Even some of the protection approaches described above require attack detection. Certain protection schemes are rather expensive, and some researchers have suggested engaging them only when an attack is taking place, which implies the need for attack detection.

Two major goals of attack detection are *accuracy* and *timeliness*.

Accuracy is measured by how many detection errors are made. A detection method can err in two ways. It can falsely detect an attack in a situation when no attack was actually happening. This is called a *false positive*. If a system generates too many false positives, this may have dire consequences, as discussed in Section 5.3.2 The other way for a detection method to err is to miss an attack. This is called a *false negative*. While any detection method can occasionally be beaten by an industrious and persistent attacker, frequent false negatives signify an incomplete and faulty detection approach.

As the attack detection drives the engagement of the response, the performance of the whole DDoS defense system depends on the timeliness of the detection. Attacks that are detected and handled early may even be transparent to ordinary customers and cause no unpleasant disruptions. Detection after the attack has inflicted damage to the victim fails to prevent interruptions, but minimizes their duration by quickly engaging an appropriate response.

The difficulty of attack detection depends to a great extent on the deployment location and the desired detection speed. Detecting an attack at the victim site is trivial after the DoS effect becomes pronounced. It is like detecting that the dam has broken once your house is underwater. Usually, the network is either swamped by a sudden traffic flood or some of its key servers are slow or have crashed. This situation is so far from the desired that the crudest monitoring techniques can spot it and raise an alert. However, denial of service takes a toll on network resources and repels customers. Even if the response is promptly engaged, the disruption is bad for business. It is therefore desirable to detect an attack as early as possible, and respond to it, *preventing* the DoS effect and maintaining a good face to your customers. Although agent machines are usually synchronized by commands from a central authority and engaged all at once, the attack traffic will take some time (several seconds to a few minutes) to build up and consume the victim's resources. This is the window where early detection must operate. What is desired is to detect that the water is seeping through a dam and evacuating the houses downstream minutes before the dam breaks.

The sensitivity and accuracy of attack detection deteriorate as monitoring is placed farther away from the victim. This is mostly due to incomplete observations, as monitoring techniques at the Internet core or close to attack sources cannot see all traffic that a victim receives, and cannot closely observe the victim's behavior to spot problems. This is like trying to guess whether a dam will break by checking for leaks at a single spot in the dam. It may happen that the other places leak profusely while the one we are monitoring is dry and safe. It also may happen that all observed places leak very little and seem innocuous, but the total amount of water leaked is enough to flood the houses downstream.

Core-based detection techniques must be very crude, as core router resources are limited. This further decreases the accuracy. On the other hand, source-based detection techniques can be quite complex. Fortunately, since sources see only moderate traffic volumes even during the attack, they can afford to engage in extensive statistics gathering and sophisticated profiling.

Since target-based detection is clearly superior to core- and source-based attempts, why do we have detection techniques located away from the target? The reason lies in the fact that autonomous DDoS defense is far simpler and easier to secure than a distributed defense. DDoS response near the source is most effective and incurs the least collateral damage, and co-locating a detection module with the response builds an autonomous defense at the spot. Similarly, core-based response has the best yield, since a core deployment at a few response points can control a vast number of attack streams, irrespective of the source and victim locations. Adding a detection mechanism to core-based response builds autonomous and stable defense in the Internet core. Balancing the advantages and disadvantages of various detection locations is another complex task for defenders.

Once the attack has been successfully detected, the next crucial task is *attack characterization*. The detection module must be able to precisely describe the offending traffic, so that it can be sifted from the rest by the response module. Legitimate and attack traffic models used in detection, sometimes coupled with additional statistics and profiling, guide the attack characterization. The goal is to obtain a list of parameters from the packet header and contents, along with a range of values that indicate a legitimate or an attack packet. Each incoming packet is then matched against the list, and the response is selectively applied to packets deemed to be a likely part of an attack. Attack characterization is severely hindered by the fact that the attack and legitimate traffic look alike. However, good attack characterization is of immense importance to DDoS defense, as it determines the amount of collateral damage and the effectiveness of the response.

Three main approaches to attack detection are *signature*, *anomaly*, and *misbehavior* detection.

Signature Detection

Signature detection builds a database of attack characteristics observed in the past incidents—*attack signatures*. All incoming packets are compared against this database, and those that match are filtered out. Consequently, the signature must be carefully crafted to precisely specify the attack, but also, ensure that no legitimate traffic generates a match. The goal is reach a zero false-positive rate, but the effectiveness of signature detection is limited to those attacks that involve easy-to-match packet attributes. For example, the Land DoS attack [CER98a] sends packets whose source IP address and source port are the same as their destination IP address and port, causing some TCP/IP implementations to crash. As no legitimate application will ever need to send a similarly crafted packet, a check for equality of source and destination IP address and port can form a valid attack signature. This kind of check is so simple that it should always be performed. Other signatures can be much more complex.

Since vulnerability attacks can be successful with very few packets, signature detection that accurately pinpoints these packets (and helps filtering mechanisms to surgically remove them from the input stream) is an effective solution. On the other hand, signature detection cannot help with flooding DDoS attacks that generate random packets similar to legitimate traffic.

In addition to victim-end deployment, signature detection can be used at the source networks to identify the presence of agent machines. One approach is to monitor control traffic between agent machines and their handlers to look for telltale signs of DDoS commands. Most DDoS tools will format their control messages in a specific manner, or will embed some string in the messages. This can be used as a signature to single out DDoS control traffic. For example, one of the popular DDoS tools, TFN2K [CERb], pads all control packets with a specific sequence of ones and zeros. Modern DDoS tools use encrypted channels for control messages or use polymorphic techniques, both of which defeat signature-based detection of control traffic.

Another approach is to look for listening network ports used for control. Some DDoS tools using the handler/agent model require agents to actively listen on a specific port. While this open port can easily be changed by an attacker, there are a handful of widely popular DDoS tools that are usually deployed without modification. Hence, a tool-specific port can frequently make a good signature for agent detection. Detecting open ports requires port scanning suspected agent machines. Most of the modern DDoS tools evade port-based detection through use of IRC channels (sometimes encrypted) for control traffic. All agents and the attacker join a specific channel to send and receive messages. While the mere use of IRC does not provide a signal that a machine is involved in a DDoS attack, if the DDoS agents use cleartext messages on the channel (as many actually do), signature detection can be performed by examining the messages sent over IRC channels. If the use of IRC is prohibited on your machines (making the presence of IRC traffic a clear signal of problems), the attacker can instead embed commands in HTTP traffic or other forms of traffic that your network must permit.

A more sophisticated detection approach is to monitor flows to and from hosts on the network and to detect when a host that formerly acted only as a client (i.e., establishing outbound connections to servers) suddenly starts acting like a server and receiving inbound connections. Similarly, you can check if a Web server that has only received incoming connections to HTTP and HTTPS service ports suddenly behaves like an IRC server or a DNS server. Some of these techniques step across the boundaries of signature detection into the realm of anomaly detection, discussed later in this section. Stepping stones may also be detected using these techniques (by correlating inbound and outbound flows of roughly equal amounts). Note that some attacker toolkits do things like embed commands in other protocols (e.g., using ICMP to tunnel commands and replies), or may use TCP as a datagram protocol, fooling some defense tools into thinking that the fact that there was never an established TCP connection implies that no communication is occurring.

Finally, it is possible to detect agents by examining each machine, looking for specific file names, contents, and locations. All popular and widely used DDoS tools have been carefully dissected and the detailed description of the tool-specific ports, control traffic features, and file signatures can be found at the CERT Coordination Center Web page [CERe] or at Dave Dittrich's DDoS Web page [Ditd]. Of course, one cannot look for file details on machines one does not own and control. Also, attackers may try to avoid detection by installing a *rootkit* at the subverted machine to hide the presence of malicious files and open ports.

Intrusion Detection Systems (IDSs) can also be used to detect compromises of potential agent machines. They examine the incoming traffic looking for known compromise patterns and drop the suspicious packets. In addition to preventing subversion for DDoS misuse, they protect the network from general intruders and promote security [ACF+99]. One major drawback of simple IDS solutions is that they often have a high alert rate, especially false-positive alerts. Newer IDSs employ combinations of operating system detection and service detection, correlating them with attack signatures to weed out obvious false alarms, such as a Solaris/SPARC-based attack against a DNS server that is directed at an Intel/Windows XP desktop that never had a DNS server in the first place.

Anomaly Detection

Anomaly detection takes the opposite approach from signature detection. It acknowledges the fact that malicious behaviors evolve and that a defense system cannot predict and model all of them. Instead, anomaly detection strives to model legitimate traffic and raise an alert if observed traffic violates the model. The obvious advantage of this approach is that previously unknown attacks can be discovered if they differ sufficiently from the legitimate traffic. However, anomaly detection faces a huge challenge. Legitimate traffic is diverse—new applications arise every day and traffic patterns change. A model that specifies legitimate traffic too tightly will generate a lot of false positives whenever traffic fluctuates. On the other hand, a loose model will let a lot of attacks go undetected, thus increasing the possibility of false-negatives. Finding the right set of features and a modeling approach that strikes a balance between false positives and false negatives is a real challenge.

Flow monitoring with correlation, described in a previous section, is another form of anomaly detection, which also combines features of behavioral models.

Behavioral Models   Behavioral models select a set of network parameters and learn the proper value ranges of these parameters by observing network traffic over a long interval. They then use this baseline model to evaluate current observations for anomalies. If some parameter in the observed traffic falls out of the baseline range by more than a set threshold, an attack alert is raised. The accuracy and sensitivity of a behavioral model depend on the choice of parameters and the threshold value. The usual approach is to monitor a vast number of parameters, tuning the sensitivity (and the false-positive rate) by changing threshold values. To capture the variability of traffic on a daily basis (for instance, traffic on weekends in the corporate network will have a different behavior than weekday traffic), some detection methods model the traffic with a time granularity of one day.

Behavioral models show definite promise for DDoS detection, but they face two major challenges:

1. **Model update.** As network and traffic patterns evolve over time, models need to be updated to reflect this change. A straightforward approach to model update is to use observations from the past intervals when no attack was detected. However, this creates an opportunity for the attacker to mistrain the system by a slow attack. For instance, suppose that the system uses a very simple legitimate traffic model, recording just the incoming traffic rate. By sending the attack traffic just below the threshold for a long time, the attacker can lead the system to believe that conditions have changed and increase the baseline value. Repeating this behavior, the attacker will ultimately overwhelm the system without raising the alert.

    While these kinds of training attacks are rare in the wild, they are quite possible and easy to perpetrate. A simple fix is to sample the observations at random times and derive model updates from these samples. Another possible fix is to have a human review the updates before they are installed.

2. **Attack characterization.** Since the behavioral models generate a detection signal that simply means "something strange is going on," another set of techniques is necessary for traffic separation. One possible and frequently used approach is to profile incoming packets looking for a set of features that single out the majority of packets. For instance, assume that our network is suddenly swamped by traffic, receiving 200 Mbps instead of the usual 30 Mbps. Through careful observation we have concluded that 180 Mbps of this traffic is UDP traffic, carrying DNS responses. Using UDP/DNS-response characterization to guide filtering, we will get rid of the flood, but likely lose some legitimate DNS responses in the process. This is the inherent problem of behavioral models, but it can be ameliorated to

a great extent by a smart choice of the feature set for traffic separation. Another possible approach is to create a list of legitimate clients' source addresses, either based on past behavior or through some offline mechanism. This approach will let some attack traffic through when the attacker spoofs an address from the list.

Standard-Based Models   Standard-based models use standard specifications of protocol and application traffic to build legitimate models. For example, the TCP protocol specification describes a three-way handshake that has to be performed for TCP connection setup. An attack detection mechanism can use this specification to build a model that detects half-open TCP connections or singles out TCP data traffic that does not belong to an established connection. If protocol and application implementations follow the specification, standard-based models will generate no false positives. Not all protocol and application implementations do so, however, as was pointed out by Ptacek and Newsham [PN98].

The other drawback of the standard-based models is their granularity. Since they model protocol and application traffic, they have to work at a connection granularity. This potentially means a lot of observation gathering and storage, and may tax system performance when the attacker generates spoofed traffic (thus creating many connections). Standard-based models must therefore deploy sophisticated techniques for statistics gathering and periodic cleanup to maintain good performance.

While standard-based models protect only from those attacks that clearly violate the standard, they guarantee a low false-positive rate and need very little maintenance for model update, except when a new standard is specified. The models can effectively be used for traffic separation by communicating the list of misbehaving connections to the response system.

Misbehavior Modeling

Instead of trying to model normal behavior and match ongoing behavior to those models, one can model misbehavior and watch for its occurrence. The simple method of detecting DDoS attacks at the target is misbehavior modeling at its most basic: The machine is receiving a vast amount of traffic and is not capable of keeping up. Yep, that's a DDoS attack. At one extreme, misbehavior modeling is the same as signature-based detection: Receiving a sufficiently large number of a particular type of packet on a particular port with a particular pattern of source addresses may be both a misbehavior model and a signature of the use of a particular attack toolkit. But misbehavior modeling can be defined in far more generic terms that would not be recognized as normal signatures. At the other extreme, misbehavior modeling is no different than anomaly modeling: If it is not normal, it is DDoS. But misbehavior modeling, by trying to capture the characteristics of only DDoS attacks, characterizes all other types of traffic, whether they have actually been observed in the past or not, as legitimate. True misbehavior modeling falls in the range between these extremes.

The challenge in misbehavior modeling is finding characteristics of traffic that are nearly sure signs that a DDoS attack is going on, beyond the service actually failing under high load. Perhaps a sufficiently large ramp-up in traffic over a very short period of time could signal a DDoS attack before the machine was actually overwhelmed, but perhaps it signals only a surge in interest in the site or a burst of traffic that was delayed somewhere else in the network and has suddenly been delivered in bulk. Perhaps a very large number of different addresses sending traffic in a very short period of time signals an attack, but perhaps it only means sudden widespread success of your Web site. It is unclear if it is possible to model DDoS behavior sufficiently well to capture it early without falsely capturing much legitimate behavior. (Such mischaracterization could be either harmless or disastrous, depending on what you do when a DDoS attack is signaled.)

5.6.3 Attack Response

The goal of attack response is to improve the situation for legitimate users and mitigate the DoS effect. There are three major ways in which this is done:

1. **Traffic policing.** The most straightforward and desirable response to a DoS attack is to drop offending traffic. This makes the attack transparent both to the victim and to its legitimate clients, as if it were not happening. Since attack detection and characterization are sometimes inaccurate, the main challenge of traffic policing is deciding what to drop and how much to drop.

2. **Attack traceback.** Attack traceback has two primary purposes: to identify agents that are performing the DDoS attack, and to try to get even further back and identify the human attacker who is controlling the DDoS network. The first goal might be achievable, but is problematic when tens of thousands of agents are attacking. The latter is nearly impossible today, due to the use of stepping stones. These factors represent a major challenge to traceback techniques. Compounding the problem is the inability of law enforcement to deal with the tens, or hundreds of thousands, of compromised hosts scattered across the Internet, which also means scattered across the globe. Effective traceback solutions probably need to include components that automatically police traffic from offending machines, once they are found. See Chapter 7 for detailed discussion of traceback techniques.

3. **Service differentiation.** Many protection techniques can be turned on dynamically, once the attack is detected, to provide differentiated service. Clients are presented with a task to prove their legitimacy, and those that do receive better service. This approach offers a good economic model. The server is generally willing to serve all the requests. At times of overload, the server preserves its resources and selectively serves only the VIP clients (those who are willing to prove their legitimacy) and provides best-effort service to the rest. A challenge to this approach is to handle attacks that generate a large volume of bogus legitimacy proofs. It may be necessary to distribute the legitimacy verification service to avoid the overload.

As each response has its own set of limitations, it is difficult to compare them to each other. Service differentiation creates an opportunity for the legitimate users to actively participate in DDoS defense and prove their legitimacy. This is the most fair to the customers, as they control the level of service they receive, not relying on (possibly faulty) attack characterization at the victim. On the other hand, service differentiation requires changes in the client software, which may be impractical for highly popular public services. Traceback requires a lot of deployment points in the core, but places the bulk of complexity at the victim and enables response long after the attack has ended. Traffic policing is by far the most practical response, as its minimum number of deployment points is one—in the vicinity of the victim. However, traffic policing relies on sometimes inaccurate attack characterization and is bound to inflict collateral damage.

Finally, there is no need to select a single response approach. Traceback and traffic policing can be combined to drop offending traffic close to its sources. Traffic policing can work with service differentiation, offering different policies for different traffic classes. Traceback can bring service differentiation points close to the sources, distributing and reducing the server load.

Traffic Policing

Two main approaches in traffic policing are *filtering* and *rate limiting*. Filtering drops all the packets indicated as suspicious by the attack characterization, while rate limiting enforces a rate limit on all suspicious packets. The choice between these two techniques depends on the accuracy of attack characterization. If the accuracy is high, dropping the offending traffic is justified and will inflict no collateral damage. When the accuracy is low, rate limiting is definitely a better choice, as some legitimate packets that otherwise would have been dropped are allowed to proceed to the victim. This will reduce collateral damage and facilitate prompt recovery of legitimate traffic in the case of false positives. Signature detection techniques commonly invoke a filtering response, as the offending traffic can be precisely described, while anomaly detection is commonly coupled with rate limiting as a less restrictive response.

The main challenge of traffic policing is to minimize legitimate traffic drops—one form of collateral damage. There are two sources of inaccuracy that lead to this kind of collateral damage: incorrect attack characterization and false positives. If the attack characterization cannot precisely separate the legitimate from the attack traffic, some legitimate packets will be dropped every time the response is invoked. The greater the inaccuracy, the greater the collateral damage. False positives needlessly trigger the response. The amount of the collateral damage again depends on the characterization accuracy, but false alarms may mislead the characterization process and thus increase legitimate drops.

How bad is it to drop a few legitimate packets? At first glance, we might conclude that a small rate of legitimate drops is not problematic, as the overwhelming majority of Internet communication is conducted using TCP. Since TCP is a reliable transmission protocol, dropped packets will be detected and retransmitted shortly after they were lost, and put in order at the receiving host. The packet loss and the remedy process should be transparent to the application and the end user. This works very well when there are only a few drops, once in a while. The mechanisms ensuring reliable delivery in the TCP protocol successfully mask isolated packet losses. However, TCP performance drops drastically in the case of sustained packet loss, even if the loss rate is small. The reason for this lies in the TCP *congestion control mechanism*, which detects packet loss as an early sign of congestion. TCP's congestion control module responds by drastically reducing the sending rate in the effort to alleviate the pressure at the bottleneck link. The rate is reduced exponentially with each loss and increased linearly in the absence of losses. Several closely spaced packet drops can thus quickly reduce the connection rate to one packet per sending interval. After this point, each loss of the retransmitted packet exponentially increases the sending interval. Overall, sustained packet loss makes the connection send less and with a reduced frequency.

While very effective in alleviating congestion, this response severely decreases the competitiveness of legitimate TCP traffic in case of a DoS attack. In the fight for a shared resource, more aggressive traffic has a better chance to win. The attack traffic rate is usually unrelenting, regardless of the drops, while the legitimate traffic quickly decreases to a trickle, thus forfeiting its fighting chance to get through. Rate limiting for DDoS response introduces another source of drops in addition to congestion, trying to tip the scale in favor of the legitimate traffic. If the rate limiting is not sufficiently selective, packet drops due to collateral damage will have the same ill effect on the legitimate connection as congestion drops did. Even if the congestion is completely resolved (the response has successfully removed the attack traffic), those legitimate connections that had severe drops will take a long time to recover and may be aborted by the application. It is therefore imperative to eliminate as many legitimate drops as possible, not only by making sure that the response is promptly engaged, but also by increasing its selectiveness.

The traffic-policing component can be placed anywhere on the attack path. Placing the response close to the victim ensures the policing of all attack streams with a single response node, but may place substantial burden on the DDoS defense system when the victim is subjected to a high-volume flood. Victim-end deployment also maximizes the chances for collateral damage, if rate limiting is the response of choice, as imperfect drop decisions affect all traffic reaching the victim. Better performance can be achieved by identifying those network paths that likely carry the attack traffic and pushing the rate limit along those paths as close to the sources as possible. This localizes the effect of erroneous drops only to those legitimate clients who share the path to the victim with an attacker. Unfortunately, this approach causes the number of the response points needed to completely control the attack to grow, as a response node must be installed on each identified path.

One technique currently used to counter large attacks that last for a long time is to start by trying to filter locally. If that is not sufficient, the victim then contacts his upstream network provider to request the installation of filters there. In principle, this manual pushing of filters back further into the network could continue indefinitely, but since each step requires human contact and intervention, it rarely is done too far into the network. One example of successful use of this technique occurred during the DDoS attack on the DNS root servers. One root server administrator contacted his backbone provider to install filters to drop certain types of packets in the attack stream, thus reducing the attack traffic on the link leading to his root server. The manual approach has some strong limitations, however. One must carefully characterize the packets to avoid collateral damage, and not all network providers will respond quickly to all customers' requests to install filters. This issue is discussed in more detail in Chapter 6.

Attack Traceback

Attack traceback has two primary purposes: to identify (and possibly shut down) agents that are implementing the actual DDoS attack, and to try to get even further back and identify the human attacker who is controlling the DDoS network. Traceback would thus be extremely helpful not only in DDoS defense, but also in cases of intrusions and worm infections when the attack is inconspicuous, contained in a few packets, and may be detected long after the attack ends. Traceback techniques enable the victim to reassemble the path of the attack, with help of the core routers. In *packet-marking techniques* [SPS+01, DFS01, SWKA00], routers tag packets with extra information stating, "The packet has passed through this router." In ICMP traceback [BLT01], additional control information is sent randomly to the victim, indicating that packets have passed through a given router. The victim uses all such information it receives to deduce the paths taken by attack packets. In hash-based traceback [SPS+01], routers remember each packet they have seen for a short time and can retrieve this knowledge in response to a victim's queries. Obviously, all these approaches place a burden on the intermediate routers, either to generate additional traffic, or to rewrite a portion of the traffic they forward, or to dedicate significant storage to keep records of packets they have seen. More overhead is incurred by the victim when it tries to reassemble the attack path. This process may be very computationally intensive and lead to additional control traffic between the victim and the core routers. As the attack becomes more distributed, the cost of the traceback increases.

Another drawback is tracing precision. It is impossible to identify the actual subverted machine. Rather, several networks in the vicinity of the attacking machine are identified. In a sparse deployment of traceback support at core routers, the number of suspect networks is likely to be very high. While this information is still beneficial if, for instance, we want to push a traffic-policing response closer to the sources, it offers little assistance to law enforcement authorities or to filtering rule generation.

An open issue is what action to take when tracing is completed. An automatic response, such as filtering or rate limiting, is the best choice, as the number of suspect sites is likely to be too large for human intervention. In this case, suspected networks that are actually innocent (i.e., networks that do not host agents but share a path with a network that does) will have their packets dropped. This is hardly fair. Another point worth mentioning is that even a perfect tracing approach up to the sending machine is useless in a reflector DoS attack. In this case, the machine sending problematic traffic is simply a public server that responds to seemingly legitimate queries. Since such servers will not themselves spoof their IP address, identification of them is trivial and no tracing is needed.

As noted in Chapter 4, even a workable traceback scheme has two other significant problems. First, in the face of traceback of DDoS flood traffic, it gets you only to the agents, not all the way back to the actual attacker (through all her handlers, IRC proxies, or login stepping stones). This may offer some opportunity to relieve the immediate attack but does not necessarily help catch the actual attacker or prevent her from making future attacks on you. Second, if a successful attack can be waged using only a few hundred or even a few thousand hosts, yet the attacker can gain access to 400,000 hosts, she can simply cycle through attack networks and force the victim to repeat the traceback and flood mitigation steps. Because these actions occur on human timescales today, the attacker would consume not only computer resources of the victim, but also human resources. Even at future automated speeds, the difficulties and costs of dealing with this sort of cycling attack could be serious. Having some kind of understanding of how a particular attack is being waged would help the victim to know when such a tactic is in use and to adjust its response accordingly.

Service Differentiation

As mentioned above, some of the protection approaches can be engaged dynamically, when an attack is detected, to provide differentiated service to those clients who can prove their legitimacy. A dynamic deployment strategy has an advantage over static deployment, as operational costs are paid only when needed. There is an additional advantage in cases when the protection approach requires software changes at the client side. Were such approaches engaged statically, the server would lose all of its legacy clients. With dynamic engagement, legacy clients are impacted only when the attack is detected, and even then the effect is degradation of their service, since the protection mechanism favors those clients that deploy software changes. As the attack subsides, old service levels are restored.

Source validation approaches can be used to differentiate between preferred and ordinary clients, and to offer better service to the preferred ones during the attack. Proof-of-work approaches can be engaged to challenge users to prove their legitimacy, and resources can be dedicated exclusively to users whose legitimacy has been proven during the attack.

CHAPTER **6**

Detailed Defense Approaches

We have seen how DDoS attacks are waged, starting with the first phase (recruitment of a large number of hosts through remote compromise and establishment of a command and control coordination infrastructure), then moving into the second phase, the actual DDoS attacks (wielding this set of refitted attack computers to implement a series of debilitating attacks on various network-attached computer systems).

In Chapter 5, we saw a high-level view of defense tactics that addresses both of these two phases. Right away it should start to become clear that there *simply is no single "solution"* that addresses both of these phases. There cannot be a single solution to such a diverse set of problems. There is, instead, an overlapping set of "solutions" (plural) that must be woven together in order to address all aspects of information assurance: the goals of integrity, availability, and confidentiality of information systems by operational implementation of protection, detection, and response capabilities.

6.1 Thinking about Defenses

Some of the defense approaches discussed in Chapter 5 are available for deployment in real networks today, as part of open source security applications and practices, as well as commercial DDoS defense systems. Other approaches are still being examined through research prototypes and simulations and are not available for immediate deployment. But the DDoS threat is here today and must be countered. What can you do to make your networks less susceptible to DDoS attacks? If your site is being used to attack someone else, how do you detect this and respond? And if you are a victim of such an attack, what can you do with the technology and tools available today to minimize your damages?

While the problem of defending against all possible DDoS attacks is indeed extremely hard, the majority of the attacks occurring today are very simple. The reason for this is the lack of awareness of the DDoS threat in many potential target networks, the poor level of preparation, and the absence of even simple defense measures. Since many potential targets are "sitting ducks," there is no need for sophistication—simple attacks do as much damage and they are easily performed. A typical DDoS attack today can be quickly foiled by a few timely preparations, the use of some available tools, and quick intelligent action by network operations staff. All three components are necessary to achieve effective defense. Preparations close obvious security holes and minimize reaction time when the attack occurs, supplying already devised response procedures. Commercially available or homegrown DDoS defense tools fend off known or simple attacks. Informed and well-trained network staff are required to deal with stealthy attacks that bypass the first two defense measures.

This chapter gives you some guidelines on how to avoid falling prey to the garden-variety DDoS attacks being launched today, and also tells you what to do if you do become the victim of a DDoS attack. Even though attackers are constantly improving their strategies, the defense measures described here will always improve your survival chances.

This book alone is not enough. In fact it is just the beginning of a long path of learning the tools and tactics of those who would attack you, and developing all the necessary skills—both technical skills with defensive tools and strategic and tactical thinking skills—that will allow you to operate within your attacker's "OODA loop" [Boy] and gain the upper hand in an attack (as mentioned at the end of Chapter 4). Other resources that you may wish to consult in learning the tools and techniques of both attackers and responders include [Hon04], with chapters on Unix forensics, Windows forensics, network forensics, and reverse engineering; [Naz03] on strategies against worms with details on the relationship between worms and DDoS, as well as both network- and host-based detection and defense strategies that are shared with DDoS tools; [Bej04] on network security monitoring, which covers a plethora of network traffic analysis tools and techniques; and [Car04] describing Windows forensics tools and techniques in great depth, including tools written by its author.

In this chapter we will also mention many Unix and Windows commands and settings. Having on hand a good book on system administration and system tuning for your particular flavor of Unix or Windows, your routing hardware, etc., would also be advisable. You should also ask the vendors of your hardware and software products about security-specific resources they produce. Many vendors have security sections of their Web page that include security tools, online documents covering secure implementation and management practices, security feature lists and comparisons, and even multimedia security training CD-ROMs or DVDs.

While the majority of attacks are simple, there are still the more advanced attacks that must be dealt with, and these are occurring at a higher frequency due to advanced attack tools like *Phatbot*. *Phatbot* is an advanced "blended threat" that includes a vast array of features, which are described in detail in Chapter 4. Networks of tens of thousands of hosts can be easily set up, and detection and cleanup of these bots can be very difficult. Training, the use of network flow monitoring (or DDoS mitigation) tools, the information provided in this chapter, the books referenced above, and some practice will allow your site to deal with this threat.

DDoS defense is an arms race—new attacks produce better defenses, which in turn entice attackers to work harder. In the future, your network may need new defense mechanisms, but the ones presented in this chapter will never be obsolete. Consider them as the foundation of your resilience to DDoS attacks. Without these, sophisticated defense mechanisms you may purchase will be like a fancy roof on a house without a solid foundation—decorative, but providing little real protection.

As discussed in Chapter 5, the design of an effective DDoS defense involves several very hard challenges. A defense system must be able to differentiate between legitimate and attack traffic, so that its response can be selective. In simple attacks, the traffic is generally somewhat differentiable from legitimate traffic, but you must be prepared to find those differences, either manually or automatically. You must strike a balance between gathering enough information to characterize the attack and not overloading your logging and analysis capabilities.

Another obstacle to designing an effective defense is the variability of the threat. A good defense system must catch the majority of the attacks, while yielding low levels of false alarms. Nothing forces attackers to generate one type of packets, or use specific packet contents, limit spoofing to certain addresses or generate packets of only a certain length, or to set an "evil bit" [Bel03] in the header of their packets to warn firewalls that these are malicious. Anything is fair game, as long as it seems legitimate, or is simply too much to handle. In particular, if you stop a DDoS attack based on one type of traffic, an observant attacker might—and in many cases will—switch to another, or may even mix or randomize her attack. Be prepared to alter your defenses accordingly.

The distributed nature of the threat makes localized solutions ineffective against some possible attacks. However, these solutions are still very effective against many real-world attacks. In practice, with today's technology most available defenses must be located close to the victim. Pushing the defenses further into the Internet core and closer to the attack sources potentially reduces collateral damage, but does not fit today's typical business models for deploying network defenses. Remote networks are generally unwilling to deploy systems that do not bring them direct benefit. Furthermore, since the attack is distributed, many deployment points may be needed to handle it completely. Enforcing wide deployment of any service in the Internet is infeasible in the short term. If the service is cooperative, such as tracing attack packets, this also raises policy issues [Lip02].

Defensive systems located near the target can themselves be easily overwhelmed by a sufficiently large attack. Consider how much traffic your defense system can handle when determining if it will be sufficient for your needs, since any attacker who exceeds this capacity is likely to be successful, regardless of the sophistication and power of your defenses. To assist in constructing a layered defense, there are many common practices and defense techniques that have been very effective in increasing resilience to attacks, handling specific attack types, and minimizing damages. The report of the Distributed-Systems Intruder Tools Workshop [CER99] held in 1999 gives a useful listing of best security practices for managers, system administrators, Internet Service Providers (ISPs) and incident response teams.[1] There are simple and straightforward steps you can take to fortify your network and make it robust and self-contained, so that it does not become easy prey. There are monitoring techniques that help you discover if you are a victim or a source of DDoS attack. If you have prepared in advance, there are approaches that will weather many DDoS attacks and minimize your damages. A determined attacker with a lot of time and resources may still be able to hinder your operation, but it will be much harder.

6.2 General Strategy for DDoS Defense

Regardless of whether your site is the victim of a DDoS attack, is being used as a stepping stone by attackers to anonymize their activity, or is hosting DDoS agents or handlers, the general defense strategies are the same. These strategies tend to fall into the classic

---

[1] While this document was created in 1999, it was written carefully to avoid becoming dated quickly. In most venues where DDoS is discussed, many of the questions that come up from audience members are answered by this document. It is still viable as a starting point for anyone wanting to understand the complexity of DDoS and how to respond to it in the short, medium, and long term.

Protect, Detect, and React categories, mirroring the general incident response life cycle [CERc, HMP+01]:

1. **Preparation.** It is important to understand how your network operates and have tools in place to perform both host- and network-level data capture and analysis, have procedures established in advance, and practice using the tools. Many preparation techniques that aim at understanding and strengthening your network will, in fact, protect you against simple attacks.

2. **Detection.** Not all attacks will cause your network to fail, so if complete failure is the only way to know when a problem exists, only the most severe problems will be detected and a larger percentage of incidents will go completely unrecognized. These unrecognized incidents can still be harming your operations and may also serve as a sign that you have an enemy out to get you. If he fails now, he might improve his attack and succeed later. Measures should be in place to detect a range of activities, with logs kept for a sufficient period of time to support forensic analysis tasks. Flow logging, for example, can also be used to detect stepping stones and multiple-system intrusions, and deal with a host of serious attacks on your network (we will discuss one tool, *SiLK*, in a moment). Intrusion Detection Systems (IDSs) can also add to the visibility of malicious activity on the network, and can be tuned in an emergency to watch for specific aspects of DDoS networks (e.g., command/control traffic, use of specific protocols or ports, or connections to/from specific suspect network blocks) [ACF+99].

3. **Characterization.** It often does not take very much captured traffic to determine the kind of DDoS tool in use. Many analyses exist of common tools [Ditf, Dith, CERb, Ditg, CER01b, DWDL, DLD00], which can guide incident response teams in understanding the role being played by hosts on their network, how the DDoS network functions, and how to efficiently communicate and cooperate with other sites. While removing agents from a specific network definitely helps DDoS response, the ultimate goal of characterization is to learn and share as much information about the attack as possible to help bring the entire DDoS network down. Any delay in gathering evidence and communicating it to law enforcement or other incident response teams and network providers can magnify the duration and significance of the damage inflicted by the attack.

   Another aspect of characterization is to determine where the attack appears to be coming from. It may not be possible to trace the attack all the way back to even one of the agents, but it should be possible to trace the attack to ingress or egress points of your network and perhaps to peers or your upstream providers (or downstream customers, if you are an ISP). Provide the outside entities with as much of the information you have gathered to characterize the attack as possible, to help them do their own traceback and mitigation. They may be in a better position to get closer to the attacker, and this is critical information for law enforcement to use in their investigation, should it come to that.

4. **Reaction.** Your reaction may be to block traffic to stop the attack, identify compromised hosts and gather evidence, and do forensic analysis, or invoke contingency plans for dealing with a severe network outage. Having established procedures makes reaction easier and faster in a time of crisis, as well as establishing standards for investigation, documentation, and reporting. As mentioned earlier, use of detection capabilities to augment reaction will also produce a better result.

5. **Postmortem analysis.** After the attack, it is very important to review whether your procedures did or did not work, how well your network provider responded, which tools provided the best or worst assistance in responding, etc. Make sure that you integrate these lessons learned back into procedures, training of staff, and contract language for your provider. Do your best to understand how severe this attack was in relation to what it could have been, to identify potential weaknesses in your planning and mitigation procedures.

We will now look more closely at the tactics involved in preparing for and responding to DDoS attacks.

6.3   Preparing to Handle a DDoS Attack

As in any risk management activity, preparation is crucial. Understanding how your network is organized and how it works will help you identify weak spots that may be a target of the attack. Fortifying those weak spots and organizing your network to be robust and self-contained will hinder most simple attacks and minimize the damage that can be inflicted. Finally, preparing emergency procedures, knowing your contacts, and having multiple ways to reach them (including out-of-band, in terms of your network), will enable you to respond quickly to an ongoing attack and improve your chances of weathering it.

6.3.1   Understanding Your Network

The DoS effect usually manifests itself through large network delays and loss in connectivity. Depending on the targeted resource, your whole network may experience a

DoS effect, or only specific services, hosts, or subnetworks may be unavailable. Understanding how your network functions will aid in risk assessment efforts by establishing:

- How important network connectivity is in your daily business model
- How much it would cost to lose it
- Which services are more important than others
- The costs of added latency, or complete loss of connectivity, to your key services

Most businesses today rely on the public Internet for daily activities, such as e-mail, ordering supplies online, contacting customers, videoconferencing, providing Web content, and voice-over-IP services. Some of those activities may be critical for the company's business, and may have no backup solutions. For instance, if supplies are ordered daily and must be ordered through online forms, or your company uses "voice-over-IP" exclusively for all business telephone calls, losing network connectivity may mean stalling the business for a few days. Other activities may have alternatives that do not require Internet access—e-mails can be replaced by telephone calls, videoconferencing by conference calls or live meetings; some activities can even be postponed for a few days. In this case, Internet access increases effectiveness but is not critical for business continuity.

Some companies make their profit by conducting business over the Internet. Take, for example, a company that sells cat food through online orders. Certain products or services are at a higher risk of loss due to even short-duration DDoS attacks. These include:

- Products with a short shelf-life that must be sold quickly, such as flowers or specialized holiday foods
- Commodities that could easily be obtained from many sources, so customers would simply leave and go somewhere else if they cannot get immediate access, such as pornography
- Time-critical transactions, such as betting on sports events, stock trading, mortgage applications, news delivery and major media events, and event or transportation ticket sales
- Low-margin, high-volume purchases that require a constant transaction rate to maintain viability of the business, such as major online booksellers and airline ticket services
- Businesses that offer free services supported by advertising, such as search engines and portals

Network connectivity is a crucial asset in these business models, and losing connectivity means losing daily revenue (possibly *a lot* of it). Additionally, if a company is well known, the fact that it was out of business for even a few hours can make headline news and damage its reputation—a fact that may lose them more business than a few hours of network outage.

The first step in risk assessment is making a list of business-related activities that depend on constant Internet access. Each item on the list should be evaluated for:

- Alternative solutions that do not require Internet access

- Frequency of the activity

- Estimated cost if the activity cannot be performed

In addition to costs relating directly to loss of connectivity, there may be hidden costs of a DDoS attack from handling extreme traffic loads, or diverting staff attention to mitigate the problem. In some cases, diverting attention and/or causing disruption of logging is a prime motivation of some DDoS attacks, overwhelming firewall or IDS logging to blind the victim to some other attack, or allowing a blatant action to go unnoticed. An attacker who wants to slip in "under the radar" can do so better if the radar screen is filled with moving dots.

For example, a DDoS attack may fill your logs. Logging traffic may amplify the DoS effect, clogging your internal network with warning messages. Understanding how your logging is set up will help you identify hot spots ahead of time and fortify them, for instance, by providing for more log space or sending log messages out of band.

Sophisticated DDoS attacks may manifest themselves not as abrupt service loss but as a persistent increase in incoming traffic load. This may lead you to believe that your customer traffic has increased and purchase more assets for handling additional load. Imagine your (or your stockholders') disappointment when the truth finally becomes clear. You may be paying for something that is not even necessary due to the way your ISP charges you. If you pay per byte of incoming bandwidth, this cost will skyrocket in such a subtle, slowly increasing attack. Some ISPs will be willing to waive this cost, but others will not. Whether they do may depend on how long the situation existed before you noticed it. Understanding how conditions of your service agreement apply to the DDoS attack case ahead of time will enable you to negotiate the contract or change the provider. Other hidden costs include increased insurance premiums and legal costs for prosecuting the attacker. If your assets are misused to launch the attack on someone else, you may even face civil liability.

Once critical services are identified, it is important to understand how they depend on other services. For instance, e-mail service needs DNS to function properly. If e-mail is deemed critical, then DNS service is also critical and must be protected.

6.3.2 Securing End Hosts on Your Network

Preparation for dealing with both phases of DDoS attacks starts with addressing end-host security issues. These include reducing vulnerabilities that could result in compromise of systems, and tuning systems for high-performance and high-resilience against attack.

Reducing Vulnerabilities on End Hosts

While the most common strategy for creating the DoS effect is to generate excess traffic, if the target host has a software vulnerability, misusing it may take only a few packets that shut down the host and effectively deny service with much less effort and exposure to the attacker. There are many attacks that function this way. Additionally, all techniques for acquiring agent machines are based on exploiting some vulnerability to gain access. Fixing vulnerabilities on your systems not only improves your security toward many threats (worms, viruses, intrusions, denial of service), it also makes you a good network citizen who will not participate in attacks on other sites.

It is not uncommon today for applications and operating systems that run on end hosts and routers to have bugs that require regular patching and upgrading. Many vendors have an automatic update system to which you can subscribe. This system will inform you when new vulnerabilities have been discovered, and it will usually deliver patches and updates to your hosts, ready to be installed. For example, Microsoft maintains a Windows update Web site (`http://www.windowsupdate.com`) where users can have their machines scanned for vulnerabilities and obtain relevant patches and updates. Users subscribing to automatic Windows updates would have them delivered directly to their computer. Red Hat, a commercial Linux distributor, maintains a Web site with security alerts and bug fixes for current products at `http://www.redhat.com/apps/support/errata/`. Users can subscribe for automatic updates at `http://www.redhat.com/software/rhn/update/`. Other desktop systems, such as MacOS, also offer software update services.

Virus detection software needs to be frequently updated with new virus signatures. In many cases this can help detect and thwart intrusion attempts on your hosts and keep your network secure. Each major virus detection product comes with an option to enable automatic updates. If you enable this option, new virus signatures will be automatically downloaded to your machine. However, any kind of automatic action may inflict accidental damage to your computer because of incompatibility between the update and other installed software, or may be subverted by an attacker to compromise your computer. Automatic features should be carefully scrutinized and supported by a form of authentication and by backups and extra monitoring to quickly detect and react to failures.

Some protocols are asymmetric; they make one party commit more resources than the other party. These protocols are fertile ground for DDoS attacks, as they enable the attacker to create a heavy load at the target with only a few packets. The TCP SYN attack, discussed in Chapter 4, is one example, based on filling the victim's connection table.

A modification of the TCP protocol, the TCP *syncookie* [Ber] patch (discussed in more detail in Chapter 5), successfully handles this attack by changing connection establishment steps so that server resources are allocated later in the protocol. This patch is compatible with the original protocol: Only the server side has to be updated. Linux, FreeBSD, and other Unix-based operating systems have deployed a TCP syncookie mechanism that can be enabled by the user (it is disabled by default). For instance, to enable TCP syncookies in Linux you should include "`echo 1 > /proc/sys/net/ipv4/tcp_syncookies`" in one of the system startup scripts. WindowsNT protects from SYN flood attacks by detecting the high number of half-open connections and modifying the retransmission and buffer allocation behavior, and timing of the TCP protocol. This option can be enabled by setting the parameter value `HKLM`→`System`→`CurrentControlSet`→ `Services`→`Tcpip`→`SynAttackProtect` in the System Registry to 1 or 2. FreeBSD implements syncookie protection by default, but if you wanted to control this setting, you would use "`sysctl -w net.inet.tcp .syncookies=1`" to enable it.

An authentication protocol is another example of an asymmetric protocol. It takes a fairly long time to verify an authentication request, but bogus requests can be generated easily. Potential solutions for this problem involve generating a challenge to the client requesting authentication, and forcing him to spend resources to reply to the challenge before verifying his authentication request. Unfortunately, this requires clients to understand the challenge/response protocol, which might not always be possible. Other alternatives are to consider whether you really need to authenticate your clients or to perform a stepwise authentication by first deploying weak authentication protocols that provide for cheap verification and then deploying strong ones when you are further along in your interactions with the client. If you have a fixed client pool, a reasonable alternative is to accept authentication requests only from approved IP source addresses. In any case, strengthening your authentication service by providing ample resources and deploying several authentication servers behind a load balancer is a wise decision. Understanding how the protocols deployed on your network function, and keeping them as symmetric as possible, reduces the number of vulnerabilities that can be misused for DDoS attack.

Many operating system installations enable default services that your organization may never use. Those services listen on the open ports for incoming service requests and may provide a backdoor to your machine. It is prudent to disable all but necessary services by closing unneeded ports and filtering incoming traffic for nonexistent services. For instance, if a host does not act as a DNS server, there is no need to allow incoming DNS requests to reach it. This filtering should be done as close to the end host as possible. For example, ideally you would filter at the host itself, using host-based firewall features (such as *iptables* or *pf* on Unix systems or personal firewall products on Windows or MacOS). This is the easiest place, resource-wise, to do the filtering but has implications if you do not control the end hosts on your network. Filtering at the local area network router (i.e., using a "screened subnet" style of firewalling) would be a good backup and is one way of implementing a robust layered security model. If your network has a perimeter firewall (which is not always the case), traffic can be blocked there as well. Trying to block at the core of your network, or at your border routers, may not be possible if your network design does not provide for sufficient router processing overhead (and this also violates the spirit of the end-to-end network design paradigm). To discover services that are currently active on your hosts, you can look at list of processes or a list of open ports or do a portscan using, for instance, the *nmap* tool—an open source vulnerability scanner freely downloadable from `http://www.insecure.org/nmap/index.html`. If you opt for port scanning, be advised that some types of scans may harm your machines. Inform yourself thoroughly about the features your port scan tool of choice supports and use only the most benign ones that do not violate protocols and scan at moderate speed.

Many DDoS attacks employ IP spoofing, i.e., faking the source address in the IP header to hide the identity of actual attacking agents. This avoids detection of the agent and creates more work for the DDoS defense system. It is a good security measure to deploy both ingress and egress filtering [FS00] at your network perimeter to remove such spoofed packets. (Because "ingress/egress filtering" can be a confusing concept, please refer to the descriptions in Chapter 4 and Appendix A.) As seen by an edge network, antispoofing egress filters remove those outgoing packets that bear source addresses that do not belong to your network. The equivalent ingress filters similarly remove those incoming packets that bear source addresses that belong to your network. Both of those packet address categories are clearly fake, and many firewalls and routers can be easily configured to perform ingress/egress filtering (as well as other types of filtering). Advanced techniques for elimination of spoofed addresses include detecting source addresses from those network prefixes that are reserved and filtering them from your input stream, or using a list of live internal network addresses to allow only their traffic to get to the outside world.

In general, fixing vulnerabilities raises the bar for the attacker, making him work harder to deny service. It protects your network from specific, low-traffic-rate attacks. In the absence of vulnerabilities that could quickly disable network services, the attacker instead must generate a high traffic rate to overwhelm your resources.

Tuning System Parameters

Beyond just fixing vulnerabilities, one of the first things that should be done in cases in which a DDoS attack is affecting a service or end system—but is not large enough to cause noticeable network disruption—is to ensure that the target of the attack is adequately provisioned and tuned. Even in cases in which DDoS mitigation tools are in place at the perimeter of your network, and are functioning as they should to scrub incoming packets and ensure that only "legitimate" requests are coming in, the server may still be overwhelmed and cease to function.

Examples of things to look for include:

- **Processor utilization.** Programs like *top*, *ps*, and *vmstat* are useful for checking processor utilization. The *uptime* program also shows processor load averages. If those programs indicate a single application that is consuming an unusually high amount of CPU time (e.g., 90%) this may be a vulnerable application targeted by a DoS attack. You will need to keep a model of normal CPU utilization to quickly spot applications gone wild due to vulnerability exploits or specifically crafted attacks.

- **Disk I/O performance.** Disk I/O performance can be determined using programs like *vmstat*, *iostat*, and *top*. If you are using NFS, the *nfsstat* program should be used. Tuning of IDE drives can be accomplished on Linux systems using *hdparm*. If disk-monitoring programs, such as *iostat*, indicate unusually high disk activity, this may be a vulnerable application under attack. Again, you will need a model of normal disk activity to be able to spot anomalies.

- **Network I/O performance.** If the network interface is saturated or there are other problems on the Local Area Network (LAN) segment, you may see dropped packets or a high rate of collisions. You can see these using the statistics option of *netstat*. Network socket state information can also be seen with *netstat*. If *netstat* indicates that you are experiencing a significant number of dropped packets and collisions when no attack is under way, then you are already running close to capacity. An attacker can tip you over into an overload situation by adding a rather small quantity of traffic. You need to improve the bandwidth on the highly utilized links if you want to avoid falling easy prey to DDoS. This observation is most important for those links that are publicly accessible. A fairly congested link on a purely internal LAN that does not directly accept traffic from the outside network is less of a risk for a DDoS attack than the same situation on the main link between your subnetwork and your ISP.

- **Memory utilization.** If memory is low, use *ps* and *top* to determine which programs have the largest Resident State Sizes (RSS). You may need to kill some of them off to free up memory. Memory is very cheap these days, so make sure that you have as much as your motherboard and budget can afford. If you cannot increase memory, yet still have problems with memory utilization, consider upgrading your hardware.

- **Swapping/paging activity.** Paging is a normal activity that occurs when portions of a program that are necessary for execution must be brought in from disk. Swapping occurs when physical memory is low and least-recently used pages of programs are written out to disk temporarily. Because disk speed is far slower than memory, any reading or writing of the disk can have significant performance impacts. You can check on paging and swapping activity and swap utilization using *vmstat*, *top*, or *iostat*.

- **Number of server processes.** Web servers typically have one process responsible for listening for new connections, and several child processes to handle actual HTTP requests. If you have a very high rate of incoming requests, you may need to increase the number of server processes to ensure that you are not overloading the existing processes and delaying new requests. Use *top*, *ps*, and *netstat* to check for overloading of server processes.

Tuning system parameters will help protect your network from small- to moderate-rate attacks, and in-depth monitoring of resource usage should ensure better detection of attacks that consume a large amount of resources.

6.3.3   Fortifying Your Network

In addition to securing the hosts on your network, there are also things you should do to improve the security of the network as a whole. These include how the network is provisioned and how it is designed and implemented.

Provisioning the Network

A straightforward approach to handle high traffic loads is to buy more resources, a tactic known as *overprovisioning*. This tactic is discussed in detail in Chapter 5. There are many ways in which overprovisioning can be used to mitigate the effects of a DDoS attack.

The problem here, from a cost perspective, is the asymmetry of resources. There is very little or no cost for an attacker to acquire more agent machines to overwhelm any additional resources that a victim may employ, while the victim must invest money and time to acquire these added resources. Still, this technique raises the bar for the attacker and will also accommodate increased network usage for legitimate reasons.[2]

One form of overprovisioning has to do with available network bandwidth for normal traffic. This approach is taken by many large companies that conduct business on the Internet. The attacker looking to overwhelm your network with a high traffic load will either target the network bandwidth by generating numerous large packets of any possible type and contents, or he will target a specific service by generating a high number of seemingly legitimate requests. Acquiring more network bandwidth than needed is sometimes affordable, and makes it less likely that bandwidth will be exhausted by the attack. A smartly configured network-level defense system sitting on this highly provisioned link will then have a chance to sift through the packets and keep only those that seem legitimate

Another form of overprovisioning is to have highly resourced servers. This can be (1) keeping hosts updated with the fastest processors, network interfaces, disk drives, and memory; (2) purchasing as much main memory as possible; or (3) using multiple network interface cards to prevent network I/O bottlenecks. Further, duplicating critical servers and placing them in a server pool behind a load balancer multiplies your ability to handle seemingly legitimate requests. This may also prove useful for legitimate users in the long run—as your business grows your network will have to be

---

[2] For instance, overprovisioning can help in the case of "flash crowds," when some popular event motivates many clients to access your network simultaneously.

expanded, anyway. Performing this expansion sooner than you may otherwise plan also helps withstand moderate DDoS attacks.

These two forms of overprovisioning can be combined in a holistic manner, ensuring fewer potential bottlenecks in the entire system. In the electric sector, for example, sites are required to have nominal utilization rates for the entire system that are no larger than 25% of capacity, to provide an adequate margin of unused processing capacity in the event of an emergency. This minimizes the chances that an emergency situation causes monitoring to fail, escalating the potential damage to the system as a whole.

If your network management and communication to the outside world is done in-band over the same network as potential DDoS targets, (e.g., if you use voice-over IP for your phone line), the DDoS attack may take out not only your services, but all means of communicating with your upstream provider, law enforcement, vendors, customers—in short everyone you need to communicate with in a crisis. The added cost of purchasing extra bandwidth can be viewed as a cheaper form of insurance.

Designing for Survivability

Since some DoS attacks send a high amount of seemingly legitimate requests for service, techniques that improve scalability and fault tolerance of network services directly increase your ability to weather DDoS attacks. Designing for survivability means organizing your network in such a way such that it can sustain and survive attacks, failures, and accidents (see [EFL+99, LF00]). Sometimes, adding survivability provisions has surprising benefits in protecting against unexpected events [Die01].

Survivability design techniques include:

- **Separation of critical from noncritical services.** Separating those services that are critical for your daily business from those that are not facilitates deployment of different defense techniques for each resource group and keeps your network simple. Separation can occur at many levels—you can provide different physical networks for different services, connect to different service providers, or use subnetting to logically separate networks. A good approach is to separate public from private services, and to split an *n*-tier architecture into host groups containing Web servers, application servers, database servers, etc. Once resources are separated into groups, communication between resource groups can be clearly defined and policed, for instance, by placing a firewall between each pair of groups.

- **Segregating services within hosts.** Rather than assigning several services to a single host, it is better to use single-purpose servers with well-defined functionality.

As an example of segregated services, having a dedicated mail server means that all but a few ports can be closed to incoming traffic and only a few well-defined packet types should be exchanged between the server and the rest of the network. It also means that monitoring server operation and detecting anomalies will be simplified. Having several services assigned to a single host not only makes monitoring and policing difficult, but finding and exploiting a vulnerability in any of these services may effectively deny all of them.

An advanced alternative for segmenting services that addresses just the issue of process separation is to use highly secure operating systems such as SELinux or TrustedBSD which implement Mandatory Access Control (MAC) for processes.[3] This will not help very much for DDoS mitigation, however, unless these systems are also configured not just to use MAC, but to also limit particular services to maximum usage of particular system resources. If both a DNS service and a Web server are run on such a machine and the Web service receives many seemingly legitimate requests that take a long time to process, MAC will state that all of them should get service. After all, the Web server must be permitted to do such things in its legitimate operations. Only enforcement of QoS guarantees for the DNS server by the OS can prevent the Web requests from eating up all the machine's resources and starving the DNS server.

- **Compartmentalizing the network.** Identifying bottlenecks in the risk assessment step should provide guidelines for reorganizing the network to avoid single points of failure. Dividing the network into self-contained compartments that communicate with the outside only when necessary enables your business to continue operation even when some portions of the network are down. For example, having a database server distributed across several physically disjoint networks that connect to the Internet via different ISPs may require a lot of management, but may enable you to continue serving database requests even if several servers are targeted by the attack or their incoming links are overwhelmed. Having a mail server for each department may mean that when the finance department is under attack, employees from the planning division can still send and receive e-mails. As always, decisions about which services to replicate and to what extent demand detailed cost/benefit analysis.

---

[3] Such systems are not yet commonly used by businesses, as their policy management aspects and debugging are quite complicated, so they will not be covered here. Still, you should watch for them to start making inroads in commercial and open-source operating system offerings in the next few years.

- **Reducing outside visibility.** If attackers are able to learn your network organization, they can also assess the risks and identify bottlenecks that can be targeted by the attack. There are numerous techniques that aid in hiding the internals of your network. Blocking ICMP replies to outside hosts prevents attackers from learning your routing topology. Using a split DNS effectively creates two separate DNS zones for your network with the same DNS names. One zone will contain a list of externally visible services that can be accessed through the firewall. Your external DNS server will serve this zone. Your external customers will be able to access only the external DNS server and will see only this list of services. Another zone will contain a list of internally accessible services that are available to your employees. This zone will be served by your internal DNS server. Your employees' machines will be configured with the address of the internal DNS server and will access these services through your internal network. Separating this information minimizes the data you leak about your internal network organization. It also provides separate access paths for external and internal clients, enabling you to enforce different policies.

  Network Address Translation (NAT) hides the internals of the network by providing a single address to the outside clients—that of the firewall. All outside clients send their requests for service to the firewall, which rewrites packets with address of the internal server and forwards the request. Replies are similarly rewritten with the firewall's address. This technique creates a burden on the firewall and may make it a single point of failure, but this problem can be addressed by distributing firewall service among several routers. Generally, if attackers can only see a large, opaque network, they must either attack the ingress points (which are probably the most capable and highly provisioned spots, and thus the easiest to defend) or use e-mail- or Web-based attacks to gain control of a host inside the perimeter and tunnel back out.

6.3.4 Preparing to Respond to the Attack

Having a ready incident response plan and defense measures that you can quickly deploy before the attack hits will make it easier to respond to the attack. Further, knowing who to contact for help will reduce your damages and downtime.

Responding to the attack requires fast detection and accurate characterization of the attack streams so that they can be filtered or rate limited. Devising detailed monitoring techniques will help you determine "normal" traffic behavior at various points in your network and easily spot anomalies. Detection, characterization, and response can be accomplished either by designing a custom DDoS defense system or by buying one of the available commercial products.

You should choose wisely how you configure and use a DDoS defense mechanism. For example, if you choose to make its actions fully automated, an attacker may be able to exploit the unauthenticated nature of most Internet traffic (at least traffic that does not use IPSec Authentication or Encapsulation features) to trick the DDoS defense system into acting incorrectly and producing a DoS effect that way. Assume an attacker knows that your site uses a DDoS defense mechanism that does not keep state for UDP flows, and that you have it configured to automatically block inbound UDP packet floods. She also knows that many of your users frequent Web sites that rely on some company's distributed DNS caching service. The cache provider has thousands of DNS servers spread around the Internet, which the attacker can determine by having her bots all do DNS lookups for the same sites and storing the results. DNS typically uses UDP for simple requests. Putting these facts together, the attacker could forge bogus UDP packets with the source address of all of the DNS caching service's servers, sending them all to random IP addresses at your site. Depending on how the DDoS defense system is programmed, it might assume that this is a distributed UDP flood attack and start filtering out all UDP traffic from these thousands of "agents" (really the caching DNS servers), preventing your users from getting to any Web sites served by this DNS cache provider, because their DNS replies are blocked as they come back.

Fully manual operation has its own problems. The reaction time can be significantly slowed, and in some cases slow defense may cause more problems than it solves. The network operations and security operations staff should both well understand the capabilities and features of the DDoS mitigation system and how best to deploy and control it. Appendix B offers a detailed overview of some currently available commercial products. This should serve only as an introduction to a wide variety of security products that are currently available. The reader is advised to investigate the market thoroughly before making any buying decisions.

Creating your own DDoS defense system generally makes sense only for large organizations with sophisticated network security professionals on staff. If your organization has those characteristics, a careful analysis of your system's needs and capacities might allow you to handcraft a better DDoS solution than that offered by a commercial vendor. Building a good defense solution from scratch will be an expensive and somewhat risky venture, however, so you should not make this choice lightly. If you do go in this direction, make sure you have a thorough understanding of all aspects of your network and systems and a deep understanding of DDoS attack tools and methods, as well as the pros and cons of various defensive approaches.

It is also important to balance the requirements of the network operations and security operations staff. Many sites separate these groups, often having an imbalance of staffing and resources dedicated to building and supporting the complex and expensive network infrastructure vis-à-vis handling security incidents and mitigation at the host level. Having these groups work closely together and share common goals improves the situation and causes less internal friction.

Many sites with large networks and high bandwidth costs are now purchasing or implementing traffic analysis tools, but often more with an eye toward cost containment and billing, as opposed to security. When an attack occurs, there is sometimes a distinct issue of not having visibility below the level of overall bandwidth utilization and router/switch availability statistics. There may not be flow- or packet content–monitoring tools in place, or the ability to preserve this data at the time of an attack to facilitate investigation or prosecution. Network traffic analysis is a critical component of response. It is said that one person's DoS attack is another person's physics experiment dataset.

There may also be a lack of tools, such as network taps, systems capable of logging packets at the network borders without dropping a high percentage of the packets, or traffic analysis programs. These tools, and the skills to efficiently use them, are necessary to dig down to the packet level, identify features of the attack and the hosts involved, etc. Many high-profile attacks reported by the press have been accompanied by conflicting reports of the DDoS tool involved, the type of attack, or even whether it was a single attack or multiple concurrent attacks. In some cases, sites have believed they were experiencing "Smurf" (ICMP Echo Reply flood) attacks inbound, because they saw a spike in ICMP packets. In fact, some host within their network was participating in an attack with an outbound SYN or UDP flood that was well within the normal bandwidth utilization of the site, and they were getting ICMP replies from the target's closed port. In other cases "attacks" have turned out to be misconfigured Web servers, failed routers, or even a site's own buggy client-side Web application that was flooding their own servers![4]

---

[4] The situation of self-inflicted DoS happens more than one would think. Some victims of "DDoS attacks" have suffered costly downtime and customer complaints for hours. Their ISPs often confirm the "attack" from packet counts and flow direction information obtained from simple network-monitoring tools, but nobody gathers even a short sample of network traffic to analyze. When expensive consultants are brought in and manage to get the provider to find a way to gather network traffic, or make an on-site call to the victim's server location, it is quickly determined that the problem has to do with a software

Investing in backup servers and load balancers may provide you with assets that you can turn on in case of an emergency. Backup servers can take the load off the current server pool or can supplement hosts that are crashing. Of course, there is a cost to having spare equipment lying around, and an attack may be over by the time someone is able to reconfigure a server room and add in the spare hardware. If you provide static services, such as hosting Web pages or a read-only database, it may be possible to replicate your services on demand and thus distribute the load. Service replication can even help if you deliver dynamic content. Contracting with a service that will replicate your content at multiple network locations and transparently direct users to the nearest replica provides high resiliency in case of a DDoS attack. Since these services are themselves highly provisioned and distributed, even if they are successfully attacked at one location, the other replicas will still offer service to some of your clients. The downside to such highly provisioned and distributed services is an equally high cost. This option may be viable financially for only very large sites. Very careful risk analysis and cost/benefit calculations are necessary, as well as investigation of alternatives for a disruption of business operations, such as insurance coverage. [5] Another consideration is that while replication services are highly provisioned, they may themselves be taken down by a sufficiently large attack, so this approach is not a panacea.

Another alternative is to consider gracefully degrading your services to avoid complete denial. For instance, when a high traffic load is detected, your server can go into a special mode of selectively processing incoming requests. Thus, some customers will still be able to receive service.

If the DDoS attack targets network bandwidth, no edge network defense will ameliorate the situation. Regardless of sophisticated solutions you may install, legitimate users' packets will be lost because your upstream network link is saturated and packets are dropped before they ever reach your defense system. In this situation, you need all the help you can get from your upstream ISP, and perhaps also their peers, to handle the problem.

Cultivating a good relationship with your ISP ahead of time and locating telephone numbers and names of people to reach in case of a DDoS attack will speed up the response when you need it. Many ISPs will gladly put specific filters on your incoming

---

bug and the "attack" is then halted in a matter of minutes. Had the victim, or its ISP, been prepared to analyze network traffic, the event would have lasted only a brief time and had minimal cost.

[5] Without recommending specific companies, search the Web for "DDoS insurance coverage" to find some options. Credit card companies, as well as some insurance companies, are now offering such protection.

traffic or apply rate limiting. Be aware of the information you need to provide in order to get maximum benefit from the filtering. Sometimes it may be necessary to trace the attack traffic and have filters placed further upstream to maximize the amount of legitimate traffic you are receiving.[6] This usually involves contacting other ISPs that will generally be unwilling to help you, given that you are not their customer. If you have a good relationship with your ISP, they will be in a far better position to negotiate tracing with their upstream peers. Specifying the responsibilities and services your ISP is willing to offer in case of DDoS attack in a service agreement will also simplify things once an attack occurs.

6.4 Handling an Ongoing DDoS Attack as a Target

Handling an ongoing DDoS attack on your network requires you to detect it, characterize the attack streams, and apply mitigation techniques. Detecting the attack is usually automated either through standard network-monitoring software or through a commercial DDoS defense system. While the attack will undoubtedly be detected once your services are crippled, early detection will provide more time for response and may even make the occurrence of the attack transparent to your customers.

Choosing a set of parameters to monitor for anomalies directly affects detection accuracy. You can choose to monitor levels of the incoming network traffic, the number of external clients with active requests (to spot the occurrence of IP spoofing), client behavior, server load, server resources, etc. A properly chosen set of parameters will not generate too many false positives, while still detecting the majority of the attacks early.

Once detected, the attack should be characterized as narrowly as possible. This includes: identifying network protocols, applications, and hosts that the attack targets; identifying source addresses used in attack packets, packet length, contents, etc.; identifying detailed attack characteristics facilitates setup of precise filtering and rate-limiting rules. This is where the border-level network-monitoring tools and skills, mentioned in the previous section, really pay off.

Mitigation techniques involve contacting your ISP and providing attack characteristics, and deploying filtering and rate limiting at your border routers, DMZ router, or firewall (if the target is within a perimeter defense). Predeploying load balancers and having hardware available, in an emergency, to increase server capacity can also be of

---

[6] Filtering is usually imprecise and inflicts some collateral damage. If the route that attack traffic takes can be identified and filtering placed as much upstream as possible, this minimizes the amount of legitimate traffic passing the filter and thus minimizes the collateral damage from the response.

use but is expensive and may take hours or days to implement (depending on where the hardware and staff are located in relationship to the network being attacked). Redirection of traffic through routing configurations may ease such topology or resource allocation changes.

If you have purchased a commercial DDoS defense system, many of those will automatically devise appropriate filtering rules that your network operations staff can then choose to deploy. Some systems can even be instructed to respond autonomously, without human supervision. They will deploy filters and notify the system administrator after the fact. If you use one of these systems, it would be wise for your administrators to keep a careful eye on any filters that is reports deploying, both to be aware of actual attacks and to ensure that the system is not mistakenly filtering legitimate traffic, as described earlier. There is a distinct possibility that a self-inflicted denial of service could result from a skillful attack.

Taking a close look at the attack packets may reveal weaknesses in the attack that can be used for effective response. For example, do all attack packets target the same server? If so, it may be possible to change the IP address of the server.

Many DDoS attack tools are poorly designed and may omit DNS lookup and hardcode your server's IP address in the attack script. A simple change of IP address will cause all the attack packets to be dropped at the last hop. Then, enlisting help from your ISP, a simple filtering rule deployed upstream should completely relieve your network of the flood. ISPs can further attempt to trace back the flood and stop it at the entry point to their network.

Realize, however, that this address mapping change technique may not work as desired if some clients have cached the mapping. This is likely to happen if the server's IP address is listed in public DNS records. Clients that have cached these records will receive a mapping to the old address that is being attacked and will thus still suffer the DoS effect. Sometimes the application itself can get around the DNS caching issue (some Web application services can do this).

UUNET's backbone security engineers claim to have had great success using a technique they have developed, called *backscatter traceback* [GMR01], for tracing flood traffic with forged source addresses back to its ingress points into UUNET's network cloud. The technique leverages several "tricks of the trade" that may be adopted by other network service providers to implement a similar capability. (In a very abstract and succinct fashion, the technique works by injecting a fault into the network and observing the effects on the smallest set of traffic illustrated in Figure 6.3 as it bounces off the artificial fault.) Note that the examples provided by UUNET assume functionality provided by Cisco routers.

The first step is to keep a black hole route ("route to Null0") installed on each of the network provider's routers so that it can be invoked quickly as needed. For example, a single IP address out of the IANA special-use prefix TEST-NET, say 192.0.2.1, can be used for this purpose, as it will never appear as a valid address in the Internet. A static route is established on each router that sends all traffic destined for 192.0.2.1 to the Null0 interface, effectively dumping the traffic. Normally, no traffic follows this route.

The next step is to configure a BGP-speaking router so that it can be used to quickly disseminate a route update to all routers whenever the need arises to black hole a real network, whether a single address or a larger network address block. A route map is used to set the next hop of matching tagged routes to the null-routed address 192.0.2.1.

When an address needs to be black-holed, a static route for the target address is installed on the above router with a tag that causes it to be processed by the route map. This static route will be propagated via the BGP routing protocol to the rest of the service provider's routers, who will now have Null0 as the next hop for the target address. Thus, all of the service provider's routers will be instructed to drop all traffic to the target address at all ingress points, effectively black-holing the address at the network edge. Operationally, the main feature of all this is to allow a black-hole route on all edge routers to be remotely triggered from a single control point via BGP.

Another necessary step is to establish a sinkhole network (i.e., a router designed to withstand heavy flood traffic to which attack traffic can be redirected for study). Attached to this router should be a workstation (e.g., the sensor in Figure 6.2) of sufficient capacity to capture and analyze the redirected attack traffic.

As mentioned above, the sinkhole BGP router advertises TEST-NET as the next hop for the target address, causing all incoming traffic destined for the target to be redirected to the Null0 interface.

The final step is to configure the sinkhole router to advertise itself as the next hop for a block of unallocated IP address space. (UUNET recommends using 96.0.0.0/3, as it is the largest unallocated address block on the planet.) The assumption here is that the flood traffic's forged source addresses will occasionally fall within this unallocated range, as they often do when the flood tool generates packets with randomly chosen source IPs. This route is advertised to all of the service provider's other routers, constrained by BGP egress filtering to guarantee that the route does not leak outside of the service provider's realm. This causes all the service provider's routers to reflect any outbound traffic destined for the unallocated range back to the sinkhole network.

We now describe in detail the backscatter using Figure 6.1. When attack traffic has been noticed, the service provider performs the following steps:

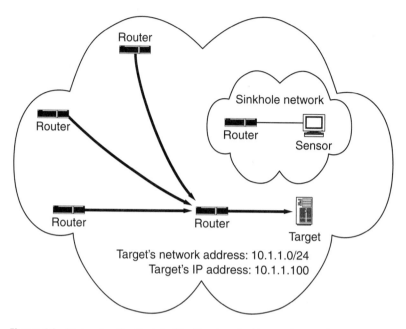

Figure 6.1 Network with attack traffic. (Reprinted with permission of Barry Greene.)

1. The sinkhole router is configured to advertise a new route for the target machine with a next hop of the TEST-NET host address. The route propagates via BGP to all of the other routers, causing all incoming attack traffic to be (temporarily) blackholed at the network edge. This causes the target to be completely unreachable for the duration of this analysis. In practice, UUNET has found that redirecting the target's traffic for 45 seconds is usually enough to capture sufficient evidence for a correct traceback to occur.

2. Another static route is added to the sinkhole router to redirect any 96.0.0.0/3 traffic to the sinkhole network. This route is also propagated to all of the other routers.

3. As the packets headed for the target, including both the legitimate packets and the spoofed attack packets, are dropped by the service provider's edge, ICMP Unreachable messages are generated by the edge routers and sent to the source addresses. This is referred to as *backscatter*.

4. Any attack traffic entering the service provider's network with a forged source address from the 96.0.0.0/3 block will cause the edge routers to generate ICMP Unreachable messages destined for the forged source addresses in 96.0.0.0/3.

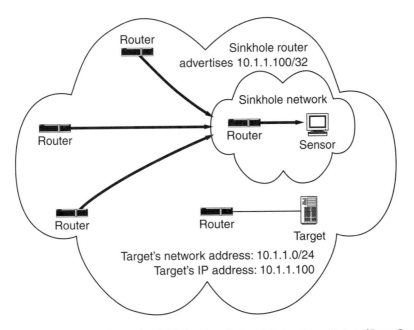

Figure 6.2 Attack traffic redirected to sink hole network. (Reprinted with permission of Barry Greene.)

5. The ICMP Unreachable messages destined for 96.0.0.0/3 will be redirected to the sinkhole network. The sinkhole network's router is configured to log incoming ICMP Unreachable messages.

6. These log messages include the source address of the edge router that generated the ICMP Unreachable message (i.e., the ingress point of the flood traffic). The traceback to the service provider's ingress point(s) is now complete. Figure 6.1 shows three such ingress points. Figure 6.2 shows further traffic analysis by a sensor.

The ISP now knows precisely which of its routers need to install defense measures (such as filtering or rate limiting) to control a long-term DDoS attack, while minimizing collateral damage to the victim and other nodes.

Note that this technique relies heavily on the assumption that the distribution of the attack traffic's forged source addresses is spread randomly over the entire IP space. The technique will be thwarted by attack traffic crafted to avoid using the unallocated space being monitored by the sinkhole network. This avoidance can be mitigated by the service provider in some cases by analyzing the attack traffic for other patterns in source address distribution and redirecting a different unallocated address range accordingly.

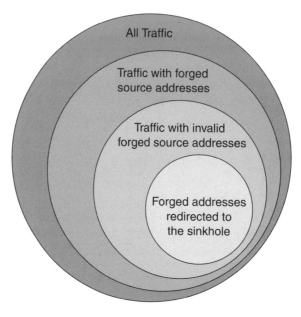

Figure 6.3   Classes of traffic directed at target

However, a clever attacker who chooses forged IP addresses only from the allocated range of IP addresses will be able to avoid this form of tracing entirely (see Figure 6.3 for an overview of traffic classes). The technique is thus imperfect, although in practice it may work successfully in the majority of cases.

6.5   Handling an Ongoing DDoS Attack as a Source

Since DDoS attacks occur regularly, this indicates that either agent-hosting sites do not care enough about their machines participating in attacks to bother stopping them, or the bandwidth available to these sites may be so great that they may not even notice the flooding. Sites should care, however. Being a good network citizen will make everyone's experience of the Internet better, and only if most online participants behave responsibly will the Internet continue to be useful. If that rationale does not sway you, consider that hosting an agent is a sure sign that your network has been compromised. In addition to participating in an attack on others, your own network and assets are at risk, and prudence dictates that you should investigate and clean up this problem.

Finally, there is a growing level of discussion of liability issues surrounding due care taken by those whose sites are used for an attack. If sufficient financial damage is incurred by a victim, and if the victim can trace the attacks back to one or more sites that are primarily responsible, then those sites may get sued. The liabilities range from failing to secure one's computers from intrusion to failing to stop an attack in progress. The sites may be found negligent for not stopping an attack, regardless of whether the attack affects their own network availability. They may also be charged with obstruction of justice by destroying evidence if they have been informed of an attack and potential legal action, yet still wiped the disks of compromised hosts and reinstalled the operating system. (The topic of liability is discussed in more depth in Chapter 8.)

The first step in handling a DDoS attack as a source is to detect that it is happening. This can in general be done by triggering an alarm whenever you notice a high outgoing traffic rate targeting a single destination or a small set of machines. While the attacker may in principle deploy numerous agent machines, instructing each of them to generate only a few packets, typical DDoS agents flood with all their might and create large traffic loads. Thus, monitoring the outgoing traffic rate for each of your machines should catch the majority of the attacks. Detecting an attempt to use IP spoofing in outgoing traffic is also a likely sign that your network is being misused for malicious purposes and requires prompt investigation.

Even if you have set up ingress/egress filtering at your border to prevent spoofed packets from leaving your network, watching internally for spoofed packets using an IDS, a firewall, or router ACLs that counts packets, may provide an early warning of trouble.

Your next step should be to determine how you can filter outgoing traffic to the target(s) and begin this filtering. While doing this, try to also take steps to identify agent machines, usually by monitoring various internal links. (Note that after you have placed filters on routers, you may no longer be able to use your network taps to gather any traffic, or to scan for handlers/agents.) Even a short sample of all network traffic to/from suspect hosts, or flows that have been identified by network monitoring tools as being DDoS-related, taken *before you apply filters* is helpful. Nobody can analyze traffic that you can no longer see, or hosts that are no longer reachable via the network. Of course, this needs to be balanced against the risk of continued damage, but if made a part of normal operating procedures for responding to a DDoS attack, it will not cause significant delays.

In the early days of DDoS, several host- or network-based DDoS agent scanning tools were available to make the task of identifying agent machines easier. In fact, the initial DDoS analyses done by David Dittrich, Sven Dietrich, Neil Long, and others in subsequent analyses over the following years included Perl-based scripts or other mechanisms that would expose and/or control the DDoS agents. (More on the historical DDoS analyses and identification of malware using scanners is found later in this chapter.)

The DDoS tool scanners mentioned above have their limitations, the major one being that tools they scan for are either obsolete or in use but with modified source code that will not be detected by file-system–level scanners or respond to network-level scanners. For Windows-based DDoS tools, such as *Knight/Kaiten* compiled with Cygwin, anti-virus software is likely to be of more help.[7] Sophisticated tools, such as *Agobot/Phatbot*, use code polymorphism and other techniques to (a) avoid detection by antivirus software, (b) detect when they are run under single-step debuggers or in a virtual machine environment, and (c) *disable* antivirus software as one of the first steps upon infecting the host. You should not fully trust any program you run on a system that has been compromised at the administrative level.

Once agent machines are found, they need to be taken off the network, their disk drives imaged (and the images preserved as evidence), examined for the attack code, and finally cleaned. Unfortunately, many DDoS attack toolkits change system directories and data to hide the presence of the code and restart the code whenever the machine is rebooted. Locating the attack code can be a long and painful process. Steps to fully clean such machines usually involve reinstallation of the operating system, and are generally similar to the procedures for cleaning up any compromised machine.

The bottom line here is that these tools will require careful analysis of the compromised host by a competent system administrator or incident responder who is familiar with forensic analysis as well as with anti-forensic techniques.

The one step in the action list just given that is most often not performed is the imaging of disk drives of attacking systems. If you have done sufficient analysis of the attack traffic, as recommended here, you will know who the victim or victims are and will have some idea of whether legal action may ensue. If the victim of the attack is, say, an online retailer, media outlet, or government agency (especially a military, intelligence, space agency, or a contractor to any of those agencies), it is highly advisable to preserve evidence before cleaning any attacking hosts. These cases also warrant notification of your own organization's legal counsel, federal law enforcement agencies, and national incident coordination centers. A breakdown in timely communication of an attack, which may be national in scope, will complicate and slow down a national-

---

[7] Antivirus software should be used in a mode that does not automatically clean up and delete things, as this destroys evidence or data that you may need to help identify command and control channels on Internet Relay Chat networks, etc.

level response. If this is a concerted attack by a terrorist organization or nation state, this failure may have national security implications.

Regardless of the pain involved, you should clean up any agent machines in your network. Apart from helping others, cleaning up those machines increases your security. An attacker who has turned your machine into an agent has broken into this machine first. She can also steal, alter, or destroy your critical information; use your machine to provide illegal services to others; or disrupt your operation. As long as she controls your computers, you are essentially at her mercy.

6.6 Agreements/Understandings with Your ISP

A recent development in several metropolitan governments is for the users to negotiate a new type of contract with their network providers that provide for specific services, and delineate responsibilities and time frames for action, in the event of attack. For example, you could negotiate some of the following services that the provider can guarantee in the event of an attack.

- **Network address agility.** Can the provider readdress portions of the network to counter an attack? This will not completely stop a DDoS attack but may be helpful in cases where an attacker is using DDoS as a masking activity to cover an existing penetration into your network. The assumption is that the attacker has done reconnaissance scanning of your network in the past, and by readdressing you are taking away her knowledge of your network and forcing her to rescan the network (and be easier to catch in the process).

- **Topological changes.** Can the provider facilitate compartmentalizing your network in order to keep some of your business functioning, even in the face of a DDoS attack?

- **Traffic capture/analysis.** Can your provider gather samples of network traffic upstream from your interface to them? This should be full-packet captures, not just headers-only or the output of *tcpdump* with its standard output captured to a file. Full-packet captures may be required to preserve evidence in case of legal action, or they may improve understanding of the attack itself. Of course, you should also have a way of capturing your own traffic inside your own network. However, if your provider uses some kind of DDoS defense mechanism, you will be unable to gather traffic on the other side of your provider's defense system and therefore they will be the only one who can capture and examine attack packets. Beyond DDoS attacks, it may be necessary to determine whether your own routing infrastructure, firewalls, or internal/DMZ hosts have been compromised.

- **Flow logging.** Similar to traffic capture, flow logging is another thing that should be done both inside and outside of your network to provide unfiltered information and for comparison. Especially if you have DDoS mitigation tools in place, you will want to regularly compare internal traffic patterns with those external to the DDoS defense perimeter, to be assured that your defense works as expected. If your staff, or that of your network provider, are able to identify missed DoS traffic or novel DDoS attacks, these facts should be reported to both your DDoS defense vendor and organizations such as the CERT Coordination Center.

  The CERT Coordination Center has an open-source, space-efficient flow logger named *SiLK* [CER04]. The *SiLK* netflow tools [GCD$^+$04] contain both a collection system and an analysis system and were developed to provide analysis tools for very large installations, such as large corporations, government organizations, and backbone network service providers. For example, the *SiLK* toolset is designed to process approximately 80 million records in less than two minutes on a Sun Microsystems 4800. One of its applications is described in Section 7.13, and the tools are available from `http://silktools.sourceforge.net/`.

- **Traffic blocking/null routing.** During times of attack, your network infrastructure may be so overwhelmed that it falls on its face. Your provider, or other networks upstream of them, will be in a better position to filter out traffic, because they are better equipped to do so, and each router in their network will see a smaller percentage of traffic than you will at the aggregation point of all DDoS flows.

- **Support for an out-of-band management network.** When your primary (or secondary, etc.) network interfaces are flooded with traffic, you may lose all ability to communicate with your network devices from the broader Internet, which means you will be able to control them only through physical presence where your network equipment is located. If your provider is able to establish an out-of-band control mechanism, be it a network connection through one of their other peering points or even a DSL or ISDN line to a terminal server within your network perimeter, you can regain remote access and may be able to route critical traffic, such as e-mail, even if your main network paths are being attacked. Again, in cases beyond DDoS attacks that require severing your main Internet connection, this could be the only way to retain remote access to your network.

- **Assistance in coordinating with their peers.** Cases of DDoS that involve source address forgery and reflection of traffic off widely distributed servers (e.g, DNS reflection, SYN-ACK reflection off routers and firewalls) may require manual traceback through many networks to determine the source. The Register.com attack mentioned in Chapter 3 is one example where a reflection attack lasted over a week and came from just a small number of hosts. Getting cooperation of the peers of your upstream provider may be very difficult, and having your upstream provider commit to working with you, even if the problem is difficult, is the first step.

It is not clear how quickly such contracts will gain acceptance, and the above items will certainly be negotiation points that may not end up in final contracts. What is clear, though, is that to date these kinds of terms have not been in contracts for several reasons: (1) An ISP's stating commitments creates a duty of performance; (2) guarantees of levels of service have a cost that is hard to calculate up front (but can mitigate losses when a crisis hits); and (3) many network providers, and many DDoS victims for that matter, have been able to ignore the issues of DDoS attacks because they have not experienced massive attacks in the past and have had no need to go through the incident response steps outlined in this chapter (but will eventually be forced to in a time of crisis). As the problem of DDoS gets more costly and damaging, which it is likely to do given the trends seen to date, these kinds of contracts will become more and more standard.

6.7 Analyzing DDoS tools

This section deals with the analysis of hosts that are suspected of being involved in a DDoS attack, including identification and analysis of malware artifacts associated with these DDoS attacks. We will start by looking at some past DDoS tool analyses that have been made public, and then move on to guiding someone in performing a similar analysis on his own. In general, one should follow the same kind of *who, where, what, when, why,* and *how* that a reporter would. Some of the goals are to explain, in sufficient detail for someone to act on this information, how the DDoS network looks and behaves, how it was set up, how an attacker uses it, and how to detect its constituent parts and tear it down.

Take a moment to study Figure 6.4. It diagrams the flow of command and control traffic, as well as DDoS attack traffic. Malware artifacts associated with the DDoS attack network are at sites A, B, C, and D, among other places.

During the attack, the victim site can detect only a huge flood of traffic or disruption in their servers' activities. The victim site can capture and analyze the attack traffic but

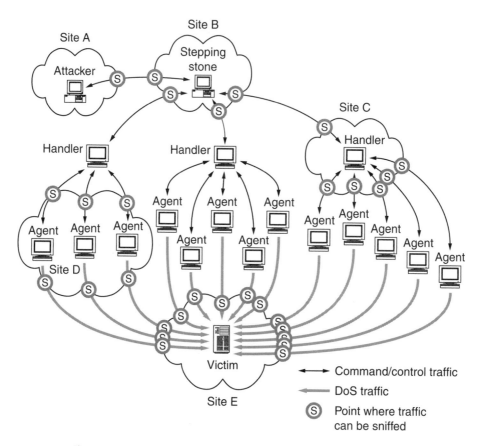

Figure 6.4   Illustration of all DDoS network traffic across all involved sites

has no access to the control traffic exchanged by DDoS network members. Further, the attack traffic cannot be captured in full (the monitoring system's hard drives would fill in minutes, if not seconds, at greater than gigabit per second speeds) but must be carefully sampled in short intervals. The compelling reason for capturing attack traffic is to understand and characterize the attack and devise appropriate selective responses. Another reason is to preserve some evidence of the attack for possible law enforcement activity. Analysis of traffic logs can prove bandwidth consumption rates, identify some of the attacking agents to do traceback, and can help verify that the attack tools the FBI may find on a suspect's system actually match the traffic that was seen coming into the victim's site. It will also help your own network engineers and incident response team or outside consultants in understanding what is going on and getting you back online quickly at a reasonable cost. There is nothing worse than paying a consultant hundreds of dollars an hour to try to guess what was happening on the network during the attack, which has stopped *two hours before he arrived* at your site, especially if the attack starts up again two hours, two days, or two weeks after he leaves.

Networks that host DDoS agents or handlers are in a much better position to gather evidence and identify the path leading to the attacker, since they can capture control traffic and malware artifacts.

6.7.1 Historical DDoS Analyses

The first public analyses of DDoS tools were performed by David Dittrich in 1999 and early 2000. Dittrich later collaborated with others, including Sven Dietrich, and Neil Long. While admittedly very technical, these analyses provide examples of all of the concepts that will be discussed below, along with references to the tools used and other related information. Anyone wanting to prepare to respond to the use of DDoS attack tools, whether at a victim site or a site hosting a DDoS handler or agent, should refer to documents on forensics, malware analysis, incident response, "Active Defense" and cyberwarfare, etc., found on Dave Dittrich's Web site [Ditd], in addition to the books referenced in Section 6.1.

The motivation for analyzing these tools was to (1) provide detailed information for peers in the incident response community that would allow detection, identification, and mitigation to occur faster; (2) facilitate law enforcement and military efforts to investigate attacks using these tools, should they be directed against critical infrastructure hosts or networks; and (3) try to anticipate what would come next and make recommendations that would prevent more severe attacks in the future. While some of these goals were accomplished, the fact that DDoS is still a growing problem five years after its appearance on the scene, with many victims just learning about it for the first time, means that this success is by no means complete.

A by-product of these analyses was the development of IDS signatures and host- and network-oriented scanners. The prototypes included in the analyses of *trinoo* [Ditf], *TFN* [Dith], *Stacheldraht* [Ditg] and *Shaft* [DLD00] were rewritten in C by Dave Dittrich, with assistance from Marcus Ranum, David Brumley, and others, and new features such as scanning by CIDR block were added. Another network-based scanner was David Brumley's *RID*.[8] Those scanners send packets to potential remote DDoS

---

[8] RID is no longer maintained but is available from Packetstorm Security at
`http://packetstormsecurity.nl/distributed/rid-1_0.tgz`.

agents or handlers and exploit vulnerabilities in DDoS tools to make them signal, "Hi, I'm here!," thus identifying compromised machines. Mark "Simple Nomad" Loveless also developed a tool called *Zombie Zapper*,[9] which not only allows detection, but also issues commands to shut down agent machines. Of course, some of the DDoS tools used passwords, and all of them could be reprogrammed to use another port, making it more difficult to find and control them.

Another way of detecting DDoS tools is to scan the file system from *within* the hosts themselves. In 2000, Mitre was contracted by the National Infrastructure Protection Center (NIPC) to write a signature-based detection tool for scanning file systems for several known DDoS tools (samples of which were provided by DDoS researchers and incident response teams). This tool, called *find_ddos* [NIP01], worked very well for identifying several DDoS handlers and agents, even if the original source code was modified prior to compiling. It must be run locally on a suspected compromised host using the system administrator account, and it is susceptible to being fooled by kernel level rootkits, which prevent it from seeing the malware in the first place. This may require that someone physically visit each potentially compromised host and boot first from trusted media to get a good scan. Using external network traffic analysis techniques, as described in this chapter, would help confirm beforehand if the host needed to be scanned or not. Network failures, reports from a victim of a DDoS attack that has identified the host, etc., can also trigger a more manually intensive internal file system scan.

6.7.2   Full Disclosure versus Nondisclosure

Before getting into details of analyzing a DDoS attack, let us digress into a brief discussion of the major points surrounding the disclosure and open discussion of computer security issues, including vulnerabilities, attack tools, and techniques. The debate involves two main positions surrounding computer security information: *full disclosure* (pro) versus *nondisclosure* (con). Without making any judgments, here are some of the main pros and cons regarding disclosure.

- **Con: You do not want to tip off the attackers.**

   By not disclosing *anything* publicly, the attackers who are using a program have no idea that anyone knows of their tools, where and how they are using them, and whether an investigation may be under way.

---

[9] Zombie Zapper is available from BINDView's Web site at http://www.bindview.com/Support/RAZOR /Utilities/Unix_Linux/ZombieZapper_form.cfm.

This assumes that the attackers are monitoring whatever channels you report to, and that they can correlate the information you provide with their own tools and activities. It is not clear when this assumption is valid or invalid.

Regardless, there is still some necessity to use discretion in what gets published, when, and where. In some circumstances, where a new attack tool is seeing use in the underground, and no known defenses exist, notification of the CERT Coordination Center, and perhaps the FBI, is warranted to provide some lead time to law enforcement investigators and incident response organizations.

- **Pro: Without knowledge of how DDoS tools work, how can you protect yourself or your network?**

    System administrators need to know how DDoS tools work, and how they appear and behave on their networks and computer systems, in order to find them and remove them. Without this knowledge, they are helpless to stop DDoS attacks or assist law enforcement.

    Vendors of computer security products and services often provide just enough information to scare potential customers into buying their products, but not enough for anyone to take self-help actions. Some of the harshest criticism of partial disclosure comes from *other vendors* or those in the Open Source community, who may be excluded from the details that would allow them to produce response tools. There is a market advantage to control of information, and that market advantage can cloud the issues and create tremendous controversy.

    Some individuals believe that the problem will not, and perhaps *cannot,* be solved by a small handful of vendors (even if they own the majority of the computer security market) because their products are not pervasive enough to provide a complete solution. Those who cannot afford the commercial products, or sites that cannot use these commercial products (like universities and ISPs), are left in a position of knowing there is a problem, but not knowing how to respond to it. These parties believe that the more widely the techniques and skills of DDoS defense are spread, the faster the overall response will be in mitigating emerging DDoS attacks.

- **Con: You do not want to help the attackers learn how to use DDoS tools or learn to build better ones.**

    Sharing analyses of DDoS tools would enable novice attackers to learn where to find DDoS tools, understand how to use them, make them more effective and less buggy, and assist them in not getting caught.

This argument assumes that attackers do not already share information about how DDoS tools work, and that they are not capable of finding bugs and improving them on their own. It is probably true that the highest-skilled attackers have both information sharing and software engineering skills at their disposal, and it is probably also true that some unskilled attackers would not be able to learn how to use these tools if analyses were not public.

Counterarguments to this include mentioning all the thousands of "hacker" Web sites and chat channels where information is shared, as well as places where pirated software, credit cards, and shell accounts are traded, which allow even unskilled attackers to gain enough systems to perform DDoS attacks without understanding the technical details of what they are doing. Those putting forward this argument try to balance the availability of information in the attacker community (which cannot readily be assessed anyway, since some of it is truly in the underground) with the benefit to defenders having this same information for use in protecting their networks. This balance cannot be accurately measured.

- **Pro: Software vendors will never discover and patch the vulnerable software or improve software writing skills if security problems are not understood.**

  Vendors of commercial software products for desktop computers, and server software for Web sites, etc., are not perfect. They produce code that contains bugs. There is no way around this, and every software product has bugs (some of which cause security problems). Unless vendors know where these security flaws are and how they can be exploited, they cannot fix them.

  This is another claim that is hard to quantify. It is true that statistics show an increase in the number of vulnerabilities that are made public each year, and there are varying frequencies of patch and security advisory releases for various software and hardware products.

- **Con: Users do not pay attention to details of attacker tools, so they do not take appropriate actions to secure their systems.**

  Very few users of computer programs take the time to study hacker tools and read hacker Web sites as a way to make purchasing decisions, or to learn how to properly configure their computers. Security researchers, who produce detailed analyses of things like DDoS tools, are not helping the average user in a meaningful way.

  The sheer number of hosts compromised (to this day!) by worms like *Nimda, Code Red, Slammer, W32/Blaster,* and *Nachi*; and hosts infected by viruses like *W32/Sobig, MyDoom,* and others that *require the user to click on attachments* show that there is a large and growing population of users who do not have sufficient skills to protect or clean up their own computers.

Of course, detailed technical analyses of DDoS tools will not help this audience, and in fact this is very rarely the audience targeted by these analyses. The goal here is getting the technical information to the technical people, and then having organizational administrators and public policy makers understand the threat and develop policies that address the problems before they become critical.

This is a classic problem in diffusion of information and organizational behavior that will probably be around as long as humans survive as a species (providing these problems do not hasten the end by themselves.) How exactly does knowledge about security flaws get from the researchers who document the vulnerabilities to executives who make business decisions about how products are manufactured, to engineers who design these products, and finally to those who purchase and use them? In this case, the researchers are documenting the vulnerabilities being exploited by attackers (e.g., the problems of TCP/IP that allow denial of service). Consumers will continue to purchase products that have these vulnerabilities. They do not know any better to demand that vendors produce products that do not have these vulnerabilities, which means engineers will not design them differently. But at the same time, CEOs will not read the analyses produced by computer security researchers, so they will not be making decisions about hiring, training, or resource allocation toward better engineering and testing to minimize the problems.

But a question still remains. Will *not discussing* these issues change the situation any faster?

- **Pro: Vendors and engineers of commercial products cannot design more robust products if they do not understand the failure modes.**

  Engineers themselves cannot design more secure products if they do not understand the vulnerabilities that exist in today's products. This may be one of the biggest benefits to sharing of technical information about DDoS, especially to router manufacturers, network engineers, software engineers, protocol writers, and application designers.

  The issue of robust software engineering may be the real key. Should consumers of software systems have to suffer for a sufficiently long and painful time with viruses, worms, computers that crash, or Web sites that cannot be reached, all in order to motivate them to change their own purchasing behavior? Do they have to be forced to change the way they configure and use their computers through legal liability, which may result from what some would argue is their own negligence?

Or do millions of consumers have to have their identities stolen and bank accounts emptied before they start to demand more secure software products?

As noted above, many of these individual pro and con points are hard to fully evaluate, so obviously the argument on both sides will continue.

6.7.3   How to Analyze Malware Artifacts

The term *malware artifact* means a program or file associated with malicious software. This includes compiled executable programs, the source code that produced them, scripts, log files, libraries, or any other file associated with an intrusion being used by the attacker. DDoS tools found on a compromised computer are one form of malware artifact, as are lists of handlers/agents and other files these DDoS tools rely on to function.

We will now take a look at the strategic and tactical issues you should consider when analyzing DDoS tools (or any malware artifacts, for that matter). To follow this material or perform the recommended analysis steps, you will need moderate Unix and Windows system administration experience and familiarity with TCP/IP networking concepts.

It is important to note that attack tools can be customized to run only on a particular host, using tools such as *Burneye* and *Shiva* [Meh03]. In essence the tools are quasi-licensed to that particular host (by "fingerprinting the host,") and will not run on any other host. This has some consequences for DDoS tool analysis and forensics, as it slows down the analysis process. On the positive side for defenders, these tools are not in widespread use, partly because of the same problems that plague all uses of cryptography. These are not trivial. The encryption of attack tools leads to a typical key management problem: If the attacker uses the same password for all his agents, then the compromise of one agent key will compromise the entire network, but if different passwords are used, then many such keys need to be remembered. At the time of writing this book, no large deployment of such *anti-analysis* and *anti-forensics* tools was publicly known. Progress has been made in breaking tools such as *Shiva* [Eag03]. The recent (2003) follow-on to *Burneye*, *objobf* [Tes], shows that attackers are well aware of code obfuscation techniques such as the ones outlined in [Wan00] and [Wro02].

The discussion below assumes that there is no anti-forensics technique being used, such as binary encryption, advanced rootkits and kernel level concealment, log alteration, etc. If such techniques are being used, this significantly increases the difficulty and skill level required of the analyst. Always remember: Just because something is not seen, that does not mean it is not there. David Dittrich has a FAQ file on

rootkits that can help you understand them, and some ways to get around them at
`http://staff.washington.edu/dittrich/misc/faqs/rootkits.faq`.

There are two things to consider at the start:

1. **Preserve evidence to avoid altering it.** Dominique Brezinski and Tom Killalea
   authored RFC3227, the *Guidelines for Evidence Collection and Archiving* [BK01]
   (also known as *Best Current Practice number 55*) to define the order and methods
   by which one should collect and preserve evidence. Other texts cover these issues
   as well, e.g., "Basic Steps in Forensic Analysis of Unix Systems" [Ditb, IAA, CIPS],
   and several examples of detailed analyses of a compromised honeypot [Spi02,
   Pro04] were performed as part of the Honeynet Project "Forensic Challenge" [Pro].

2. **Be very careful when analyzing malware.** You should *never run malware you find
   on a system* unless you are using a secure, isolated, and contained environment. You
   should either use a newly installed system that you plan to wipe and reinstall after
   analysis, or use a virtual machine environment that does not allow write operations
   to the guest operating system's file system. This way you do not run the risk of
   the malware getting loose (in the case of worms), or damaging your system if the
   attacker has booby-trapped it to do damage when run by someone other than the
   attacker. Having the host be isolated from your production network will prevent
   possible disruption from flooding, etc.

How Does the Malware Function?

In order to classify the malware, prioritize the response, and focus energies, it is helpful
to know its purpose and function. Is it a scanner? Is it a remote exploit? How about a
rootkit component or a log cleaner? If it is a DDoS tool, are you analyzing a handler, or
an agent? Does it include features of a blended threat, where it can do DDoS, scanning,
remote shell, self-upgrade, and serve you up the latest first-run movies in VCD (Video
Compact Disc) format on an IRC channel platter?

The Internal Signature of the Malware

How can someone identify this malware artifact? It may have several different signatures. Try to identify and provide examples of as many of them as possible. These
include:

File System Signature   What directory was the malware artifact found in? What
file name was used? When were the files created? What are the checksums or fingerprints
of all components? If it is still running, what open file handles does it hold?

On Unix, use *lsof* (LiSt Open Files), which shows open file handles, sockets, current working directory, program that is running, etc. A *Stacheldraht* agent, seen with *lsof,* would look like this:

```
# lsof -c ttymon
COMMAND PID  USER  FD   TYPE  DEVICE  SIZE     NODE   NAME
ttymon  437  root  cwd  DIR   3,1     1024     37208  /usr/lib/libx/...
ttymon  437  root  rtd  DIR   3,1     1024     2      /
ttymon  437  root  txt  REG   3,1     324436   37112  /usr/lib/libx/.../ttymon
ttymon  437  root  mem  REG   3,1     243964   29140  /lib/libnss_files-2.1.1.so
ttymon  437  root  mem  REG   3,1     4016683  29115  /lib/libc-2.1.1.so
ttymon  437  root  mem  REG   3,1     342206   28976  /lib/ld-2.1.1.so
ttymon  437  root  3u   sock  0,0              779    can't identify protocol
ttymon  449  root  cwd  DIR   3,1     1024     37208  /usr/lib/libx/...
ttymon  449  root  rtd  DIR   3,1     1024     2      /
ttymon  449  root  txt  REG   3,1     324436   37112  /usr/lib/libx/.../ttymon
ttymon  449  root  0u   inet  811              TCP    *:32222 (LISTEN)
ttymon  449  root  3u   sock  0,0              779    can't identify protocol
```

In this example, the name of the program is ttymon, although it may not show up that way in a process listing (programs can change their apparent name in Unix). One can identify the *current working directory* of the process (FD column, or *file descriptor*, with a value of cwd), which is /usr/lib/libx/.../. (Note the use of the directory name with three dots. This creates a hidden directory in Unix, which is a tactic intended to fool novice Unix administrators into not noticing the attacker's files.) There may be other files related to the malware stored in this same directory, including perhaps a list of agents, if this node is serving as a DDoS handler. The example also indicates that the process is listening on port 32222/tcp (line with TCP *:32222 (LISTEN)), and that it has a raw socket open for sniffing (the column with TYPE of sock and unidentifiable protocol). The program itself is identified as ttymon (FD value of txt).

A somewhat similar Windows program to *lsof* would be Foundstone's *FPort* program. A *Power* bot as seen with *FPort* would look like this:

```
FPort v1.33 - TCP/IP Process to Port Mapper Copyright 2000 by
Foundstone, Inc. http://www.foundstone.com


Pid  Process          Port  Proto Path
884  inetinfo   ->    21    TCP   C:\WINNT\System32\inetsrv\inetinfo.exe
884  inetinfo   ->    25    TCP   C:\WINNT\System32\inetsrv\inetinfo.exe
```

```
884    inetinfo   ->      80    TCP    C:\WINNT\System32\inetsrv\inetinfo.exe
1400   winnt      ->     100    TCP    C:\winnt.exe
444    svchost    ->     135    TCP    C:\WINNT\system32\svchost.exe
884    inetinfo   ->     443    TCP    C:\WINNT\System32\inetsrv\inetinfo.exe
8      System     ->     445    TCP
736    MSTask     ->    1044    TCP    C:\WINNT\system32\MSTask.exe
884    inetinfo   ->    1052    TCP    C:\WINNT\System32\inetsrv\inetinfo.exe
660    sqlservr   ->    1056    TCP    C:\MSSQL7\binn\sqlservr.exe
8      System     ->    1067    TCP
660    sqlservr   ->    1433    TCP    C:\MSSQL7\binn\sqlservr.exe
1400   winnt      ->    2350    TCP    C:\winnt.exe
1400   winnt      ->    2351    TCP    C:\winnt.exe
1400   winnt      ->    2352    TCP    C:\winnt.exe
1400   winnt      ->    2353    TCP    C:\winnt.exe
       [hundreds of lines removed . . .]
1400   winnt      ->    2646    TCP    C:\winnt.exe
1400   winnt      ->    2647    TCP    C:\winnt.exe
1400   winnt      ->    2648    TCP    C:\winnt.exe
772    termsrv    ->    3389    TCP    C:\WINNT\System32\termsrv.exe
884    inetinfo   ->    4700    TCP    C:\WINNT\System32\inetsrv\inetinfo.exe
1152   nt         ->    4836    TCP    C:\inetpub\scripts\nt.exe
1152   nt         ->   12624    TCP    C:\inetpub\scripts\nt.exe
444    svchost    ->     135    UDP    C:\WINNT\system32\svchost.exe
8      System     ->     445    UDP
260    lsass      ->    1027    UDP    C:\WINNT\system32\lsass.exe
220    winlogon   ->    1046    UDP    C:\WINNT\system32\winlogon.exe
248    services   ->    1051    UDP    C:\WINNT\system32\services.exe
884    inetinfo   ->    1064    UDP    C:\WINNT\System32\inetsrv\inetinfo.exe
564    llssrv     ->    1087    UDP    C:\WINNT\System32\llssrv.exe
464    spoolsv    ->    1217    UDP    C:\WINNT\system32\spoolsv.exe
884    inetinfo   ->    3456    UDP    C:\WINNT\System32\inetsrv\inetinfo.exe
1152   nt         ->   12623    UDP    C:\inetpub\scripts\nt.exe
```

The lines with the names winnt and nt in the Process column are associated with the bot's functions. To identify what files were created around the same time, one can use forensics tools that reveal file Modify, Access, and Change (MAC times) time stamp history. For Unix there are free forensics tools such as *The Coroner's Toolkit* (http://www.porcupine.org/forensics/) or *Sleuthkit* (http://www.sleuthkit.org /sleuthkit/docs/ref_timeline.html). *Sleuthkit* was written by Brian Carrier, originally as a research project that helped win him second place in the Honeynet Project

"Forensic Challenge" [Pro]. This toolkit will help you construct a time line of file system modifications, recover deleted files, and otherwise do static analysis of a copy of a compromised host's file system. To illustrate this, here is a time stamp listing from a host running the *mstream* [CER01b, DWDL] DDoS tool, generated by *Sleuthkit* (see instructions about creating file activity timelines with *Sleuthkit* at http://www.sleuthkit.org/sleuthkit/docs/ref_timeline.html):

```
Apr 13 2000 16:02:42  12060 .a. -rwxr-xr-x root/www root  /bin/chown
                      12660 m.. -r-sr-xr-x root/www bin   /bin/login
Apr 13 2000 16:02:43   2048 m.c drwxr-xr-x root/www root  /bin
                      12660 ..c -r-sr-xr-x root/www bin   /bin/login
                     168748 .a. -rwxr-xr-x root/www root  /usr/bin/as
                      64796 .a. -rwxr-xr-x root/www root  /usr/bin/egcs
                      64796 .a. -rwxr-xr-x root/www root  /usr/bin/gcc
                      64796 .a. -rwxr-xr-x root/www root  /usr/bin/i386-redhat-linux-gcc
                     168496 .a. -rwxr-xr-x root/www root  /usr/bin/ld
                      12656 m.c -rws--x--x root/www root  /usr/bin/old
                      12656 m.c -r-xr-xr-x root/www bin   /usr/bin/xstat
                       2315 .a. -rw-r--r-- root/www root  /usr/include/_G_config.h
                       1313 .a. -rw-r--r-- root/www root  /usr/include/alloca.h
  [ many lines deleted ]
                        178 .a. -rw-r--r-- root/www root  /usr/lib/libc.so
                      69638 .a. -rw-r--r-- root/www root  /usr/lib/libc_nonshared.a
                       6162 .a. -rw-r--r-- 1046     squid /usr/src/linux/include/asm-i386
/errno.h
                       1492 .a. -rw-r--r-- 1046     squid /usr/src/linux/include/asm-i386
/socket.h
                        277 .a. -rw-r--r-- 1046     squid /usr/src/linux/include/asm-i386
/sockios.h
                        305 .a. -rw-r--r-- 1046     squid /usr/src/linux/include/linux/errno.h
Apr 13 100 16:02:44     702 m.c -rwxr-xr-x root/www root  /etc/rc.d/rc.local
                       1024 m.c drwxr-xr-x root/www root  /root/.ncftp
                          9 m.c lrwxrwxrwx root/www root  /root/.ncftp/history
                          9 m.c lrwxrwxrwx root/www root  /root/.ncftp/log
                          9 m.c lrwxrwxrwx root/www root  /root/.ncftp/trace
                      29696 m.c drwxr-xr-x root/www root  /usr/bin
                      17016 m.c -rwxr-xr-x root/www root  /usr/bin/rpc.wall
                       8460 .a. -rw-r--r-- root/www root  /usr/lib/crt1.o
                       1124 .a. -rw-r--r-- root/www root  /usr/lib/crti.o
                       1892 .a. -rw-r--r-- root/www root  /usr/lib/gcc-lib/i386-redhat-linux
```

```
/egcs-2.91.66/crtbegin.o
  [ many lines deleted ]
Apr 15 2000 05:55:09   1024 m.c drwxr-xr-x root/www root  /var/named
                       1024 m.c drwxr-xr-x root/www root  /var/named/ADMROCKS
Apr 15 2000 05:56:19  20437 .a. -rwxr-xr-x root/www root  /usr/sbin/tcpd
Apr 15 2000 05:56:20     34 .a. -rw-r--r-- root/www root  /usr/libexec/awk/addy.awk
                      35628 .a. -rwxr-xr-x root/www root  /usr/sbin/in.telnetd
Apr 15 2000 05:56:26 159576 .a. -rwxr-xr-x root/www root  /usr/bin/pico
                        975 .a. -rw-r--r-- root/www root  /usr/share/terminfo/v/vt200
                        975 .a. -rw-r--r-- root/www root  /usr/share/terminfo/v/vt220
```

From this listing, the following observations can be made:

- On April 13 at 16:02, /bin/chown was run (note .a. for access time stamp.)

```
Apr 13 2000 16:02:42  12060 .a. -rwxr-xr-x root/www root    /bin/chown
```

- At the same time, /bin/login was modified (note m.. for modify time stamp).

```
12660 m.. -r-sr-xr-x root/www bin    /bin/login
```

- Also at the same time, the compiler egcs and gcc was run and /bin/old and /bin/xstat were created.

```
168748 .a. -rwxr-xr-x root/www root  /usr/bin/as
 64796 .a. -rwxr-xr-x root/www root  /usr/bin/egcs
 64796 .a. -rwxr-xr-x root/www root  /usr/bin/gcc
 64796 .a. -rwxr-xr-x root/www root  /usr/bin/i386-redhat-linux-gcc
168496 .a. -rwxr-xr-x root/www root  /usr/bin/ld
 12656 m.c -rws--x--x root/www root  /usr/bin/old
 12656 m.c -r-xr-xr-x root/www bin   /usr/bin/xstat
```

- Simultaneous access to .h files in the system include directory /usr/src/linux /include/, indicates that the program being compiled uses network libraries.

```
6162 .a. -rw-r--r-- 1046   squid  /usr/src/linux/include/asm-i386/errno.h
1492 .a. -rw-r--r-- 1046   squid  /usr/src/linux/include/asm-i386/socket.h
 277 .a. -rw-r--r-- 1046   squid  /usr/src/linux/include/asm-i386/sockios.h
 305 .a. -rw-r--r-- 1046   squid  /usr/src/linux/include/linux/errno.h
```

- Next, the /etc/rc.d/rc.local file is replaced (note m.c for modify and i-node change time stamps).

```
Apr 13 100 16:02:44  702 m.c -rwxr-xr-x root/www root /etc/rc.d/rc.local
```

Further examination of this file (not shown in the example) revealed that the change was to include the line `/usr/bin/rpc.wall` at the end of the file, thus restarting the agent on each reboot.

- `ncftp` logging files were also replaced. Further analysis showed that they were deleted and turned into links to `/dev/null` to disable logging of file transfers over the network using `ncftp` program.

```
1024 m.c drwxr-xr-x root/www root    /root/.ncftp
   9 m.c lrwxrwxrwx root/www root    /root/.ncftp/history
   9 m.c lrwxrwxrwx root/www root    /root/.ncftp/log
   9 m.c lrwxrwxrwx root/www root    /root/.ncftp/trace
```

- The program `/usr/bin/rpc.wall` was modified, and C runtime libraries were loaded.

```
8460 .a. -rw-r--r-- root/www root    /usr/lib/crt1.o
1124 .a. -rw-r--r-- root/www root    /usr/lib/crti.o
1892 .a. -rw-r--r-- root/www root    /usr/lib/gcc-lib/i386-redhat-linux
/egcs-2.91.66/crtbegin.o
```

If anti-forensic techniques such as sophisticated rootkits or kernel changes are being employed, some of this file system information would not be available and it would not be as easy to infer what exactly occurred and in what order. The same holds for the situation in which the system is not examined right away, but instead used for a long time, thus overwriting file access information.

Surface Analysis   Surface analysis of malware artifacts attempts to understand the purpose and behavior of the program by examining the files installed on the system by an attacker.

For example, strings embedded in the malware artifact or file types containing malware code (e.g., shell scripts, executable objects, libraries, as reported by programs such as *file* on Unix) contain useful information. Knowing the file type helps narrow the search while investigating files on the system. Scripts are easy to read, and may reveal how a toolkit works, how it was installed, and how it is hidden. Keep in mind that simply looking at executable files with a pager or editor is not a very good idea, as it can affect your terminal screen.

Also keep in mind that surface analysis alone is very unreliable. It can be easily defeated using simple techniques, and sometimes strings are embedded to trick the

unwary analyst into thinking a program is something other than what it really is, or to
waste the analyst's time going down a blind alley.

For example, running a *file* for a malware artifact associated with the *ramen* worm
produces the following report:

```
1:          ASCII text
2:          ELF 32-bit LSB executable, Intel 80386, version 1,
            dynamically linked (uses shared libs), not stripped
asp:        ASCII text
asp62:      ELF 32-bit LSB executable, Intel 80386, version 1,
            dynamically linked (uses shared libs), not stripped
asp7:       ELF 32-bit LSB executable, Intel 80386, version 1,
            dynamically linked (uses shared libs), not stripped
bd62.sh:    Bourne shell script text
bd7.sh:     Bourne shell script text
getip.sh:   Bourne shell script text
hackl.sh:   Bourne shell script text
hackw.sh:   Bourne shell script text
l62:        ELF 32-bit LSB executable, Intel 80386, version 1,
            dynamically linked (uses shared libs), not stripped
l7:         ELF 32-bit LSB executable, Intel 80386, version 1,
            dynamically linked (uses shared libs), not stripped
lh.sh:      Bourne shell script text
login:      ELF 32-bit LSB executable, Intel 80386, version 1,
            dynamically linked (uses shared libs), not stripped
net.tgz:    gzip compressed data, deflated,
            last modified: Thu Jan 25 00:39:04 2001, os: Unix
ps.tgz:     gzip compressed data, deflated,
            last modified:Tue Jan 23 23:37:26 2001, os: Unix
ramen.tgz:  gzip compressed data, deflated,
            last modified: Thu Jan 25 13:37:47 2001, os: Unix
randb62:    ELF 32-bit LSB executable, Intel 80386, version 1,
            dynamically linked (uses shared libs), not stripped
randb7:     ELF 32-bit LSB executable, Intel 80386, version 1,
            dynamically linked (uses shared libs), not stripped
s62:        ELF 32-bit LSB executable, Intel 80386, version 1,
            dynamically linked (uses shared libs), not stripped
s7:         ELF 32-bit LSB executable, Intel 80386, version 1,
            dynamically linked (uses shared libs), not stripped
scan.sh:    Bourne shell script text
```

```
start.sh:        Bourne shell script text
start62.sh:      Bourne shell script text
start7.sh:       Bourne shell script text
synscan62:       ELF 32-bit LSB executable, Intel 80386, version 1,
                 dynamically linked (uses shared libs), stripped
synscan7:        ELF 32-bit LSB executable, Intel 80386, version 1,
                 dynamically linked (uses shared libs), stripped
td:              ELF 32-bit LSB executable, Intel 80386, version 1,
                 dynamically linked (uses shared libs), stripped
update.c:        ASCII text
w62:             ELF 32-bit LSB executable, Intel 80386, version 1,
                 dynamically linked (uses shared libs), not stripped
w7:              ELF 32-bit LSB executable, Intel 80386, version 1,
                 dynamically linked (uses shared libs), not stripped
wh.sh:           Bourne shell script text
```

The above output indicates that there are several Bourne shell scripts that make up the core of the worm (e.g., scan.sh, start.sh, start62.sh, and start7.sh) as well as a number of precompiled programs (the items identified as ELF 32-bit LSB executable, Intel 80386, version 1, dynamically linked (uses shared libs), stripped). Further examination of the executable files shows that they perform the scanning, the exploitation of remote vulnerabilities to spread the worm. Closer analysis of this worm kit revealed that the file td was a *Stacheldraht* agent!

Network State Signature   What network connections does the malware create?

Noticing network connections will give you information about the "last hop" stepping stone from which the attacker broke into your machine, or if your machine *is* the stepping stone, it will also tell you where the attacker bounced to. Sockets in the ESTABLISHED state are active. The LISTEN state means that a server process (or peer-to-peer application) is waiting for new connections to be initiated.

On Unix, you can use either *netstat* (which will list all network sockets) or *lsof*. Here is what the output of *netstat* on a Linux system shows you on a sample agent machine:

```
# netstat -an --inet
Active Internet connections (servers and established)
Proto Recv-Q Send-Q Local Address    Foreign Address        State
tcp    0      0     0.0.0.0:12345      0.0.0.0:*             LISTEN
tcp    0      0     10.10.10.3:2222    10.10.10.10:32965     ESTABLISHED
```

```
tcp      0        0    10.10.10.3:2222    0.0.0.0:*         LISTEN
tcp      0        0    10.10.10.3:22      10.10.10.2:33354  ESTABLISHED
tcp      0        0    0.0.0.0:22         0.0.0.0:*         LISTEN
raw      0        0    0.0.0.0:1          0.0.0.0:*         7
raw      0        0    0.0.0.0:6          0.0.0.0:*         7
```

In this case, one can tell by the lines showing `Proto` values of `raw` that some process has opened a raw socket. This by itself is suspicious as raw sockets bypass operating system handling of network communication and are frequently misused to send spoofed packets. There is also a process listening on port 12345/tcp (`Proto` equal to `tcp` and `Local Address` equal to `0.0.0.0:12345`), and two established connections to ports 22/tcp and 2222/tcp. (`Foreign Address` of `10.10.10.10:32965` and `10.10.10.2:33354`.) Further examination of suspicious processes on a given machine has indicated that there is an exploited *SSH* daemon, detailed in [Dit01]. The listening port on 12345/tcp resulted from the buffer overflow exploit on the vulnerable server.

Another suspicious sign is the program placing a network interface in promiscuous mode. Promiscuous mode allows a program to see all packets on the LAN segment, not just those that are supposed to be for the Network Interface Card (or NIC) of this particular computer, and is used for sniffing other users' communications. One can use the *ifconfig* command on Unix to see if the NIC is in promiscuous mode. (Be aware that rootkits that replace the *ifconfig* command, or replace kernel-level process calls, will "lie" to you about the promiscuous mode flag in the NIC's driver. You may still see system log messages showing the NIC entering/exiting promiscuous mode, or you may have to use other means to get around the rootkit.)

Process State Signature What processes are created by the malware, and how do they show up in process listings? Sometimes blended threats will include several programs that all run in the background: a backdoor shell, a file transfer server, an IRC bot, an IRC bouncer, a sniffer, and perhaps a DDoS agent. The parent–child relationships between these processes can tell you something about how they were started on the system (perhaps from a buffer overflow in a Web server, which might make them all share a common *httpd* parent process).

On Unix, you can use the *ps* (simple process listing), *pstree* (a tree version, showing parent–child–grandchild relationships between processes), and/or the *top* command (show processes continually, with those using the most resources at the top of the list).

System Log Signature   What was logged by the system? On Unix, start with the *syslog* daemon and look at the files it keeps. This may (if the attacker has not wiped or deleted the log files) show some signs of his entry and activity. To illustrate this, here is a sample log file excerpt:

```
XXX 11 15:26:11 XXXX in.fingerd[864]: connect from XXX-XXX-14.XXXXXXXXX.XXX
XXX 11 15:26:11 XXXX in.telnetd[865]: connect from XXX-XXX-14.XXXXXXXXX.XXX
XXX 11 15:26:11 XXXX telnetd[865]: ttloop: peer died: Try again
XXX 11 15:26:12 XXXX in.pop3d[866]: connect from XXX-XXX-14.XXXXXXXXX.XXX
XXX 11 15:26:13 XXXX in.telnetd[867]: connect from XXX-XXX-14.XXXXXXXXX.XXX
      .
      .
      .
XXX 12 05:36:20 XXXX in.telnetd[1126]: connect from DDDDDD.XXXXXX.XXX
      .
      .
      .
XXX 12 11:01:52 XXXX in.telnetd[1213]: connect from EEEEEEE.XXX.XXX
XXX 12 11:02:21 XXXX su: XXXXX on /dev/ttyp1
      .
      .
      .
XXX 12 11:04:28 XXXX in.rlogind[1229]: connect from CCCCCCCC.XXXXXXXX.XXX
XXX 12 11:04:44 XXXX in.rlogind[1230]: connect from CCCCCCCC.XXXXXXXX.XXX
      .
      .
      .
XXX 12 11:08:57 XXXX su: XXXXX on /dev/ttyp1
XXX 12 11:11:19 XXXX su: XXXXX on /dev/ttyp1
      .
      .
      .
XXX 12 11:33:05 XXXX in.telnetd[1290]: connect from AAAAAA.XXXXXX.XXX
XXX 12 11:33:16 XXXX login: 1 LOGIN FAILURE FROM AAAAAA.XXXXXX.XXX, XXX
XXX 12 11:33:21 XXXX login: 2 LOGIN FAILURES FROM AAAAAA.XXXXXX.XXX, XXX
      .
      .
      .
XXX 12 11:34:02 XXXX su: XXXXX on /dev/ttyp1
XXX 12 11:41:52 XXXX wu.ftpd[1327]: connect from BBBBBBB.XXXXXX.XXX
XXX 12 11:41:57 XXXX ftpd[1327]: USER XXXXX
XXX 12 11:41:59 XXXX ftpd[1327]: PASS password
XXX 12 11:42:00 XXXX ftpd[1327]: SYST
XXX 12 11:42:01 XXXX ftpd[1327]: CWD /tmp
XXX 12 11:42:06 XXXX ftpd[1327]: TYPE Image
XXX 12 11:42:06 XXXX ftpd[1327]: PORT
XXX 12 11:42:06 XXXX ftpd[1327]: STOR mountd
```

```
XXX 12 11:42:08 XXXX ftpd[1327]: QUIT
XXX 12 11:42:08 XXXX ftpd[1327]: FTP session closed
XXX 12 12:00:25 XXXX in.telnetd[1342]: connect from AAAAAA.XXXXXX.XXX
```

The entries from 15:26:11 to 15:26:13 show what appears to be a port scan. The lines with `in.telnetd[1213]` and `in.telnetd[1290]` show connections using *telnet,* followed by successful use of `su` to elevate privileges. The lines following the `wu.ftpd[1327]` *FTP* daemon connection show a login, and transfer of a file `mountd` (the attacker's mount daemon exploit program) to the `/tmp` directory. This leads you to both the last hop point of entry information for the attacker, which can be correlated with other logs to find other systems the attacker may control, as well as a directory in which to start looking for evidence.

An attacker's access attempts may also be logged in the application level logs, like *Apache's* `access_log` and `referrer_log` files, Microsoft's Internet Information Server (IIS), or the standard Windows Event Logs. Here is an example of a buffer overflow exploit attempt found in an *Apache* log file contained on a Unix system:

```
==> /var/log/apache/access_log <==
[deleted host ip] - - [07/Aug/2001:17:19:35 -0400] "GET
/scripts/..%c1%9c../winnt/system32/cmd.exe?/c+ping.exe+"-v"+igmp+
"-t"+"-l"+65000+[deleted target ip]+"-n"+7000+"-w"+0" 404 -
```

This shows the attempted exploitation of the Unicode directory traversal vulnerability in Windows IIS to run the `ping.exe` program to attack some site with a distributed ICMP Echo Request flood. It did not work in this case (note the 404 HTTP failure error code) because Unix does not have a file called `/winnt/system32/cmd.exe` (or `ping.exe` for that matter), but the attacker blindly tried anyway.

The External Signature of the Malware

What TCP and UDP ports show up when scanned from the outside? Often, malware will include a backdoor, IRC bot, or other code, which will be listening on a TCP or UDP port. Performing a half-open scan (only sending SYN packets and seeing the response) is one way of detecting them.

You can use *nmap, Nessus,* or other port scanners to perform half-open scans from outside your network. Compare the information gathered this way with the information gathered from internal examination with programs like *lsof* on Unix, or *FPort* on

Windows. Here is what a Windows host running the *Power* bot blended threat looks like when scanned with *nmap*:

```
Starting nmap V. 2.53 by fyodor@insecure.org (www.insecure.org/nmap/)
Interesting ports on XXXXXXXXXXXX (192.168.1.225):
(The 65522 ports scanned but not shown below are in state: closed)
Port        State      Service
21/tcp      open       ftp
23/tcp      open       telnet
25/tcp      open       smtp
80/tcp      open       http
100/tcp     open       newacct
135/tcp     open       loc-srv
139/tcp     open       netbios-ssn
443/tcp     open       https
445/tcp     open       microsoft-ds
1025/tcp    open       listen
1026/tcp    open       nterm
4836/tcp    open       unknown
12624/tcp   open       unknown


TCP Sequence Prediction: Class=random positive increments
                         Difficulty=17052 (Worthy challenge)
Remote operating system guess: Windows 2000 RC1 through final
release
```

In this case, the last line shows there was a listening backdoor on port 12624/tcp, which gives the prompt "Password:" if you connect to it. Note here that one should be *very careful* about just randomly connecting to listening ports on an infected host! You have no idea how the program works, what it might do if you connect to it, whether it reports connections to the attacker, and so on. It is best to try to get copies of the program and analyze them on a safe, isolated, throw-away system, or to passively capture network traffic first and analyze it to determine how the program may function from what it exposes to you on the network.

This is where the anti-analysis features mentioned earlier come into play. The malware may be programmed to prevent you from tracing it, or dumping its memory. It may employ per-block in-memory decryption, so even if you can dump memory, it will be hard to determine any strings, passwords, or embedded IP addresses or domain names. If the malware also encrypts traffic on the network, it becomes extremely difficult to do runtime, or dynamic, analysis. If you run across anything that goes beyond your abilities to analyze, ask around for help (start with organizations like the CERT Coordination Center). If you determine that you do have a very advanced tool on your hands, make sure you also report this immediately to your local FBI or Secret Service office, and do your best to preserve as much evidence as you can about the intrusion [BK01].

Some programs do not have listening ports, instead watching for special packets using embedded commands in ICMP Echo Reply, UDP, or crafted TCP packets that are not part of any established connections. These are a form of *covert channels* when they are used for command and control. If they eventually open up a port for the attacker to connect to, they are called a *closed port backdoor*.

The Department of Defense defines covert channel to be *any communication channel that can be exploited by a process to transfer information in a manner that violates the systems security policy.* In the context of DDoS, this means using some protocol in a way that was not intended, for the purpose of command and control of DDoS handlers or agents. For example, *Stacheldraht* used ICMP Echo Reply packets sent between handler and agents to communicate that the agent was still alive. You can see the words "skillz" and "ficken" in these packets (which somewhat defeats the covertness of the communication, but using ICMP packets nonetheless is not something that a network operator or system owner would typically ever see if they were not looking for it). Following is the illustration of some ICMP packet contents captured as part of a *Stacheldraht* agent's covert command and control channel:

```
ICMP message id: 10.0.0.1 > 192.168.0.1 ICMP type: Echo reply
45 E 00 . 04 . 14 . 01 . 0F . 00 . 00 . 40 @ 01 . E9 . 53 S 0A . 00 . 00 . 01 .
C0 . A6 . 00 . 01 . 00 . 00 . B4 . 13 . 02 . 9A . 00 . 00 . 00 . 00 . 00 . 00 .
00 . 00 . 00 . 00 . 00 . 00 . 00 . 00 . 00 . 00 . 00 . 00 . 00 . 00 . 00 . 00 .
73 s 6B k 69 i 6C l 6C l 7A z 00 . 00 . 00 . 00 . 00 . 00 . 00 . 00 . 00 . 00 .
00 . 00 . 00 . 00 . 00 . 00 . 00 . 00 . 00 . 00 . 00 . 00 . 00 . 00 . 00 . 00 .
 .
 .  [60 lines of zeros deleted]
 .
00 . 00 . 00 . 00 .

ICMP message id: 192.168.0.1 > 10.0.0.1 ICMP type: Echo reply
45 E 00 . 04 . 14 . 04 . F8 . 00 . 00 . 40 @ 01 . E5 . 6A j C0 . A6 . 00 . 01 .
0A . 00 . 00 . 01 . 00 . 00 . CE . 21 ! 02 . 9B . 00 . 00 . 00 . 00 . 00 . 00 .
00 . 00 . 00 . 00 . 00 . 00 . 00 . 00 . 00 . 00 . 00 . 00 . 00 . 00 . 00 . 00 .
```

```
66 f 69 i 63 c 6B k 65 e 6E n 00 . 00 . 00 . 00 . 00 . 00 . 00 . 00 . 00 . 00 .
00 . 00 . 00 . 00 . 00 . 00 . 00 . 00 . 00 . 00 . 00 . 00 . 00 . 00 . 00 . 00 .
.
.  [60 lines of zeros deleted]
.
00 . 00 . 00 . 00 .
```

A closed port backdoor might accept special UDP or ICMP packets, which tell it to "open up a listening TCP socket on 12345/tcp and bind a shell to it." The attacker then has a small window of time (perhaps just seconds) to connect to the server port; otherwise, it closes again and goes back to waiting for another covert command. This makes it much harder to detect the backdoor from the network, but still allows the attacker full access whenever it is needed.

The Network Traffic Signature of the Malware

Get full packet captures of network traffic to/from the infected host. In a case in which the attacker is using anti-forensic techniques that would prevent you from restarting the program yourself in a closed environment, these traces must be gathered *while* the attacker is using the tool.

It is also best to collect the traffic as close to the suspect computer as possible (i.e., on the same LAN segment), or at least at the border of your network so you can capture all traffic in and out of the suspect computer. One factor that will complicate things is the use of fully switched networks, especially ones that are centrally managed and for which subnet owners are not provided with port mirroring (known on Cisco hardware as Switched Port Analyzer, or SPAN). Without this ability, the switch will provide only a subset of traffic that is associated with the IP addresses of devices on the same switch port, plus any broadcast Ethernet traffic. (Critical Networks maintains a Web page with information on sniffers and network taps that may be of use: http://www.criticalnets.com/resources/index.html).

Start by getting an overall view of the "scene of the crime" by gathering high-level statistics of network flows. One public domain program for Linux that works well is *tcpdstat* [Cho00]. A version modified by Dave Dittrich at the University of Washington [bDD02] ports the code to Linux and adds some new protocols and features (like peak bandwidth use). Here is a view of a traffic capture with [bDD02] to/from a suspected DDoS agent:

```
DumpFile:      suspect.dump
Id:            200203221735
StartTime:     Fri Mar 22 17:35:42 2002
```

```
EndTime:      Sat Mar 23 13:13:25 2002
TotalTime:    70663.53 seconds
TotalCapSize: 3414.13MB
CapLen:       1514 bytes
# of packets: 167707807 (15702.13MB)
AvgRate:      2.07Mbps      stddev: 2.89M      PeakRate: 12.16Mbps


### IP flow (unique src/dst pair) Information ###
# of flows: 91  (avg. 1842942.93 pkts/flow)
Top 10 big flow size (bytes/total in %):
 54.8%  9.1%  5.7%  5.2%  5.1%  5.1%  3.6%  3.5%  2.4%  2.2%


### IP address Information ###
# of IPv4 addresses: 68
Top 10 bandwidth usage (bytes/total in %):
 100.0% 54.8%  9.1%  5.8%  5.2%  5.2%  5.2%  3.6%  3.5%  2.5%
### Packet Size Distribution (including MAC headers) ###
<<<<
 [   32-   63]:     768292
 [   64-  127]:  165385712
 [  128-  255]:       3256
 [  256-  511]:        310
 [  512- 1023]:       3309
 [ 1024- 2047]:    1546928
>>>>


### Protocol Breakdown ###
<<<<
protocol      packets                bytes                bytes/pkt
-----------------------------------------------------------------------
[0] total     167707807 (100.00%)    16464877084 (100.00%)    98.18
[1] ip        167707807 (100.00%)    16464877084 (100.00%)    98.18
[2] tcp         2312006 (  1.38%)     2223505740 ( 13.50%)   961.72
[3] ftp              12 (  0.00%)             742 (  0.00%)    61.83
[3] http(s)           5 (  0.00%)             300 (  0.00%)    60.00
[3] http(c)           5 (  0.00%)             322 (  0.00%)    64.40
[3] sunrpc            4 (  0.00%)             268 (  0.00%)    67.00
[3] ident            40 (  0.00%)            2732 (  0.00%)    68.30
[3] socks            10 (  0.00%)             799 (  0.00%)    79.90
[3] squid             3 (  0.00%)             180 (  0.00%)    60.00
[3] icecast           2 (  0.00%)             120 (  0.00%)    60.00
```

```
[3] irc6667            6303 (  0.00%)            669118 (  0.00%)  106.16
[3] http-a                2 (  0.00%)               134 (  0.00%)   67.00
[3] other           2305620 (  1.37%)        2222831025 ( 13.50%)  964.09
[2] icmp             398486 (  0.24%)          27952528 (  0.17%)   70.15
[2] res_255       164997315 ( 98.38%)       14213418816 ( 86.33%)   86.14
>>>>
```

We can see from the StartTime: and EndTime: lines that the capture period was just under a day. The average traffic (AvgRate:) rate was 2.07 Mbps, with peaks (PeakRate:) going up to 12.16 Mbps. This one host *alone* could take out a 10-Mbps network! Looking further, we see that 98% of the traffic ([2] res_255) is not even a valid protocol! It is a reserved IP protocol value that is not supposed to be used. This would slip past some tools that expect only TCP, UDP, and ICMP, but provides nice ground for formulation of filtering rules. As attack traffic is using an invalid protocol number, filtering traffic based on this signature will inflict no collateral damage.

Another program that may work better (although it is slightly harder to read at first) is *Aguri* [CKK]. The following example includes real IP addresses, but they come from the author's own published paper.

```
%%!AGURI-1.0
%%StartTime: Thu Mar 01 00:00:00 2001 (2001/03/01 00:00:00)
%%EndTime: Sun Apr 01 00:00:00 2001 (2001/04/01 00:00:00)
%AvgRate: 14.91Mbps
[src address] 4992392109177 (100.00%)
0.0.0.0/0        87902964189 (1.76%/100.00%)
 0.0.0.0/1      206637364377 (4.14%/14.78%)
 0.0.0.0/2      205796877844 (4.12%/7.12%)
   60.0.0.0/6    97928228974 (1.96%/3.00%)
        62.52.0.0/16 51875058871 (1.04%/1.04%)
     64.0.0.0/8  100831910967 (2.02%/3.51%)
       64.0.0.0/9 74610984109 (1.49%/1.49%)
 128.0.0.0/2     142349668983 (2.85%/13.33%)
  128.0.0.0/3    197067746696 (3.95%/10.48%)
    128.0.0.0/5  202911635757 (4.06%/5.45%)
      133.0.0.0/8 69142535628 (1.38%/1.38%)
             150.65.136.91    54123094932 (1.08%)
   192.0.0.0/4   212653628837 (4.26%/38.41%)
     192.0.0.0/6 88855538654 (1.78%/1.78%)
       202.0.0.0/7 235853368912 (4.72%/14.70%)
```

```
  202.0.0.0/9          117196493427 (2.35%/6.77%)
            202.12.27.33     160473669718 (3.21%)
          202.30.143.128/25  60239291958 (1.21%/1.21%)
          203.178.143.127 94031811680 (1.88%)
   204.0.0.0/6  228960094456 (4.59%/17.68%)
   204.0.0.0/8 125458765333 (2.51%/7.58%)
          204.123.7.2       87103414877 (1.74%)
          204.152.184.75   165733431144 (3.32%)
   206.0.0.0/7 164036959478 (3.29%/5.51%)
    206.128.0.0/9        53526598302 (1.07%/1.07%)
   207.0.0.0/8 57628266965 (1.15%/1.15%)
  208.0.0.0/4   282590640975 (5.66%/31.72%)
   208.0.0.0/6  116047154301 (2.32%/22.20%)
   209.0.0.0/8 140888988219 (2.82%/11.78%)
          209.1.225.217    238192306019 (4.77%)
          209.1.225.218    209160635530 (4.19%)
   210.0.0.0/7 154008321340 (3.08%/3.08%)
    216.0.0.0/9          192899750315 (3.86%/3.86%)
%LRU hits: 86.82% (1021/1176)
```

A paper on *Aguri* [CKK] explains the summary output this way: "In the address profile, each row shows an address entry and is indented by the prefix length. The first column shows the address and the prefix length of the entries. The second column shows the cumulative byte counts. The third column shows the percentages of the entry and its subtrees."

This illustration shows that the "top talker" (by source address) is 209.1.225.217, with 4.77% of the total traffic. *Aguri* can read *tcpdump* files, so a packet capture taken using the *libpcap* format [10] should quickly confirm which specific host may be involved in a DoS attack. (For example, if this host were sourcing a significant portion of the 14.91- Mbps average, that would be suspicious and may warrant further investigation.)

It has also happened before that worms like *Slammer*, or DDoS tools like *mstream*, will cause router instability because the source addresses they forge are in multicast address space, or otherwise force the router CPU to process them as part of egress filtering, which effectively erases or disables router settings. The lesson here is to never

---

[10] *libpcap* is the library that *tcpdump* uses for saving files.

assume hardware will not fail or that a parameter that was set at one time is still set the same way at the present time.

Once you have isolated a suspect system, and you can filter out the attack traffic, start looking at other flows for command and control traffic. *Trinoo,* for example, was very obvious and chatty on the network. In the following code we show some *trinoo* communication captured with *ngrep* program.

You can see the commands the attacker types in the right column, including the password to connect to the handler (betaalmostdone), the password between the handler and agents (144adsl), the prompts from the handler (trinoo>), and the commands the attacker types in (for example, msize 32000, dos 216.160.XX.Y and quit.) The leftmost column indicates the protocol (T for TCP, and U for UDP). The TCP stream is the command shell to the handler, and the UDP stream is the command and control channel between the handler and the agent(s).

```
# ngrep -x ".*" tcp port 27665 or udp port 31335 or udp port
27444 interface: eth0 (192.168.0.200/255.255.255.0) filter: ip and
( tcp port 27665 or udp port 31335 or udp port 27444 ) match: .*

U 192.168.0.1:32892 -> 10.0.0.1:31335
  2a 48 45 4c 4c 4f 2a                            *HELLO*

T 192.168.100.1:1074 -> 10.0.0.1:27665 [AP]
  ff f4 ff fd 06                                  .....

T 192.168.100.1:1074 -> 10.0.0.1:27665 [AP]
  62 65 74 61 61 6c 6d 6f   73 74 64 6f 6e 65 0d 0a   betaalmostdone..

T 10.0.0.1:27665 -> 192.168.100.1:1074 [AP]
  74 72 69 6e 6f 6f 20 76   31 2e 30 37 64 32 2b 66   trinoo v1.07d2+f
  33 2b 63 2e 2e 5b 72 70   6d 38 64 2f 63 62 34 53   3+c..[rpm8d/cb4S
  78 2f 5d 0a 0a 0a                                x/]...

T 10.0.0.1:27665 -> 192.168.100.1:1074 [AP]
  74 72 69 6e 6f 6f 3e 20                          trinoo>

T 192.168.100.1:1074 -> 10.0.0.1:27665 [AP]
  62 63 61 73 74 0d 0a                             bcast..

T 10.0.0.1:27665 -> 192.168.100.1:1074 [AP]
```

```
   4c 69 73 74 69 6e 67 20    42 63 61 73 74 73 2e 0a    Listing Bcasts..
   0a                                                     .


T 10.0.0.1:27665 -> 192.168.100.1:1074 [AP]
   31 39 32 2e 31 36 38 2e    30 2e 31 2e 20 20 20 0a    192.168.0.1.
   0a 45 6e 64 2e 20 31 20    42 63 61 73 74 73 20 74    .End. 1 Bcasts t
   6f 74 61 6c 2e 0a 74 72    69 6e 6f 6f 3e 20          otal..trinoo>


T 192.168.100.1:1074 -> 10.0.0.1:27665 [AP]
   6d 74 69 6d 65 72 20 31    30 30 30 0d 0a             mtimer 1000..


T 10.0.0.1:27665 -> 192.168.100.1:1074 [AP]
   6d 74 69 6d 65 72 3a 20    53 65 74 74 69 6e 67 20    mtimer: Setting
   74 69 6d 65 72 20 6f 6e    20 62 63 61 73 74 20 74    timer on bcast t
   6f 20 31 30 30 30 2e 0a                               o 1000..


U 10.0.0.1:1025 -> 192.168.0.1:27444
   62 62 62 20 6c 34 34 61    64 73 6c 20 31 30 30 30    bbb l44adsl 1000


T 10.0.0.1:27665 -> 192.168.100.1:1074 [AP]
   6d 74 69 6d 65 72 3a 20    53 65 74 74 69 6e 67 20    mtimer: Setting
   74 69 6d 65 72 20 6f 6e    20 62 63 61 73 74 20 74    timer on bcast t
   6f 20 31 30 30 30 2e 0a                               o 1000..


T 10.0.0.1:27665 -> 192.168.100.1:1074 [AP]
   74 72 69 6e 6f 6f 3e 20                               trinoo>


T 192.168.100.1:1074 -> 10.0.0.1:27665 [AP]
   6d 73 69 7a 65 20 33 32    30 30 30 0d 0a             msize 32000..


U 10.0.0.1:1025 -> 192.168.0.1:27444
   72 73 7a 20 33 32 30 30    30                         rsz 32000


T 10.0.0.1:27665 -> 192.168.100.1:1074 [AP]
   74 72 69 6e 6f 6f 3e 20                               trinoo>


T 192.168.100.1:1074 -> 10.0.0.1:27665 [AP]
   64 6f 73 20 32 31 36 2e    31 36 30 2e 58 58 2e 59    dos 216.160.XX.Y
   59 0d 0a                                              Y..
```

```
T 10.0.0.1:27665 -> 192.168.100.1:1074 [AP]
    44 6f 53 3a 20 50 61 63      6b 65 74 69 6e 67 20 32    DoS: Packeting 2
    31 36 2e 31 36 30 2e 58      58 2e 59 59 2e 0a          16.160.XX.YY..

U 10.0.0.1:1025 -> 192.168.0.1:27444
    61 61 61 20 6c 34 34 61      64 73 6c 20 32 31 36 2e    aaa l44adsl 216.
    31 36 30 2e 58 58 2e 59      59                         160.XX.YY

T 10.0.0.1:27665 -> 192.168.100.1:1074 [AP]
    74 72 69 6e 6f 6f 3e 20                                 trinoo>

T 192.168.100.1:1074 -> 10.0.0.1:27665 [AP]
    71 75 69 74 0d 0a                                       quit..

T 10.0.0.1:27665 -> 192.168.100.1:1074 [AP]
    62 79 65 20 62 79 65 2e      0a                         bye bye..

T 192.168.100.1:1075 -> 10.0.0.1:27665 [AP]
    62 65 74 61 61 6c 6d 6f      73 74 64 6f 6e 65 0d 0a    betaalmostdone..

T 10.0.0.1:27665 -> 192.168.100.1:1075 [AP]
    74 72 69 6e 6f 6f 20 76      31 2e 30 37 64 32 2b 66    trinoo v1.07d2+f
    33 2b 63 2e 2e 5b 72 70      6d 38 64 2f 63 62 34 53    3+c..[rpm8d/cb4S
    78 2f 5d 0a 0a 0a                                       x/]...

T 10.0.0.1:27665 -> 192.168.100.1:1075 [AP]
    74 72 69 6e 6f 6f 3e 20                                 trinoo>

T 192.168.100.1:1075 -> 10.0.0.1:27665 [AP]
    6d 70 69 6e 67 0d 0a                                    mping..

T 10.0.0.1:27665 -> 192.168.100.1:1075 [AP]
    6d 70 69 6e 67 3a 20 53      65 6e 64 69 6e 67 20 61    mping: Sending a
    20 50 49 4e 47 20 74 6f      20 65 76 65 72 79 20 42     PING to every B
    63 61 73 74 73 2e 0a                                    casts..

U 10.0.0.1:1025 -> 192.168.0.1:27444
    70 6e 67 20 6c 34 34 61      64 73 6c                   png l44adsl

U 192.168.0.1:32894 -> 10.0.0.1:31335
    50 4f 4e 47                                             PONG
```

```
T 10.0.0.1:27665 -> 192.168.100.1:1075 [AP]
   74 72 69 6e 6f 3e 20    50 4f 4e 47 20 31 20 52    trinoo> PONG 1 R
   65 63 65 69 76 65 64 20  66 72 6f 6d 20 31 39 32    eceived from 192
   2e 31 36 38 2e 30 2e 31    0a                        .168.0.1

T 192.168.100.1:1075 -> 10.0.0.1:27665 [AP]
   71 75 69 74 0d 0a                                    quit..

T 10.0.0.1:27665 -> 192.168.100.1:1075 [AP]
   62 79 65 20 62 79 65 2e    0a                        bye bye..
```

It was the simplicity of the protocol, and the lack of encryption or authentication of commands between the handler and agent, that allowed David Dittrich's scanner and *Zombie Zapper* to detect and/or control *trinoo* agents. Not all DDoS tools are this easy to detect and manipulate.

Real-time monitoring of network traffic can sometimes be a controversial topic for two reasons. First, you are capturing electronic communication in real time, which is covered by state and federal wiretap (or electronic communication privacy) statutes. Be careful to understand the exemptions defined in these laws to know if you are complying with or violating them. Not just anybody can monitor traffic on any given network. Second, you are leaving a known compromised host in operation, and thus in the control of an attacker. If you are a network operator, your primary goal is to get the system off the network to make the network regain stability and have it cleaned as soon as possible. However, if you are an incident responder, researcher, or law enforcement agent investigating a crime, your primary goal is to get as much network traffic as possible, which implies keeping the infected host on the network. These two contradictory goals must be balanced, hopefully getting as much traffic as is reasonable before shutting off wall ports. Another option to collect a sufficient amount of malicious traffic while minimizing its bad effects is to use devices like the Honeynet Project's "honeywall" (http://www.honeynet.org/tools/cdrom) or other layer two filtering bridges configured to block outbound traffic that exceeds specific bandwidth limits or uses specific ports and protocols. A device like the honeywall provides protection for the network infrastructure and makes logging traffic much easier.

The type of traffic that can be obtained by sniffing is determined by the role your site plays in the DDoS network. Does your site host a handler or an agent? Is it the victim of the DDoS attack? Are you just a transit provider, routing packets between other parties? Each of these situations provides a different perspective on the DDoS network and different opportunities to capture traffic for analysis or investigation by law enforcement authorities.

Figure 6.4 on page 184 illustrates a DDoS network in action. In this diagram, *Site A* is where the attacker is located. She uses a stepping stone at *Site B*, to connect to handlers at several locations, including *Site C*. There could be many, many different stepping stones used by the attacker. We depict only one stepping stone here. The handlers, in turn, relay attack commands to all of the agents they are controlling at numerous sites, one of which is shown as *Site D*. All of the agents then unleash a flood of packets toward the victim at *Site E*. That is the aggregation point for all traffic, and may be knocked out entirely by the flood.

As you can see, trying to relate the attack on the victim to the attacker requires tracing packet flows back from *Site E*, through all intermediary sites until you get back to *Site A*. If the attacker disconnects from the stepping stone at *Site B*, or switches to another stepping stone, the trail is broken. If she uses multiple stepping stones, instead of just the one depicted here, traceback gets harder. If logs are cleaned on each stepping stone, or they are used only once, traceback becomes even more challenging.

Now let us take a look at what traffic you can capture, based on your perspective in the network. In all of the figures in this section, the traffic that can be captured by sniffing at the network border is depicted by a circle with an "S" in it.

From the perspective of a network hosting agents, you can see the command and control traffic coming in from a handler (perhaps not all of them) to the agents at your site, and you can see the outbound DDoS attack traffic from this subset of agents going to the victim. This is shown in Figure 6.5.

Most sites will fall into this category, since there are typically far more compromised hosts used as agents than there are handlers, stepping stones, or victims (usually combined). A site hosting agents has a responsibility to identify and clean up the compromised hosts, lest they be used over and over for continued attacks. At sites with small incident response teams, or none at all, the typical cleanup is "wipe the drive, reinstall the OS, get back online." As discussed in Section 6.5, this has potential negative consequences. One consequence is that, unless you also patch the system to current levels, you will be placing the same vulnerability back on the system and it will be compromised again. Another is the destruction of evidence. At least some data collection and preservation is typically warranted in the case of large attacks. A better response is to restore the system from a recent, known clean backup that already has software patches installed. Alternatively, do the operating system installation and patching from CD-ROMs you have prepared while the system is disconnected from the network entirely. Ask the vendor or distribu-

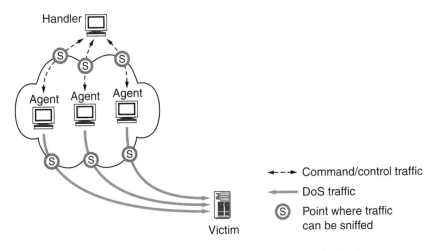

Figure 6.5 Illustration of attack and control traffic seen from site hosting agents

tor of your operating system of choice how to produce a patch CD-ROM for such use. Windows users can try things like Microsoft's Security Readiness Kit (found at http://www.microsoft.com/technet/security/readiness/default.mspx), or if you are using Red Hat Linux, by downloading and creating CDs from the packages in their errata Web pages http://www.redhat.com/errata/. Doing less than that can expose newly cleaned machines to repeated intrusions, sometimes nearly immediately. (Note that if you have a PC on the network of a large Internet 2 educational site, and you try to install a Windows 2000 or XP system from the original CD-ROMs distributed with your computer dating prior to 2003, that system has a high probability of being infected with *W32/Blaster, Nachi,* or some other currently active worm or bot in less than one minute, that is, *before the installation is even complete!*)

In some cases, the command and control traffic would expose all of the agents in the DDoS network. In other cases, DDoS handlers keep track of all the agents within a file. Knowing that your site is hosting agents, you can identify the victim and assist them in identifying all of the agents in the DDoS network by monitoring traffic at their site, and you can assist the site hosting the handler in recovering information about a large percentage of the agents and perhaps take down the entire network. Working with the site hosting the handler also gets one hop closer to the attacker.

Moving now to the site hosting the handler, one can capture only command and control traffic. The traffic rate will be much lower, and the view of the agents in a DDoS network provides more information because the handler communicates with agents at numerous sites. The view from the site hosting the handler is depicted in Figure 6.6.

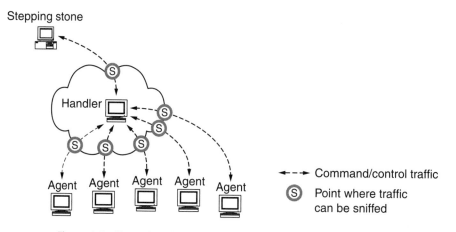

Figure 6.6   Illustration of control traffic seen from site hosting a handler

Note that now both parts of the command and control traffic are visible: the connection from the attacker to the handler's user interface, as well as the traffic to/from a set of agents. Capture all packets to and from the handler, including the data portion of packets (not just headers). Keep these logs secure.

If the attacker is not using an encrypted channel, you also get to see the passwords, user account names, and command syntax of the DDoS tool. This alone may give you enough information to determine what tool is in use, just from watching traffic from outside the handler. Host-level forensics are also an option here for recovering even more information, and preservation of evidence should be carefully done in the event that law enforcement is involved later in the process. Note that you should consider *very, very carefully* any actions that would take control of the DDoS network in any way. The best advice is to get law enforcement involved as soon as you understand how the DDoS network functions and provide a report to them.

You also want to attempt to identify the stepping stones used for incoming connections to the handler. Keep track of all of them, and determine if there is more than one IP address or network block that is favored by the attacker. What time of day are connections most often made? Identify the sites involved, and very carefully attempt to contact them, perhaps by going through their upstream providers, to make sure that you do not end up reporting the DDoS network to the attacker or one of her friends! If you get cooperation from the other sites, they can then attempt to identify other upstream stepping stones, and maybe even other handlers in the network (or networks) being used by the attacker.

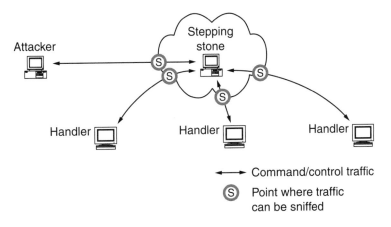

Figure 6.7   Illustration of control traffic seen from site hosting a stepping stone

Now we will look at the site that is hosting the stepping stone. Here we have only a partial view of the command and control traffic between the attacker and the handlers. There is no more visibility beyond the handlers to agents. This is illustrated in Figure 6.7.

Monitoring at the stepping stone may reveal more handlers, and following this trail may ultimately lead to identification of the attacker's location, other stepping stones, or even more agents. Over time, a pattern of behavior of the attacker can be determined, and in some cases active connections to handlers can be identified during the point of an attack.

If law enforcement is involved, they are now able to use search warrants and subpoenas to get more information about accounts used by the attacker, perhaps even hitting upon the attacker's own computers and accounts. At worst, they are able to identify the previous stepping stone in use by the attacker and continue to follow the chain backward toward the attacker.

As you may be seeing by now, the process of traceback is slow, tedious, and labor intensive. It requires some pretty detailed understanding of network capture and analysis tools and techniques, preestablished mechanisms to capture traffic at the network borders, knowledge of what kind of DDoS tool is being used, how the tool functions and presents itself on hosts and the network, and the skills to put all of this together. Taking out an entire DDoS network is a hard problem, but it can be done.

While doing this level of tracing requires many skills and is labor intensive, it has proven successful in the real world. One of the authors, David Dittrich, has personally used the techniques described in this chapter to take down entire DDoS networks, some numbering in the hundreds of hosts (see the time line of DDoS activity leading up to the February 2000 attacks referenced in Chapter 3). Of course, Dittrich wrote the analyses of several of these early tools, and intimately knows how they work. On the other hand, these analyses are freely available on many sites in the Internet to allow anyone who is motivated and resourceful to know everything publicly available about these same tools. Anyone can use the techniques described in these analyses to do the same. Many people have done just that, including some talented members of federal law enforcement in several countries, and DDoS attackers have been brought to justice using these methods of investigation. Similar analyses of newly discovered DDoS tools continue to be written by people around the world. Of course this effort takes skill, discipline, and time and generally makes a profit only for security companies who resell this public information or use it in products they sell. The upside is the reward that comes from knowing that you have contributed to improving the state of computer security on a global scale. Luckily for all, there is a large supply of people with these qualifications and who share this belief.

Malware Command and Control

What ports or protocols are used for command and control? Does the program use password protection or encrypt communications or files? What are the passwords or cryptographic keys, and where can they be found? How are agents identified to handlers (and vice versa) and can you get a complete list of them all?

Earlier, we discussed several examples of looking at network traffic. The analyses of *trinoo* [Ditf], *TFN* [Dith], *Stacheldraht* [Ditg], *Shaft* [DLD00], and *Power* [Dita] all provide further examples of how to identify DDoS agents on the network.

This is some of the most sensitive information, and you should think very carefully about how to disclose this, to whom, and when. It would be very inappropriate, and perhaps very dangerous and a potential legal liability, to provide information that allows another attacker to take over and use a large DDoS network. For example, if you explain that someone has established a bot network on the Dalnet IRC channel *#NotARealChannel,* and he is using a particular bot with a password of *notapassword*, then anyone with basic knowledge of the bot in question could take over the entire botnet and use it for his own purposes.

The Source Code Lineage of the Malware

Attack programs are often shared in the computer underground, in source code form and in compiled binary form. When source code is shared, features of two or more programs may be exactly the same (e.g., how IP header checksums are computed or shell code is injected into overfilled buffers in order to force execution of code on the stack). By knowing how program code is shared and changed from program to program, it is sometimes possible to trace a program back to its author, or to use an existing signature detection method to identify code variants. An entire class of programs may share the same set of known signatures, but a new program that appears on the scene for the first time may go undetected or get packets past existing DDoS mitigation tools. These are all reasons to want to understand how a program developed over time.

You may have only a compiled binary, not the source code, for the particular malware artifact in hand. This makes it harder to distinguish lineage, but not entirely impossible in all cases. There are still symbols that may exist in the symbol table, strings used for prompts and messages to the user, etc., that can be identified and compared to some well-known artifacts.

Many programs borrow heavily from others, be it specific attack features, exploit shell code, cryptographic libraries, etc. Some (like *knight.c*) were coded originally in C for Unix systems, but have been compiled under portable C compiler environments like Cygwin on Microsoft Windows. Some people will simply assume that if the program was originally written for Unix, it will not work on Windows and can not be easily ported to different operating systems.

Who Is Using the Malware?

Going back to 1999, DDoS was most often used for a sort of "drive-by shooting on the Information Superhighway." Attackers were continuously fighting wars using DDoS to take down opponents' machines and IRC channels. However, DDoS is now becoming a component of crime in the form of acts like extortion or rigging online bids. Sometimes a disgruntled ex-employee will attack her former company to exact revenge for a believed false termination. One day a terrorist organization or nation state may use DDoS as a force multiplier in an attack on another state's critical infrastructure. Knowing who is attacking—attribution, in legal and military terminology—can be important.

This is another sensitive subject, though. While capturing traffic to and from suspected compromised hosts, you may get IP addresses of stepping stones, handlers/agents, or direct connections from the attacker's main systems. Beginners have been known to connect from their parents' PC on a DSL line that can be traced directly to a phone number by their ISP. Others have used stolen credit cards to dial in to "no charge" ISPs that do not even have accounts or caller-ID capable switches for their modem pools, resulting in near total anonymity from anywhere in the world. Knowing either of these things tells you something about the attacker (but even if she is connecting from an identifiable DSL or cable modem line, that *still* does not mean the attacker is sitting at that particular keyboard!).

To Whom Should You Provide the Analysis, and When?

Anyone who is involved in DDoS—either victims or sites whose computers were compromised and used as stepping stones or DDoS handlers or agents—has some responsibility to not only clean up his machines, but to report the incident to others and to help in mitigating the problem. As time goes on, and as DDoS attacks become more prevalent and more damaging, the legal situation may likely change in such a way that failing to act appropriately, not reporting participation, or not helping to stop DDoS attacks may incur liability on the part of those involved. Establishing policies and procedures before this becomes an issue is the best course of action, and the best time to start is right now.

In most cases, the DDoS attack will span multiple jurisdictions, within your own country or between several countries around the world. Many attacks these days involve the attackers spreading DDoS agents around the world, and using stepping stones in two or more countries before connecting to the DDoS handlers. This makes it *much harder* to attribute the attack and identify suspects. A good place to start is by contacting your local representatives of federal law enforcement agencies (in the United States that would include the FBI and the Secret Service). It is best to contact these agencies in advance, and get to know them (and let them get to know you) so that it is easier to reach out to the right person in a timely manner when an attack hits. Once law enforcement officers know who you are and understand your skill level and areas of expertise, they will trust your reports more and can prioritize their response appropriately.

Federal law enforcement agencies are (as Australians would say) "up to their armpits in alligators." The more complete and readable your analysis, with an executive summary and high-level overview of the attack itself, the easier their job will be. Getting bit-image copies of compromised hosts used to attack, and full packet traces of network attack and command and control traffic (time stamped, cryptographically fingerprinted, and kept secure for chain-of-custody purposes, etc.) all help make a potential case.

You should also report the incident, in similar detail (but perhaps without some of the more sensitive information from your own site) to national-level incident response centers, such as the CERT Coordination Center in the United States. These organizations often have liaisons with federal law enforcement and other organizations with a larger view of the attack landscape. By correlating events across a larger population, they can identify and help prioritize national-level responses to very large events. Organizations like the CERT Coordination Center also have liaisons to similar institutions abroad and can facilitate cross-border incident response. Contact information for the CERT Coordination Center is provided in Chapter 9.

If you are a network service provider, it would be good to notify your customers if they are victims, or sources, of DDoS attacks. Many ISPs see DDoS as being more of a bandwidth problem, opting to simply add capacity to prevent the network from becoming unstable. Their support staffing can be stretched thin, and it can be very time-consuming trying to explain to a customer (who may know very little about network administration) that his computer was compromised and is being used to attack others, and to assist in the cleaning process. Some ISPs gain notorious status for being unresponsive to DDoS problems.

Lastly, ISPs and NSPs should likewise report large DDoS events to law enforcement and incident response organizations, as described above. For the same reasons, but at a higher level, they have a responsibility to report events, especially if they see these events as being widespread through their association with other network providers. Consult your legal staff to establish policies and procedures for reporting.

What to Keep Private

As mentioned earlier, there are many pieces of information that you should think twice, or even five times, about releasing.

Some pieces of information, like your own internal IP addresses of compromised production hosts, you may never want to release. It may be best to anonymize these, but leave the times and source addresses of attacking hosts intact for investigators. If the event does end in court, you or your company may be required to release the information at that point for use in court. In order to accommodate this, the anonymization must be reversible with a key so that information is preserved and can be released during a trial.

Keep in mind, however, that IP addresses are not authenticated and can easily be spoofed, so they do not serve as a completely reliable source of information identifying a particular computer, let alone an individual. Attackers can, and do, control DNS servers that allow them to also map IP addresses to DNS names at will, so it is important to do reverse mappings to show how DNS names translate at a given point in time. (Provide both IP address and current DNS mapping in your reports, showing the time and time zone to which the mapping corresponds.) It is necessary to have several sources of information, preferably authentication logs used to obtain the IP address in the first place, to help correlate and ensure proper identification.

During your investigation, you may determine that one or more of your own computers are attacking someone, or you may obtain IRC traffic or command/control traffic from a DDoS handler or agent that identifies victims of DDoS attacks. You do *not* want to be responsible for providing information that opens other hosts up to abuse because you have essentially given account/password information allowing their remote control, or for them to be trivially taken over by someone else. Of course, someone else may find them and take them over anyway before you release information, but at least you could not be accused of providing the means. The IP addresses of victims are another thing that you want to consider carefully before releasing, and then you may want to talk to the victim sites and allow them to release their own information.

Names of individuals involved (especially if suspected of performing a DDoS attack) should be held closely, but provided to law enforcement. Releasing names of suspects, or making statements about them and their skill level publicly, can sometimes result in their *attacking you* in retaliation. Perhaps worse, if you cannot prove your allegations you might be sued for libel.

CHAPTER 7

Survey of Research Defense Approaches

Immediately after the first large-scale attacks, much research was dedicated to the new problem of stopping, eliminating, and somehow filtering out DoS attacks targeted at end-host systems. While DDoS was a relatively new problem, related research existed in congestion control, mitigation of simple DoS attacks, fault tolerance, and survivability.

During the CERT Coordination Center's Distributed System Intruder Tools (DSIT) Workshop [CER99] mentioned in Chapter 3, the initial ideas about DDoS defenses were formed. This workshop produced a report that laid out an array of defensive responses ranging from protection to detection and reaction, in a near-, mid-, and long-term time frame, for managers, researchers, system administrators, network operators, and incident response teams.

The DDoS attack networks at the time ranged from several hundred up to over 2,000 hosts, small by the standards of 2004, but viewed as extremely large at the time. (The first DDoS tools could only handle a dozen or so agents, so this was an increase of two orders of magnitude in size in just a few months. It took four more years to increase by two more orders of magnitude.) DDoS networks of only a few dozen to a few hundred hosts allowed for small(er) solutions in response to the threat.

Many research approaches attempted to solve smaller subproblems of a very complex problem. They are more varied than the commercial solutions discussed in Appendix B, but not necessarily realistic. Due to the sensitive nature of network traffic data and the complexity of the phenomenon, it is difficult to fully understand the effects of DDoS. Many prototypes are tested in lab-only environments without background or operational traffic. Some (falsely) assume that attack traffic is mostly spoofed, which is clearly untrue, and others assume certain knowledge about the topology of the network, or access to oracles that can tell whether given traffic is DDoS or not. Others require substantial modifications to the Internet infrastructure that would make it incompatible with existing protocols and client applications, or are impractical for technical, policy, or political reasons.

This book does not survey all the existing research approaches—there are a lot of them and the list keeps growing. We discuss a few of them in this chapter. Limitations of space and the frequent appearance of new systems prevent us from covering all DDoS defense research, and the inclusion or exclusion of a particular project in this chapter should not be considered either a recommendation or a criticism of that project.

7.1   Pushback

Pushback, proposed by Mahajan, et al. [MBF+02], emerged from discussions within the original DDoS research group at the CERT Coordination Center DSIT workshop [CER99]. The idea, taken from practice, is that network operators try to push back offending traffic toward the source, either crudely by unplugging a network cable in the router and watching whether the bad traffic stops, or by observing network traffic on monitoring equipment. Rate limits propagating outward from the victim (pushback) then alleviate the pressure on the victim, allowing it to exchange traffic and effectively survive for a moment while the offending sources are stopped or removed. This assumes that the offending traffic is not evenly distributed across all possible ingress points.

There are two techniques at play here: local Aggregate Congestion Control (ACC) and pushback. Local ACC detects the congestion at the router level and devises an attack signature, or more appropriately in this context, a *congestion signature*, that can be translated into a router filter. The signature defines a high-bandwidth aggregate, a subset of the network traffic, and local ACC determines an appropriate rate limit for this aggregate. Pushback propagates this rate limit for the aggregate to the immediate upstream neighbors that contribute the largest amount of the aggregate's traffic. This mechanism works best against DDoS flooding-style attacks and flash crowds, as they share common traits, and tries to treat these phenomena from a congestion control point of view. Too broad a specification of the aggregate signature or policy can lead to benign traffic being limited, as shown in experiments [IB02], and too narrow a specification can allow attackers to bypass the protection. Pushing an imperfect response upstream limits collateral damage at the possible cost of catching less attack traffic. Generally, pushback seems to require contiguous deployment patterns in routers. Existing approaches cannot push the rate limit past a router that does not understand the pushback method. Pushback also requires routers to maintain state about traffic flows, which is an additional burden.

7.2   Traceback

Some of the first proposals for defending against DDoS included means to perform traceback to the agents of a DDoS network. The assumption is based on some DDoS tools spoofing the sources and relatively low numbers of agents (100–2,500). In the 1999–2000 time frame, it seemed inconceivable that larger networks with over 100,000 hosts [CER03] would exist in the near future.

An early proposal, ICMP Traceback by Bellovin, et al. [BLT01], was to send an ICMP packet, probabilistically every n (early proposals included $n = 20,000$) packets, containing a portion of the captured packet, from the observing router to the destination. The disadvantage is that under heavy attack, a target may miss those packets due to congestion of the network equipment, and some networks do not allow ICMP messages to travel across their border router. Even though the sampling of $1/n$ occurs, it does create additional traffic in the direction of the victim, which adds to the congestion.

Subsequent proposals used a technique called Probabilistic Packet Marking (PPM). Again, every 20,000 network packets to a destination, a router would mark a packet with a reference to itself.[1] Such a low sampling frequency was chosen to avoid a heavy burden on the router infrastructure due to marking a high volume of traffic during a flooding attack. By analyzing several marked packets from a given source, the victim of the flood would try to build a path back to the attacker, or at least to the edge closest to the attacker on the marking infrastructure. The initial proposal by Savage et al. [SWKA00] did not have any provisions for authentication for those markings, but a later proposal added authentication and integrity checking [SP01]. Several techniques along these lines have been proposed, including single-bit techniques [Adl02]. One drawback is that a sufficiently spread DDoS attack network could stay below the limits of sampling. Some musings by Waldvogel [Wal02] on how PPM techniques could be fooled outline further problems PPM faces with regard to deception and denial of service techniques. One of the PPM schemes [SWKA00], at least, claims to provide

---

[1] The IP identification field in the IP header is proposed to bear this mark. This field is used for assembly of fragmented packets. As only about 0.25% [SWKA00] of Internet traffic is fragmented packets, many packet-marking schemes use this field to put their marks in. It is likely that these schemes are not interoperable.

some benefit without contiguous deployment, unlike the Pushback scheme. For an evaluation of Savage et al.'s packet-marking techniques, see Park et al. [PL01].

The hash-based traceback technique [SPS$^+$01] asks participating routers to remember *each* packet they see, but for a limited time. This enables tracing of one-packet attacks such as "Ping of Death," but only if the query is fast. The Source Path Isolation Engine (SPIE) remembers packets by computing hashes over the invariant portions of an IP header (e.g., TTL and checksums removed). For additional space trade-offs, weak hashes, rather than strong cryptographic hashes, are deployed in the form of Bloom filters [SPS$^+$02]. This *passive* recording capability does not have to exist inside the router even though hardware design considerations for inclusion in routers were discussed [SPS$^+$02]. The SPIE designers thought of a way to place a passive tap on each interface of the router. Some critics initially thought it would be too expensive to add one device per interface, so the SPIE device was extended to be a SPIEDER with multiple connections to each interface cable on the router. Although the weak hashes allow for false positives, they are quickly disambiguated through multiple hash functions applied at different routers as the distance increases from the victim. The victim initiates a traceback request through an alternate network (real or virtual) connecting the traceback manager, the data-generation agents, and the routers. Due to the high volume of traffic on backbone networks, the time between receipt of an offending packet and the request for a traceback should be on the order of a few minutes, depending on network capacity and traffic [SMS$^+$01].

Dean et al. [DFS01] take an algebraic approach to the traceback problem. Similar to Savage et al. [SWKA00], this technique embeds partial tracing information into IP packets at the router level. This new scheme uses algebraic techniques to encode path information into packets and to reconstruct them at the victim site. The authors hope to gain more flexibility in the design and improvements in discarding attacker-generated noise and providing multiple-path traceback.

PPM and algebraic traceback schemes make several assumptions. We quote:

1. Attackers are able to send any packet.

2. Multiple attackers can act together.

3. Attackers are aware of the traceback scheme.

4. Attackers must send at least thousands of packets.

5. Routes between hosts are generally stable, but packets can be reordered or lost.

6. Routers cannot do much per-packet computation.

7. Routers are not compromised, but not all routers have to participate.

These assumptions clearly differentiate these techniques from a single-packet technique like hash-based traceback [SPS+02]. The authors of [DFS01] discuss efficiency compared to Savage et al., as space requirements vary between 18 and 21 bits. In some cases, they achieve slightly better results for path reconstruction, but the number of false positives remains high. Aside from packet marking, an out-of-packet scheme is considered, similar to Bellovin [BLT01]. The authors realize that further algorithm improvement is necessary, and trade-offs need to be explored. This concept needs further refining, but could develop into a promising concept in the long run.

Two serious problems exist for traceback solutions:

1. Traceback solutions often become unacceptably complex and expensive when there are large numbers of sources or when sources are well distributed.

2. Traceback, in and of itself, does nothing to stop an attack. If perfect, it identifies the edge networks containing all DDoS sources. Does one then cut them off? Persuade them to clean up the DDoS agents? Counterattack? There are no good answers, except those that presume that one can characterize the attack well enough to distinguish the attack packets from all other packets. If one can do that, traceback may no longer be needed, as offending packets can be filtered using the characterization. Lacking such a DDoS oracle, one option would be to dynamically deploy filters or rate limiters close to identified sources. This would localize collateral damage and stop the flood of attack traffic. However, this calls for a complex and distributed system with the potential to inflict high damage when wrong, so it is not likely to lead to real-life deployment.

7.3   D-WARD

D-WARD, proposed by Mirkovic et al. [Mir03, MPR02], was developed at UCLA under sponsorship by the DARPA Fault Tolerant Network (FTN) program, which sponsored several other DDoS projects. This source network–based system aims to detect attacks before or as they leave the network that the DDoS agent resides on. It is an inline system (transparent to the users on the network) that gathers two-way traffic statistics from the border router at the source network and compares them to network traffic models built upon application and transport protocol specifications, reflecting normal (legitimate), transient (suspicious), and attack behavior. Models are built at two granularities: for each communication with a single destination (called a "flow") and for individual connections. Based on this three-tiered model (attack, suspicious, benign/normal), D-WARD applies rate limits at the router on all the outgoing traffic to a given destination, preferring legitimate connection traffic, slightly slowing down suspicious traffic, and severely slowing down (what it perceives as) attack connections. Rate limits are dynamic and change over time, based on the observation of the attack signal and policed traffic aggressiveness. Less aggressive traffic will be more lightly policed.

Like most research systems, D-WARD was tested with a homegrown set of DDoS benchmarks, and, again like most research systems, it performed well on those benchmarks. However, the D-WARD system also underwent extensive independent testing (also known as "red teaming") toward the end of the DARPA FTN program cycle. Those experiments indicate that D-WARD has the ability to quickly detect those attacks that create anomalies in two-way traffic, such as heavy floods, including some on-off or pulsing attacks. D-WARD effectively controls all traffic, including the attack traffic, and has very low collateral damage and a low level of false positives. It promptly restores normal operations upon the end of the attack(s). By rate limiting the attack traffic rather than blocking it, this system quickly recovers from false positives. By design, it stops attacks at the source networks; thus, it requires wide deployment (covering a majority of actual sources) to achieve the desired effectiveness. Unless a penalty for hosting DDoS agents is imposed on source networks, this is not a system that network operators would eagerly deploy, as D-WARD does not provide a significant benefit to the deployer. However, it may be possible to integrate it with other defense mechanisms (such as COSSACK in Section 7.8) that require source network action, to provide selective response.

In summary, D-WARD's advantage lies in the detection and control of attacks, assuming that attack traffic varies sufficiently from normal traffic models. Due to the fact that D-WARD selectively rate limits traffic, it has low collateral damage, and attack response is relatively fast. On the downside, attackers can still perform successful attacks from networks that are not equipped with this system.

7.4 NetBouncer

NetBouncer, proposed by O'Brien [O'B], also emerged from the DARPA FTN program. It is a client-legitimacy mechanism that sits on the network of a potential victim/target. Ideally, it gets positioned at the choke point of the network and aims to allow packets only from "legitimate" clients or users. Several tests for legitimacy are performed on the client, e.g., a ping (ICMP Echo request) test to see whether there is an actual client behind the packet that was received by the target, and also a Reverse Turing Test [vABHL03]. The reader may have seen such a test when registering for an e-mail account on the Yahoo e-mail service: The client is asked to enter a phrase or word displayed in a very noisy image, something that we assume only a human could do, not a machine.[2] Other tests investigate whether an ongoing connection falls within the protocol specifications (for example, is it truly a real-time video streaming connection?) and, if not, NetBouncer terminates the connection.

Once the client has proven that he is indeed legitimate, he is added to the pool of legitimate clients and is given preferential treatment over the not-yet-legitimate clients. This pool is managed using Quality of Service techniques and guarantees fair sharing of resources between all the legitimate clients. To prevent an attacker from inheriting the credentials of a legitimate client, the legitimacy expires after a certain time and needs to be reassessed using the same or a different test.

Can such an approach work? It can defeat many spoofed attacks, since the challenge must reach the true source of the packet for the network transaction to complete. The available network resources are fairly shared among the clients that have proven their legitimacy. Because the legitimacy tests are stateless, the system itslf cannot be the target of state-consumption attacks.

However, NetBouncer assumes certain properties of clients, such as the ability to reply to pings (i.e., check the presence of a client), which not all clients support, especially those behind firewalls and home DSL routers with additional security features turned on. Although a client is legitimate, he is not protected against impersonation attacks, i.e., an attacker can abuse the fact that a legitimate client has done all the necessary work to prove his legitimacy to NetBouncer and then attack the network faking that legitimate client's source IP address. Also, the system is not immune to resource exhaustion due to a large number of legitimate clients (a "flash crowd" effect). Further, like all target-side defenses, it can be overwhelmed by pure volume of packets on the incoming wire. A sufficiently large DDoS network can overwhelm NetBouncer and similar approaches, since the attackers can flood all but the most massive network connections in front of the defense system.

Like all the better DDoS defense schemes, NetBouncer has its advantages and limitations. On the positive side, it appears to provide good service to legitimate clients in the majority of cases. As it sits inline on the network, meaning that it does not have a visible presence on the network akin to a network bridge, it does not require modifications to the servers and clients on either protected network or the

---

[2] An interactive example of such a Reverse Turing Test can be found on the CAPTCHA page at http://www.captcha.net/.

hosts connecting to the same. The deployment location is close to the victim and it does not require cooperation with other NetBouncers. On the negative side, attackers can perform successful attacks on the victim/target by impersonating legitimate clients or recruiting a large number of agents, both of which are easily achieved through spoofing and sufficient recruitment, respectively. Additionally, NetBouncer makes certain assumptions about the legitimate clients that are not always shared by all such clients and will cause them to be excluded from accessing the protected resources. The legitimacy tests put a significant burden on NetBouncer itself and can exhaust the resources of the defense mechanism.

7.5   Secure Overlay Services (SOS)

Keromytis et al. propose Secure Overlay Services (SOS) [KMR02] as a DDoS defense, with the goal of routing only good traffic to the servers. Traffic that has not been confirmed to originate from good users/clients is dropped. Clients must use an overlay network, essentially a network sitting on top of the existing network, to get authenticated and reach the servers.

Clients must first contact the *access points* of the overlay network, the gatekeepers that will check the legitimacy of each client before letting her into the network. These access points send the packets to a so-called *beacon* via a routing algorithm called *Chord*, which decides where packets go on this overlay network. The beacons, in turn, send the packets to *secret servlets*. The latter are the only nodes on the overlay network that can penetrate the firewall of the protected network. These secret servlets then tunnel the packets to the firewall, which will allow only the packets from the secret servlets' source addresses to reach the protected network. The built-in redundancy of the overlay network assures that if a node should fail, other nodes will step forward and assume its role.

SOS is meant for communicating with a network protected with a firewall, e.g., a private enterprise network. The test for legitimacy of packets is pushed out to the access points on the overlay network, which leaves the firewall working on dropping attack packets and accepting connections from its trusted secret servlets. The built-in redundancy of the SOS network, as well as the secrecy of the path taken by the packets from the source to the final destination, contribute to the resistance against DoS attacks on SOS itself.

Like pure target-side solutions, SOS could potentially be overwhelmed by a bandwidth attack on the firewall that allows only approved packets through. Routing restrictions require core routers to check source addresses on packets before routing them. Routers do not currently do that very quickly, so, in practice, keeping the IP addresses of the target and firewall secret is the real answer. If attackers are unable to route traffic directly to the target machine or firewall (due either to routing restrictions or secrecy of their IP addresses), the only way to generate a flood at the firewall is by going through the overlay network. The overlay network will take careful steps to prevent bad traffic from being sent to the protected system. Only flooding attacks capable of overwhelming all of the entry points into the overlay network will succeed, and the defender can configure many of those and increase their numbers if necessary.

If routing restrictions or secrecy of the protected system's addresses are not possible, however, attackers will be able to bypass the SOS overlay and send DDoS packets directly to the firewall. Should that happen, SOS offers no more protection against a flooding attack than any victim-end solution.

In summary, SOS does provide communication of a legitimate client with the protected, albeit private, server and/or network. It also offers resilience to node failure, as surviving nodes will assume the role of failed nodes, and resilience against denial of service on the system itself. On the other hand, the SOS system is designed to work with private services only, since it requires changes in client software and an extensive overlay infrastructure. There is also a WebSOS [CMK+03] variant that works with a public Web server and uses CAPTCHA [vABHL03] for legitimacy, which limits WebSOS's use to human Web browsing. Clients must know of the access points in order to get to the protected services, and using CAPTCHA requires human presence. Also, the use of an overlay network by SOS and WebSOS redefines the routing topology and creates a longer or slower route to the destination. Recent research by Andersen et al. [ABKM01] has shown that careful construction and use of an overlay can sometimes actually offer better performance than use of standard Internet routing, so it is possible that there will be no significant loss in speed due to the use of SOS. Current results [KMR02], however, show twofold to tenfold slowdown.

7.6   Proof of Work

A different way to approach the DDoS problem is to consider the subproblem of the connection depletion attack. Many connections are initiated by an attacker to deplete the number of open connections a server can maintain. A defense goal is to preserve these resources during such an attack. As a defense, the server starts handing out challenges [SKK+97, JB99, WR03], not unlike the ones in NetBouncer, to the client requesting a connection. This happens at the TCP/IP protocol level, since the system aims at protecting the resources involving network connections. The server distributes a small cryptographic puzzle to its clients requesting a connection, and waits for a solution. If the client solves the puzzle within a certain time window, the appropriate resources are then allocated within the network stack (the portion of the operating system that handles network communication). Clients that fail to solve the puzzles have their connections dropped.

This is the proof-of-work approach explained in detail in Chapter 5. However, this approach will work *only* against connection depletion attacks, not other types of flooding attacks, such as UDP flooding attacks. Such attacks achieve their goal merely by placing packets on the target's network link. Anything the target does upon receipt of them to check their validity is too late. Bandwidth has already been expended.

This approach forces the attacker to spend time and resources prior to achieving a successful connection to a server or target, and slows down the rate at which he can deplete the resources of the server from any given host/client. While this has a low overhead (the server still must generate *and* verify the puzzles), the actual TCP/IP protocol implementation on both ends (client and server) must be modified for this approach to work. This defense does not address problems such as distributed attacks in which the attacker generates sufficient requests to exhaust the server resources (by sheer number) or attacks that exhaust puzzle-generation resources and consume the capacity of the network pipe leading to the server, or flash crowd type of attacks.

By analogy, one can also consider using Reverse Turing Tests [vABHL03] for countering DDoS attacks, as proposed by Morein et al. [MSC+03].

7.7 DefCOM

DefCOM, proposed by Mirkovic et al. [MRR03], is pursued jointly at the University of California Los Angeles and the University of Delaware. It is a distributed system that combines source-end, victim-end, and core-network defenses. It detects an ongoing attack and responds by rate limiting the traffic, while still allowing legitimate traffic to pass through the system. It is composed of three types of nodes (routers or hosts): alert generators that detect an attack; rate limiters that enforce simple rate limits on all traffic going to the attack's target; and classifiers that rate-limit traffic, separate legitimate packets from suspicious ones and mark each packet with its classification. Alert generator and classifier nodes are designed for edge-network deployment, while rate-limiter nodes are designed for core deployment.

In case of an attack, the likely detection point is at the alert generator within the victim network, and a likely classifier engagement point is close to the source networks. DefCOM traces the attack from victim to all active traffic sources (attack or legitimate) using an overlay network and exchanging statistics between defense nodes.

The rate limit is deployed starting from the victim, and propagates to the leaves on the traffic tree (classifiers close to sources). Packet marks, injected by classifiers, convey information about the legitimacy of each packet to rate-limiting nodes. Rate limiters allocate limited bandwidth preferentially first to packets marked legitimate, then to those marked suspicious, and finally to nonmarked packets. This creates three levels of service, giving best service to legitimate packets.

Any firewall could assume alert generator functionality. Core routers would have to be augmented with a mark-observing capability to perform rate-limiter functionality. D-WARD was described as a likely candidate for classifier functionality. However, separation of legitimate from attack traffic does not need to be as good as D-WARD's. A classifier node can simply mark traffic it deems important for the source network's customers as legitimate. As long as classifiers obey rate-limit requests, this traffic will not hurt the victim.

In summary, DefCOM's design is an interplay of detection at the target/victim network, rate limiting at the core, and blocking of suspicious/attack traffic at source networks. Using D-WARD as its initial classifier system, DefCOM also reaches further out into the core to handle attacks from networks not outfitted with classifiers watching for bad traffic. DefCOM claims to handle flooding attacks while inflicting little or no harm to legitimate traffic. Due to the overlay nature of the system, DefCOM lends itself to a scalable solution and does not require contiguous deployment thanks to the use of peer-to-peer architecture, but it does require a wider deployment than victim-end defenses. As a drawback, handling damaged or subverted nodes in the overlay network may be hard, and DefCOM is likely to operate badly if they are not handled. At the time of writing, DefCOM exists only as a design and fragments of an implementation, so it should be considered as a promising new idea rather than a complete, ready-to-deploy solution.

7.8 COSSACK

COSSACK, proposed by Papadopoulos et al. [PLM+03] and developed by the University of Southern California/ISI, aims to prevent attacks from ever leaving the source networks, i.e., the networks harboring the DDoS agents. So-called *watchdogs,* a plug-in to the free lightweight intrusion detection system Snort [Sou], detect a potential attack by analyzing and correlating traffic across the source networks. Based on the correlation (timing, type of traffic), the correlating entities are able to suppress the similar and simultaneous traffic as a group action.

This technique acts at the source network, triggered by a notification from the target of a DDoS attack, by filtering out the apparently offending traffic. However, if the legitimate traffic gets matched by the correlation engine, leading to a false positive, then that legitimate traffic will get dropped by COSSACK.

A major assumption of this technique is the deployment of watchdogs at the source networks. The source networks are being prevented from becoming attack sources, but a network without a watchdog can still participate in a DDoS attack. This drawback is common to systems requiring source-end deployments. No modifications are required at the protocol or application level for the source networks. The communication between the watchdogs is not scalable, as they use multicast communication.

7.9 Pi

Pi, proposed by Yaar et al. [YPS03], is a victim-based defense, building on previous packet-marking techniques [SP01], that inserts path identifiers into unused (or under-used) portions of the IP packet header. The main idea is that these path identifiers or fingerprints are inserted by the routers along the network path. The target or victim would then reject packets with path identifiers matching those packets that have been clearly identified as part of an attack.

In the basic Pi marking scheme, each participating router marks certain bits in the IP identification field of the IP packet.[3] The placement of the mark within this field is defined by the value of the packet's TTL (time to live) field. A mark is a portion of the hash of the router's IP address. Since the TTL value is decremented at each router, a contiguous path of the packet is built as it gets closer to the victim. One can decide to stop marking within a certain hop distance of the victim network to increase reachability of this scheme.

Pi filtering can take place once the marking scheme has been installed in the infrastructure. This scheme assumes that the victim knows how to identify the bulk of the attack traffic, for instance, by selecting a large portion of incoming traffic bearing the same mark. Filters then drop all traffic with the given mark. Inadvertently, some legitimate traffic sharing the mark with the attack (because it shares the path to the

---

[3] As mentioned when discussing traceback schemes, packet-marking approaches are not interoperable as they all place their marks in the same field in the IP header.

victim due to the fluctuating and adaptive nature of the network) will be dropped, too.

Pi claims to work after the first attack packet has been identified (*if* it can be identified by the target), to maintain IP fragmentation, work without inter-ISP cooperation, and with minimal deployment. Pi is likely to suffer the same problems from flooding attacks on the box running the defensive mechanism or its incoming network link as most other victim-side defenses.

7.10   SIFF: An End-Host Capability Mechanism to Mitigate DDoS Flooding Attacks

Yaar et al. [YPS04] propose to mitigate DDoS flooding attacks using an end-host capability mechanism that splits Internet traffic into two classes: privileged and unprivileged. End hosts can exchange *capabilities* that will be used in privileged traffic. Routers will then verify these capabilities statelessly. These capabilities are assigned in a dynamic fashion, so misbehaving (that is, attacking) hosts can have their capabilities revoked. Contrary to other approaches (e.g., in Section 7.5), this scheme does not require an overlay mechanism, but it does require a modification of the clients and servers, and also routers.

The end hosts would use a handshake protocol to exchange capabilities, and then that privileged traffic would be expedited by the network, in contrast to the unprivileged traffic which does not get precedence. There are provisions in place to prevent flooding with privileged traffic by an unauthorized user, e.g., by someone who tries to forge the capabilities (implemented by markings in each packet). Should an end host with capabilities start flooding, then the credentials for privileged traffic can be revoked for that end host.

The authors of this mechanism propose two avenues: a next-generation Internet incorporating these techniques and a retrofit for the current network protocols in IPv4. It is unclear that these avenues will prove fruitful.

In summary, this technique makes several assumptions, including the assumption that client and server update the TCP/IP protocol software to incorporate modifications necessary for the new capabilities. The advantage is that no inter-ISP or intra-ISP cooperation is necessary. However, it is also assumed that spoofing is limited, and processing and state maintenance are required at each router. The new network protocol requires marking space in the IP header, cooperation of clients and servers, that each router marks packets,[4] and that routes between hosts on the network remain stable. These assumptions are quite restrictive, compared to what can happen in a real network.

7.11   Hop-Count Filtering (HCF)

Hop-Count Filtering, proposed by Jin et al. [JWS03], is a research project at the University of Michigan, aimed at defending against DDoS by observing the TTL value (time to live, the number of hops or routers a packet will travel before getting discarded to avoid network loops—the value gets decremented at each router the packet traverses) in inbound packets. Deployed at victim/target networks, it observes the proper TTL value for any given source address on the network that enters the victim/target network, attempts to infer a hop count (that is, the distance of the sender from the defense) and builds tables that bind a given IP to the hop count.

The system makes guesses of hop counts starting with the observed TTL value and guessing the initial TTL value that was placed in the packet at the sender. There are only a few such values that operating systems use and they are fairly different, which facilitates correct guesses. The hop count is then the difference between the initial TTL and the observed one.

Hop-count distributions follow the normal distribution (bell curve), as there is sufficient variability in the TTL values. If an attacker wanted to defeat this scheme, he would have to guess the correct TTL value to insert into a forged packet, so that the deduced hop count matches the expected one. Spoofing becomes difficult, as the attacker now has to spoof the correct TTL value associated with a given spoofed source address and, augmented by the appropriate difference in hop counts between attacking and spoofed address, malicious traffic becomes easier to model.

In the general operation, the hop-count filter is passive while it is analyzing traffic and matches it to the established incoming tables of assumed hop counts. If the number of mismatches crosses an established threshold, the scheme starts filtering. The incoming tables are constantly updated by examining a random established (e.g., successful) TCP connection to a site within the protected network. Note that this scheme tries to prevent spoofed traffic. Nothing prevents an attacker from launching an attack with true sources and carrying the correct TTL values, and thus attacks using

---

[4] As mentioned when discussing traceback schemes, packet-marking approaches are not interoperable as they all place their marks in the same field in the IP header.

large bot networks or worms with DDoS payloads, which do not need to spoof source addresses to be successful, will still be a problem. Since these types of attacks are easy today, attackers would simply adopt this method over source address forgery to get around such defenses.

Like other victim-side defenses, this approach cannot help defend against flooding attacks based on overwhelming the link coming into the machine that is checking the TTL values.

7.12   Locality and Entropy Principles

Two general and related themes are being investigated by several researchers. We will highlight the principles these themes are exploring—locality and entropy, which relate to self-similarity.

7.12.1   Locality

In his worm-throttling paper, Williamson [Wil02] discusses throttling a spreading worm by using the concept of locality: People communicate only with a fixed number of other people on a regular basis, read a limited number of similar Web pages per day (e.g., CNN, New York Times, *Wired*), and send mail to a given set of people. Behind this thought is the small-world model of social networks of Watts [Wat99]. McHugh extends this model in his locality approach for dealing with outsider threat [McH03]: Is there a model for attack behavior or, more to the point, is there a complement to good behavior that is based on small networks (tightly connected) of networked hosts? There may be some way of characterizing DDoS and worm behavior using this principle based on known worm and DDoS data; work continues in this area.

7.12.2   Entropy

Another way of looking at this problem is to consider the self-similarity of attack traffic. Kulkarni et al. [KBE01] propose to investigate whether the attack packets can be easily compressed when considered in a stream, as an indication that a machine-generated stream (the attacker generates repetitive packets aimed at one or more targets, with low entropy, low complexity, and high compressibility) is present rather than a human-generated stream (which tends to be more chaotic, with high entropy).

Similarly, a research project by Schnackenberg et al. [FSBK03] looks at the source address entropy of the network packets. Based on a study of DDoS data inserted into a collection of network traffic collected at the border of the New Zealand national network, it appears that the entropy of source addresses present during a DDoS attacks is significantly different from what is present in the rest of the traffic (and considered normal everyday traffic without attacks). A prototype for this approach exists.

7.13   An Empirical Analysis of Target-Resident DoS Filters

Collins and Reiter [CR04] present an empirical analysis of target-resident DoS filters, such as Pi (see Section 7.9), HFC (see Section 7.11), Static Clustering (SC), and Network-Aware Clustering (NAC). Both SC and NAC monitor the behavior of a range of source addresses and build a baseline model of this behavior. Under attack, traffic from these source addresses is compared against the baseline model to classify it as legitimate or attack. SC groups addresses into fixed-size ranges, while NAC uses ranges derived from routing tables.

With the help of replicated Internet topologies (obtained from CAIDA, among others), this analysis runs the filtering mechanisms against actual DDoS data collected using a space-efficient network flow data collection system, the System for internet-Level Knowledge (SiLK) [CER04, GCD+04], developed by the CERT Coordination Center.

In their summary for spoofed traffic (Figure 7.1), Collins and Reiter point out that even though HCF has a low false-negative rate, this is due to the assumption that the true hop count of each network packet can accurately be determined. This is clearly not the case, as compromised hosts can manipulate the TTL field of each sent packet, yielding a possible false hop count. Pi, SC, and NAC do reasonably well. Pi appears to be immune to spoofing. Both SC and NAC do well since the distribution of spoofed traffic allows for easier filtering versus "normal" traffic.

In drastic contrast, the learning algorithms for *attacker learning* compared to *normalcy learning* allow for the superiority of SC and NAC in the nonspoofed traffic case (see Figure 7.2)

As Collins and Reiter emphasize, the results should not be overvalued, as this represents work in progress. These results do provide us, however, with insights into realistic analysis—with real-life and not simulated DDoS data—of the DDoS mitigation mechanisms outlined above.

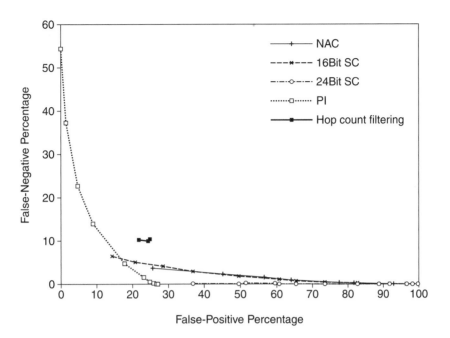

Figure 7.1 Summary of analyses of spoofed traffic. (Reprinted with permission of Michael Collins.)

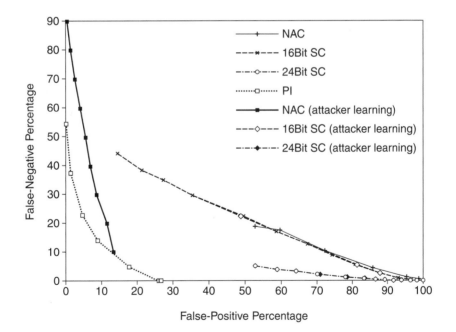

Figure 7.2 Summary of analyses for nonspoofed traffic. (Reprinted with permission of Michael Collins.)

7.14   Research Prognosis

There was a rich explosion of DDoS defense approaches immediately after the DDoS phenomenon became widely known. The results of this research include many of the projects discussed in earlier sections. As the preceding discussion suggests, and the similar discussion in Appendix B also indicates, the existing approaches have not solved the entire DDoS problem in provable ways. Some solutions clearly stop some attacks, and some solutions claim they will stop most attacks. What is the actual prognosis for future research in this field? Is there reason to believe that a more complete solution to the problem is on the horizon? Answering these questions requires better information about how proposed DDoS solutions perform.

A problem with the existing research is that there is no convincing evidence that any proposed approach actually works against broad classes of DDoS attacks. Most researchers have tested their systems against particular DDoS toolkits, with traces of real DDoS attacks, or with parameterized traffic generation capable of emulating a wide variety of attacks. A few researchers have had outsiders perform significant tests on their systems, though that approach is expensive and not necessarily convincing. But there is no known set of tests that everyone agrees represent the necessary and sufficient evidence that a DDoS solution works well enough to rely upon. Collins and Reiter [CR04] have made a start on comparing some DDoS defense systems against real attacks.

DDoS solutions that require major changes (such as altering behavior of core routers, changing fundamental Internet protocols, or deploying new software on all machines in the Internet) will never be implemented without far more convincing evidence that they would work if their price was paid. In particular, it would be depressing if major changes were made in the Internet to counter today's DDoS attacks, only to discover that slightly altered attacks bypass the expensive new defenses. This issue points out one serious advantage that target end systems have: they typically cost less to deploy, so if they do not work, less has been lost. Overall, we need to have a far deeper understanding of the nature of the attacks and the characteristics of proposed defenses before we should accept anyone's claim to possess a silver bullet against DDoS.

7.14.1   Slowing Innovation

One dispiriting fact is that few really new approaches have come out as of the time of writing. Researchers have brought older ideas to maturity and improved the systems that incorporate them, but most of the ideas being developed come from the original explosion of DDoS defense approaches.

Since this crop of approaches does not seem terribly likely to produce solutions capable of dealing with all DDoS attacks, a complete response to the DDoS threat would seem to depend on new approaches. The authors hope that some new approaches will be suggested in the future that invigorate the DDoS research field

Refinements/Combinations of Earlier Ideas

In the absence of new approaches, some researchers have investigated whether combinations of existing approaches can achieve more complete coverage of the DDoS problem. DefCOM [MRR03] is one such example. These systems offer some hope of dealing with the overall problem. The researchers postulate that the weaknesses of one portion of the system will be covered by the strengths of other parts. Of course, it is possible that exactly the opposite is true: The strengths of one may be undermined by the weaknesses of the others.

Until truly fresh approaches are found, however, the available choices are to improve one approach or to combine several approaches. Thus, we should expect to see more interesting and clever combinations of defenses in the future.

7.14.2   Several Promising Approaches

We should not be too pessimistic. Academic researchers quest for complete solutions at practically no cost. In the real world, something less is often good enough. For many people, solid implementations of some of the kinds of solutions described in this chapter and Appendix B may prove to offer sufficient protection from DDoS attacks at acceptable costs. For example, companies that do business with a limited set of trusted customers might get sufficient protection from a solution like SOS, or companies that can afford large bandwidth links into their defense nodes can be protected by certain sets of the victim-end solutions.

7.14.3   Difficult Deployment Challenges

Some of the most promising solutions depend on either widespread deployment or deployment at some key locations in the core of the Internet. Neither of these deployment patterns is easy to achieve. Widespread deployment most usually arises because the software in question is extremely attractive to users, and most of the solutions that require such deployment lack features that excite the ordinary user. In particular, software that helps protect other users' computers, but does not help protect the installer, has had difficulty achieving much market penetration.

Approaches like traceback and pushback that require deployment in many nodes in the core face a different problem. The institutions that run the machines on which these deployments must occur have critical requirements for the performance of their systems. They cannot afford to pay heavy performance penalties on a per-packet basis, since they carry so many packets. Even more critical, they cannot afford to install features in their routers that decrease stability or cause other forms of disruption in normal service. There must be extremely compelling evidence of benefit, acceptable performance, and stability before there is any hope of installing functionality at these sites. Further, there is no real hope of installing it at all of them, so only solutions that provide significant benefit in partial deployments have any chance of real-world use.

CHAPTER 8

Legal Issues

This chapter deals with the legal aspects of defending against DDoS attacks, or pursuing criminal or civil remedies against perpetrators of DDoS attacks. It provides a cursory overview of the subject, and is by no means intended to provide legal advice. It is based on current law existing in the United States; thus, readers in other countries will need to consult their local laws for further guidance.

Because of differences among jurisdictions, especially among countries, all readers are encouraged to consult with a qualified attorney to obtain specific advice regarding situation- and jurisdiction-specific legal options. (All dollar amounts shown are in U.S. dollars.)

That said, the reader can learn much about the practicalities of using the legal system in response to DDoS attacks by examining how the legal system generally functions; the basic processes of discovery, investigation, and prosecution; and civil litigation. Since this process is complex and deliberate, the rate at which a case moves through it can vary depending on how well prepared a party is beforehand. Knowing what to expect and some of the proper things to do may improve the party's chances of obtaining a favorable outcome.

8.1 Basics of the U.S. Legal System

Before addressing some of the steps to follow in initiating legal proceedings, it is helpful to understand the pathways through the U.S. legal system. Many other legal systems throughout the world are similar, but laws can and do vary significantly, even within similar systems.

There are fundamentally two distinct types of law: *criminal law* and *civil law*. Depending on the circumstances of a DDoS attack, criminal and/or civil actions may be brought.

A *criminal action* is brought by the government against an individual for violation of criminal statutes, but only after that individual has been charged with violation of such a statute. The types of criminal acts associated with DDoS attacks fall into two categories—misdemeanor or felony, depending on the gravity of the crime. Criminal actions can be brought at the state or federal level depending on whether state or federal laws have been violated, and the location of the parties involved. Essentially, in order for the government's attorney to have a successful prosecution of a defendant, the state must prove *beyond a reasonable doubt* that the defendant committed the crime or crimes alleged by the government. Penalties may include monetary fines, imprisonment, or both.

Civil actions are the result of disputes between individuals for which a legal remedy may exist. These are typically matters such as breach of a contractual agreement, or breach of a duty imposed by law. In the case of DDoS attacks, causes of action may include negligently failing to secure computers used to attack someone, or negligent interference with commercial activity. There are four requirements for a suit charging negligence: (1) The injured party, the plaintiff, must show that a duty was owed by the defendant to do or not do something; (2) the plaintiff must show that the duty was breached by the defendant; (3) the plaintiff must also show that the defendant was the cause of the harm to the plaintiff; and (4) the plaintiff must have been harmed in such a way that damages may be awarded.

In a civil suit, the plaintiff (the party bringing the suit against the defendant) must prove, by a *preponderance of the evidence,* that the defendant is responsible for the plaintiff's injury. The court then determines an appropriate remedy, which can include the assessment of monetary damages or directing a party to perform (or refrain from performing) some action. This is known as a suit in *tort* (as opposed to a suit in *contract*).

A special type of civil action that may apply in DDoS attacks is a *class action suit*. A class action is usually an action brought by a representative plaintiff against a defendant or defendants on behalf of a class of plaintiffs who have the same interest in the litigation as their representative and whose rights can be more efficiently determined as a group than in a series of individual suits. In recent years, several high-profile class action suits have been brought by consumers in the United States; thus, readers may be familiar with the lawsuits brought by victims of asbestos poisoning, tobacco addiction, leaky silicone breast implants, and a particular type of intrauterine birth control device.

Since criminal actions are the responsibility of the government, a victim should report suspected crimes to the appropriate authorities [1] and provide them with sufficient evidence of the alleged acts and the harm caused by those acts. Such evidence will allow the government's attorney to determine applicable laws and whether or not to proceed with prosecution. In order to assess the likelihood of obtaining a successful prosecution, the authorities need to know things such as the location of the victim, the type and monetary amount of damage suffered, etc.

It also helps to have evidence that can lead to the identity of a suspect. This is important for two reasons.

First, victims should be prepared to at least gather some samples of network attack traffic and other log information that confirms that an attack is actually taking place. It is not uncommon for a victim who suspects he is under attack, and may even believe he "knows who is attacking and why," to later learn from a consultant that the problem is actually a bug in a Web application, insufficient resources on a server, or a misconfiguration of hardware or software. It is advisable to first perform some level of capture and analysis of network traffic and server logs before contacting the authorities.

Second, both civil and criminal actions require that an individual, or group, be identified and brought into the legal process. You cannot sue, and the police cannot jail, an unknown entity. In the case of many DDoS attacks, the complexity of the "crime scene" may prevent a direct identification of a suspect. Even if a suspect can be identified, he may reside in another country, and it may be difficult, if not impossible, to bring him before the presiding judicial authority. Extradition may be an option in certain criminal cases, but not for civil actions. Furthermore, the United States does not have an extradition treaty with every foreign government. Thus, this option may

---

[1] We will not attempt to provide guidelines for when to contact legal authorities, which authorities to contact, what to present to them, etc. The reader is encouraged to have someone from their organization's incident response and/or legal teams reach out to both your state and federal law enforcement agencies and discuss the process with them, well in advance of needing to contact them in the event of a DDoS attack. This not only establishes a relationship, but also helps to understand the process and expectations in the event that law enforcement must become involved. In fact, some corporations find it useful to understand precisely the preferred facts, report formats, methods of transmitting/receiving digital data, standards for digital evidence collection and preservation, etc., so as to bring nearly "ready-made" case materials to law enforcement, significantly speeding up the legal process. References provided throughout this chapter will also assist in developing your incident response capabilities to mesh better with the needs of the legal system.

not be available in every case in which the culprit is a citizen or resident of a foreign country.

8.2   Laws That May Apply to DDoS Attacks

On the criminal side, the primary federal law that applies to most DDoS-related attacks is the Computer Fraud and Abuse Act, or 18 U.S.C. §1030.[2]

An example of this law being applied to DoS attacks is the case of *United States v. Dennis* in the District of Alaska in 2001 [ws]. In 2001, a former computer systems administrator in Alaska pled guilty to one misdemeanor count for launching three e-mail-based DoS attacks against a server at the U.S. District Court in New York. He was charged under 18 U.S.C. §1030(a)(5) with "interfering with a government-owned communications system."

Other DDoS-related attacks mentioned elsewhere in this book, such as the extortion attempts against online gambling sites and online business, may fall under 18 U.S.C. §1030(a)(7), which covers extortionate threats. Analysis of a Congressional Research Service report [fra] suggests such attacks may also violate

- 18 U.S.C. §1951 (extortion that affects commerce)
- 18 U.S.C. §875 (threats transmitted in interstate commerce)
- 18 U.S.C. §876 (mailing threatening communications)
- 18 U.S.C. §877 (mailing threatening communication from a foreign country)
- 18 U.S.C. §880 (receipt of the proceeds of extortion)

The act of breaking into hundreds or thousands of computers to install DDoS handlers and agents may violate 18 U.S.C. §1030(a)(3) (trespassing in a government computer). If a sniffer is used to obtain passwords as part of this activity, the attacker may have violated 18 U.S.C. §1030(a)(6) (trafficking in passwords for a government-owned computer) or 18 U.S.C. §2510 (wiretap statute).

---

[2] United States Code, abbreviated as *U.S.C.*, is the complete body of constantly revised laws defined at the federal level in the United States. It is divided into *titles*, then subdivided further into *sections/subsections*. *10 U.S.C* means Title 10 of the United States Code. The symbol § stands for *section/subsection*. Titles and sections/subsections also have *common names* that identify them based on the legislation that created or amended them. So the complete reference to the Computer Fraud and Abuse Act, which is Title 10, Section 1030, would be *10 U.S.C. §1030*. Subsections are further identified by subordinate letters and numbers in parentheses, so subsection *a* and sub-subsection *3* would be identified as *10 U.S.C. §1030(a)(3)*. For more information on United States Code, see http://www.law.cornell.edu/uscode/.

Even an *attempt* to violate any of the sections of 18 U.S.C. §1030 listed above is itself a violation of 18 U.S.C. §1030(b).

On the civil side, 18 U.S.C. §1030(g) creates a civil cause of action for violation of subsection (a)(5)(B), which includes any of the following:

1. Loss to one or more persons during any one-year period (and, for purposes of an investigation, prosecution, or other proceeding brought by the United States only, loss resulting from a related course of conduct affecting one or more other protected computers) aggregating at least $5,000 in value.

2. The modification or impairment, or potential modification or impairment, of the medical examination, diagnosis, treatment, or care of one or more individuals.

3. Physical injury to any person.

4. A threat to public health or safety.

5. Damage affecting a computer system used by or for a government entity in furtherance of the administration of justice, national defense, or national security.

Damages include only economic damages, and the civil action must be brought within two years of the act or when the damage was discovered.

Another civil action surrounding a DDoS attack against a business, which prevents customers from engaging in business with the victim and thus damages its business, would be "Tortious Interference with Business Relationship or Expectancy." To prove this, the plaintiff (the DDoS victim) would have to show several things, including such elements as knowledge of the business relationship between the victim and its customers, knowledge that the action (the DDoS attack) would disrupt this relationship, knowledge that the result would cause damage to the victim, proof that the defendant caused such disruption and damage, and proof that the victim has suffered a loss. (Here is where careful evidence collection and realistic incident cost estimation become very important.)

The Department of Justice Cybercrime Web site [fra] also lists these laws as applying to computer intrusion cases:

- 18 U.S.C. §1029 (fraud and related activity in connection with access devices)
- 18 U.S.C. §1362 (communication lines, stations, or systems)
- 18 U.S.C. §2510 et seq. (wire and electronic communications interception and interception of oral communications)
- 18 U.S.C. §2701 et seq. (stored wire and electronic communications and transactional records access)

- 18 U.S.C. §3121 et seq. (recording of dialing, routing, addressing, and signaling information)

This is a representative, yet not exhaustive, list of laws that may apply. Readers are urged to consult with an attorney and local/federal law enforcement agencies in their jurisdiction in order to learn more about what legal options exist in the event of a DDoS attack, and how to prepare to exercise these options when and if a DDoS attack occurs. It is also important to understand your responsibilities and potential liabilities in the event that your own systems are taken over and used to attack someone else, in which case you may be the defendant, not the plaintiff, in a civil suit.

8.3   Who Are the Victims of DDoS?

If we start with the premise that DDoS attacks are actually two-phased attacks—first breaking into thousands of computers and installing malware on them to use for attacking, and then using them to wage one or more DDoS attacks—then it follows that a significant amount of damage is actually spread out over a very large number of sites, in many jurisdictions, and over an extended time period. And that is before any DDoS flooding even takes place. Arguably, there may be more damage in aggregate from the cleanup of all the DDoS handlers and agents than is suffered by smaller DDoS victims, but there have certainly been DDoS attacks against large sites with high income from advertisers who may suffer multimillion-dollar losses from attacks that last only a few hours to a few days.

Not only are damages spread out, but so is the evidence necessary to attribute the attack to a specific individual or group and pursue criminal prosecution or civil remedies. As described in Chapters 5 and 7, traceback can be difficult, if not practically impossible. The network traffic associated with the attack that proves what tool was used, how the DDoS network was controlled, and who did it, is spread out and highly volatile. Once the DDoS network ceases to function, there is no more network traffic—nothing left to capture.

The quality of incident response by all parties involved can and does affect the overall investigation, yet the distributed nature of DDoS attacks may mean that these parties are in different countries, with different languages, time zones, and entirely different legal systems. Victims whose systems were used as handlers and agents may simply "wipe and reinstall" the operating system and applications, destroying evidence in the process. Network providers at those sites, or the DDoS flooding victim site, may not focus at all on capturing network traffic, instead only acting to stabilize the network. In doing this, they fail to capture highly important evidence at the only time it may be present. In cases of extortion, it may be easier to follow the money than to follow the packets. (This is touched on by Lipson [Lip02].)

In the past few years, victims of the second phase of DDoS attacks (the flooding) have included:

- Internet Relay Chat (IRC) networks.

- Web sites associated with government agencies, such as the NSA, FBI, NASA, Department of Justice, and the Port of Houston in Texas.

- Web sites associated with news organizations, such as Al-Jazeera, CNN, and the *New York Times*.

- Terrorist-related Web sites.

- Web sites associated with opposing sides in political conflicts (e.g., Arab/Israeli, Indian/Pakistani, U.S./China).

- Web hosting sites, such as Rackspace.com and Rackshack.com.

- Online gambling or pornography sites.

- Anti-spam sites.

- Major telecommunication providers or ISPs, such as British Telecom, Telstra, and iHug.

- Major online businesses, such as Microsoft, Amazon, eBay, SCO, and Akamai.

The motivations for DDoS attacks are varied, including: simple pranks; grudges for perceived personal slights or denigration; making a political statement; exhibiting rage; for personal aggrandizement within peer groups; attempting to gain financial advantage in betting or auction scenarios; extorting money.

It is not easy to generalize about why someone would be attacked, but it is usually not hard to find reasons why someone may wish to bring harm to your organization. It then takes only sufficient technical skill, or the ability to engage (perhaps by hiring) someone who does have these skills. It is believed by many that it is only a matter of time before a terrorist organization or nation-state actor will use DDoS attacks for some political or military objective, perhaps directing the attacks against the critical infrastructures that support the United States economy. It would be unwise to believe that your site is entirely immune from being attacked, and this possibility should be weighed appropriately in your risk assessment, your continuity of operations policies and procedures, and your insurance portfolio.

8.4 How Often Is Legal Assistance Sought in DDoS Cases?

Each year, the FBI and Computer Security Institute (CSI) do a survey of security professionals in government and corporate environments. The 2004 survey is described in Appendix C (Section C.1). The key finding to note in this year's survey was that the 269 reporting institutions calculated total reported costs from DoS attacks of $26,064,050. DoS is the most costly kind of cyberattack this year, nearly twice as costly as the next largest category, theft of proprietary information (at $11,460,000 in losses).

The author of an article introducing the 2003 survey [McC03] makes an interesting statement regarding investigation of such crimes:

> The FBI generally has a trigger point of $5,000 for a cybercrime it will pursue. Given the number of incidents and the limited number of agent-hours that can be devoted to cybercrimes, this is certainly understandable. However, it is important to remember that Cliff Stoll's famous investigation detailed in *The Cuckoo's Egg* (1989) [Sto89], which turned up major holes in the highly sensitive Mitre Corp.'s phone system and ended up uncovering a spy, began with a discrepancy of only a few pennies.
>
> Obviously, the initial monetary loss should not be the sole factor that determines whether authorities decide to investigate a particular cybercrime. Unfortunately, I can't think of any other criteria that could be applied to better effect. So for the foreseeable future, companies will probably have to rely on internal resources to investigate most computer crimes. Outsourcing may be possible, but that would require companies to divulge sensitive data to outsiders, and in any case, there just aren't that many trained cybersnoops available.

A report on the British Computer Misuse Act (CMA) by the "All Party Internet Group" [api04] (both described in more detail in Section 8.10) also covers the topic of the viability of prosecution of DoS attacks. In paragraphs #59 and #60 their report states,

> We received written and oral evidence from [the Association of Remote Gambling Operators, new trade body for online bookmakers] about the criminal DDoS attacks that are currently being made on gambling websites both in the UK and elsewhere. These attacks are accompanied by monetary demands (for amounts between $10,000 and $40,000) to make the attacks stop. ARGO told us that their members would not give in to this blackmail, but that the impact on the gambling businesses had been very severe indeed. The National Hi-Tech Crime Unit (NHTCU) has become involved in the

investigation, but the perpetrators are believed to be based abroad, which sets some limits upon what they are able to quickly achieve.

Almost every respondent from industry told us that the CMA is not adequate for dealing with DoS and DDoS attacks, though very few gave any detailed analysis of why they believed this to be so. We understand that this widespread opinion is based on some 2002 advice by the Crown Prosecution Service (CPS) that s3 [subsection 3] might not stretch to including all DoS activity. Energis and ISPA told us that they knew of DoS attacks that were not investigated because "no crime could be framed."

Taking a look at another source of data, based on the numbers of incidents detected by groups such as CAIDA and Arbor Networks, it is probably safe to say that a very, very small percentage of the thousands of actual attacks per week ever result in legal action (either criminal or civil). Since a very large proportion of the attacks that occur on a regular basis are directed at IRC networks and their users—IRC being a free service, meaning no concrete monetary losses associated with the DDoS flooding—it follows that the actual damages from the majority of DDoS *floods* are also low. It is very unlikely that, even if reported, the FBI would expend scarce resources to investigate these attacks. Reporting would, seemingly, do very little good.

Of course, there are victims of DDoS flooding attacks who lose access to not only their servers, but sometimes their entire network and parts of their upstream provider's network (which may spill over to other customers of that same provider). In these cases, there may be significant financial losses, and these losses may be spread across multiple primary and collateral victims. (For example, the incident involving the Port of Houston was the by-product of an attack on a third party using the port's computers, which disrupted ship movement and may have financially impacted those shippers and even *the shippers' customers*!) Worse yet, consider situations in which irreparable loss is suffered as a result of an attack (for example, loss of data from instrumentation, say on scientific experiments at remote locations) or loss of life.

These are all, however, the second-phase victims of DDoS attacks. When you look at the first phase of DDoS attacks, in which thousands of computers are compromised, the damages could potentially really add up and are, for the most part, "hidden" costs.

Let us take a look at a simple example of the two phases of a DDoS attack. Imagine that an individual breaks into 1,000 computers to create a DDoS botnet. (A thousand hosts is a relatively small botnet these days. A large botnet would be in the hundreds of thousands.) The attacker then uses this DDoS botnet to attack a small business that sells consumer electronics products exclusively through their Internet Web site. During the attack, which we will imagine lasts six days, the victim would have made $500 in net revenue per day.

The obvious loss here is to the DDoS victim, who has suffered a net revenue loss of $3,000. Depending on overhead, cash on hand, and time of year, this loss could be significant to this victim. For example, is this the last week before Christmas when this single week accounts for 20% of yearly revenue? Add on top of that the cost of dealing with the attack itself, which can add up rapidly (especially if handled by a consultant, who may charge well over $100 per hour).

For simplicity, let us say the compromised computers that were used in the attack are all owned by broadband customers running Windows XP, and assume that all of them learn that their computers have been compromised and all of them want to clean up their problem. Each of these 1,000 users takes her computer in to a local computer service company, which charges $100 to back up the computer's hard drive, wipe the drive, reinstall Windows XP and all its current patches, reinstall all the users' applications, and restore the data files. The individual damage to each user is $100 plus her wasted time and loss of use of her computer, but added up we have a real financial cost of $100,000 (well above the $5,000 limit for prosecution). If these were business computers, the loss would instead be lost wages for the person who cleans up the system, plus some amount of lost productivity of the user of the computer. Adding in benefits and overhead, it could be several times this $100-per-system figure.

Any of these victims could report this problem to law enforcement, but the vast majority typically will not. There are perhaps two similar situations that exist. One is the most prolific graffiti tagging, which causes similar small amounts of actual monetary losses due to damage, spread over a large area. (Even then, it is rare that a tagger can tag tens of thousands of locations around the globe.) Another is spam, where the spammer consumes the resources of many sites around the Internet for sending or relaying the spam messages.

If the preceding victims decided to report the problem, and if they were able to adequately preserve evidence and provide useful reports to the FBI or Secret Service, these federal agencies would be in a better position to efficiently and effectively investigate and prosecute a larger number of cases and thus obtain the deterrent effect that laws and law enforcement are supposed to provide. Making it easier for victims to do the right thing and encouraging them to regularly report computer crimes are keys to improving this situation.

Besides the amount of damages, there are other factors that cause many businesses' reluctance to report computer crimes. Many corporate victims want to avoid any negative publicity for fear that they will lose their customers' trust, that their competitors will use information about an incident to their advantage, and that shareholders or others may bring lawsuits against the corporation or its executives. Some corporate executives are also not convinced that law enforcement either understands the needs of businesses (e.g., fearing that they may come in and seize critical systems) or that law enforcement is capable enough to help.

Also, some victims do not care very much about involving law enforcement. If the attack stops, they are satisfied. At most, they may investigate purchasing defenses to help in the event of future attacks. That's probably most true of relatively small businesses. There is an overhead cost associated with dealing with law enforcement on any issue, and many businesses may consider that overhead more expensive than the attack, or at least an added cost to the attack that they cannot afford to bear. They may also have what they believe to be sufficient insurance coverage and are satisfied with making a claim, or they may simply wish to assume any remaining risk above and beyond their existing insurance coverage.

8.5 Initiating Legal Proceedings as a Victim of DDoS

If your network and/or security operations staff can confirm that an attack is under way and that your systems have been impacted enough to cause monetary and/or physical damage, it is time to decide how to move forward. It is assumed here that your own staff, and that of your upstream network provider(s), have already identified and attempted to use all available technical measures to mitigate the attack, and that these efforts have not been adequate to bring the network back to reliable functioning.

At this point, management is faced with a decision as to whether or not to start legal proceedings.

8.5.1 Civil Proceedings

Discussed in this chapter are several theories of tort that could be used, but a victim will immediately be faced with two problems.

First, who are you going to sue? Trying to identify the perpetrator of a DDoS attack by direct traceback will be almost impossible. He may be foolish enough to brag on an IRC channel about his attack or may even contact you directly (he would have to contact you if this were an extortion attempt). However, actually identifying a physical person sitting at a keyboard and proving that he caused the damage will be very, very difficult.

Second, there is no obvious case law surrounding use of civil litigation against DDoS attackers, or even downstream liability for that matter. This may change over time, but at present this will be a hard path to follow.

8.5.2 Criminal Proceedings

Criminal proceedings are easier to initiate, but they, too, suffer the same problem of identifying the attacker. At least with a criminal investigation, law enforcement has powers of subpoenas, search warrants, and seizure of evidence to help identify the attacker, provided they have the resources and desire to pursue the case. As mentioned before, how well victims preserve, process, and present the evidence will have an impact on law enforcement's ability to pursue the case.

Start now, before an attack occurs, by reviewing the guidance provided on the Department of Justice's Cybercrime Web page (`http://www.cybercrime.gov/reporting .htm`). In case you did not read this in advance and are currently under attack, the numbers to call for reporting computer crimes at the time of publication of this book are +1-202-323-3205 for the National Infrastructure Protection Center (NIPC) Watch Desk, and +1-202-406-5850 for the U.S. Secret Service's Electronic Crimes Branch.

You should also consider reporting the incident to the CERT Coordination Center. The CERT Coordination Center is a trusted third party, who will not release any information about a victim site, the attack, etc., without the victim's express permission. Reporting to both federal law enforcement and the CERT Coordination Center also provides valuable visibility at a national level of potential large-scale cyberattacks or attacks targeted at specific critical infrastructure sectors, such as banking, telecommunications, energy, etc. The CERT Coordination Center can be contacted at `cert@cert.org` or +1-412-268-7090.

Organizations may also have other reporting requirements. For example, if your organization is in the financial sector, you may be required to file a Suspicious Activity Report (SAR) with the Securities and Exchange Commission [sar]. Even if you are not in the financial sector, you may wish to consult this same reference and use the SAR as a model for collecting information and constructing a narrative with which to report the incident to federal law enforcement.

8.6 Evidence Collection and Incident Response Procedures

Chapter 6 goes into some detail on the type of network- and/or host-related information to gather when investigating a DDoS attack. Other references cover the topic of evidence collection, chain of custody, investigation of computer crime, and digital forensics [CERd, NIoJa, NIoJb, oECFL, Uni, IAA, oJb, CIPS, oJa].

The important things to keep in mind when collecting information that may be used as evidence are:

- **Volatility of evidence.** Evidence has a life cycle which dictates how long it lives, and therefore how quickly you must move to preserve it. Put another way, the order in which you collect your evidence should be arranged so as not to disturb other evidence and change attributes, such as file time stamps, or outright destroy it, for example, by overwriting disk space. See RFC 3227 for more information [BK01].

- **Chain of custody.** Maintaining a record of who collected the information, when, and how, and then keeping track of all subsequent handoffs of the information to others is called the *chain of custody.* This includes integrity checks, such as cryptographically strong hash values (e.g., SHA1 or better), which provide a unique signature of the contents. (Even better is a cryptographic time stamp of the file, which not only proves the fingerprint of the file, but also the time at which that fingerprint was made.) If it cannot be proved in court that this chain was maintained, an argument can be made that the evidence may have been tampered with, was accidentally modified from booting the system, or is incomplete.

- **Records kept as a normal course of business.** Logs and other records showing access and the like should be kept as a normal course of business in order to be admissible as evidence. You will be better off when these records are required for use in court if you have a standard practice that involves their collection.

See section V in the Department of Justice document "Searching and Seizing Computers and Obtaining Electronic Evidence in Criminal Investigations" [CIPS] for more information about evidence in computer crime cases.

8.7 Estimating Damages

So how exactly does a victim calculate losses? Even though computer crime cases go back decades, there was little firm guidance from state or federal legislatures in the United States on how to calculate damages from computer security incidents, let alone a definition of what "losses" were in these cases. This led to a great deal of confusion, and situations in which widespread intrusions involving dozens of sites were not investigated, because no single victim was willing or able to show a loss that exceeded the $5,000 limit necessary to trigger federal statutes, such as the Computer Fraud and Abuse Act (CFAA) (18 U.S.C. §1030).

Under the original CFAA, it was unclear whether damages could be aggregated. This meant that DDoS attacks that involved hundreds or thousands of sites that were hosting a handful of agents each, if they even calculated damages at all, would suffer "losses" only in the low thousands of dollars. Since each site would be looked at in isolation, conceivably none would meet the $5,000 limit, so pursuing prosecution would not be justified. If the victim was simply a public IRC server that did not have any paying customers, their losses could similarly be less than the $5,000 limit. There would be no case, even if in reality that one individual attacker had caused aggregate damages for a series of attacks that ran into the tens of thousands of dollars.

In some cases where there were multiple charges, for example, when a sniffer was used to capture user passwords as they were transmitted over the network, prosecutors would use the federal wiretap statute or "trafficking in access devices" (that is, the passwords) as the basis on which to prosecute. In other cases in which the suspect possessed credit card numbers, statutes involving trafficking of credit card numbers would be used. None of these statutes required proving a minimum amount of monetary damages (or any monetary damages at all).

A court decision in 2000, however, in the case *United States v. Middleton* did set a precedent in calculating damages. Nicholas Middleton worked as a system programmer for an ISP named Slip.net. He had intimate knowledge of how the system worked. He became dissatisfied with his job at Slip.net, and he quit. After quitting, he continued to use an account that Slip.net had given him, and used special computer programs to elevate privileges and delete accounts and files. His former employer tracked this activity to his account, and reported it to authorities. Middleton was arrested for causing damage to a "protected computer" without authorization, in violation of 18 U.S.C. §1030(a)(5)(A) and was later convicted [mid].

In the instructions to the jury on calculating damages, the court in *Middleton* stated:

> The term "loss" means any monetary loss that Slip.net sustained as a result of any damage to Slip.net's computer data, program, system or information that you find occurred.
>
> And in considering whether the damage caused a loss less than or greater than $5,000, you may consider any loss that you find was a natural and foreseeable result of any damage that you find occurred.
>
> In determining the amount of losses, you may consider what measures were reasonably necessary to restore the data, program, system, or information that you find was

damaged or what measures were reasonably necessary to re-secure the data, program, system, or information from further damage.

Middleton appealed, but a higher court held that the calculation of damages was valid and that the "losses" suffered by the victims of computer crimes could reasonably include a wide range of harms, including the costs of:

1. Responding to the attack

2. Conducting a damage assessment

3. Restoring the system and data to their condition prior to the attack

4. Any lost revenue or costs incurred due to the interruption of services

The USA Patriot Act of 2001 [oJa] amended 18 U.S.C. §1030(e)(11) to codify the decision of the courts in *Middleton*. Under these changes, the government is now able to aggregate "loss resulting from a related course of conduct affecting one or more other protected computers"[3] over a period of one year.

This also allows for including both attack phases of a DDoS attack, such that any subset of damages from the many sites involved can be aggregated, more easily getting above the $5,000 jurisdictional threshold. Of course, this does not mean that the FBI will investigate every case that involves damages over $5,000, but it does make it easier to meet the minimum required limit of damages.

8.7.1   A Cost-Estimation Model

A model that is helpful for calculating such damages was developed as part of a study by a group of Big 10 (plus 1) universities. Called the "Incident Cost Analysis and Modeling Project" (or ICAMP) [oIC], the group used the following type of analysis.

• Persons affected by the incident were identified and the amount of time spent/lost due to the incident was logged.

• Staff/faculty/student employee time cost was calculated by dividing the individual's wage rate by 52 weeks and 40 hours per week to come up with an hourly rate. The wage rate is then multiplied by the logged hours, and varied by $+/- 15\%$.

• A benefit rate of 28% is added (an average of the institutions in the study) to come up with a dollar loss per individual.

---

[3] The term *protected computer* is defined in 18 U.S.C. §1030(a)(5)(B)(i).

Title	Hours	Cost/Hr	Total	−15%	+15%
Incident investigator	37	$33.65	$1,245.05	$1,058.29	$1,431.81
System administrator*	3	$33.65	$100.95	$85.81	$116.09
Benefits @ 28%			$348.61	$296.32	$400.91
Subtotal (salary and benefits)			$1,694.61	$1,440.42	$1,948.81
Indirect costs			$0.00	$0.00	$0.00
Total labor cost			$1,694.61	$1,440.42	$1,948.81
Median cost +/−15			$1,694.61	+/−$254.20	

* Expected time for system reinstallation

Figure 8.1 Incident cost table

- The total of all individuals' time, plus incidental expenses (e.g., hardware stolen/
  damaged, phone calls to other sites), is then calculated using a simple spreadsheet
  approach.

This model is described in more detail in a FAQ (frequently asked question) file
that was authored by David Dittrich [Dite], which includes references to an Excel
spreadsheet that can be used as an example in calculating damages from an incident.
The model is elaborated on in an article in *SecurityFocus Online* entitled, "Developing
an Effective Incident Cost Analysis Mechanism" [Ditc].

Figure 8.1 shows an example of the incident costs associated with a break-in to a
single computer. It includes only the response costs incurred by an incident investigator
and the administrator of the system. Both of their salaries, when broken down to an
hourly rate, are $33.65. You simply multiply these salaries by the number of hours
spent, then include benefits and overhead costs. (In this example, there are no indirect
costs.) Totaling up these costs, and including an error factor of +/− 15%, shows
that the cost of cleanup for this single host is $1,695 +/− $254. The hardest part of
this process is simply getting those involved to keep track of time spent, then doing
the bookkeeping to aggregate damages within your organization. Many universities
in the United States will frequently have hundreds or even thousands of computers
compromised by a given worm or automated exploit, costing the better part of a day
or more of time per computer to restore each affected computer to functionality. The
total length of time to clean up all affected systems may extend to several weeks, or

even months, in real time. The result is an unrecognized loss of productivity across the institution of hundreds of thousands of dollars per incident.

8.8 Jurisdictional Issues

The above discussion of damage estimates and limits includes the term "jurisdictional threshold." Since we are talking about federal statutes in the United States, this means the agency that will prosecute the computer crime is the United States Attorney's Office, which means that the Federal Bureau of Investigation or Secret Service will be the investigative agency. The damages must be aggregated within, for example, an FBI field office.

Let us look at the FBI field office in the Central District of California. From their Web page [fbi], they describe their jurisdiction this way:

> The Los Angeles Field Office of the Federal Bureau of Investigation (FBI) has investigative jurisdiction over the federal Central District of California. The Central District is comprised of seven counties: Los Angeles, Orange, Riverside, San Bernardino, San Luis Obispo, Santa Barbara, and Ventura.
>
> The Los Angeles Field Office territory is the most populated [in all of the FBI's territories] with 18 million people residing within 40,000 square miles. The Los Angeles Field Office has the third greatest number of Special Agents in the FBI.
>
> The Los Angeles Field Office headquarters is located at 11000 Wilshire Boulevard in Los Angeles. The field office also has ten satellite offices known as Resident Agencies, which are located in Lancaster, Long Beach, Palm Springs, Riverside, Santa Ana, Santa Maria, Ventura, Victorville, West Covina, and at the Los Angeles International Airport.

What this means is that the aggregate amount of damage being estimated for prosecution within the jurisdiction of the Los Angeles field office includes only those victims in the area described above. The easier it is for the FBI's various field offices to correlate incidents and calculate aggregate damages, the better chance they will be able to quickly identify a jurisdiction that meets the limit and to move forward with an investigation. All victims of computer intrusions who wish to support law enforcement (and to have a viable legal deterrent to computer crime) should take this into consideration and be prepared to produce accurate and timely damage estimates, e.g., using the methods discussed above.

Another jurisdictional issue has to do with which laws apply to a given computer crime. Is a sniffer a violation of state electronic communications privacy laws, or federal electronic communications privacy laws, or both? How about computer trespass statutes? These are typically state laws, if trespass into computers is recognized at all. There is a federal Computer Fraud and Abuse Act, which may also have a state version.

Many large cities have police resources for investigating computer crimes, but these resources are often very limited. More and more crimes are beginning to involve the use of computers as instrumentalities of crime and/or repositories of evidence. As these crimes increase, the resources of local law enforcement will become even more strained. Much computer forensic analysis is handed off from local police to county or state police services, who may have more resources and training (although still not enough to investigate all cases involving computers). Regional computer forensics centers and joint FBI/Secret Service Task Forces are being formed across the country and are augmenting and coordinating computer forensic analyses and computer crime investigations, but there is still much to be done to keep up with the increase in number of digital devices that can be used for crimes, including things like PDAs, wrist watches, cell phones, digital cameras, and key-chain memory sticks.

8.9   Domestic Legal Issues

Let us now revisit the earlier attack scenario, only this time it is a much larger attack. Our attacker now breaks into 100,000 computers and builds a series of large bot networks. The attacker now goes after a site that receives on the order of $1 million per day in advertising revenue. The attacker has taken her time and knows the available bandwidth to the victim site, and understands the network topology and response capabilities of the victim's upstream providers. She uses only sufficient numbers of DDoS agents at a time to take the site down, assuming it will be cleaned up over time by incident response teams and the attack capacity of the botnet will decrease over time. She brings in new attack networks at just the right time to keep the pain at a sufficiently high level. Using this tactic, the attacker can keep the attack going for more than a week.

Legal counsel for any victim should consider the following issues when determining what advice and which course of action to take after an attack:

- **Negligence on the victim's part.** Consider whether there was negligence on the part of your client. Some issues to address are: (1) what precautions did the victim take prior to the attack to prepare for the possibility of an attack; (2) did the victim do an adequate risk assessment and balance defenses with insurance coverage to mitigate financial risk; (3) how did the victim respond to the attack once it was aware of the attack; and (4) was the response justifiable morally, ethically, and legally?

Addressing the preceding issues is important because it is likely that your client/victim may be called to account to shareholders, customers, subcontractors, or any others who may be financially harmed as a result of an inadequate or a legally questionable response by the victim.

The main message here is that counsel and client should perform an adequate risk assessment that addresses the prevention, detection, and reaction elements of information assurance.

- **Criminal culpability**. Consider whether your client/victim is able to identify a suspect in the attack, either through communications by the attacker that reveal an identity, involve a consistent communication method that can be traced back to the attacker, or through the legal discovery or investigative processes. It is best to provide this information to federal law enforcement as soon as possible to allow them an opportunity to investigate.

  Where a suspect cannot readily be identified by the victim, the possibility of investigation still exists. However, if the attacker has taken advanced measures to cover her tracks and thereby remain anonymous, the possibility of a successful prosecution becomes much more difficult, if not impossible.

  Either way, as mentioned in Section 8.7 regarding losses in criminal prosecutions, sufficient economic injury to the victim must be shown in order to meet the statutory limits required to pursue prosecution. Thus, it is important that any victim thoroughly assesses and collects evidence of the harm caused by an attacker.

- **Liability**. There are two primary types of liability that could apply in DDoS attacks. There is direct or "attacker" liability for the harm caused by an attacker, and indirect, or "downstream" liability, for the harm caused by those sites whose systems are compromised and used for an attack.

  In an attacker liability suit, the person or persons responsible for the attack are sued. However, in a downstream liability suit, the plaintiff would be trying to prove negligence on the part of the owner of computers that were compromised and used to launch an attack against a third party. As previously mentioned, proving negligence involves showing, by a preponderance of the evidence, that four factors exist:

  1. The defendant owed a duty of care to the plaintiff to secure their computers against compromise and abuse.
  2. The defendant breached, or violated, that duty.
  3. The breach of that duty was the actual and proximate cause of injury to the plaintiff.

4. The injury suffered by the plaintiff can be addressed by the awarding of damages.

The key here is establishing a duty of care which is judged using a "reasonable person" standard (i.e., what would a reasonable person do to secure her computer, and did the defendant fail to do at least the same?). In other words, negligence cannot exist where there is no preexisting duty, or where a duty cannot be established.

Laws that establish some form of requirement for computer security include the Gramm-Leach-Bliley Act [Ele], which suggests a number of security measures that banks, credit unions, and other financial institutions should implement to protect their computer databases (and institutes civil and criminal penalties for businesspeople who do not adequately protect personal or financial information from compromise due to computer intrusions).

In the health care field, there is the Health Insurance Portability and Accountability Act (HIPAA) of 1996 [hip], which holds system administrators, information security officers, and administrators financially liable for disclosure of health-related information that could result from a computer intrusion.

It is important to note that liability cases are usually brought in local courts. Thus, trial venue may become another important factor that comes into play (e.g., where did the "damage" actually occur?).

8.10   International Legal Issues

Earlier, the relationship among city, state, and federal law enforcement was mentioned. Often, there are collaborative difficulties between law enforcement agencies at the various government levels. For example, county sheriffs may consider a crime to be in their jurisdiction and search and seize computers, only to have the FBI show up and claim jurisdiction, having to then argue about which agency has priority of possession over the evidence and the manner in which it was collected and handled. These issues get even more complicated when taken up to the international arena.

Criminal law is very well defined in the United States with regard to computer crimes. Internationally, however, there is very little law concerning computer intrusions. Laws concerning computer systems and electronic forms of data and property are quite different from country to country. In certain countries, computer data (information) is not considered property at all. (For more on international legal issues, see [int, oE, IAA, Lip02].)

In 1999, a study of available national legal codes concerning computer crimes in 50 countries around the world was performed by Ekaterina Drozdova, Marc Goodman, Jonathan Hopwood, and Xiaogang Wang. This study found that 70% of these countries had computer crime statutes,[4] while 30% had few or no laws covering computer-related crimes.[5] It is worth noting that a nation's not having explicit statutes concerning computer crime does not mean that computer crime is legal there. The nation may use existing principles of law as applied to the new realm of computers instead. That has its strengths (well-established and understood laws) and its weaknesses (the analogy between the cyber and noncyber situations might be strained).

In November 2001, the Council of Europe released its final draft of the *Convention on Cybercrime,* [oE], which provides guidelines for members of the European Union in how to formulate harmonious laws regarding computer misuse. Chapter II, Section 1, states guidelines for formulating substantive criminal law as it pertains to several offenses. For our purposes, the critical elements are the unauthorized access of computers, data interference, system interference, and misuse of computing devices. These cover both phases of DDoS attacks. The Convention states that "each party shall adopt such legislative and other measures as may be necessary to establish as criminal offenses under its domestic law, when committed intentionally, the access to the whole or any part of a computer system without right."

The *Convention on Cybercrime* attempts to address some of the legal imbalance found in the Drozdova survey. It states, "Given the cross-border nature of information networks, a concerted international effort is needed to deal with such misuse." Chapter III defines the guidelines for international cooperation. Article 23 expresses the general tenor for the principles governing international cooperation:

> The Parties shall co-operate with each other, in accordance with the provisions of this chapter, and through application of relevant international instruments on international co-operation in criminal matters, arrangements agreed on the basis of uniform or reciprocal legislation, and domestic laws, to the widest extent possible for the purposes of

---

[4] The countries with computer crime statutes were Australia, Austria, Bulgaria, Canada, Finland, France, Germany, Greece, India, Israel, Italy, Japan, Malaysia, Mexico, the Netherlands, Norway, the People's Republic of China, Portugal, Romania, Russia, Singapore, South Africa, Spain, Sweden, Switzerland, the United Kingdom, and the United States.

[5] The countries with few or no computer crime laws were Argentina, Brazil, Chile, Costa Rica, the Czech Republic, Denmark, El Salvador, Ecuador, Hungary, Iceland, Ireland, Jordan, Luxembourg, New Zealand, Oman, Panama, Peru, Poland, Saudi Arabia, Trinidad and Tobago, Tunisia, the United Arab Emirates, and Venezuela.

investigations or proceedings concerning criminal offenses related to computer systems and data, or for the collection of evidence in electronic form of a criminal offense.

Remaining articles define principles of extradition and other principles requiring mutual assistance among nations.

Extradition is important in cases in which crimes are committed by a foreign-based individual, and the victim's government wishes to bring a suspect from another country before a court having proper jurisdiction. The case of Onel de Guzman, author of the "I Love You" computer virus, provides an example. Laws in the Philippines at the time de Guzman launched this virus did not consider computer data to be property, and the Philippines had no laws on their books covering computer intrusion or damage. The FBI quickly tracked the attack to de Guzman and had the cooperation of the Philippines federal police. However, when asked by the FBI to arrest de Guzman, courts in the Philippines could not help. Nothing could be done, despite the significant estimated worldwide damages, which ran into the millions of dollars.

In addition to needing a law under which to bring a criminal action, another requirement is that the act must be illegal under both jurisdictions in order for an extradition request to be honored. This is known as "dual criminality." In the de Guzman case, he could not be brought back to the United States to stand trial here because he did not break any existing Philippines law.

In order to obtain extradition of a suspect from another country to the United States, federal law enforcement agents in the United States must first draft charges and go through a process called "letters rogatory," which involves the Department of State's producing the letters and delivering them to the foreign nation's state representatives, who then in turn provide them to the foreign government's federal law enforcement agents, who then issue a warrant for the suspect's arrest, serve this warrant, and prepare to deliver the suspect to the United States federal law enforcement agents. Mutual Legal Assistance Treaties (MLATs) that are established in advance speed up this process greatly, as does having a Legal Attache (LEGAT) from the United States FBI or Secret Service already in the foreign country and working closely with their federal law enforcement agency. Of course, the foreign government may refuse to arrest or extradite the suspect, which can cause a delay or derail a case. Interpol is one international police organization that tries to bridge this gap of international jurisdictional issues [BN].

The outlined legal procedures are clearly expensive, heavyweight, and slow. Thus, one cannot rely on them to help much in stopping an ongoing DDoS attack of international origins. At best, they may allow eventual prosecution of the perpetrator.

There are also issues of national defense that can come up in cases of massive DDoS attacks against corporations or agencies that provide "critical infrastructures," such as banking, transportation, energy, telecommunications, etc. When does an attack on a business move from a criminal matter to a national security situation? Who is really attacking, and what damage do they intend to cause? While it may be clear that a direct attack on a military command-and-control network by a foreign entity that is clearly associated with a foreign military or intelligence agency could be interpreted as an act of war, it is not clear when or how a set of DDoS attacks on banks and airlines by an unknown entity would be interpreted as an act of war.

8.11 Self-Help Options

In the prior sections, we have seen many of the issues and impediments to federal criminal prosecution that lead some executives to doubt the ability of federal law enforcement agencies to pursue criminal legal remedies, and some of the options for civil remedies available to victims. There still are some who wish to take matters into their own hands and "do something" about being attacked.

This subject is sometimes called Active (Network) Defense, Computer Network Defense (CND) Response Actions, or the extreme form, the popular media term *hack back*.[6,7]

This is a complex and controversial topic that is gaining in prominence in computer security conferences and discussion lists. David Dittrich maintains a section of his Web page that includes a significant amount of material on the topic (see `http://staff.washington.edu/dittrich/activedefense.html`). The as yet unpublished *Handbook on Information Security* [Bid05] will include an article by Kenneth Himma and David Dittrich titled, "Active Response to Computer Intrusions" that covers this topic.

---

[6] The federal government has been given guidance on CND response actions that can be taken by military personnel. According to a Congressional Research Service report [Ser], p. 18, states, "The guidance, known as National Security Presidential Directive 16, was signed in July 2002, and is intended to clarify circumstances under which an information warfare attack by DOD would be justified, and who has authority to launch a computer attack."

[7] While some use the term *Active Defense* (or Active Network Defense), this subject is also known as Computer Network Defense Response Actions (CND-RA). The popular media term *hack back* overemphasizes the most extreme forms of CND-RA. A new term, *Active Response Continuum*, is proposed by David Dittrich in [Bid04] to reflect that there is a measured progression of response actions that should be thoughtfully considered.

One option that has very little real chance of working is attempting to counter a DDoS attack with a DDoS attack. There are just too many reasons why this is simply a foolish option to pursue.

- It is too easy for a moderate to highly skilled attacker to build large DDoS attack networks that cannot be overwhelmed by a counterattack. Moderate-sized botnets can easily reach 10,000 to 30,000 hosts, and large botnets of 140,000 hosts were seen as early as 2003 [Fis03]. There is simply no way that a victim can counter this kind of available bandwidth without further damaging its own network.

- Going after smaller subsets of bots, say in the 1,000 to 5,000 range, has similar problems with trying to match firepower, and if the attacker controls 140,000 hosts, it would be impossible to keep up with the influx of new attacking hosts, 1,000 here, 1,000 there, for as long as the attacker has more resources.

- Attacking back to attempt to disable hosts can have side effects that are unpredictable. Since such an attack may be disproportional to the traffic coming out of the DDoS agents, the owner of those systems may turn around and press charges against you. The attacker may control a host that is used for patient care, process control, etc., but using it to attack may not cause it to fail completely. Your counterattack, specifically designed to disable the host completely, may cause more damage than the original attacker, and you may be found by a court to be legally responsible for this damage.

- Can the desired goal be attained without risking even greater retaliation? If you do not know who is attacking you, and you do not know whether they have already penetrated your network or not, it is impossible to expect that a counterattack that is limited to attempting to remove their access to compromised hosts will actually achieve that goal. If you fail, and they have control of other resources in your own network that you are not aware of, they may simply use these to increase the damage to your network.

The bottom line is that a counterattack against a DDoS attack is almost certainly guaranteed to fail, or to cause more damage than it prevents. Such a counterattack is also likely to violate computer crime statutes at the state and/or federal level, and to potentially also violate statutes in other nations (where some of the DDoS agents and handlers you will be attacking may be located) and further increase your legal risk exposure. Regardless of how much it may seem to be worth the risk, the chances that your resources, knowledge about the attacker, skill level, and ability to execute a tactical and strategic counteroffensive, *and* do it in an ethically and legally justifiable manner, are very, very slim at best. Even if you were to succeed in such a counterattack, you would be creating congestion and harming many other Internet users who have nothing to do with either you or the attacker.

At this point in time, your best course of action is to follow the guidance in Chapter 6 to collect evidence of the attack, and to then contact the sites that are involved in the attack as well as federal law enforcement agencies, and to work cooperatively with all sites involved to respond to the situation.

8.12   A Few Words on Ethics

Not all problems are best solved by legal action. Our world operates because most of us agree on many ethical principles and normally act according to those principles. Should we not apply those principles just as much to our cyber behavior as our real-world behavior? Doing so would have a couple of implications concerning DDoS. We do not presume to provide moral answers here, but we would like to bring up a few questions.

First, if one ascribes to the ethical principle that it is wrong to needlessly harm others, one should consider if it is ever right to launch a DDoS attack against anyone, whether it be an offensive or defensive act. You will do them harm. You may very well do harm to third parties who you did not intend to strike. Is that right?

When viewed from the perspective of someone wishing to use DDoS as an offensive tool, there is no ethical justification. Even when viewed from a defensive perspective, as a countermeasure to an attack on you, DDoS is still hard to ethically justify.

Second, if you believe that it is unethical to offer assistance to another who is doing wrong, is it ethical of you to leave your computer in a state that makes it easy for a DDoS attacker to compromise? This is not a simple or trivial point. How much effort do you need to take to secure your computer? What if fixing a known problem requires crippling functionality that you rely on? This issue can be resolved only by considering one's own personal morality and circumstances, but we urge all readers to spend a moment or two thinking about whether they are doing enough to protect their own computers, not just for selfish reasons, but to make it less likely that your computer assets will be used to perform a DDoS attack on another site.

There will always be people who have morality that allows them to perform actions like DDoS attacks without compromising their principles, and those who do not care for morality at all. So relying on morality to stop DDoS attacks is unrealistic. But perhaps applying a bit more simple morality to the cyberworld might stop a few attacks or make DDoS attacks a bit harder to perpetrate.

The ethical issues surrounding self-help options are covered in more depth in the same article, "Active Response to Computer Intrusions," in the forthcoming *Handbook on Information Security* [Bid05] mentioned earlier, as well as in articles by the University of Washington professor Kenneth Einar Himma ("The Ethics of Tracing Hacker Attacks through the Machines of Innocent Persons," [Him04a] and "Targeting the Innocent: Active Defense and the Moral Immunity of Innocent Persons from Aggression" [Him04b]).

8.13   Current Trends in International Cyber Law

A recent subject of discussion regarding liability of owners of the hosts that are compromised and used for DDoS attack is a pair of laws in Italy regarding civil and criminal negligence. To see how they apply, a hypothetical scenario will be used.

Let us say that A is the victim of a DDoS attack, and this attack can be traced to one or more computers owned by B. If a post-mortem analysis of B's computer is performed, and it shows that B has not applied the "minimum security measures," then A has a civil cause of action against B and can bring suit in Italian civil court for an article called "damage refund" under the Italian civil code. (This is similar to what was discussed in Section 8.9.)

What is more, there is a law in Italy (196/2003) called the "Privacy Law." This law requires that the appropriate/minimum security measures for information security are mandatory if an information system stores sensitive, personal, and judiciary-related data. If an incident occurs, and the owner of the information system is found not to be compliant with the law, they may be levied a penalty of 50,000 euros and three years in jail. This means that if A is attacked using a compromised host owned by B, and B's compromised machine contains sensitive data, and a post-mortem analysis (even conducted by the police) demonstrates that the minimum security measures were not applied, then B may be brought in front of the court for violation of both laws.

This privacy law is new, so as of publication of this book there was no case law to cite. Italian Web sites that store personal information will have a privacy statement mentioning law 196/2003.

As discussed in Section 8.2, the primary law in the United States that may apply to DDoS attacks is the Computer Fraud and Abuse Act. The example cited, *United States v. Dennis*, prosecuted a DoS attack under 18 U.S.C. §1030(a)(5), "interfering with a government-owned communications system." This law clearly applies to government-owned systems, and other "protected computers." A very good explanation of its application to date, and some proposed changes to the way that the terms *unauthorized* and *access* are interpreted, can be found in a 2003 *New York University Law Review* article by Orin S. Kerr [Ker03].

A similar law to the CFAA in the United Kingdom is the Computer Misuse Act (CMA). During the early part of 2004, a group called the All Party Internet Group (APIG)[8] held an inquiry into the CMA [api04]. Their inquiry notes the same cases of DDoS-related extortion attempts cited in Chapter 3, and the efforts of the British High Tech Crimes Unit to investigate them. They also cite the same case of a DoS attack involving the Port of Houston. Further, they point out the same issue of the two phases of DDoS attacks, stating:

> In general, where a DDoS attack takes place then an offense will have been committed because many machines will have been taken over by the attacker and special software installed to implement the attack. Even when a system is attacked by a single machine, an offense will sometime be committed because the contents of the system will be altered.

Their recommendation is the creation of a new offense of "impairing access to data."

An even more interesting recommendation made by APIG is founded on the same evidence discussed earlier in this chapter of limited resources on the part of law enforcement, and the impression of some victims that there is no effective law enforcement response option available to them in all but the largest cases. This situation creates a negative value in their opinion of laws that are on the books, but provide no realistic deterrent due to very low prosecution rates. Their recommendation is to build on an ancient right, preserved under s6(1) of the Prosecution of Offenses Act of 1985, for individuals to bring private prosecution. They explain that the first step is for the individual making the claim to "lay an information" before a magistrate, who then decides whether or not to issue a summons. If he does, a criminal trial will ensue.

To implement this recommendation, they suggest following the recommendations of another group, EURIM (the European Information Society Group). In a EURIM-IPPR e-crime study working paper titled, "Working Paper 4: Roles and Procedures for Investigation" [eur04] recommends several things:

- Creation of joint private industry/law enforcement crime units, and establishment of guidelines for the creation, governance, and operation of such units.

- Develop guidelines with industry for handling requests from private investigation teams for supporting services for which only law enforcement are authorized.

---

[8] APIG is made up of parliamentarians from the House of Commons and House of Lords, and provides a discussion forum for Internet-related issues for the purpose of informing debate in Parliament.

- Develop a scheme for the exchange of investigative and forensics experience, best practices, and tools within communities.

- Investigate with representatives of law enforcement, industry, and other interested parties the possibility of investigators and others in industry with appropriate skills and experience being accredited to work to the same legal and operational standards and guidelines as law enforcement when involved in e-crime investigations.

The effect of these two bodies of recommendations would be to (1) make criminal the act of denying access to data and information systems; (2) create a cadre of trained computer security professionals in private industry who have special, but limited, authority to investigate these crimes (perhaps closely involved with law enforcement); and (3) to permit these private security service companies to bring private prosecutions under the CMA (with the right reserved by the Director of Public Prosecutions to take over, decline to provide evidence, or withdraw the case).

Relating the APIG proposal back to the United States, this proposal includes components that are similar to those put forward in the United States in a 1998 law review article by Stevan D. Mitchell and Elizabeth A. Banker entitled, "Private Intrusion Response" [MB98]. This paper came out of work during the Clinton administration by the President's Commission on Critical Infrastructure Protection (PCCIP), in the Critical Infrastructure Assurance Office (CIAO) [pcc97, itCD97].

It will likely take some time—and much needed debate—before the issues brought up in these proposals are resolved. Similarly, it will take time before there is enough case law under new statutes to determine if a positive effect has been achieved on reducing cybercrime in general, or the use of DDoS as a means of engaging in other criminal activities.

CHAPTER 9

Conclusions

As we have seen, distributed DoS attacks are a genuine threat that cause serious damage to many Internet users. The losses being suffered have escalated from being merely annoying to actually being debilitating and disastrous for some users. There is every reason to believe that the rate and seriousness of DDoS attacks will increase. The current limited level of losses caused by DDoS is probably not due to successes in defending against them, difficulties in perpetrating the attacks, or lack of attractive targets to attack. Rather, the level of loss is related more to the motivations and desires of those who are perpetrating the attacks. As more unprincipled and dissatisfied users of the Internet observe the success of DDoS attacks, we should expect the frequency and severity of such attacks to increase.

There are existing examples suggesting that we will indeed see such a trend. Politically motivated DDoS attacks have taken place (such as the attack against Al-Jazeera). DDoS attacks have been used to state political opinions (like the attacks on SCO in protest of their intellectual property claims on Unix and Linux source code). A company in Great Britain may have been put out of business by a DDoS attack. Criminals have begun to investigate ways to turn DDoS attacks into profits (extortion attempts based on threats of unleashing DDoS attacks). For example, Mybet, a German Internet gambling site, was recently hit with a DDoS attack that prevented customers from reaching it for 16 hours, causing more lost income than the extortion attempt associated with the attack demanded [Leb]. Many British gambling sites, including iBetX, William Hill, TotalBet, UKbetting, and SportingOptions, have been targeted by similar attacks when they refused to pay the extortionist's price [Leyb]. Because of the low technological barrier required to become the commander of an army of DDoS agents that can then be directed at any Internet target, we can expect that DDoS attacks will become more frequent and more targeted toward achieving aims of these sorts.

As long as DDoS attacks prove effective in achieving such aims, attackers are likely to continue using them. Until we find a reasonable defense against some kinds of DDoS attacks, we should expect to see their incidence, power, and seriousness increase. Why? Because network bandwidth, processor speed, and number of available systems that can be attacked and compromised all continue to increase, as does the sophistication of attacker tools for compromising computers and using them to attack. Nor is it common for a DDoS attacker to be arrested, let alone prosecuted or convicted, so legal deterrents are not yet effective. Existing commercial defenses are not likely to be sufficient to stem the tide of increasing attacks.

Obviously, then, something needs to be done. But the way ahead is not clear. Many intelligent researchers have been examining the DDoS problem for several years now, and we do not lack for a variety of approaches to creating a sufficient defense against DDoS attacks. What's lacking is any consensus among those researchers on which of the approaches actually show sufficient promise to take the step beyond research prototypes to make them effective solutions for real-world deployment. Full consensus has not even been achieved on the nature of the entire problem, even at the level of a common agreement on exactly what constitutes a DDoS attack.

A major reason for the lack of consensus is that we lack any convincing method of demonstrating the effectiveness of solutions. Each researcher or commercial provider performs some series of tests that give them sufficient confidence about their approach to make claims that it works, to some extent, at least. Some of these tests amount to little more than trying a few DDoS attacks against the proposed defense and declaring victory once the defense stops them. Even the best of these tests are rarely more than using parameterized traffic generators with a variety of settings to generate many different forms of attacks, perhaps coupled with some limited blue team/red team testing. No one in either the research or commercial community has provided really convincing evidence that their system handles a wide variety of possible DDoS attacks, nor have they provided a methodology for a head-to-head comparison of proposed DDoS solutions. One outstanding problem, then, that must be overcome before we have any real hope of combating real-world DDoS threats is to find a way to test how well a proposed defensive mechanism works.

We do not propose to go into all the reasons why determining the efficacy of a DDoS mechanism is difficult, but we will suggest a few major ones:

- Security metrics of any kind are hard to come by.

- There is not even complete understanding among all those involved in DDoS defense on what the actual goal of the defense should be. Some claim it should stop the onslaught of the attack traffic, at all cost. Others claim it should make sure legitimate traffic gets through. Both goals are important, since stopping the bad traffic benefits everyone, but getting the legitimate traffic through prevents the DDoS attackers from achieving their real goal.

- There is no well-defined statement of what kind of attacks a good DDoS defense mechanism must handle to be labeled successful.

- There is no common testing methodology or large enough testing environment in which to perform comparisons.

- Any convincing testing methodology would need to observe the behavior of the system in the face of realistic traffic, and producing simulations or generating such traffic is not trivial.

- Skills and strategy/tactics in incident response against DDoS attacks are still not widespread enough to generate sufficient demand for a solution or the motivations to engineer networks that would accommodate such solutions. Without strong demand, the research and development required to understand and evaluate DDoS attacks and defenses will not be performed.

Fortunately, some researchers have recognized this problem and are now starting to tackle it in an organized way. The National Science Foundation and the Department of Homeland Security have funded research to investigate DDoS measurements and benchmarking, and a program to build a substantial testbed for performing evaluations of DDoS and other cybersecurity solutions [USC]. Many of the researchers in the DDoS community are contributing in other ways: by holding workshops and discussions of these issues, by writing papers that seek to better define the DDoS threat, and by investigating both the breadth of the potential DDoS problem and the space of possible solutions.

All of these efforts, however, are mere precursors to finding a fabric of layered solutions that address all aspects of the DDoS problem, from the ability to take control of huge numbers of computers and do with them as the attacker desires, to creating network-level autoimmune-style actions, to improving the efficiency of human incident response. Few in the DDoS research community seem to believe that any proposed solution, in its present form or with minor improvements, would stand up particularly well to the benchmarks and testbeds we hope to have in a few years, much less prove of great efficacy in halting the DDoS threat in the real world. The character of the DDoS threat will evolve over time, probably becoming more difficult to handle. Therefore, even if some existing system handled all of today's threats well, it would be unlikely to be a complete solution for the future. A more reasonable hope is that better understanding of the performance, strengths, and weaknesses of different defense approaches will ultimately provide guidance on truly effective solutions. Thus, there will be much more research to be done before we can claim to have a full understanding of the problems associated with DDoS attacks and effective countermeasures to the DDoS threat, in the same way that we have relatively good understanding of the nature of viruses and effective ways to handle them.

We must remember that these relatively effective tools for handling other security threats have not eliminated those threats. They have merely reduced them to manageable levels. The same is nearly certain to be true for DDoS threats. The Internet is not just waiting for a magic switch to be thrown that will, at whatever cost, eliminate DDoS attacks forever. Rather, we eventually hope to reach the point where vigilant system administrators who can afford to spend moderate amounts of money on their defenses and even greater amounts of their time on properly configuring them and running them will usually be able to handle common DDoS attacks.

There is good reason to believe we will never be able to make DDoS attacks impossible. Ultimately, a DDoS attack can consist of a vast number of requests coming in to a site that are indistinguishable from real requests for that site's resources. In many ways, a DDoS attack is a flash crowd with a bad attitude. The physical world's solutions for dealing with situations in which more people want something than can get it are usually imperfect, and we are unlikely to do much better in cyberspace. However, these sorts of solutions are good enough for most purposes in the real world, and are similarly likely to be good enough for handling most DDoS attacks. Our goal need not be perfection, but just to reduce the threat to the point where we all know how to live with the possibility of DDoS attacks and how to handle them when they do occur. To achieve this more realistic goal, we should enlist all tools at our disposal, including social, financial, legal, and political solutions, as well as purely technical ones.

Any solution we do produce that limits the threat of DDoS to a manageable level will have to be continually improved. Like all other security problems, defending against DDoS attacks is akin to an arms race. As defenses make particular forms of DDoS attacks ineffective, the attackers will seek new weak points that permit them to resume the attacks. The defenders must then improve their defenses to counter those attacks, and the attackers go back to the drawing board to find new ways around the better defenses. Other cybersecurity problems are also arms races, and they have been dealt with sufficiently well to allow us all to go about our cyberbusiness with reasonable safety. It is always possible to invent a new virus that existing virus protection programs will not detect, but once that happens, the virus protection providers find a way to stop it and everyone gets back to business. Similarly, increasingly sophisticated DDoS attacks can quite possibly be met by increasingly powerful defenses.

9.1   Prognosis for DDoS

Given that we expect attacks to become more sophisticated in response to improved defenses, what will the DDoS attacks of the future look like? Answering this question is inherently speculative, and even more so since attacks of the future are likely to be characterized by how they avoid the defenses of the future, and we do not currently have a good sense of what these defenses will be. With those caveats, here are our best guesses on the future of DDoS attacks.

9.1.1   Increase in Size

DDoS attacks of the future are likely to be larger than those perpetrated today. Armies of compromised machines numbering in the tens or hundreds of thousands seem readily available on the black market. A strongly motivated opponent can probably draft a larger army than that. A million-node DDoS network is not beyond the bounds of possibility; indeed, some evidence suggests that such a network might already exist. Thus, researchers would be prudent to investigate defenses that could handle such an immense attack. A system administrator armed only with today's best target-side defense tools is unlikely to be able to handle an army of anything close to that size, and it may well be that even in the future handling such large armies will require assistance from outside the ISP of the attack's target.

9.1.2   Increase in Sophistication

Chances are that any successful DDoS defense mechanism will be most effective against attacks that are unsophisticated, especially attacks whose packets are all similar and easy to characterize. Thus, attackers are likely to move away from such attacks to attacks that consist of widely varying types of packets. Indeed, they have already made first steps in that direction. Existing DDoS attack toolkits allow many variations. For example, attackers can vary the proportions of packets that use particular transport protocols; they can alter their spoofing characteristics; or they can vary patterns of which machines in a DDoS army attack at what times, allowing pulsing attacks.

The more sophisticated the defense tools get at picking out the characteristics of attack packets from the entire stream of packets, the more sophisticated the attackers are likely to become. For example, if entropy measurements prove effective in detecting which packets comprise the attack flow, attackers might try to control the entropy of various attack packet characteristics to confuse the defense systems.

In one way, we might see less sophistication in attacks. With a large enough army, an attacker can overwhelm most targets by having each of his machines send a single packet, something as innocuous as a packet requesting that a connection be opened. By mere volume, these packets could overwhelm a server, and finding any difference between the packets sent by legitimate clients trying to open a connection and attackers seeking to overwhelm the service would be challenging.

9.1.3   Increases in Semantic DDoS Attacks

Researchers have discovered a number of ways in which a target machine can be kept busy with a relatively low volume of requests, so-called *algorithmic attacks*. Attacks on application hash tables, discussed in Chapter 4, have been demonstrated, for example. Others are likely to be discovered and perpetrated in the future.

Generally, these kinds of denial of service problems will be best handled by changing the algorithm under attack to be less susceptible (akin to handling TCP SYN floods), but for some such attacks defenders may be able to use systems that observe the patterns of packets and can deduce which are part of the attack. Then the attack packets could be dropped, altered, or otherwise treated specially to prevent them from causing a DoS attack.

Defending against this type of algorithmic attack will have the good and bad properties of virus defenses. Specific attacks will require specific fixes, but when those fixes are made, that particular attack will become ineffective. Further, finding a new effective attack will require some work by the attacker. Whether genuine creativity will be required or mere slogging persistence will be enough remains to be seen. Regardless, even if a silver bullet is discovered that handles volume-based DDoS attacks, it is unlikely to also handle algorithmic attacks.

9.1.4   Infrastructure Attacks

Another likely trend in DDoS is that attackers may increasingly choose to target something other than the end machine. Effectively, sometimes without knowing it, attackers are already flooding links somewhere upstream of the target machine, but explicitly targeting something else is less common today. One well-known attempt was the attack on the root DNS servers mentioned earlier. The attack obviously attempted to flood those servers, but very likely the true goal was to deny service to the wider Internet by making name lookups slow or impossible. Some DDoS attacks have already targeted routers or other parts of the Internet's infrastructure. DDoS attacks could again strike DNS servers, or they could be targeted at interrupting the spread of routing information, or they could be specifically designed to overwhelm firewalls, perhaps including algorithmic attack characteristics that cause particularly poor firewall performance.

It is highly likely that this kind of DDoS attack will eventually become part of more sophisticated attacks on both cyber and real-world targets. Attackers wishing to achieve their goals may start by separating their victim from the rest of the network, or cutting off their communications with a particular remote partner. A DoS attack would thus be merely one stage in a more complex plan, in the same way that disabling an alarm is only one step in burglarizing a building.

What might become the target of an infrastructure attack? Anything other than a source node and a destination node that is still required to perform some important action. Beyond DNS servers, routers, and firewalls, other examples might include key distribution servers, certificate servers, LDAP servers, or back-end cookie-based authentication servers. Some electronic cash schemes require online checking of the cash's validity by a third party. How will they behave if that third party is unavailable due to a DDoS attack? Spam control services often distribute blacklists or other information to their clients over the network. Attackers are already launching DDoS attacks on them to prevent this service from being effective. Perhaps a future worm will combine its spread with DDoS attacks on the virus signature distribution sites of the major security software companies. The possibilities are likely to be limited only by either the imagination of DDoS attackers or that of the designers of new Internet services.

9.1.5   Degradation of Service

We might see a trend toward degradation of service rather than denial of service. Current DDoS attacks try to make a service completely inoperable. If they are effective, they are usually also detected, at which point steps can be taken to stop them. But what if the attacker merely wanted to make your network heavily loaded at all times? Normal customers would get through, but would suffer slow service from your site. Detection would be much harder, since it would not be clear that anything was seriously wrong. Most of the promising DDoS defense strategies assume that the attack is crippling and are designed to detect and respond to that effect. They might not detect or remedy a mere slowing down of your network.

Degradation-of-service attacks lack the kind of instant gratification that casual DDoS perpetrators seem to desire. However, as a tool of economic warfare, they are much more attractive. A competitor's reputation can be damaged, or he can be forced to make investments in more hardware or bandwidth without any commensurate increase in his business. Someone who wants to keep an undesired news story from receiving wide attention could just make it slow and difficult to get to the site storing the information. Subtlety does not yet seem to be a characteristic of the typical hacker, but time may lead to more sophistication and more complex goals. Such sophistication has been observed in other types of cyberattacks, and will surely come to DDoS, as well.

9.1.6   Motivations for Attacks

The bulk of the DDoS attacks that we have observed to date appear to be typical activities of the hacker subculture. Either they are designed to demonstrate the hacker's abilities or they are part of an ongoing undercover war among hacker communities. However, there are disturbing signs suggesting that those with more serious and dark motives are starting to embrace DDoS as a tool, and we should expect such trends to increase.

The two major areas of increase are likely to be in politics and crime. We have already mentioned existing examples of both. DDoS is an effective tool for silencing an opponent, at least in the increasingly important world of the Internet. That makes DDoS a good tool for certain kinds of political warfare. Politics should be taken here in its broadest sense, not just applying to national candidates, but to international activities, advocacy for and against various political views, and perhaps even to the elections themselves. Those designing electronic voting systems should beware of connecting them to the Internet during elections, or at least be prepared to provide proper operation of the system despite DDoS attacks causing network disconnections.

Criminals have already embraced the extortion possibilities of DDoS. Cleverer criminals are likely to find more inventive uses of the attack to achieve their goals. Delivery of burglar alarm signals over the Internet would be at risk from such attacks, for example. As police operations increasingly rely on networking, criminals will be increasingly able to prevent coordination by law enforcement. A carefully planned DDoS attack might be able to manipulate the stock market or serve as an adjunct to other kinds of fraud.

Increasing use of *Voice-Over IP* (VoIP) services makes them a new candidate for DDoS attacks, causing disruption of business services that were formerly performed over very well-secured and difficult-to-attack infrastructures. Convergence of services (such as e-mail and text messaging, voice services, and geo-location) in cell phones and other wireless devices that are starting to use the Internet for their functions will become another target for DDoS attacks. Many of the application-level vulnerabilities discussed in this book—which were mostly solved in the computer world—are recurring as TCP/IP stacks and applications are ported to small, low-powered wireless devices. The result is that old DoS and DDoS attacks will work again against a new, weaker target base. For example, many Internet cell phones may lock up if old Windows TCP/IP packet fragmentation attack tools are used against them.

Generally, as our society relies more on having Internet communications ubiquitously available, the motivations for selectively disrupting them will increase. In the future, the preferred elementary school student excuse for not having completed an assignment might switch from "the dog ate my homework" to "DDoS took down the class Web site."

9.1.7   Overall Prognosis

At the most general level, the future of DDoS is improved defenses followed by improved attacks. Attackers will move away from the attacks we can readily handle and toward the attacks we find most challenging to deflect. Because the fundamental nature of a DDoS attack is "too much of a good thing," chances are that we will never be totally free of them, in some form or other. DoS attacks pop up every so often in the real world and are often hard to deal with. The automation of the Internet merely makes them easier for an individual to perpetrate, but not necessarily any easier to handle.

The border between the physical world and the cyberworld has already been breached. A paper by researchers at AT&T Research [BRK02] describes a variant of DDoS attack using a U.S.-based mail carrier for transporting massive amounts of catalogs and brochures ordered "automagically" from online Web forms to the physical target. A subsequent real attack on a notorious real-world spammer's home followed about a month later (see http://www.infomaticsonline.co.uk/News/1137552). His postal mailbox was inundated with a flood of catalogs, sales offers, and other postal junk mail, sent to him by irate Internet users tired of receiving spam from him. The idea has been extended by Jakobsson et al. into the concept of *untraceable e-mail cluster bombs* [JM].

One lesson that readers should take from this book is that systems put in the Internet are at risk from many attacks, DDoS among them, and it is not currently possible to fully protect nodes in the Internet. Recent worm incidents have caused unfortunate problems for many Internet-connected systems. As technology allows us to make use of computers and networks for ever-widening classes of applications, it is vital to keep in mind the risks one faces when something is moved onto a network accessible by all. The most important applications, such as control of power grids, hospital equipment, transportation, and military systems, demand especially careful thinking before making them Internet-accessible.

9.2   Social, Moral, and Legal Issues

DDoS is a problem that is unlikely to be solved by any single person or entity. It is a problem for society as a whole. As we have seen, it is difficult for any single computer or network to fully defend itself from all feasible attacks. Help is required to handle huge flooding attacks, at least. There must be a social aspect to DDoS defense.

Social problems are most commonly dealt with using either shared morality or legal authority. Given the many different attitudes people have toward the proper moral behavior of computer and network users, and the international scope of the Internet (and, hence, the DDoS problem), engaging shared morality to make inroads against DDoS attacks seems like an uphill struggle. Perhaps each of us can do our part, taking a bit of extra care to secure our own machine so that it does not become part of someone else's DDoS problem, but we cannot hope to solve the DDoS problem quickly this way.

Legal actions are somewhat more promising. As described in Chapter 8, many countries, including the United States, have existing laws that are relevant to DDoS attacks, and also have law enforcement agencies that are interested in DDoS attacks and might be able to help. However, the difficulty in tracking down the culprit limits the degree to which law enforcement approaches can be used, at least today. Also, the large numbers of attacks and the limited resources of law enforcement make it impossible for police and federal agents to investigate all DDoS attacks.

However, if you have suffered large damages and are well prepared to work with law enforcement authorities, legal avenues may prove helpful. If you think you might need to resort to legal action against DDoS attacks in the future, you should make preparations now. You should know whom to contact, understand how to gather evidence they can use, and be prepared to help law enforcement in their investigations.

Currently, few DDoS attackers have been caught, prosecuted, and convicted, which limits the desired deterrent effect of laws against performing these attacks. In the future, more successful prosecutions of DDoS perpetrators and better national and international mechanisms for dealing with the legal aspects of DDoS attacks may discourage all but the most motivated attackers.

9.3 Resources for Learning More

While we believe we have provided a good overview of many important aspects of the DDoS problem, there is a lot more information available than we could hope to fit into this book. Also, research into DDoS attacks and potential defense mechanisms is ongoing, and there is sure to be interesting new information available shortly after this book has gone into print, too late for inclusion. We will now tell you about a number of resources you can use to learn more about DDoS attacks and defenses and to keep up to date on the latest research and news in the field.

The resources we will describe are in several categories. First, we will discuss Web sites that have useful information. Next, we will discuss mailing lists. Then we will talk about conferences and journals that typically publish DDoS-related research.

9.3.1 Web Sites

- **CERT Coordination Center.** One of the most important Web sites for getting information about any type of computer security problem is `http://www.cert .org/`. This Web site belongs to the CERT Coordination Center (CERT/CC), a university-based, government-supported organization that is tasked with keeping on top of newly emerging computer security problems and providing authoritative information about the nature of the problems. The CERT Coordination Center also helps provide information about measures that should be taken in response. The CERT Coordination Center Web site maintains a current list of known vulnerabilities and ongoing security problems, along with advice on fixing those problems. They have a repository of white papers and other information useful in understanding different forms of attacks and defensive mechanisms. The CERT Coordination Center performs research on survivability of computer systems in the face of various attacks, and many conclusions and results from this research are available from their Web site. The CERT Coordination Center also runs educational programs to train computer professionals in understanding and dealing with common security problems.

The CERT Coordination Center was the first organization of its kind, founded in 1988, but it is by no means the only one in the world. In fact, the CERT Coordination Center has helped many incident response teams around the world get started by providing training, advice, and resource materials. For example, Australia's AusCERT and Germany's DFN-CERT were two of the first that the CERT Coordination Center assisted in getting started, and Japan's JPCERT Coordination Center was another that benefited from early CERT Coordination Center help. The CERT Coordination Center was a founding member of FIRST (Forum of Incident Response and Security Teams; `http://www.first.org/`), which now has over 100 members. There are more than 300 incident response teams worldwide.

The CERT Coordination Center Web site is the first place to go to seek assistance in handling a security problem you are not familiar with, including brand new attacks that have suddenly popped up on the network. They produce quick, reliable, detailed reports of new types of attacks. The CERT Coordination Center also has a mailing list through which it delivers alerts of new attacks as soon as they have been verified and properly characterized.

- **Dave Dittrich's DDoS Web page.** One of the authors of this book maintains a Web page that contains links to large numbers of pages containing interesting material related to DDoS at `http://staff.washington.edu/dittrich/misc/ddos/`. This page focuses particularly on DDoS attack tools, but contains much useful and interesting information on other aspects of DDoS attacks and defenses, including research papers, white papers analyzing particular attacks and tools, links to Web sites of commercial providers who sell DDoS defense products, news stories on DDoS attacks, articles and papers offering advice on protecting against DDoS attacks and related security problems (such as IP spoofing), discussions of legal issues concerning DDoS, and links to Web sites belonging to other DDoS researchers.

- **Dshield.** Dshield gathers information about new and ongoing attacks from various sources and provides attack characterizations and other relevant information. This Web site's primary purpose is to disseminate firewall rules to allow people to filter out new attacks as quickly as possible, but they provide a wide variety of other interesting and useful information about the kinds of attacks going on at the moment and the latest techniques for handling those attacks. Dshield's home page is `http://www.dshield.org/`.

- **CAIDA.** CAIDA, the Cooperative Association for Internet Data Analysis, does precisely what its name suggests: It gathers and analyzes data concerning the performance of the Internet. CAIDA is not specifically dedicated to DDoS measurement, but has done work on measuring the prevalence of DDoS attacks in the Internet [MVS01], and analysis of DDoS attacks is well within their charter and areas of interest. More recently, they published an analysis of a large DDoS attack on SCO. Their Web site has both of these resources posted, and may feature future work on measuring DDoS. CAIDA's home page is `http://www.caida.org/`.

9.3.2   Mailing lists

- **SANS**. The Systems, Audit, Network, and Security Institute (SANS) provides information about many issues of properly installing, running, and maintaining computers and networks. Their Web site (`http://www.sans.org`) contains much interesting and useful information, but the *SANS Newsbites* newsletter is of particular interest. This newsletter is published weekly and delivered by e-mail to its subscribers. Several editors (who include some of the most respected names in computer security) scan the recent world news concerning issues of computer security and provide short descriptions of the most important stories, usually with Web links to the original, full-length versions. While not limited to stories on DDoS, major DDoS attacks and significant new developments in DDoS defense mechanisms are usually covered in this newsletter. To subscribe, you need to set up a free account at the SANS Web portal: `https://portal.sans.org/login.php`.

  SANS also publishes a weekly summary of known security flaws in various hardware and software systems called *@Risk: The Consensus Security Vulnerability Alert*. Generally, this newsletter does not directly discuss DDoS issues, but it may highlight vulnerabilities that will allow attackers to enlist particular machines as agents for DDoS attacks, or semantic-level problems that allow denial of service on particular systems without flooding. It is a good resource for keeping track of which of your systems might need patching. It can be subscribed to in the same way as *SANS Newsbites*, described above.

- *Cryptogram*. Bruce Schneier, a noted author and researcher on issues of computer security, publishes a monthly newsletter called *Cryptogram*, also usually delivered by e-mail. This newsletter contains Web links to many important recent stories on issues of computer security, but it represents a more definite editorial voice and opinion than *SANS Newsbites*, whose primary goal is to bring important news to the attention of readers. *Cryptogram* does not concentrate on DDoS issues, but frequently contains stories on the subject. For more information on *Cryptogram*, including subscription information, go to `http://www.counterpane.com/crypto-gram.html`.

- *IEEE Cipher*. This newsletter is distributed by the IEEE Computer Society's Technical Committee on Security and Privacy. It contains announcements of upcoming conferences in the field, summaries of important results reported at such conferences, book reviews, and other materials of interest to those working in the computer security field. It is produced bimonthly, and you can obtain more information on its contents and how to subscribe by visiting `http://www.ieee-security.org/cipher.html`.

- *RISKS Digest*. The ACM Committee on Computers and Public Policy produces a digest of important information concerning risks faced by various users and groups due to reliance on computer and networking technology, moderated by Peter G. Neumann. Many of these risks arise from security concerns, some of them from DoS threats. *RISKS Digest* can be read over the Web (at `http://catless.ncl.ac.uk /Risks`) or through a moderated network newsgroup (*comp.risks*). If these options are not open to you, visit `http://catless.ncl.ac.uk/Risks/info.html#subs` for other ways to subscribe to this digest.

9.3.3   Conferences and Workshops

There is no single conference or workshop devoted to research on DDoS attacks and defenses. Instead, papers on these subjects tend to appear in the major computer security conferences and many leading networking conferences. Since these conferences cover a much broader range of topics, one must look through a conference program or proceedings to pull out the papers related to DDoS, but nowadays it is common for most of the conferences listed below to have one or more DDoS-related papers each time they are held. Many of the most important papers on DDoS issues were published by one of these conferences.

- **IEEE Symposium on Security and Privacy**. Held annually, typically in May. This conference covers the entire range of security research, but often contains some papers on DDoS. For example, the 2003 IEEE Symposium on Security and Privacy contained a paper on using puzzle auctions to defend against DDoS [WR03]. For further information, go to `http://www.ieee-security.org` and search their conference list.

- **USENIX Security Symposium**. Held annually, typically in summer. This conference covers the entire range of computer security problems, so DDoS papers appearing here often prove to be important and influential. For example, USENIX 2001 contained a paper on inferring the frequency and characteristics of DDoS attacks using the backscatter technique [MVS01]. For further information, go to `http://www.usenix.org/events/`.

- **Annual Computer Security Applications Conference**. Held annually, typically in December. This conference tends to concentrate on security at the application level, but has broad coverage of security issues. For example, ACSAC 2003 contained a paper discussing an extension of IP traceback techniques to deal with reflector attacks [CL03]. For further information, go to `http://www.acsac.org/`.

- **Infocom**. Held annually, typically in March or April. This is a large conference covering all topics in networking. For example, Infocom 2001 contained a paper on authentication of marking for traceback solutions to DDoS [SP01]. For further information, go to `http://www.ieee-infocom.org/`.

- **ACM SIGCOMM Conference**. Held annually, typically in August. This conference covers the entire range of networking topics and sometimes will have papers on DDoS issues. For example, SIGCOMM 2002 contained the SOS paper describing that DDoS defense system [KMR02]. For further information, go to `http://www.acm.org/sigcomm/sigcomm.html`.

- **IEEE International Conference on Network Protocols (ICNP)**. Held annually, typically in October or November. This conference covers the entire range of networking topics and sometimes has papers on DDoS issues. For example, ICNP 2002 contained a paper on the D-WARD DoS defense system [MPR02]. For further information, go to `http://www.ieee-icnp.org/`.

- **Network and Distributed System Security Symposium (NDSS)**. Held annually, typically in February in San Diego, California. NDSS covers a wide range of issues concerning network security, including DoS issues. In recent years, the symposium has typically published one or two papers on DoS issues each year. For example, a major paper on implementing the pushback defense strategy appeared in NDSS 2002 [IB02]. For further information, go to `http://www.isoc.org/isoc/conferences/ndss/`.

- **New Security Paradigms Workshop (NSPW)**. Held annually, typically in September. This workshop looks for papers on very new issues in computer security and is most likely to publish papers on entirely new approaches to DDoS defense. The papers are more typically about ideas and approaches than completed systems or studies. For example, NSPW 2003 contained a paper on forming alliances between DDoS defense nodes [MRR03]. For further information, go to `http://www.nspw.org`.

- **Black Hat Briefings**. Several conferences, held internationally each year. This venue concentrates on practical solutions to real security problems, drawing an audience of working professionals in the fields of networking, system administration, and security. This conference is more likely to draw attendees from the hacker community than some of the more academically oriented conferences. For more information, go to `http://www.blackhat.com/`.

- **CanSecWest**. One conference, held in Vancouver, British Columbia, Canada, each year (plus a new Asia-Pacific version held in Japan). This venue concentrates on computer security research of various forms, both theoretical and practical, drawing a similar audience to that of the Black Hat Briefings. Its single-track model, held over three days, allows everyone to hear every talk. For more information, go to `http://www.cansecwest.com/`.

- **The IEEE Information Assurance Workshop**. Held annually, typically in June, at the U.S. Military Academy at West Point, New York, (also known as the "West Point Workshop"). This conference covers the entire range of information assurance research, including papers on DDoS, information warfare, etc. For further information, go to West Point's Web site: `http://www.itoc.usma.edu/workshop/`.

- **The USENIX Technical Conference**. In addition to the Security Symposium mentioned previously, the USENIX Association holds a general annual technical conference, typically in June or July. This conference has papers and tutorials on hot and important topics in operating systems, networking, and related areas, including security. Some papers on DDoS defense may appear in this conference. For more information, go to `http://www.usenix.org/`. The USENIX Association runs a wide variety of conferences on topics in systems and networking areas, and sometimes runs one-time workshops or starts new conferences on hot topics, so it is worthwhile to look at their Web site's list of upcoming conferences occasionally. The same observation is true of the ACM and IEEE.

9.3.4   Magazines and Journals

A number of publications often contain useful articles on DDoS attacks. We will not cover newspapers and popular magazines directed to the general community, though these may sometimes contain useful articles on DDoS, but will concentrate on the more technical publications.

- *ACM Transactions on Information and System Security (TISSEC)*. The Association for Computing Machinery's main journal on security issues. Covering the entire range of security issues, *ACM TISSEC* will only occasionally contain articles on DDoS, but they are likely to be detailed versions of important work. For example, one of the major articles on IP traceback appeared here in an extended version [DFS02]. For more information, go to `http://www.acm.org/pubs/tissec/`.

- *IEEE Security and Privacy*. A relatively new magazine that publishes articles that combine technical depth with good comprehensibility by a typical computer professional. This publication is likely to have surveys, general descriptions of problems and solutions, and articles helping readers to understand general problems rather than more academic articles on detailed descriptions of particular systems. For more information, go to `http://www.computer.org/security/`.

- *IEEE Transactions on Dependable and Secure Computing*. A new publication starting in 2004 that will publish scholarly papers on fields of reliability and security. Since it is a recent publication, describing what will appear there is premature, but it seems likely to be a premiere venue for high-quality work on security threats and defences, including DDoS characterization and defense. For more information, go to `http://www.computer.org/tdsc/index.htm`.

- *Journal of Computer Security*. This journal covers a broad range of computer security issues, and may sometimes contain papers on DDoS issues. For more information, go to `http://www.csl.sri.com/programs/security/jcs/`.

- *IEEE/ACM Transactions on Networking*. A highly respected publication that prints academic papers on all aspects of networking. Some issues may contain papers on DDoS issues. For example, one issue of IEEE/ACM Transactions on Networking contained a paper on single-packet IP traceback [SPS+02]. For more information, go to `http://www.ton.cc.gatech.edu/`.

- *Computer Communications Review*. This magazine issued by the ACM emphasizes quick publication of timely information on important new topics in networking. Some issues may contain papers on DDoS issues. For more information, go to `http://www.acm.org/sigcomm/ccr/`.

- *USENIX ;login:*. This bimonthly publication is included in all USENIX Association memberships, and covers a wide range of topics concerning the design, administration, and use of Unix and Linux systems. It publishes many articles that are helpful for system administrators of Unix machines, including occasional articles on DDoS topics. For more information, go to `http://www.usenix.org/publications/login/`.

9.4 Conclusion

We wish to leave you with a final thought, quoted from the wise words of Douglas Adams [Ada80]: "Don't Panic!"

Yes, DDoS attacks are real. Yes, they are serious. Yes, defensive measures are in their infancy and are not always effective against all attacks. And, yes, real people have suffered economic and other forms of damage from DDoS attacks. However, it is equally true that most sites in the Internet have never suffered a DDoS attack (and perhaps never will), most DDoS attacks that do occur are not that serious, and most of these real DDoS attacks can be handled with methods and tools that are available today. We have outlined these defensive approaches in this book. If you take the steps to prepare yourself, the chances are excellent that even should someone direct a DDoS attack at your doorstep, you will withstand the flood and recover quickly.

There is no cause for panic in the foreseeable future, either. As we said earlier, we expect that DDoS attacks will become more common and that use of DDoS attacks for serious purposes, from political statements to crime, will become more prevalent. However, there is much research going on to gain greater understanding of the DDoS threat and to provide more effective and powerful defensive tools. All of the major players in the Internet, including the backbone providers, ISPs, operating systems builders, router and switch manufacturers, governmental and nongovernmental agencies with Internet responsibilities, professional societies of network and system administrators, and the entire computer networking research community, regard DDoS attacks as one of the most significant threats to the future growth and stability of the Internet. All of these groups are committed to providing the Internet's users with the best possible protections against DDoS attacks. As the threats become worse, rest assured that these groups will do all they can to counter them. You have allies in this fight, and powerful ones at that. Ultimately, we believe that the future of DDoS defense is not a silver bullet technical solution, but stronger cooperation on both the human and the technical level.

Now that you have overcome any panic you might have, you should take a realistic second look at your own situation. Is your organization in a position that might be threatened by a DDoS attack? Have you made reasonable preparations to handle such an attack should one occur? If not, and if you are not comfortable with the risk of a DDoS attack dropping your organization off the Internet for some period, now is the time to make those preparations. Many of them are simple, painless, and even cost free. Most of them will have secondary benefits, like also protecting you against other threats or increasing your knowledge and awareness of how your network operates. If you delay taking these precautions, you are putting yourself unnecessarily at risk.

Finally, while we have done the best we can to educate you, our readers, about the threat of DDoS and the methods available to deal with that threat, we must reiterate that neither the threat nor the defensive methods will stay static. After we have finished writing and you have finished reading this book, progress will march on for the attackers and the defenders alike. Taking the steps we outline will help you today, but remember that one of those steps, a particularly important one, is periodically surveying the world of threats and the measures you have taken to counter them. Tomorrow's attacks will be different than today's, and perhaps new countermeasures will be required to deal with them. Like most other security issues, you must remain vigilant. Keep learning, keep watching, keep improving your defenses. Those who follow this final advice are likely to be among the fortunate group who do not fall prey to the DDoS attacks of the future.

APPENDIX A

Glossary

The following is a glossary of terms associated with DDoS.

- **agent**   A malware program responsible for performing actions under control of a handler. In the context of DDoS, this would be the program that floods a victim. Other agents could be responsible for distributed sniffing, distributed file service, distributed password cracking, etc. An agent in a classic handler/agent network does not directly respond to user commands, instead having these commands relayed to it from a handler. IRC bots, on the other hand, do (in most cases) respond directly to commands from the attacker.

    See also *army, bot, botnet, handler.*

- **amplification**   Attacks that use amplification use some kind of request that will elicit a response that is larger in size, or number of replies, than the original query. For example, if an incoming ICMP Echo Request packet is 100 bytes, and the attacker can trick 100 hosts into replying, the result is 10,000 bytes out for every 100 bytes of requests, or a 100-fold amplification. Similarly, if a forged DNS request comes in that is some 80 bytes long, but causes a reply that is 400 bytes long, a fivefold amplification is obtained. Amplification attacks typically also involve IP spoofing; for example, in the Smurf attack the attacker spoofs the IP address of the victim.

- **anomaly detection**   A variety of defense approaches that aim to detect the occurrence of a DDoS attack (or some other malicious activity) by monitoring network state or traffic for anomalies. The defense system usually builds a model of normal network behavior—the baseline model. It then continuously monitors a large number of parameters and periodically compares observations with the baseline. Mismatches trigger the attack detection.

See also *signature detection* and *misbehavior detection*.

- **army** An informal term used to describe the collection of compromised hosts that a DDoS attacker coordinates to perform a DDoS attack. For *blended threats* (such as Phatbot), these hosts can also provide many services besides DDoS, such as anonymous proxying, keystroke monitoring and sniffing, spam delivery, etc. Such collections more closely resemble classic client/server architectures than the army analogy suggests. All such collections organized to perform attacks are often generically referred to as a *network*, both in and outside the DDoS context.

  See also *agent*, *blended threat*, *bot*, *botnet*, *handler*, and *network*.

- **artifact** Used in conjunction with *malware*, meaning something left behind on a compromised system. Typically a program or script, but it can also be just a text file containing information, e.g., a README file.

  See also *malware*.

- **BGP** Border Gateway Protocol is a protocol that is used between Internet routers to exchange routing information. Through this exchange, routers learn how to reach foreign IP addresses (not residing on their network). BGP is the Internet's major routing protocol. For more information see RFC 1771 at `http://www.ietf.org/rfc/rfc1771.txt`.

- **blended threat** A term, coined by incident response organizations in Australia in 1998, referring to *malware* packages that provide more than one type of service to an attacker, such as file service for pirated media, IRC control functions, scanning, sniffing, proxy services for anonymity, and DDoS. An example of a blended threat that is bundled into a single self-updating and self-propagating program is *Phatbot*. See `http://www.lurhq.com/phatbot.html` for a high level description of *Phatbot* functions.

  See also *artifact* and *malware*.

- **BNC** Also known as *bounce*, this is an IRC relay program. It functions like a password-protected (usually) proxy server that accepts an incoming, possibly encrypted, connection on a high-numbered TCP port, such as 12345, and then makes a connection out to a preprogrammed IRC server, typically on the normal IRC server port of 6667. It serves as one type of stepping stone.

  See also *stepping stone*.

- **bot**   Short for *robot*, this is an IRC client program that runs in the background and watches for certain strings to show up in an IRC channel. When it sees those strings, the bot is programmed to perform some action, such as invite someone into an IRC channel, give them operator permissions, scan a netblock looking for vulnerable hosts, or perform a DoS attack.

    See also *artifact*, *blended threat*, *botnet*, and *malware*.

- **botnet**   A network of bots that all synchronize through communication in an IRC channel. Botnets have been known to grow to as large as over 400,000 hosts, although most are typically in the hundreds of bots up to the tens of thousands of bots. Botnets can be established on any normal IRC channel, although more frequently compromised systems at sites with high availability and bandwidth, such as research universities, are used as "rogue" IRC servers explicitly for control of botnets. This makes them harder to detect and dismantle, as there is not an IRC operator (IRCop) monitoring the server. Botnets have also been known to channel-hop, and sometimes to even hop between IRC networks, to avoid detection. An IRC channel has limited capacity, so a botnet may need to span multiple channels. IRC bots sometimes employ encryption to protect their communication, which makes detection of botnets much more difficult.

    See also *bot, blended threat,* and *malware*.

- **challenges**   Messages sent by some security mechanisms to alleged clients of the network or host they protect, to determine the validity of their traffic. Depending on the type of challenge, the responder might need to demonstrate that he really initiated contact (as opposed to an attacker *spoofing* his address), or he might need to demonstrate that a live human user is initiating the communication (a *Reverse Turing Test*). *Puzzles* are a special kind of challenge.

    See also *puzzles*.

- **CIDR (Classless Internet Domain Routing)**   A means of specifying the address of a network, and the number of bits used for its netmask, in one term. It replaces the old class designations in IP addresses (e.g., *Class C* addresses were divided into 24 bits of network address followed by 8 bits for host address and start with bits 110). Thus, a Class C network address of 192.168.100.0 would be written in CIDR notation as 192.168.100.0/24. This is also called a *netblock*.

- **collateral damage**   Loss, delay, or other negative effects experienced by nonmalicious traffic or a device (host, router, etc.), due to the action of a security mechanism. Sometimes this term also refers to similar damage done by a DDoS attack to a site or traffic that is not itself a target.

- **Datagram** See *packet*.

- **DNS** Domain Name Service is an Internet service that maps names such as `www.example.com` to IP address 192.0.34.166 and vice versa. DNS is provided by numerous DNS servers distributed all over the Internet. DNS information is vital for most Internet services such as e-mail and Web service, and as such is heavily cached to provide redundancy and rapid response. For more information see RFCs 1034, 1035, and 1591 at `http://www.ietf.org/rfc/rfc1034.txt`, `http://www.ietf.org/rfc/rfc1035.txt`, and `http://www.ietf.org/rfc/rfc1591.txt`.

- **egress filtering** Filtering traffic passing through a router as it leaves a network (as opposed to *ingress filtering*, which is entering a network) to prevent spoofing, to eliminate nonroutable addresses, or to restrict IP protocols.

  See also *IP header* in Chapter 4 and *IP spoofing*, Section 4.5, and the sidebar covering ingress/egress filtering that accompanies that section.

- **exploit** A piece of code that takes advantage of an existing vulnerability in a program to violate administrative rules. The usual goal of exploit programs is to gain access to a machine, escalate user's privileges or do some kind of damage. The exploit code is given to a vulnerable program either locally (e.g., attacker typing a reply to program's request on a keyboard) or remotely (e.g., attacker sending exploit over the network to a remote server, such as Web server).

  See also *malware*.

- **false negatives** Failures of a monitoring, auditing, or alerting system to detect the presence of something it is looking for. This may be a malicious event for an IDS, an open port when scanning, detection of a DDoS attack, etc. Such failures may allow an attack to continue unhindered, or render a defense system ineffective.

  See also *false positives*.

- **false positives** False indications of the presense of something being looked for by a monitoring, auditing, or alerting system. False positive alerts in a detection system waste time in response to non-events. In a DDoS defense system, they can lead to engaging the defense system often when no attack is ongoing. This can lead those who are monitoring the system to disregard alerts or turn off the defenses.

  See also *false negatives*.

- **filtering** Generally, dropping packets based on some well-defined and easily observed characteristic of the packets. Many DDoS defense mechanisms use filtering of some kind to counter the flood. There are many kinds of filtering, based on the location where performed and the criteria used: *Ingress filtering* and *egress fil-*

tering are examples. Unlike *rate limiting*, filtering tends to imply that all packets matching the targeted characteristics are dropped, whether or not their quantity is troublesome.

See also *egress filtering*, *ingress filtering*, and *rate limiting*.

- **flooding**   Attacking a host by sending a deluge of traffic (meaningful or meaningless, it does not matter) that overwhelms either the host or the network. Examples of flooding attacks are *ping floods* (send large amounts of ICMP Echo Request packets), *UDP floods* (send large amounts of UDP packets), and *SYN flooding* (barraging the host with connection requests that are never finalized).

- **handler**   A malware program responsible for controlling a large number of *agents* who perform some distributed function. In the context of DDoS, the handler provides the attacker with a front end (typically a command-line shell) that provides status, control of when attacks start and stop, selection of attack method and duration, and sometimes automated update and communication with other users.

  A handler can be a discrete program (a *malware artifact*) found on a compromised computer, or it may be an IRC channel, in the case of DDoS botnets.

  See also *agent*, *malware*.

- **ingress filtering**   Filtering traffic passing through a router as it enters a network (as opposed to *egress filtering*, which is leaving a network), e.g., to prevent spoofing, to eliminate nonroutable addresses, or to restrict IP protocols.

  See also *IP header*, *IP spoofing*, Section 4.5, and the sidebar on ingress/egress filtering that accompanies that section.

- **IP header** The portion of an IP packet containing control information that describes how to handle the packet. RFC 791 [Ins81a] defines the Internet protocol datagram headers as shown in Figure A.1

  What follows the header is the data (often called the *payload*) being sent to the destination. There is a checksum to help detect whether the header has been corrupted, but there is nothing to authenticate any of the fields in the header. (This is the reason that someone can spoof source addresses, by simply putting any value they wish into the *Source address* field and sending the packet off on its journey.) RFC 791 can be found at `http://www.ietf.org/rfc/rfc0791.txt`.

  Some research DDoS defense schemes require inserting a mark into the IP header. Such marks are usually inserted into fields that are deemed unused or hardly used, such as the *Identification* field.

  See also `http://www.networksorcery.com/enp/protocol/ip.htm`.

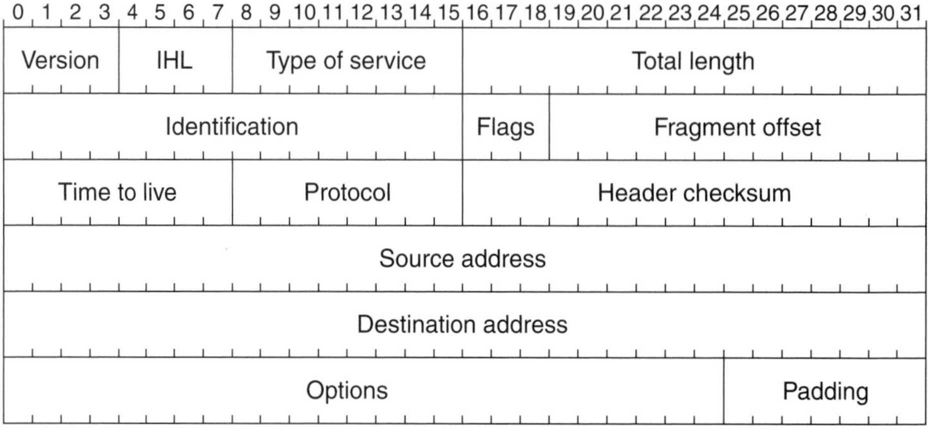

```
 0  1  2  3  4  5  6  7  8  9 10 11 12 13 14 15 16 17 18 19 20 21 22 23 24 25 26 27 28 29 30 31
```

Version	IHL	Type of service	Total length
Identification		Flags	Fragment offset
Time to live	Protocol	Header checksum
Source address
Destination address
Options	Padding

Figure A.1 Illustration of *IP header* as explained in RFC 791

- **IP spoofing**   There are two fields in an IP packet header that give information about the sender and intended recipient of the packet—*source address* and *destination address*, respectively. In IPv4, there is no enforcement that these addresses are correct, which means that an attacker can put any address she wants in the source address field of a packet and inject it into the network (where the router will dutifully route the packet on to the intended recipient). This is known as *spoofing*, or *source address forgery*. The attacker must have administrative privileges on a compromised machine in order to perform IP spoofing.

   By forging the address of a host at another site and sending a service request packet to a service port that is actively listening, the attacker can trick the receiving host into sending responses, not to the host that sent them, but to the host whose address was forged in the packet. This causes a *reflection* and sometimes *amplification* of traffic, and is one way that spoofing is used in DDoS.

   See also the discussion of how to prevent IP Spoofing at the border of a network in Section 4.5 and the sidebar discussion of ingress/egress filtering in Chapter 4. One of the primary uses of ingress/egress filtering discussed in this book is for prevention of IP Spoofing.

   See also *amplification, IP header,* `http://en.wikipedia.org/wiki/IP _spoofing`, and *reflector*.

- **IRC (Internet Relay Chat)**   A distributed network of servers that relay text chat messages from server to server, and to any clients connected to one of the IRC servers. IRC has been in use since the late 1980s, and has emerged from BITNET

RELAY, a VMS-based network chat program. There are many IRC networks, such as Dalnet, EFnet, and Undernet. IRC predates, and is not directly compatible with, instant messaging protocols such as AIM, ICQ, Jabber, etc.

- **ISP (Internet Service Provider)**   This typically refers to a tier two network provider, or provider of Internet services to end customers (e.g., dialup, broadband, cable modem, or wireless).

  See also *NSP*.

- **malware**   A blend of the words *malicious software*. Malware is any program that an attacker uses to do her thing, be it scanning, sniffing, hiding, breaking into more systems, or performing denial of service on some system.

  See also *agent*, *artifact*, *bot*, and *handler*.

- **misbehavior detection**   A variety of defense approaches that aim to detect the occurrence of a DDoS attack (or some other malicious activity) by monitoring network activity looking for behavior that matches predefined models of bad behavior. Unlike *signature detection*, these models are more generic and are created based either on observation of known DDoS attacks or deduction of characteristics of a denial of service on a machine or network. The system then continuously monitors a large number of parameters and periodically compares observations with the models. Matches trigger the attack detection.

  See also *anomaly detection*, *false positive*, *false negative*, and *signature detection*.

- **netblock**   See *CIDR*.

- **network**   A term that reflects a functional relationship between distributed and coordinated computers, similar to social networks, criminal networks, and client/ server networks. It is often used interchangeably with *army* in the context of DDoS attacks, though that term should not be taken to suggest that DDoS attacks are the only danger from such collections of attack machines. *Blended threats* (such as *Phatbot*) provide a wide variety of services for attackers, with the same host providing both a pirate music service and participating in a DDoS attack, and the fact that the attacker can use the host for these and many other types of misbehavior at a moment's notice is the greatest threat.

  See also *agent*, *army*, *blended threat*, *bot*, *botnet*, *network*, and *handler*.

- **NSP (Network Service Provider)**   This term typically refers to a tier one, or "backbone" (or "transit") network provider, or a provider of network service to edge networks, or ISPs.

  See also *ISP*.

- **packet**   Data is routed across the Internet in chunks called *packets* or *datagrams* via a protocol called IP protocol. Each packet has an IP header specifying who sent this packet and where it is going, and some control information.

  For a tutorial on TCP/IP, see `http://www.ietf.org/rfc/rfc1180.txt`

  See also *protocol* and *IP header*.

- **port**   Communications over the network between two computers using the TCP/IP protocol suite is done over *ports*, or numbered interface slots maintained by the TCP/IP stack. Services are usually assigned special *well-known ports*, such as port 22 for SSH, or port 80 for HTTP. To specify port 80 on a specific protocol, such as TCP, you would use *80/tcp* in a log file or in an output of a monitoring program.

  In a DoS attack using a SYN flood, an attacker may, for instance, target one or both of ports 22/tcp and 80/tcp, hoping that his SYN requests on those ports can make the TCP/IP stack fill up with half-open connections and refuse any new ones.

  See also *protocol* and *TCP/IP*.

- **protocol**   Communication over the network between two computers using the TCP/IP protocol suite is done using one of many different transport *protocols*. These are different predetermined mechanisms for communication that are defined by standards.

  Datagrams, or *packets*, are routed across the Internet using the *IP* protocol. IP is defined by RFC 791: `http://www.ietf.org/rfc/rfc0791.txt`.

  The two most commonly used transport protocols in the TCP/IP suite are *TCP* (the *Transmission Control Protocol*) [Ins81b] and *UDP* (the *User Datagram Protocol*.) [Pos80].

  TCP is defined by RFC 793: `http://www.ietf.org/rfc/rfc0793.txt`.

  UDP is defined by RFC 768: `http://www.ietf.org/rfc/rfc0768.txt`.

  There is also a control message protocol, *ICMP* (*Internet Control Message Protocol*) [Pos81], which can tell hosts that networks are not available, hosts are not available, and ports are not available, or can be used to tell if a host is alive or not. (Of course, there are many other things that ICMP can do, as well.) ICMP is defined by RFC 792: `http://www.ietf.org/rfc/rfc0792.txt`.

  ICMP is commonly used for DDoS attacks to send a datagram flood, or to exploit improperly configured routers in a *Smurf* attack.

  There are also many application protocols that provide vocabulary for client and server applications, such as the SSH protocol for secure remote terminal access, the HTTP protocol for Web services, and the FTP protocol for transferring files. These application protocols generate packets that are then "wrapped" with TCP or UDP protocol information and sent to their destination. They are then unwrapped by the destination application and processed. For a list of the currently defined application protocols, see `http://www.iana.org/assignments/protocol-numbers`.

- **puzzles** A special kind of *challenge* message used by some DDoS defense mechanisms. The defense mechanism will allow a certain client's traffic through to a potential target only after the client has solved the puzzle, which generally takes a significant amount of time. If working properly, DDoS nodes are unable to solve puzzles quickly enough to perpetrate an effective attack. Puzzle approaches are also referred to as *proof-of-work* systems.

    See also *challenges*.

- **rate limiting** Allowing only some predefined quantity of traffic (defined in number of packets and/or bytes per second) to traverse a particular network link. Rate limiting is used by many DDoS defense mechanisms. Unlike *filtering*, rate limiting tends not to drop all traffic matching the characteristics it is looking for, and might drop no traffic at all, if the quantity is low enough.

    See also *filtering*.

- **reflector** A host that is used to attack another site, but without having to compromise and install any DDoS agent on it first. In fact, it may be completely patched and secure, or may even be a firewall itself! It is simply used to reflect, or relay, packets from one host to another host by virtue of the fact that the source address in the incoming request was forged and the reply thus goes to the victim, not the true sender of the packet. (This is different from *unwitting agents*.)

    See also *IP spoofing* and *unwitting agents*.

- **rootkit** A set of programs or operating system kernel modification that hides the presence of an intruder on a system. This may be done by replacing common operating system commands, or by altering what operating system commands can see by diverting system calls.

    See also *malware*.

- **signature detection** Attack detection approaches based on remembering data or communication patterns seen at the time of previous attacks, and looking for similar patterns in current traffic. The defense system usually builds a database of known patterns (signatures) and continuously monitors incoming traffic looking for those patterns.

    See also *anomaly detection*, *false negative*, *false positive*, and *misbehavior detection*.

- **source address forgery** See *IP spoofing*.

- **spoofing**   See *IP spoofing*.

- **stepping stone**   A general term used to describe an attacker's use of indirection for connections. A stepping stone can be a stolen account that an attacker uses to log on, then connect to another host; an unrestricted proxy (e.g., SOCKS or HTTP) that is used to relay a connection; a compromised host with a *IRC* "bounce" (e.g., *BNC*) program or other backdoor installed by the attacker. These are often used for gaining anonymity.

   Attackers will often use multiple stepping stones, chaining them together across multiple continents and time zones. They may disable logging and wipe out log files, or install a rootkit before using the stepping stone, or they may use it once (from another stepping stone) and then never use the host again, making it impossible to track the attacker.

   See also *BNC*.

- **TCP/IP**   The name of a suite of protocols that form the foundation of the Internet. For the purposes of this book, the primary protocols in the TCP/IP suite that come up are the transport protocols *TCP* and *UDP*, the routing protocol *IP*, and the control message protocol *ICMP*.

   For a tutorial on TCP/IP, see `http://www.ietf.org/rfc/rfc1180.txt`.

   See also *packet*, *IP header*, *protocol*, and *port*.

- **traceback** An attempt to trace the true origin of a packet or a stream of packets. Because of *IP spoofing*, merely assuming that the packet was sent by the node specified as the source address in its *IP header* is not always effective, so other methods of tracing packets to their origin are required.

- **troll**   A name given to someone who acts in a malicious manner in a public forum, such as a newsgroup or e-mail list. One method used is to send a highly inflammatory message that is intended to stir controversy resulting in lengthy arguments and degradation of discourse. Some even aim to degrade things to the point where people abandon the group entirely.

   See also `http://en.wikipedia.org/wiki/Internet_troll`.

- **unwitting agent**   A term that researchers use to refer to computers that are used for DDoS attack by exploiting a vulnerability that allows an attacker to run commands remotely on the system. An example is the *Power* bot [Dita], which used the Windows Internet Information Server Unicode Directory Traversal vulnerability to run PING.EXE, sending a flood of ICMP Echo Request packets at its victim.

The attacker's bots simply use a list of vulnerable hosts, sending each one an HTTP GET request that starts the flooding.

There is a primary subtle difference between an "unwitting agent" and other DDoS attack scenarios. In an unwitting agent scenario, the attack is done using legitimate programs already installed on the computer, but started by way of exploiting a vulnerability to run the program. This is different from a worm that uses an exploit to cause the system to run attacker code, but contains its own attack payload and runs in memory (e.g., *Slammer* or *Code Red*), and is also not a reflection attack as described by Vern Paxson [Pax01], which includes tricking an otherwise secure server into replying to forged service requests.

See also *agent* and *blended threat*.

APPENDIX B

Survey of Commercial Defense Approaches

As mentioned in Chapter 3, shortly before the turn of the millennium, DoS attacks became more frequent and their effect more devastating. Numerous companies sprang to the challenge of designing effective and practical DDoS defenses. On the one hand, they had a hard task of designing an effective victim-end defense that can successfully handle high-volume attacks and guarantee low collateral damage. The victim-end deployment was dictated by an economic model—customers needed a solution they could deploy themselves and gain immunity against the attacks. Infrastructure (core-based) and source-end solutions were unlikely to sell. On the other hand, commercial solutions did not need to meet the challenge of "completely handling the problem," as research approaches do. It was sufficient to build a product that works today for existing attacks, then upgrade it should new threat models occur. This resulted in several highly practical solutions that appear to have good performance and do not incur high processing or storage cost.

To their credit, all commercial solutions deviated from the signature-based detection and filtering model established by intrusion detection systems. Rather, they attempted to devise versatile anomaly-based models, selecting multiple traffic and host behavior features and training their systems to recognize ranges of these features that are seen during normal operation. Detection of features that fall outside a baseline range signals an attack. This approach shows promise to handle diverse DoS attacks and other network threats such as worms, viruses, insider threats, and peer-to-peer file sharing. Unlike research approaches that focused mainly on dropping the attack traffic even when this inflicts collateral damage, commercial solutions recognized the need to identify and protect legitimate users' traffic while controlling the attack. A lot of effort is thus invested in sophisticated algorithms for traffic profiling and separation at the victim-end.

A common downside of commercial products appears to be the inability to spot and handle sophisticated attacks. For instance, those attacks whose features blend into feature ranges incorporated in baseline models will go undetected. So will attacks that attempt to retrain baseline models to suit their needs, by introducing anomalous traffic slowly over time. Randomized attacks are also likely to defeat the characterization process in commercial products. Finally, some levels of false positives are likely to occur when traffic and host patterns change for legitimate reasons, e.g., due to a flash crowd.

A prevalent trend among commercial DDoS defenses is to offer a myriad of utilities for monitoring network usage and easy management and restructuring of the network, in addition to protection functionality. This increases the value and appeal of the product. Since DDoS is an infrequent (although devastating) event from the point of view of a single network, investment in a product purely focusing on DDoS defense may take a long time to pay off. On the other hand, defense products regularly monitor network traffic looking for anomalies as a sign of the attack. Collected information, presented through a user-friendly interface, is valuable for network monitoring and management, thus making the defense product useful on a daily basis.

This appendix surveys a subset of currently available commercial DDoS solutions, and its goal is to provide the reader with a solid understanding of a variety of protection, detection, and response techniques deployed in those products. **The authors in no way wish to promote or endorse the solutions discussed in this appendix.**

Further, the authors did not themselves test any of the mentioned products for several reasons: (1) since there is currently no agreement in the security community on benchmark suite or testing methodology for DDoS defense product evaluation, test results would have doubtful merit; (2) obtaining sample products from vendors and subjecting them to tests requires the vendors' consent, which is sometimes hard to get (see [And02]); and (3) testing takes a lot of time, effort, and skilled staff to be done properly. The authors can thus make no informed opinion on how the discussed products perform in practice, or which ones are better than others. The information presented in this appendix is based **solely on vendors' claims**. It is gathered from product white papers (on Web pages, for example) and through personal communication with product developers, heavily distilled and summarized to provide design facts and omit performance claims. Its only purpose is to show you what is out there in the commercial world.

The list of solutions presented in this book is by no means exhaustive. In an ever-changing market, it would be impossible to account for all commercial products that provide effective DDoS defense. In our opinion, the products discussed herein form a representative set of commercial solutions available today. You should investigate the market yourself before buying any DDoS defense product and assure yourself that the product provides the desired security guarantees to your network.

The material in this appendix is likely to soon become obsolete as new products appear and old ones are withdrawn from sales.

B.1   Mazu Enforcer by Mazu Networks

Mazu Enforcer combines anomaly and signature DDoS detection and deploys filtering to respond to attacks. Anomaly detection is performed by building behavioral models of legitimate traffic. The user specifies *triggers*—traffic characteristics whose behavior should be monitored and incorporated in the model. There are two types of triggers. *Bandwidth triggers* describe the amount of inbound and outbound traffic of various types. Total inbound packet or byte rate, outbound TCP packet rate, or inbound ICMP packet rate are all examples of bandwidth triggers. *Suspicious traffic triggers* describe specific traffic whose excess may overwhelm network resources. Fragmented packets, TCP SYN packets, and the ratio of inbound to outbound TCP packets represent examples of suspicious traffic triggers. Once the triggers have been defined, Enforcer monitors the values of these parameters over time, recording their distributions within the baseline model of the network traffic. Another utility, Threshold Advisor, examines the recorded trigger distributions and guides the definition of thresholds that will be used for anomaly detection. The Threshold Advisor displays the average, maximum, and user-selected percentile value for each trigger, and makes a recommendation for threshold value. Figure B.1 depicts the sample trigger types along with their threshold values. In addition to trigger distributions and thresholds, the baseline model contains the distributions of packet attributes: payload hash and packet header fields, such as source and destination addresses, source and destination ports, TTL, and protocol.

During normal operation, the Enforcer records trigger values and compares them with the defined thresholds to detect anomalies. Once an anomaly is detected, Enforcer alerts the operator of the attack and starts the characterization process, devising appropriate traffic filters. The goal of this process is to accurately describe and surgically separate the attack from the legitimate traffic. The Enforcer first observes each packet attribute (payload hash and header fields), and attempts to identify parameter values that describe the highest volume of the inbound traffic. For instance, assume

Bandwidth Triggers

● Total inbound byte rate	1,820,458 bytes/second
● Total inbound packet rate	38,078 packets/second
● Inbound TCP packet rate	37,108 packets/second
● Inbound TCP byte rate	1,706,968 bytes/second
● Inbound UDP packet rate	970 packets/second
● Inbound UDP byte rate	113,490 bytes/second
● Inbound ICMP packet rate	0 packets/second
● Inbound ICMP byte rate	0 bytes/second

Suspicious Traffic Triggers

● Inbound fragmented IP packets	0 packets/second
● Inbound TCP SYN packet rate	50 packets/second
● Unacknowledged inbound TCP SYNs	0 packets
● Traffic from reserved addresses	75 packets/second
● TCP ratio (inbound/outbound)	1 packet/second
● Packets with suspicious payload	0 packets/second

Figure B.1   Illustration of the Mazu Enforcer trigger types along with the corresponding threshold values. (Reprinted from Mazu Enforcer white paper with permission of Mazu Networks.)

that 80% of all incoming packets have a TTL value of 23 or 25, and the other 20% have uniformly distributed values from 10 to 250. The characterization process would then identify values 23 and 25 for the TTL parameter. The next step is to compare the distribution of the identified values with the historical distribution for a given packet attribute stored in the baseline model. Assume that a baseline model indicates that, historically, the majority of packets have uniformly distributed TTL values between 10 and 250. The identified distribution of values clustered at 23 and 25 then significantly differs from the historical distribution, which in this example makes a TTL value a suitable parameter for differentiating between the legitimate and the attack packets. If, on the other hand, the distribution of the identified values were similar to that indicated by a historical model (i.e., if packets usually had their TTL values clustered around 23 and 25), the TTL parameter could not be used to perform traffic separation.

Once the separation parameters (and their values) are identified, Enforcer recommends the appropriate filters. Five types of filters are supported:

1. **Cisco router ACL filters.** These are standard Cisco router filters that describe traffic using source and destination addresses, port numbers, and the protocol field. ACL filters, if accepted by the operator, are not deployed by Enforcer, but rather are installed in the downstream router.

2. **High-performance Mazu filters.** In addition to the descriptive ability of ACL filters, Mazu filters can describe packets using TTL values, packet length, and the payload hash. Since more descriptive power equals better traffic separation, Mazu filters are likely to inflict lower collateral damage than the ACL filters.

3. **Mazu expression filters.** Operators have the ability to specify their own filters describing a combination of any packet attribute and value ranges, using Boolean expression constructs.

4. **TCP SYN flood filters.** Enforcer offers protection against TCP SYN flood attacks, with filters that can be engaged preemptively. TCP SYN flood filters track stale half-open TCP connections and generate resets to free server resources.

5. **Payload filters.** Fragments of packets seen in known incidents, such as *Nimda* and *Code Red* spread, are used to filter out known malicious traffic.

Enforcer also makes an attempt to forecast the expected impact of each recommended filter, with the goal of predicting the filter's effectiveness in stopping the attack traffic and the likely amount of collateral damage. This prediction is easily made by calculating the percentage of the inbound traffic matching the filtering rule. The collateral damage prediction is derived by calculating the percentage of traffic described by the baseline model that matches the filtering rule. Figure B.2 illustrates a sample filter forecast for two recommended filters. The packet attribute (high-performance Mazu) filter is predicted to reduce the incoming traffic by 63%, and inflict no collateral damage. The ACL filter is predicted to reduce the incoming traffic by 65% and inflict 3% of collateral damage. Enforcer can run in active, passive, or hybrid mode. Active mode places the Enforcer inline, between the entrance router connecting the network to the Internet and the firewall sitting in front of the network. Passive mode places a wiretap on the line connecting the router and the firewall. Hybrid mode combines the passive mode during normal operation with the ability to reroute traffic through the Enforcer and trigger the active mode once the attack has been detected.

Enforcer literature specifies that it has an interactive traffic visualization and analysis tool which can be queried to display statistics on historical or current traffic across many dimensions. Such a tool should facilitate network management.

B.2 Peakflow by Arbor Networks

Peakflow is a family of security products, built on the common Peakflow Platform, which provides an architecture for extensive data collection and anomaly detection.

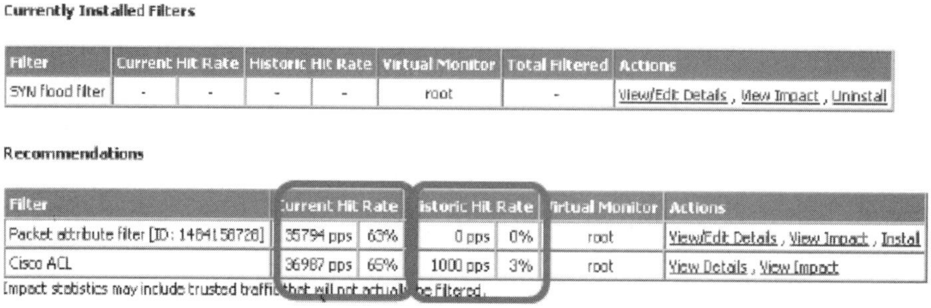

Currently Installed Filters
Filter | Current Hit Rate | Historic Hit Rate | Virtual Monitor | Total Filtered | Actions
SYN flood filter | - | - | - | - | root | - | View/Edit Details, View Impact, Uninstall
Recommendations
Filter | Current Hit Rate | Historic Hit Rate | Virtual Monitor | Actions
Packet attribute filter [ID: 1484158728] | 35794 pps | 63% | 0 pps | 0% | root | View/Edit Details, View Impact, Install
Cisco ACL | 36987 pps | 65% | 1000 pps | 3% | root | View Details, View Impact
Impact statistics may include trusted traffic that will not actually be Filtered.

Figure B.2 Illustration of the Enforcer's forecast of filter impact. (Reprinted from Mazu Enforcer white paper with permission of Mazu Networks.)

SECURITY
POLICY
PEERING
NW ENGINEERING
API
NETWORK-WIDE ANOMALY DETECTION
Perimeter AD
DoS, zero-day worms, inter-router threats, router attacks
Internal AD
Zero-day threats, abuse, misuse
MEASURE, AGGREGATE, CORRELATE
FLOW DATA
Src, Dst, Port, Protocol, Device
ROUTING DATA
Topology, Connectivity
SECURITY DATA
NIDS

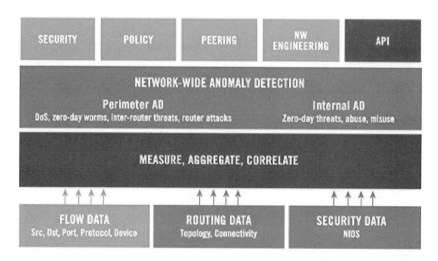

Figure B.3 Illustration of the Peakflow Platform. (Reprinted from Peakflow white paper with permission of Arbor Networks.)

The Peakflow Platform, shown in Figure B.3, collects three kinds of data about network state.

1. Flow data, describing the traffic seen at each network device. This is a breakdown of traffic characteristics, including source and destination addresses and port numbers, and the transport protocol.

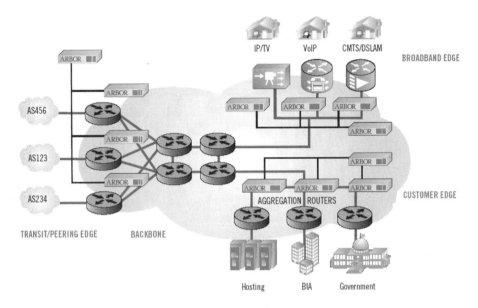

Figure B.4   Peakflow SP deployment within a service provider's network. (Reprinted from Peakflow white paper with permission of Arbor Networks.)

2. Routing data, describing the network connectivity.

3. Security data, collected from network intrusion detection systems (NIDSs) distributed throughout the network, describing detected intrusion attempts.

Flow data is collected through distributed passive sensors that tap the network links, while routing and NIDS data is imported from existing network routers and intrusion detection systems. Collected data is used to build baseline models of normal network behavior. Peakflow Platform aggregates and correlates data measured during network operation, looking for anomalies that disagree with the baseline model. The Peakflow white papers specify that, in addition to DDoS, detected anomalies can be used to detect other security problems, such as Internet worms spreading in the network, router attacks, insider threats, and misuse of network resources.

Peakflow SP is a security product for service providers, which aims at protecting the deploying network from external threats and enhancing network management. Figure B.4 illustrates the deployment of Peakflow SP (shapes labeled "Arbor") within a service provider's network. Peakflow SP consists of two modules:

1. Peakflow DoS, which attempts to detect and mitigate network threats.

2. Peakflow Traffic, which monitors and displays network statistics at different levels, which should facilitate network management.

Peakflow DoS uses Peakflow Platform to monitor network state, detect anomalies, and provide a fingerprint of the offending traffic. The fingerprint describes numerous traffic characteristics, including the source and destination ports and IP addresses, transport protocol, etc. The observations at different network points are then correlated and compared, looking for the presence of the fingerprint. Peakflow DoS thus attempts to trace the offending traffic and reconstruct its trajectory through the network. This action should identify network devices affected by the threat and facilitate easy mitigation. For instance, if a worm is detected in the network, the tracing process aims to identify all infected machines so that they can be cleaned by the operators. Attempted threat mitigation can be performed by Peakflow DoS itself policing the offending traffic through filtering, sinkhole routing or blackhole routing. Another option is that Peakflow DoS recommends filtering or rate-limiting rules to network routers. Peakflow DoS white papers also specify that the product generates detailed reports of the handled anomalies, which should facilitate forensics.

Peakflow Traffic uses Peakflow Platform to monitor, aggregate, and display data on network traffic and routing, which should facilitate network management. One goal of this monitoring process is to enable service providers to monitor behavior of their peers and optimize transit and peering arrangements. The other goal is to enable providers to monitor their customer traffic, which should help devise accurate pricing schemes and understand network utilization. Peakflow Traffic white papers specify that the product can profile network traffic at different granularities—peer-to-peer, AS-to-AS, and pop-to-pop—by various parameters, such as AS number, ASPath attribute, application, or next-hop router. Peakflow Traffic literature also specifies that the product can detect routing anomalies such as route failures, suspicious BGP announcements, routing instability, can alert network operators, and provide detailed information to support mitigation. The product also offers detailed reports that can be exported in various formats and used to support network management decisions.

Peakflow X is a security system that aims to detect and mitigate internal threats within a company. Figure B.5 illustrates the deployment of Peakflow X (shapes labeled "Arbor") within a service company's network. Peakflow X organizes monitored hosts into groups based on similar operational policies and behavior. This creates a map of network usage with a goal to help operators to understand communication patterns between and within groups, profiled by network service, and possibly restructure the

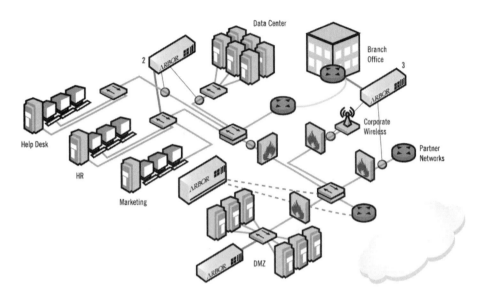

Figure B.5   Peakflow X deployment within a company's network. Shapes labeled "Arbor" represent Peakflow modules monitoring traffic via inline taps (small circles on the links) and switches (shapes with arrows). (Reprinted from Peakflow white paper with permission of Arbor Networks.)

network to better use its resources. Grouping further aims to facilitate development of common policies for devices that have similar functionality. For instance, all Web servers could be grouped and managed together. Peakflow X uses Peakflow Platform to build baseline models of normal traffic patterns and to detect anomalous behavior. Peakflow X white papers specify that the product works together with NIDSs to tune NIDS behavior and disable signatures likely to generate false positives. It can also correlate NIDS signature detection with anomaly detection from Peakflow Platform, providing higher-confidence alerts. When a threat is detected, Peakflow X generates a threat alert, assigning it a priority level based on the sensitivity of target and protocol threat. The system also maintains a detailed log of historical network usage which aims to facilitate forensics and provide information for network engineering decisions.

B.3   WS Series Appliances by Webscreen Technologies

Webscreen is primarily an inline security system, which aims to protect *Web servers* from DDoS attacks. Webscreen is deployed between a Web server (or a firewall) and

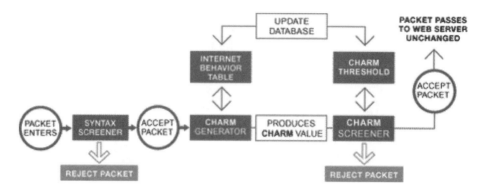

Figure B.6   Processing of an incoming packet by a Webscreen appliance using CHARM technology. (Reprinted from Webscreen's white paper with permission of WebScreen technology, Inc.)

the rest of the Internet. It examines each incoming packet using proprietary CHARM technology, attempting to assess a packet's legitimacy. This packet processing is depicted in Figure B.6. CHARM technology monitors the behavior of users accessing the Web server during normal operation, building a baseline model of legitimate access patterns for each user and recording them in the Internet behavior table. Webscreen attempts to detect the occurrence of the attack by noting the change in traffic levels and user access patterns, in comparison with server resource utilization. Each incoming packet is then assessed for legitimacy and acted on accordingly. A packet is first screened by Syntax Screener, which checks whether the packet is properly formed. Packets that appear malformed will be dropped. A packet then passes through the CHARM Generator and is assigned a CHARM value using the data stored in the Internet behavior table for a given source address, and relating this data to packet contents. The vendor provides no details on how the CHARM value is generated. This value is then compared to the dynamic threshold by the CHARM Screener. The threshold value is dynamically adjusted according to the perceived server resource use— higher resource use results in higher thresholds. Only those packets whose CHARM value is greater than the threshold are allowed to reach the server. Packets deemed legitimate are also used to update the baseline models in the Internet behavior table. This approach appears to favor the known legitimate users, protecting their traffic during the attack, and it may reject first-time users whose access coincides with the attack.

Webscreen Technology, Inc. offers three products that essentially provide the same protection functionality but operate at different scales. WS2 is designed for 2-Mbps throughput, monitors up to 500,000 source IP addresses, and works to protect up to eight IP addresses. WS100 and WS1000 both monitor up to 8 million source IP addresses and work to protect up to 512 IP addresses. WS100 is designed for 100-Mbps throughput and WS1000 is designed for 1-Gbps throughput.

B.4   Captus IPS by Captus Networks

Captus IPS is an inline, policy-based product that aims to detect and mitigate network threats. It provides policy language that administrators can use to specify fine-granularity security polices. Traffic features that can be used in policy specification include:

- Source and destination IP addresses and ports, and traffic protocol and flags.
- Traffic rate and duration of match required for trigger conditions.

Traffic features can be combined within a policy rule using AND and OR Boolean operators. Additionally, traffic can be grouped into areas, with multiple policies defined over a given area. Policies are used to define the desired condition of the network. A typical policy rule includes at least one match statement and one trigger statement. A match statement instructs Captus IPS to monitor traffic with specified characteristics, e.g., a given source and destination port and transport protocol. A trigger rule compares monitored traffic features with specified thresholds, such as flow rate or expected packet size. Rule violation results in an attack alert. Captus IPS white papers specify that the product can detect DoS attacks, Internet worm and virus propagation, peer-to-peer file sharing, port scans, spam, and insider threats. Captus IPS mitigation options include notifying network operators and shaping, redirecting, or denying traffic. The chosen option depends on the action specified in the violated policy rule.

Captus IPS View is a centralized management console for configuration, management, and monitoring of multiple Captus IPS devices. Captus IPS View white papers specify that the product provides network state visualization and report generation and detailed logging of traffic and attack data. Figure B.7 depicts deployment of Captus IPS and Captus IPS View devices within a company's network.

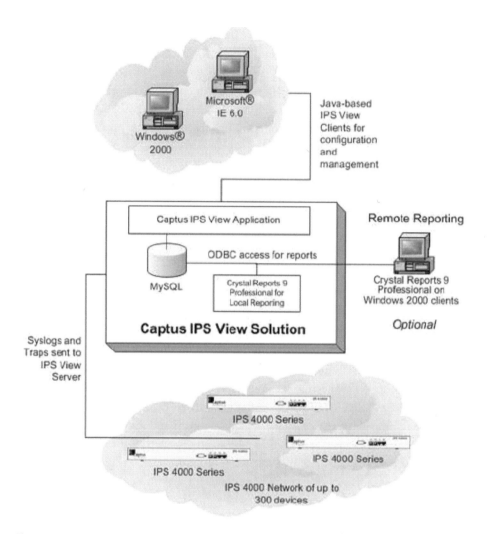

Figure B.7 Deployment of Captus IPS and Captus IPS View devices within a company's network. (Reprinted from Captus products white paper with permission of Captus Networks Corporation.)

B.5 MANAnet Shield by CS3

MANAnet Shield is a family of products that aim to offer protection from both incoming and outgoing DDoS attacks:

- MANAnet FloodWatcher is a passive device that detects anomalies in network traffic that could be a sign of an incoming DDoS attack and alerts administrators.

- MANAnet Linux Router implements path-enhanced IP (PEIP—CS3 technology to defeat IP spoofing). It also attempts to enforce fair sharing of network resources based on PEIP information using CS3 technology called Place-Based Fair Queueing (PLFQ). The router can deploy rate-limiting rules as a response to incoming DDoS attacks, at the request of its neighbors, or on its own accord.

- MANAnet Firewall offers firewall functionality with PEIP and PLFQ and issues rate-limiting requests when a DDoS attack is detected.

- MANAnet Reverse Firewall is an inline device that aims to detect and throttle outgoing DDoS attacks.

MANAnet FloodWatcher monitors incoming and outgoing network traffic, collecting statistics on multiple traffic parameters. The collected data is compared to operator-set thresholds to detect anomalies. Offending traffic is then profiled and network operators are alerted about the attack and provided with a devised attack signature.

MANAnet Linux Router is a router implementing two proprietary technologies: PEIP, with a goal to defeat IP spoofing; and PLFQ, with a goal to provide fair resource sharing among legitimate users. PEIP modifies each packet with additional information to discern the path that the packet takes through a MANAnet-protected network. The first router on the path will append its IP address to the packet. Subsequent routers will enumerate their incoming interfaces, and append the number of the interface on which a packet was received to the path information. Packets that are replies to service requests preserve the path information from the request. Reply-specific path information is appended to the preserved request path. This should provide useful information in case of reflector DDoS attacks, where the path of reply traffic would be the same in all packets, but the request paths would differ. For instance, assume that three attackers—A, B, and C—send DNS requests to server S, faking a victim's address V. All replies will carry an identical path from S to V, but they will also carry different paths for request packets indicating A, B, and C. PEIP information aims to help V drop offending replies (to requests from A, B, and C), while still being able to send DNS requests to S and receive replies. The IP address in the beginning of the path information is called a *visible source*. A MANAnet Linux Router subjects incoming traffic to the proprietary queueing algorithm PLFQ with a goal to assign a fair share of resources to each visible source. A visible source that is particularly misbehaving (sending large amounts of traffic) may be additionally restrained by the router deploying a rate limit on traffic from this source. Contiguous MANAnet routers organize themselves into *cooperative neighborhoods* and work together to build PEIP information and attempt to trace incoming attacks back to an ingress point into the neighborhood. Figure B.8 depicts two cooperative neighborhoods.

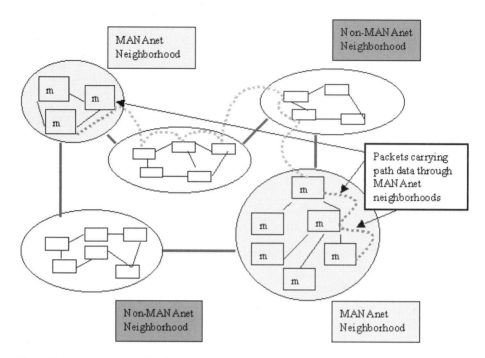

Figure B.8 MANAnet neighborhoods cooperate to defend against DDoS attacks. (Reprinted from
MANAnet white paper with permission of CS3, Inc.)

MANAnet Firewall implements the standard firewall functionality and adds three
new features:

1. The ability to decode PEIP information and perform PLFQ packet scheduling.

2. The ability to perform Historical Place-Based Fair Queueing (HPLFQ). The vendor
    does not offer much information on this option, except that the goal of HPLFQ
    is to ensure fair service to new requests with respect to the recent service history of
    their paths.

3. The ability to detect and rate-limit packets that are deemed "unexpected" by the
    firewall. The MANAnet Firewall keeps track of each established TCP connection,
    defining a range of expected sequence numbers to be seen in the incoming pack-
    ets. This range is inferred by observing the acknowledgment and TCP window
    information from the connection's outgoing packets. Incoming TCP packets with
    sequence numbers matching the defined range are called *expected* and sent to their
    destination. TCP packets that do not match the sequence number range, TCP SYN,

UDP, and ICMP packets are called *unexpected*. These packets will be rate limited in case of an attack by being placed in different processing queues at the MANAnet Firewall and assigning a limited share of resources to each queue. Packets within the queue will be processed applying PLFQ. The product white papers specify that this creates a possibility for legitimate users to have their unexpected packets served even during a DDoS attack.

MANAnet Reverse Firewall applies MANAnet Firewall functionality to the outgoing traffic. It aims to detect outgoing DDoS attacks and responds by placing a rate limit on the amount of unexpected packets that are allowed to leave the network. In this case, packets that cannot be readily identified as replies to incoming TCP packets are called unexpected. The Reverse Firewall also deploys PEIP and PLFQ with a goal to offer fair service to legitimate users within the deploying network. The PEIP information in dropped packets should help network operators locate compromised machines within their network.

B.6   Cisco Traffic Anomaly Detector XT and Cisco Guard XT

Cisco Security products offer a family of solutions intended to mitigate DDoS attacks. Solutions come in two flavors:

1. Cisco Traffic Anomaly Detector XT aims to detect denial-of-service attacks, worms, and other threats by passively monitoring network traffic.

2. Cisco Guard XT is an inline solution that aims to mitigate attacks by policing offending traffic.

The Detector learns normal traffic patterns and builds baseline models of normal activity over time, using proprietary Multi-Verification Process (MVP) architecture. The Detector stores state for each session (e.g., a TCP connection) and verifies each incoming packet within the context of its session state, source, destination, and protocol. Monitored traffic is compared to baseline models using proprietary MVP technology to detect anomalous behavior. Upon attack detection, the Detector provides its corresponding Guard product with information about the attack's target IP (or several target IPs). All traffic destined to the target IP is then diverted using proprietary Cisco technology through the Guard product, which examines each packet and classifies it as either legitimate or attack. The packet verification process again uses MVP architecture, and subjects each packet to five-stage inspection designed to identify and block the suspicious traffic while allowing legitimate packets to pass:

1. **Filtering**. The Guard initially enforces user-configurable static filters to block obvious and known attacks. Dynamic filters are defined and imposed in real time by later stages of the MVP process, based on specific anomalies detected during the inspection.

2. **Active verification**. The Guard uses proprietary mechanisms with a goal to detect and discard spoofed packets.

3. **Anomaly recognition**. This module monitors all traffic that has not been dropped by Filtering and Active Verification modules, and compares it to baseline models to detect anomalies. Baseline models attempt to capture legitimate behavior at source IP and protocol granularity, using numerous parameters, including the total traffic volume, distribution of packet sizes and port numbers, distribution of packet interarrival times, the number of concurrent flows, higher-level protocol characteristics, the ratio of inbound to outbound traffic, etc. Traffic that deviates significantly from the baseline is identified as attack. The Anomaly Recognition module then creates and imposes a series of dynamic filters at the Filtering module to block the newly discovered attack source.

4. **Protocol analysis**. This module processes flows identified as suspicious by the Anomaly Recognition module with a goal to identify application-specific attacks, such as incomplete or erroneous service requests. It then creates and imposes a series of dynamic filters at the Filtering module to block the newly discovered attack source.

5. **Rate limiting**. This module deploys per-flow and per-protocol traffic shaping, applying a target resource–specific policy. This policy is learned over time, with a goal of setting the appropriate rate limit without human intervention.

Figure B.9 depicts the Guard's attack mitigation process. The Guard looks for signs that the attack has stopped and then restores diverted traffic to its original path. Detector and Guard are designed to be used as stand-alone solutions, as well as in joint operation. Figure B.10 depicts a recommended deployment of Detector and Guard products within a network. Both Detector and Guard products claim to generate detailed traffic

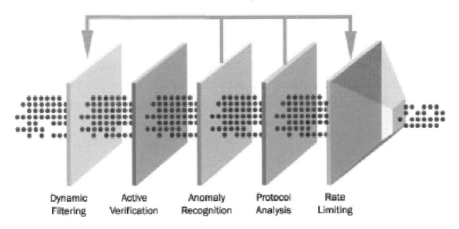

Figure B.9   Attack mitigation process in Cisco Guard and Cisco Guard XT

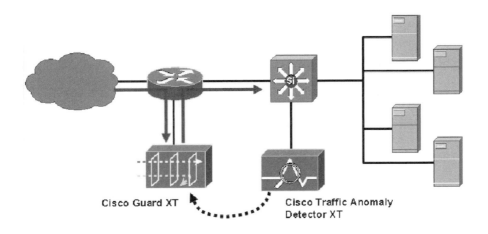

Figure B.10   A recommended deployment of Guard and Detector products within a network

reports that can be used by operators to examine network usage or to perform attack forensics. Figures B.9, B.10, and the text in this section have been reproduced by Prentice Hall with the permission of Cisco Systems, Inc. Copyright © 2004 Cisco Systems, Inc. All rights reserved.

B.7   StealthWatch by Lancope

StealthWatch aims to detect DDoS attacks by deploying anomaly detection. It profiles traffic at the host granularity and builds baseline models of each host's activity, including services provided and requested by each host and the corresponding traffic volumes. Upon completing an initial training period, the host models are locked in place. Stealth-Watch also builds legitimate traffic models at a flow granularity, where Lancope defines a flow as any communication between two hosts, using a specific transport protocol and a specific destination port. During normal operation, each communication between hosts is assessed against corresponding flow and traffic models, and possibly using IDS-provided signature detection, and the source host is assigned a Concern Index denoting the level of suspicion. Each network host has a separate Concern Index threshold. When a host's Concern Index exceeds the threshold, StealthWatch raises an alarm alerting the network administrator about suspicious host behavior. The vendor provides no details about the process of calculating the Concern Index or assigning host-specific thresholds. The StealthWatch white papers claim that this detection mechanism can be used to detect DoS attacks, worms, and insider threats.

By profiling individual hosts, StealthWatch also facilitates division of network resources into Virtual Security Zones. Hosts with similar network and application behaviors are grouped together into zones, facilitating zone-based security policy definition and enforcement, with a goal to help network management.

StealthWatch white papers specify that the product preserves detailed flow statistics and can display them using a variety of graphical views, which aim to facilitate network management and attack forensics.

StealthWatch can be deployed outside the firewall with a goal to protect a network from external threats, or inside the firewall with a goal to protect key segments from internal threats. Figure B.11 depicts a sample StealthWatch deployment inside a company's network. The StealthWatch Management Console is a centralized management console for monitoring, configuration, and management of multiple StealthWatch devices. Its white papers specify that the product coordinates intelligence and attack alerts from these devices, offering a global view of network usage and security.

B.8   Summary

After surveying the above solutions, several questions may have occurred to the reader.

- **Are the preceding solutions the only ones that handle the DDoS problem?** Not by any means. It was impossible to collect and survey all the existing DDoS solutions

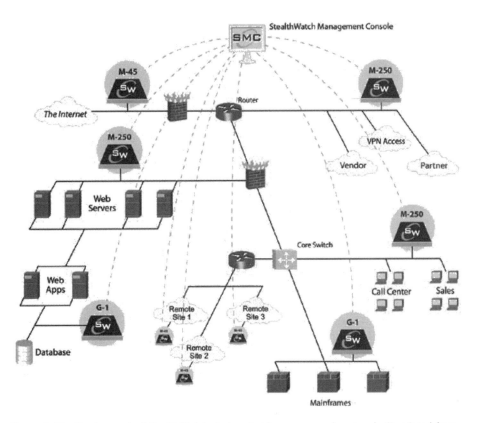

Figure B.11 Deployment of StealthWatch devices inside a company's network. (Reprinted from StealthWatch white paper with permission of Lancope.)

in this book, first, because space is limited and, second, because the market scene is continuously changing.

- **Are the preceding solutions better than those that were not surveyed?** This is a hard question to answer. Due to the lack of common evaluation methodology for DDoS defense solutions, it is impossible even to compare surveyed solutions to one another. It would be even more far-fetched to compare one of those to another solution not surveyed in this book. Rather, we believe that the selected solutions represent popular attack detection and mitigation approaches that are currently favored by the commercial community. Other solutions that you may find on the market are likely not to be drastically different from the surveyed ones. The overview of the functionalities offered by the preceding solutions should provide you with a list of features you can look for in a DDoS solution.

- **So which one is the best?** Ah, another hard question! There is currently no agreement in the DDoS defense community about the methodology for DDoS solution evaluation. Thus, even if we obtained and tested a sample of each of the systems discussed, we would have a hard time designing tests that everyone would accept as realistic and appropriate. This situation might change in the next few years. A number of ongoing research projects are examining the proper methods of evaluating DDoS defense solutions. The NSF also funded a project in 2003 to build a large DDoS research testbed [USC]. Answering questions about the relative performances of different research and commercial DDoS defense mechanisms may be more feasible when these projects have reached fruition.

In an attempt to provide more useful information to the reader, we summarize the capabilities found in the preceding solutions in Table B.1. As with the earlier material in this appendix, the summary is based solely on vendor claims in product white papers and does not reflect any of the authors' or publisher's opinions.

Table B.1   Summary of Commercial Product Features

Featured Products	
Mazu Enforcer	Enforcer.
Peakflow	Peakflow SP for service providers offering external attack mitigation and traffic management functionality and Peakflow X for companies offering internal attack mitigation functionality.
Webscreen	WS2, WS100, and WS1000 provide the same attack detection/mitigation functionality at different scales.
Captus	Captus IPS for attack mitigation and Captus IPS View for management of multiple Captus IPS devices.
MANAnet	FloodWatcher for attack detection, Router and Firewall for incoming attack mitigation and Reverse Firewall for outgoing attack mitigation.
Cisco	Traffic Anomaly Detector XT provides attack detection functionality. Guard XT provides attack detection mitigation functionality.
StealthWatch	StealthWatch provides attack detection functionality and StealthWatch Management Console for management of multiple StealthWatch devices.

Table B.1 *(continued)*

Deployment	
Mazu Enforcer	Active, passive, and hybrid.
Peakflow	Active for Peakflow SP, passive for Peakflow X.
Webscreen	Active.
Captus	Active.
MANAnet	Passive for FloodWatcher; active for Router, Firewall, and Reverse Firewall.
Cisco	Passive for the Detector, active for the Guard.
StealthWatch	Passive.

Attack Detection	
Mazu Enforcer	Anomalies are detected in incoming traffic by monitoring various traffic parameters and comparing them against bandwidth and suspicious traffic triggers.
Peakflow	Anomalies are detected in network state by monitoring various traffic parameters, routing data and NIDS data, and correlating observations.
Webscreen	Anomalies are detected by building legitimate-host behavior models and noting change in traffic levels and user access patterns in comparison to server resource use.
Captus	Anomalies are detected through traffic monitoring and comparison with operator-defined policies. Policy violation triggers attack detection.
MANAnet	Anomalies are detected by monitoring various traffic parameters and comparing monitored values to operator-set thresholds.
Cisco	Anomalies are detected by monitoring traffic patterns and comparing them to baseline models built over time.
StealthWatch	Anomalies are detected by building models of host activity and traffic levels, then comparing monitored communication against these baseline models. Each source host is assigned a Concern Index. Attack is detected when the Concern Index exceeds the host-specific threshold.

Table B.1 (*continued*)

	Attack Response
Mazu Enforcer	Develop and install appropriate filters, or recommend ACL filters to be installed by CISCO routers.
Peakflow	Develop and install appropriate filters, perform sinkhole or blackhole routing of the suspicious traffic or recommend filters to be installed by network routers.
Webscreen	Drop packets whose CHARM value falls below the dynamic threshold. Threshold value depends on the level of server resource use.
Captus	Notify operators; shape, redirect, or deny suspicious traffic.
MANAnet	Rate-limit unexpected packets, perform PLFQ.
Cisco	Divert suspicious traffic through the Guard and police it using multiple verification methods to identify and block malicious packets.
StealthWatch	Alert network administrator about suspicious hosts.

	Extra Features
Mazu Enforcer	Projected filter impact before installation. Traffic visualization and analysis tools.
Peakflow	Peakflow DoS (part of Peakflow SP) claims to provide offending traffic tracing and identification of affected network devices. Peakflow Traffic (another part of Peakflow SP) claims to profile traffic at peer-to-peer, AS-to-AS, and pop-to-pop granularity. Peakflow X organizes monitored hosts into groups facilitating group management. It also claims to tune NIDS devices and correlate their data with its anomaly detection. Both Peakflow Traffic and Peakflow X claim to offer detailed traffic and attack reports.
Webscreen	None.
Captus	Claims to offer network state visualization, report generation, and detailed logging of traffic and attack data.
MANAnet	Claims to be able to trace the offending traffic to the network ingress point.
Cisco	Claims to offer detailed traffic and attack logging and report generation.
StealthWatch	Hosts with similar behavior are grouped into zones and managed collectively. Claims to offer detailed flow statistics logging and display in a variety of graphical views.

APPENDIX C

DDoS Data

Relatively little reliable data is available on the DDoS problem. Because of its distributed nature and the difficulties of measuring Internet-wide phenomena, direct measurements of the most important characteristics of DDoS attacks (how often they occur, how long they typically last, how heavy the attack flow is, how many agent sites are typically used, the composition of the attack traffic, etc.) are difficult to obtain.

Here, we summarize the reliable data that is publicly available that addresses such questions. Most of the sources we discuss were mentioned earlier in this book, but here we gather all the information into a single place, for the purpose of drawing the best picture possible of the measurable characteristics of DDoS attacks. We do not include reports about particular attacks, with the exception of a small amount of data concerning the combined attack on the DNS root servers that was perpetrated on October 21, 2002. We include some details on this attack because it was one of the larger attacks, its characteristics have been published by a reliable source, and it was an attack on the Internet as a whole, rather than on a single machine.

By its nature, the data provided here is a snapshot. We hope that more data of this kind will be published, as new techniques for gathering it are developed and more sites provide assistance in data gathering.

We present data from the following sources here:

- *The 2004 CSI/FBI Computer Crime and Security Survey*
- A paper on the use of the backscatter technique to infer DDoS attacks [MVS01]

- A paper describing the use of several techniques to analyze a number of observed actual attacks [HHP03]

- A presentation on data gathered by researchers on DDoS activity on a moderately large network over the course of six months

- A brief report on characteristics of the attack perpetrated on the DNS root servers in October 2002

Each is discussed in a separate section.

C.1   2004 CSI/FBI Computer Crime and Security Survey

Annually, the Computer Security Institute (CSI) and the FBI release the results of a survey they perform on the prevalence and character of computer crime. The 2004 survey data was gathered voluntarily from over 486 participants in the United States of America, covering business, government, educational, and medical facilities. Some respondents have only a few employees, while others have tens of thousands. The survey queries the respondents on many issues concerning computer security and cybercrime, of which DDoS is only one. Responses are voluntary, and not all responders answer all questions. Based on these facts about the source of the data, an important caveat for the following discussion is that there is no evidence to show that the respondents were representative of the kinds of Internet sites that suffer DDoS attacks most frequently, or of those that see the most powerful DDoS attacks.

One element of the survey is a question about the kinds of attacks that the institution has observed being perpetrated on its computers. DDoS attacks are one of the classes of attacks in the survey. Page 9 of this report contains a chart describing this data. Table C.1 extracts information from this chart describing the percentage of respondents who were targeted by a DDoS attack for the last five years.

Although this data shows that DDoS incidence has declined from the previous years, a significant percentage of all respondents (17%) suffered at least one DDoS attack in the past year. In some other cases, the respondent might not have recognized that an attack took place, though generally the participating institutions are both technically adept and aware of the nature and characteristics of different kinds of attacks, so they are likely to have noticed all but the most trivial attacks.

One further table from this report offers more depressing news. Each respondent provided an estimate of the loss suffered due to various forms of attacks on his institution over the course of the year. The report adds up the costs for each attack type over all institutions. The total reported cost of DDoS attacks by reporting institutions (total

Table C.1   Percentage of CSI/FBI cybersecurity survey
responders who observed a DDoS attack during
1999–2004

Year	Percentage of Respondents Observing DDoS Attack
2000	27
2001	36
2002	40
2003	38
2004	17

269) was \$26,064,050. DoS was the most costly kind of cyberattack this year, being followed by theft of proprietary information, which was responsible for the loss of \$11,460,000—less than half of the DDoS-inflicted loss.

This data shows that the potential cost of being unable to handle a DDoS attack is quite high, suggesting the value of taking the steps to protect your network that were outlined in Chapter 6.

The annual *CSI/FBI Computer Crime and Security Survey* can be obtained from the Computer Security Insitute's Web site, `http://www.gocsi.org/`.

C.2   Inferring Internet Denial-of-Service Activity

The paper described here was written by David Moore (of CAIDA) and Geoffrey Voelker and Stefan Savage (of the Department of Computer Science and Engineering at the University of California at San Diego). It was published in the 2001 USENIX Security Symposium.

The authors used a clever insight to get an overall picture of the amount and characteristics of DoS activity in the Internet as a whole.[1] They observed that many (though not all) DDoS attacks use general IP spoofing to hide the sources of the attack. An IP address is chosen more or less at random from the range of legal addresses and used as the putative source address of an attack packet. There are a vast number of attack packets, so sooner or later each possible IP address is used in some attack packet.

---

[1] In actuality, various researchers (including Dave Dittrich and Sven Deitrich, two of this book's authors) had been using this technique for some time to observe DDoS activity [DLD00], but, for various reasons, they were unable to publish data from their studies. See also `http://seclists.org/incidents/2000/Apr/0026.html`.

Further, many packet types used in typical attacks will generate a response, assuming they actually get delivered to the target of the attack. The response might merely be a packet indicating an error, but a response packet usually will get returned to the supposed sender of the attack packet. Since spoofing was used, the response does not go to the machine that sent the attack packet, but to the machine whose address was spoofed in the attack packet's source address field.

The authors of this paper realized that if one set up a network of machines that had no real users or services, and should never receive any legitimate traffic at all, any packets that it did receive would be part of some kind of attack. Some of them would be part of a DDoS attack, and, since those packets would be recognizable as response packets of various sorts (unlike the kinds of packets generated by random port scanning or worms), they could be separated out from the remainder of the traffic. They could then provide insight into which machines in the Internet were currently under attack, and perhaps insight into the character, duration, and size of the attack. The authors called the packets arriving at their test network due to responses to DDoS packets *backscatter*. The overall technique of inferring DDoS activity based on these packets and their characteristics is often called the *backscatter technique*.

There are a number of caveats that the authors themselves bring up about interpreting these results. Perhaps the three most important are that the results do not capture data on attacks that did not use generally randomized IP spoofing, that attack packets that would not tend to generate responses are not represented in the data, and that congestion and other effects certainly caused the dropping of an unknown number of attack packets and responses to those packets. All of these caveats suggest that the numbers reported here were underestimations of the actual DDoS activity, though it is impossible to know by how much. Despite these shortcomings, this study represents the best data we have available on overall prevalence of DDoS attacks in the Internet. All other available data measures DDoS activity only on a small portion of the Internet.

CAIDA, an organization devoted to measuring important characteristics of the Internet, had a large space of unused network addresses that could be configured for this purpose, so the authors of this paper performed a large study of the traffic received at these addresses, analyzing the data in various ways to obtain insight into the DDoS phenomenon. Their data, gathered over the course of three weeks in 2001, remains the best large-scale, Internet-wide description of DDoS attacks.

Full details of the study and its results can be found in [MVS01], but we will repeat their major results here. Over the three-week period, they observed over 12,805 separate attacks on more than 5,000 different targets in more than 2,000 DNS domains. The largest attack they observed contained more than 600,000 packets per second,

Table C.2 DDoS attack distribution by protocol, from the paper "Inferring Internet Denial-of-Service Activity"

Protocol	Percentage of attacks	Percentage of Attack Packets
TCP	91.8	66.00
UDP	3.3	0.25
ICMP	2.3	33.66
Protocol 0	2.2	0.06
Other	0.4	0.03

an immense number of packets that could not be handled by most machines in the Internet.

The study's traces were gathered in three segments, each lasting around one week. They typically observed 20 or more attacks per hour. During one hour-long period, they observed 150 attacks. In this case, most of the targets were on a common network.

The technique also allowed the researchers to deduce the type of packets used in the attack, by characterizing the type of response. Around 60% of all responses were TCP, some being SYN ACKs (probably indicating a SYN attack), some being TCP RSTs or RST ACKs (probably indicating a TCP-based attack that sent unexpected TCP packets), and a few being some other kind of TCP packets. Thirty-seven to forty percent of the responses were some kind of ICMP packet. The largest-volume attacks seemed to generate ICMP TTL exceeded responses. The authors were unable to identify exactly what mechanism was being exercised in these attacks.

From this and other data, the authors were able to deduce the protocol used in the attack. Table C.2 (derived from Table 5 in their paper) summarizes these results.

Thus, while the majority of both attacks and attack packets are TCP-based, other protocols are in use for attacks. For this data, particularly, one must bear in mind that the study does not capture information on DDoS attack packets that do not generate responses. So, for example, if a particular UDP streaming protocol does not cause the target to generate a response denying improper packets or querying the source, all attack packets using that protocol would be unaccounted for by this methodology. So this data cannot tell us the frequency of DDoS attacks that use packets that do not generate responses.

The backscatter technique also allowed the researchers to determine the duration of attacks. The methods they used to deduce durations (which are related to the methods used to determine when attacks started and stopped, which in turn were used to count overall number of attacks) are described in the paper. The results, in brief, were that most attacks were short. Fifty percent lasted less than 10 minutes, 80% less than 30 minutes, and 90% less than one hour. But there were some very long attacks. One percent of the attacks lasted more than 10 hours, and dozens of attacks went on for several days. These results should suggest to you the danger you are in if you cannot respond to a DDoS attack. It need not stop on its own, unless the attacker wants it to. For practical purposes, if you cannot stop it, you are at the attacker's mercy indefinitely.

The researchers were also able to shed some light on what kinds of sites were suffering attacks. The response packets they received had the target's IP address in the source field, allowing the researchers to attempt a reverse DNS lookup on that address.[2] Not all addresses resolve under reverse lookups, and a bit less than 30% of the addresses the researchers observed proved not to be resolvable in this way. Of those that were resolvable, many appeared to be home machines using dial-up or DSL connections (deduced by particular strings appearing in the names of these machines). Two to three percent of the attacks were targeted at name servers of various types, and 1 to 3% of the attacks were targeted at routers. Thus, attacks on the infrastructure are a reality, and are not limited to the single case of the October 2002 attacks on the DNS root machines.

The top-level domains (TLDs) of the machines under attack showed a broad range of targets, with machines in the .net and .com domains receiving a lot of attacks. This analysis did turn up the surprising result that machines in Romania (identified by the .ro TLD name) were attacked nearly as often as .net and .com machines, and that Brazilian machines (with the .br TLD name) were also very commonly targeted. The authors did not have a good explanation for the frequency of attacks on targets in this country.

The full paper provides many other interesting measurements. One more we will comment on here is the degree to which particular nodes were subjected to multiple attacks. The study found that nearly two thirds of the nodes attacked were attacked only once in their traces. Nearly a fifth of the nodes were attacked twice. However, a few unfortunate nodes were attacked dozens of times, and one unlucky node received more than 100 attacks. The lesson is that a determined adversary may return to his attack, even if you take temporary measures to stop him, as has frequently been seen in practice. The best way to minimize damage from repeated attacks is to develop well in advance the monitoring and response strategies (such as mentioned in Chapter 6)

---

[2] Unlike a normal DNS lookup, which translates a human-readable name to an IP address, a reverse DNS lookup translates an IP address to a human-readable name. The DNS service supports both forms of lookup.

that you can easily engage over and over again. While automated defenses may fend off simple attacks, defeating a determined attacker who repeatedly targets your network will require all the skill and attention of your operations staff.

Once the technique of backscatter was described, other entities began to perform their own studies using the technique. CAIDA was particularly well positioned to perform this study, as they own a lightly utilized /8 network that represents 1/256 of the total IP address space. Most others running such experiments (an exception being the University of Michigan's Internet Motion Sensor; see `http://ims.eecs.umich.edu/`) have far fewer addresses that they can configure to receive backscatter traffic, increasing the noise in their measurements.

Relatively little other backscatter data has been reported. One recent paper [GMP04] discussed applying spectral analysis statistical techniques to backscatter data to determine a number of characteristics. In particular, this study looked at determining the actual start and end times of attacks, looking only at TCP SYN ACK backscatter packets. They did not concentrate on providing the same kind of analysis as the earlier paper, so the results are not directly usable to confirm the findings of [MVS01].

C.3   A Framework for Classifying Denial-of-Service Attacks

This paper, written by Alefiya Hussain, John Heidemann, and Christos Papadopoulos, of the USC/Information Sciences Institute, analyzes data obtained from observing traffic in a particular ISP over the course of five months. The researchers used automated methods to pull possible DoS attacks from the observed traffic, then analyzed these flagged portions of the traffic by hand to remove any false positives. They acknowledge that the results are not a perfect count of all DoS attacks that occurred, but that was not the point of their research, anyway. Their goal was to analyze actual DoS traffic using various methods, statistical and otherwise, to deduce interesting information, such as whether the attack originated at a single site or at multiple sites and whether it was a direct attack from a set of DDoS agents or a reflector attack.

They observed 80 separate attacks. The first method they used to analyze the attacks was to examine the headers of the attack packets. Using techniques such as checking the ID and TTL fields of packets, they were able to make strong inferences about which of the attacks were distributed and which came from a single source in 67 of the 80 cases. They then used statistical techniques (primarily arrival rate analysis, ramp-up behavior, and spectral analysis) to further examine their data.

Header examination allowed them to determine that 37 of the attacks appeared to be single sourced, 10 multisourced, and 20 were reflector attacks. They could make no firm determination on the other 13 attacks. As in the backscatter experiments, they determined that TCP was the most popular protocol to use in the attack, followed by ICMP. UDP and protocol 0 were less frequently used. Five of the attacks used more than one protocol.

The rates of the attacks that they observed varied from 300 packets per second to 98,000 packets per second. Not surprisingly, the high-rate attacks tended to be distributed, with the low-rate attacks being more commonly single sourced. Reflector attacks had intermediate rates.

Ramp-up analysis looked at how quickly the attack reached its peak. The researchers' hypothesis was that single-sourced attacks would usually reach their peak quickly, while multisourced attacks would increase more gradually, based on variations in the attack start times at different agents and varying amounts of time for the first packets from different agents to reach the target. The paper presents sample graphs from two of the 67 they analyzed, showing ramp-up times of three seconds and fourteen seconds, respectively. The former is classified with high confidence as a distributed attack in which IP spoofing was not used, while the researchers postulated that the latter was an attack from multiple machines on the same subnetwork, using subnet spoofing.

The researchers then applied spectral analysis on the packet arrival times to their data, on the hypothesis that it would allow them to distinguish single-sourced attacks from multisourced attacks, despite the use of spoofing. To simplify their idea, spectral analysis measures how similar the traffic is to itself over time. Single-sourced attacks were hypothesized to show a high similarity under spectral analysis for the entire course of the attack, even at very high data sampling rates, while multisourced attacks would show variations at high enough sampling rates of the data.

Using the 67 previously classified attacks, the researchers determined that there were indeed characteristically different spectra for the two types of attacks. Single-sourced attacks had dominant high frequencies, while multisourced attacks had dominant low frequencies. Reflector attacks showed their own characteristic spectral behavior. They confirmed these results by applying the techniques to a smaller second set of data gathered from USC's network, and by running experimental DoS attacks, capturing the packets, and using the techniques on these.

The paper discusses use of the techniques for detecting attacks and characterizing them in a live detection and defense system. For the purposes of this appendix, the important points are that they give a per-ISP view of the frequency of significant DoS attacks (around 80 in three months) and they point out that single-sited DoS attacks were still common at the time they performed their study, five months between mid-2002 and early 2003.

C.4   Observations and Experiences Tracking Denial-of-Service Attacks across a Regional ISP

Researchers associated with the University of Michigan were able to observe all network activity on a regional ISP that offered service to most of the state of Michigan's educational institutions for an extended period. They used *Netflow* to sample packets from this network and looked for misuse patterns. They gathered data for six months. Unfortunately, this data has not been collated into a formal publication, to date, but a Powerpoint presentation delivered in May 2001 that was based on the data is available on Arbor Networks' Web site, `http://www.arbornetworks.com/downloads/research37/nanogSlides4.pdf`. This discussion is based on that presentation.

Overall, the researchers observed nearly 2,000 DoS attacks in the six months covered by their study. Around 75% of the attacks flowed from their network to the outside world, with the remainder being directed at targets attached to their ISP. (Not surprisingly, given that the ISPs major customers were schools and universities, there was a strong correlation between the frequency of attacks and the academic year.) They observed an average of 12 attacks per day, significantly more than was observed in the USC/ISI study.

These researchers observed flooding attacks based on various kinds of TCP, ICMP, and UDP packets. Some attacks clearly were performing fully random IP spoofing, while others were spoofing within a /24 subnet. Analysis of the packets allowed the researchers to deduce that a number of well-known DDoS toolkits were being used by attackers.

Over the course of the study, the researchers observed increasing sophistication on the part of the attackers. Subnet spoofing attacks dominated fully random spoofing attacks by a 3 to 1 ratio. 60–90% of the attacks they observed lasted 15 minutes or less, but, like the CAIDA/ UCSD study, they observed some very long-lasting attacks.

In terms of magnitude, the largest 5% of the attacks they observed filled the pipes of their ISP, indicating that these attacks probably caused serious trouble for many people other than the target.

The targets of the attacks varied, with .net, .com, and .edu addresses dominating. Again, this finding is largely consistent with the CAIDA/UCSD results. Also like the CAIDA/UCSD study, they found many attacks were targeted at autonomous systems that provided cable modem or DSL services to home customers.

This study turned up a much higher incidence of DDoS attacks than the USC/ISI study—2,000 in six months versus 80 in three months. One possible explanation for the difference is that the USC/ISI study was unable to capture data from all points in the ISP under consideration. It is also likely that the ISP studied here was larger in scope than the ISP studied by USC/ISI. On the other hand, the presentation of the data from the Michigan regional study is somewhat sketchy, so it is hard to find the same level of detail as in the USC/ISI study. Thus, from only these two data points, it is hard to generalize whether your ISP will see 25 to 30 attacks per month or, more likely, 350 per month.

While it is tempting to compare the results of this study (11 attacks per day) with the results of the backscatter study (20 attacks per hour), these datasets were obtained at a different time, using different techniqes, and are not directly comparable. The University of Michigan study observed only attacks that were either (1) launched from compromised hosts within their network, or (2) were sourced from outside their network and targetting victim systems within their network, while the CAIDA backscatter study observed only the effects of attacks that used random spoofing and required the victim to generate a reply. It is obvious that while both studies can advance our knowledge of current trends in the DDoS field, neither of them can yield high-confidence estimates of attack frequency. At best, we get a lower bound on the frequency of specific attack types, but no data on how prevalent these types of attacks are as opposed to other types. There is promise in future research that combines both of these sources of data: actual attack traffic from DDoS agents and blackhole monitor data.

This presentation suggests that the researchers, some of whom are now associated with Arbor Networks, are deploying their observation technology in other networks, and have observed an increase in attack severity and sophistication. They also suggest that they are observing more attacks directed against network infrastructure, though this presentation provides few details.

C.5   Report on the DDoS Attack on the DNS Root Servers

Paul Vixie, Gerry Neeringer, and Mark Schleifer, who run three of the DNS root servers, wrote a brief report on what they observed and were able to deduce about the DDoS attack on the DNS root servers. There are other reports available on details of particular DDoS attacks, but the nature of this attack makes it of more general interest.

As stated earlier, the attack occurred on October 21, 2002. It lasted for a little over an hour. Each root server was attacked with a volume of between 50 and 100 Mbps, with a total attack volume of something like 900 Mbps, which translates to around 1.8 Mpackets/sec. The attack traffic was a mixture of protocols, including ICMP, TCP SYNs, TCP fragments, and UDP. The attack was synchronized to attack all 13 DNS root servers, making it clear that it was completely intentional.

The attack used randomized IP spoofing, with some care taken to ensure that nonroutable addresses tended not to be chosen.

The authors indicate that some of the root name servers became unreachable from parts of the Internet due to congestion effects, either close to the servers or further upstream. None of the servers were overwhelmed in the sense that they could not answer all queries that were delivered to them, but some servers did not receive all queries that were sent to them, again due to congestion.

Some of the root servers were continuously reachable from virtually all monitoring locations for the entire duration of the attack. These servers achieved their immunity by overprovisioning their networks, so that the flood did not congest their pipes or any pipes in their vicinity.

No users reported any problems receiving DNS root service during the attack, which is not surprising. In the first place, most DNS requests rely on caching to avoid trips to these servers. Also, since some of the servers were available continuously from all locations, the system's design would reroute queries to those servers eventually, leading to a few seconds' delay, rather than failure.

One point the report makes is that the entire attack might have gone unnoticed, were it not for automatic monitoring tools that quickly made the increase in traffic obvious. This point suggests that if you are not already running some kind of network monitoring on your local network, you should start doing so. Otherwise, it may take you some time to determine that problems you are experiencing are due to DDoS attack, rather than some other failure or attack.

Finally, the authors and other authorities who run the DNS root servers took this attack to heart, even though it did not cripple their vital service. They have taken important measures to protect their systems against future attacks, including widespread mirroring of the content and ensuring that there is sufficient topological and geographic diversity in root server locations so that no attacks on a small set of network choke points can cripple the service. We should all take a lesson from their prudence and take similar proactive steps to protect our networks before they succumb to a DDoS attack.

This report can be found on line at `http://d.root-servers.org/october21.txt`.

C.6   Conclusion

The preceding sections describe the bulk of the publicly available data on the frequency, size, duration, and character of DDoS attacks. (More data exists from studies that are not available to the public.) Much of it is a few years old. There is only one group known to the authors to be doing continued backscatter analysis using an unused /8 network over a long period of time (see `http://monkey.org/~jose/presentations/ddos.d/`). Similar sources of data have not been widely available to date, and this has made research very difficult to pursue. This situation is expected to change as a result of an HSARPA-funded project to collect various types of data for analysis and testing purposes. (See `http://www.computerworld.com/securitytopics/security/story/0,10801,96011 ,00.html`)

But it is a fair bet that attacks are no less common. It is clear, as well, that the sophistication of attacks is increasing. The data from these various studies also make clear that DDoS attacks target a wide range of systems, from home users on dial-up lines, to large businesses, to important pieces of the Internet's infrastructure.

References

[ABKM01] D.G. Andersen, H. Balakrishnan, M.F. Kaashoek, and R. Morris, "Resilient Overlay Networks," *Proceedings of 18th ACM Symposium on Operating Systems Principles (SOSP 2001)*, October 2001, pp. 131–145.

[ACF+99] J. Allen, A. Christie, W. Fithen, J. McHugh, J. Pickel, and E. Stoner, *State of the Practice of Intrusion Detection Technologies*, Technical Report CMU/SEI-99-TR-028, Software Engineering Institute, 1999.

[Ada80] D. Adams, *Hitchhiker's Guide to the Galaxy*, Harmony Books, 1980.

[Adl02] M. Adler, "Tradeoffs in Probabilistic Packet Marking for IP Traceback," *Proceedings of the 34th annual ACM Symposium on Theory of Computing*, ACM Press, 2002, pp. 407–418.

[AJ] A. Jesdanun, "New computer Virus Variant Floods Web Sites of Anti-Spam Activists," Associated Press, 3 Dec 2003, http://www.securityfocus.com/news/7575.

[AJB00] R. Albert, H. Jeong, and A.L. Barabási, "Error and Attack Tolerance in Complex Networks," *Nature*, vol. 406, no. 6794, July 2000, pp. 378–382.

[And02] M. Andress, "Denial of Service: Fighting Back," *Network World Fusion*, 2 Sep 2002, http://www.nwfusion.com/reviews/2002/0902rev.html.

[api04] *Revision of the Computer Misuse Act: Report of an Inquiry by the All Party Internet Group*, June 2004. The report and background files are available at http://www.apig.org.uk /computer_misuse_act_inquiry.htm.

[Bar64] P. Baran, *On distributed communications*, Memoranda RM-3420-PR, RM-3103-PR, RM-3578-PR, RM-3638-PR, RM-3097-PR, RM-3762-PR, RM-3763-PR, RM-3764-PR, RM-3765-PR, RM-3766-PR, RM-3767-PR, RAND Corporation, August 1964.

[Bar02] A.L. Barabási, *LINKED: The New Science of Networks*, Perseus Books, 2002.

[BBC$^+$04] A. Bavier, M. Bowman, B. Chun, D. Culler, S. Karlin, S. Muir, L. Peterson, T. Roscoe, T. Spalink, and M. Wawrzoniak, "Operating System Support for Planetary-Scale Network Services," *Proceedings of the USENIX First Symposium on Networked Systems Design and Implementation (NSDI 2004)*, March 2004, pp. 253–266.

[Bej04] R. Bejtlich, *The Tao of Network Security Monitoring: Beyond Intrusion Detection*, Addison-Wesley, 2004.

[Bell] D.E. Bell and L.J. LaPadula, *Secure Computer Systems: Mathematical Foundations and Model*, Technical Report M74-244, The MITRE Corp., Bedford, MA, 1973.

[Bid05] H. Bidgoli Ed., *The Handbook of Information Security*, John Wiley & Sons, 2005.

[BCC$^+$98] B. Braden, D. Clark, J. Crowcroft, B. Davie, S. Deering, D. Estrin, S. Floyd, V. Jacobson, G. Minshall, C. Partridge, L. Peterson, K. Ramakrishnan, S. Shenker, J. Wroclawski, and L. Zhang, "Recommendations on Queue Management and Congestion Avoidance in the Internet," IETF RFC 2309, April 1998, `http://www.ietf.org/rfc/rfc2309.txt`.

[bDD02] D. Dittrich (modified application), *tcpdstat (uw mods)*, 2002, `http://staff.washington.edu/dittrich/misc/core02/tcpdstat-uw.tgz`.

[Bel03] S. Bellovin, "The Security Flag in the IPv4 header," IETF RFC 3514, April 2003, `http://www.ietf.org/rfc/rfc3514.txt`.

[Ber] D.J. Bernstein, "SYN Cookies," `http://cr.yp.to/syncookies.html`.

[Bin00] BindView Corp., "The Naptha DoS Vulnerabilty," November 2000, `http://www.bindview.com/Support/RAZOR/Advisories/2000/adv_NAPTHA.cfm`.

[BK01] D. Brezinski and T. Killalea, "Guidelines for Evidence Collection and Archiving," IETF RFC 3227, February 2002, also Best Current Practice 55, `http://www.ietf.org/rfc/rfc3227.txt`.

[BLT01] S. Bellovin, M. Leech, and T. Taylor, "ICMP Traceback Messages," Internet draft, work in progress, October 2001.

[BN] M. Ward, "Interpol Patrols the Web," BBC Online News, 30 Jun 2000, `http://news.bbc.co.uk/1/hi/sci/tech/812764.stm`.

[Bon97] V.J. Bono, "7007 Explanation and Apology," April 1997. Appears in NANOG mailing list, `http://www.merit.edu/mail.archives/nanog/1997-04/msg00444.html`.

[Boy] Col J.R. Boyd, "Boyd's OODA loop" from "the Essence of Winning and Losing," `http://www.d-n-i.net/fcs/ppt/boyds_ooda_loop.ppt`.

[BR00] D. Bruschi and E. Rosti, "Disarming Offense to Facilitate Defense," *Proceedings of the New Security Paradigms Workshop (NSPW 2000)*, ACM Press, September 2000, pp. 69–75.

[BR01] D. Bruschi and E. Rosti, "AngeL: A Tool to Disarm Computer Systems," *Proceedings of the New Security Paradigms Workshop (NSPW 2001)*, ACM Press, September 2001, pp. 63–69.

[BRK02] S. Byers, A.D. Rubin, and D. Kormann, "Defending against an Internet-Based Attack on the Physical World," *Proceedings of the 2002 ACM workshop on Privacy in the Electronic Society*, ACM Press, November 2002, pp. 11–18.

[Bru] D. Brumley, *RID*, http://packetstormsecurity.nl/distributed/rid-1_0.tgz.

[BS03] J. Bellardo and S. Savage, "802.11 Denial-of-Service Attacks: Real Vulnerabilities and Practical Solutions," *Proceedings of the 12th USENIX Security Symposium*, August 2003, pp. 15–28.

[Car04] H. Carvey, *Windows Forensics and Incident Recovery*, Addison-Wesley, 2004.

[CERa] CERT Coordination Center, "CERT Advisory CA 1997-28, IP Denial-of-Service Attacks," December 1997, http://www.cert.org/advisories/CA-1997-28.html.

[CERb] CERT Coordination Center, "CERT Advisory CA 1999-17, Denial-of-Service Tools," December 1999, http://www.cert.org/advisories/CA-1999-17.html.

[CERc] CERT Coordination Center, "Handbook for computer security incident response teams (CSIRTS)," December 1998; revised April 2003, http://www.cert.org/archive/pdf/csirt-handbook.pdf.

[CERd] CERT Coordination Center, "How the FBI Investigates Computer Crime," http://www.cert.org/tech_tips/FBI_investigates_crime.html.

[CERe] CERT Coordination Center, Web page, http://www.cert.org/.

[CER96] CERT Coordination Center, "CERT Advisory CA 1996-21, TCP SYN Flooding and IP Spoofing Attacks," September 1996; revised November 2000, http://www.cert.org/advisories/CA-1996-21.html.

[CER98a] CERT Coordination Center, "CERT Advisory CA 1998-13, Vulnerability in Certain TCP/IP Implementations," December 1998, http://www.cert.org/advisories/CA-1998-13.html.

[CER98b] CERT Coordination Center, "CERT Summary CS 1998-02, SPECIAL EDITION—Denial of Service Attacks Targeting Windows 95/NT Machines," March 1998, http://www.cert.org/summaries/CS-98.02.html.

[CER99] CERT Coordination Center, "Results of the Distributed-Systems Intruder Tools Workshop," December 1999, http://www.cert.org/reports/dsit_workshop-final.html.

[CER00] CERT Coordination Center, "CERT Advisory CA 2000-21, Denial-of-Service Vulnerabilities in TCP/IP Stacks," November 2000, http://www.cert.org/advisories/CA-2000-21.html.

[CER01a] CERT Coordination Center, "CERT Advisory CA 2001-19, "Code Red" Worm Exploiting Buffer Overflow in Its Indexing Service DLL," January 2001, http://www.cert.org/advisories/CA-2001-19.html.

[CER01b] CERT Coordination Center, "CERT Incident Note IN 2000-05, "Mstream" Distributed Denial of Service Tool," May 2000, http://www.cert.org/incident_notes/IN-2000-05.html.

[CER01c] CERT Coordination Center, "CERT Incident Note IN 2001-07, W32/Leaves: Exploitation of previously installed SubSeven Trojan Horses," July 2001, http://www.cert.org/incident_notes/IN-2001-07.html.

[CER03] CERT Coordination Center, "CERT Advisory CA 2003-08, Increased Activity Targeting Windows Shares," March 2003, http://www.cert.org/advisories/CA-2003-08.html.

[CER04] CERT Coordination Center, "SiLK: System for Internet-Level Knowledge," 2004, http://www.cert.org/analysis/silk.html.

[Cho00] K. Cho, K. Mitsuya, and A. Kato, "Traffic data repository at the WIDE project," *Proceedings of the USENIX Annual Technical Conference*, June 2000, pp. 263-270, http://citeseer.ist.psu.edu/cho00traffic.html.

[CIPS] Computer Crime and U.S. Department of Justice Intellectual Property Section, Criminal Division, "Searching and Seizing Computers and Obtaining Electronic Evidence in Criminal Investigations," http://www.cybercrime.gov/searchmanual.pdf.

[CKK] K. Cho, R. Kaizaki, and A. Kato, "Aguri: An Aggregation-Based Traffic Profiler," *Proceedings of the Second International Workshop on Quality of Future Internet Services*, LNCS 2156, Springer Verlag, September 2001, pp. 222-242, ftp://ftp.csl.sony.co.jp/pub/kjc/papers/aguri.ps.gz.

[CL03] Z. Chen and M.C. Lee, "An IP Traceback Technique against Denial-of-Service Attacks," *Proceedings of 19th Annual Computer Security Applications Conference(ACSAC 2003)*, December 2003, pp. 96–105.

[CMK+03] D.L. Cook, W.G. Morein, A.D. Keromytis, V. Misra, and D. Rubenstein, "WebSOS: Protecting Web Servers from DDoS attacks," *Proceedings of the 11th IEEE International Conference on Networks (ICON 2003)*, September 2003, pp. 455–460.

[CN] C. Nuttall, "Crime Gangs Extort Money with Hacking Threat," *The Financial Times*, 11 Dec 2003, http://www.rense.com/general44/hack.htm.

[CNN] CNN, "FBI Web Site Hacked Last Week," 26 Feb 2000, http://www.cnn.com/2000/TECH/computing/02/26/fbi.hackers/.

[Con] Internet2 Consortium, Internet 2 Web page, http://www.internet2.edu/.

[CR04] M. Collins and M.K. Reiter, "An Empirical Analysis of Target-Resident DoS Filters." *Proceedings of IEEE Symposium on Security and Privacy*, May 2004, pp. 103–114.

[CW03] S.A. Crosby and D.S. Wallach, "Denial of Service via Algorithmic Complexity Attacks," *Proceedings of 12th USENIX Security Symposium*, August 2003, pp. 29–44.

[Del] M. Delio, "Microsoft Crashes: The Fallout," *Wired News*, 26 Jan 2001, http://www.wired.com/news/business/0,1367,41454,00.html.

[Dev] The Cygwin Developers, *The Cygwin GNU development environment for Windows*, http://www.cygwin.com.

[DFS01] D. Dean, M. Franklin, and A. Stubblefield, "An Algebraic Approach to IP Traceback," *Proceedings of the Network and Distributed System Security Symposium (NDSS)*, February 2001, pp. 3–12.

[DFS02] D. Dean, M. Franklin, and A. Stubblefield, "An Algebraic Approach to IP Traceback," *ACM Transactions on Information and System Security (TISSEC)*, vol. 5, no. 2, 2002, pp. 119–137.

[Die01] S. Dietrich, "Survivability with a Twist," *USENIX ;login: Security Issue*, November 2001, http://www.usenix.org/publications/login/2001-11/pdfs/dietrich.pdf.

[Dita] D. Dittrich, "Analysis of the "Power" Bot," August 2001, http://staff.washington.edu/dittrich/misc/power.analysis.txt.

[Ditb] D. Dittrich, "Basic Steps in Forensic Analysis of UNIX Systems," 2001, http://staff.washington.edu/dittrich/misc/forensics/.

[Ditc] D. Dittrich, "Developing an Effective Incident Cost Analysis Mechanism," *Security Focus*, 12 Jun 2002, http://online.securityfocus.com/infocus/1592.

[Ditd] D. Dittrich, "Distributed Denial of Service (DDoS) Attacks/Tools," 2000, http://staff.washington.edu/dittrich/misc/ddos/.

[Dite] D. Dittrich, "Estimating the Cost of Damages Due to a Security Incident," 2000, http://staff.washington.edu/dittrich/misc/faqs/incidentcosts.faq.

[Ditf] D. Dittrich, "The DoS Project's Trinoo Distributed Denial of Service Attack Tool," October 1999, http://staff.washington.edu/dittrich/misc/trinoo.analysis.txt.

[Ditg] D. Dittrich, "The Stacheldraht Distributed Denial of Service Attack Tool," December 1999, http://staff.washington.edu/dittrich/misc/stacheldraht.analysis.txt.

[Dith] D. Dittrich, "The Tribe Flood Network Distributed Denial of Service Attack Tool," October 1999, http://staff.washington.edu/dittrich/misc/tfn.analysis.txt.

[Dit01] D. Dittrich, "Analysis of SSH CRC32 Compensation Attack Detector Exploit," November 2001, http://staff.washington.edu/dittrich/misc/ssh-analysis.txt.

[DLD00] S. Dietrich, N. Long, and D. Dittrich, "Analyzing Distributed Denial of Service Tools: The Shaft Case," *Proceedings of 14th USENIX Systems Administration Conference (LISA 2000)*, December 2000, pp. 329–339, http://www.adelphi.edu/~spock/lisa2000-shaft.pdf.

[DMS04] R. Dingledine, N. Mathewson, and P. Syverson, "Tor: The Second-Generation Onion Router," *Proceedings of the 13th USENIX Security Symposium*, August 2004, pp. 303–320, http://freehaven.net/tor/tor-design.pdf.

[DWDL] D. Dittrich, G. Weaver, S. Dietrich, and N. Long, "The Mstream Distributed Denial of Service Attack Tool," May 2000, http://staff.washington.edu/dittrich/misc/mstream.analysis.txt.

[Eag03] C. Eagle, "Strike/counter-strike: Reverse Engineering Shiva," Proceedings of BlackHat Federal 2003, October 2003, http://www.blackhat.com/presentations/bh-federal-03/bh-federal-03-eagle/bh-fed-03-eagle.pdf.

[EFL+99] R.J. Ellison, D.A. Fisher, R.C. Linger, H.F. Lipson, T.A. Longstaff, and N.R. Mead, "Survivability: Protecting your critical systems," *IEEE Internet Computing*, vol. 3, no. 6, 1999, pp. 55–63.

[el] SANS UNISOG e-mail list, Thread on Register.com DNS Attack, http://staff.washington.edu/dittrich/misc/ddos/register.com-unisog.txt.

[Ele] Electronic Privacy Information Center, *The Gramm-Leach-Bliley Act*, http://www.epic.org/privacy/glba/.

[eur04] EURIM Group, *Working paper 4: Roles and Procedures for Investigation*, May 2004, http://www.eurim.org/consult/e-crime/dec03/ECS_WP4_web_031209.htm.

[fbi] FBI Los Angeles field office, Web page, http://losangeles.fbi.gov/.

[Fis03] D. Fisher, "Thwarting the Zombies," *eWeek*, March 31, 2003.

[Flo00] S. Floyd, "Congestion Control Principles," IETF RFC 2914, September 2000, http://www.ietf.org/rfc/rfc2914.txt.

[fra] C. Doyle, "Cybercrime: A sketch of 18 U.S.C. §1030 and Related Federal Criminal Laws," http://www.ipmall.info/hosted_resources/crs/RS20830_031124.pdf.

[FS00] P. Ferguson and D. Senie, "Network Ingress Filtering: Defeating Denial of Service Attacks which Employ IP Source Address Spoofing," IETF RFC 2827, May 2000, http://www.ietf.org/rfc/rfc2827.txt.

[FSBK03] L. Feinstein, D. Schnackenberg, R. Balupari, and D. Kindred, "Statistical Approaches to DDoS Attack Detection and Response," *Proceedings of 3rd DARPA Information Survivability Conference and Exposition (DISCEX 2003)*, April 2003, pp. 303–314.

[Gam] G. Byrne, "Security Issues of Online Gaming," *GameDev.net*, http://www.gamedev.net/reference/articles/article2062.asp.

[GCD⁺04] C. Gates, M. Collins, M. Duggan, A. Kompanek, and M. Thomas, "More Netflow Tools for Performance and Security," *Proceedings of the 18th USENIX Large Installation System Administration Conference (LISA 2004)*, November 2004.

[GMP04] K. Giles, D. Marchette, and C. Priebe, "On the Spectral Analysis of Backscatter Data," *Proceedings of the 2004 Hawaii International Conference on Statistics, Mathematics, and Related Fields*, June 2004.

[GMR01] B.W. Gemberling, C.L. Morrow, and B.R. Greene, "ISP Security: Real World Techniques," October 2001, http://www.nanog.org/mtg-0110/greene.html.

[GOM03] T.H. Grubesic, M.E. O'Kelly, and A.T. Murray, "A Geographic Perspective on Commercial Internet Survivability," *Telematics and Informatics*, vol. 20, no. 1, February 2003, pp. 51–69.

[Gra] P. Gray, "DDoS Attack Cripples Uecomm's AU links," *ZDNet*, 20 Mar 2003, http://www.zdnet.com.au/news/security/0,2000061744,20273027,00.htm.

[Gre02] B. Greene, *BGPv4 Security Risk Assessment*, Cisco white paper, June 200, http://www.cymru.com/Documents/barry2.pdf.

[Har] A. Harrison, "Cyberassaults Hit Buy.com, eBay, CNN, and Amazon.com," *Computerworld*, 9 Feb 2000, http://www.computerworld.com/news/2000/story/0,11280,43010,00.html.

[Har68] G. Hardin. "The Tragedy of the Commons," *Science*, vol. 162, 1968, pp. 1243-1248.

[Hex01] H. HexXer, "CodeGreen." Appears in a mailing list and is available in the archives, 2001, http://archives.neohapsis.com/archives/vuln-dev/2001-q3/0575.html.

[Hon04] The Honeynet Project, *Know Your Enemy: Learning about Security Threats*, 2nd Edition, Addison-Wesley, 2004.

[HHP03] A. Hussain, J. Heidemann, and C. Papadopoulos, "A Framework for Classifying Denial of Service Attack," *Proceedings of ACM SIGCOMM 2003*, August 2003, pp. 99–110.

[Him04a] K.E. Himma, "The Ethics of Tracing Hacker Attacks through the Machines of Innocent Persons," *International Journal of Information Ethics*, 2004.

[Him04b] K.E. Himma, "Targeting the Innocent: Active Defense and the Moral Immunity of Innocent Persons from Aggression," *Journal of Information, Communication, and Ethics in Society*, vol. 2, no. 1, January 2004.

[hip] *Health Insurance Portability and Accountability Act (HIPAA)*, http://www.hipaa.org/.

[HMP⁺01] A. Householder, A. Manion, L. Pesante, G. Weaver, and R. Thomas, *Managing the Threat of Denial-of-Service Attacks*, Technical Report, CERT Coordination Center, October 2001, http://www.cert.org/archive/pdf/Managing_DoS.pdf.

[HWLT01] K.J. Houle, G.M. Weaver, N. Long, and R. Thomas, *Trends in Denial of Service Attack Technology*, Technical Report, CERT Coordination Center, October 2001, `http:/ /www.cert.org/archive/pdf/DoS_trends.pdf`.

[IAA] European Commission – Information Society, "Handbook of Legislative Procedures of Computer and Network Misuse in EU Countries," `http://europa.eu.int/information_ society/eeurope/2005/all_about/security/handbook/text_en.htm`.

[IB02] J. Ioannidis and S.M. Bellovin, "Implementing Pushback: Router-Based Defense Against DDoS Attacks," *Proceedings of Network and Distributed System Security Symposium (NDSS)*, February 2002, The Internet Society.

[Ins81a] Information Sciences Institute, "Internet Protocol," IETF RFC 791, September 1981, `http://www.ietf.org/rfc/rfc0791.txt`.

[Ins81b] Information Sciences Institute, "Transmission Control Protocol," IETF RFC 793, September 1981, `http://www.ietf.org/rfc/rfc0793.txt`.

[int] T.L. Putnam and D.D. Elliott, *International Responses to Cyber-crime*, Hover Press, `http:/ /www-hoover.stanford.edu/publications/books/fulltext/cybercrime/35.pdf`.

[itCD97] *Toward Deterrence in the Cyber Dimension*, Report to the President's Commission on Critical Infrastructure Protection, 1997, `http://www.timeusa.com/CIAO/resource/pccip /DeterrenceCyberDimension.pdf`.

[JB99] A. Juels and J. Brainard, "Client puzzles: A Cryptographic Countermeasure Against Connection Depletion Attacks," *Proceedings of the Networks and Distributed System Security Symposium (NDSS)*, March 1999, pp. 151–165.

[JKR02] J. Jung, B. Krishnamurthy, and M. Rabinovich, "Flash crowds And Denial of Service Attacks: Characterization and Implications for CDNS and Web Sites," *Proceedings of 11th International World Wide Web Conference*, May 2002, pp. 293–304.

[JL] J. Leyden, "Sobig linked to DDoS attacks on Anti-spam Sites," *The Register*, 25 Sep 2003, `http://www.theregister.co.uk/content/56/33059.html`.

[JM] M. Jakobsson and F. Menczer, "Untraceable E-mail Cluster Bombs: On Agent-Based Distributed Denial of Service," Preprint is available at `http://www.informatics.indiana .edu/markus/papers/0305042.pdf`.

[Jou00] F. Jou, "Design and Implementation of a Scalable Intrusion Detection System for the Protection of Network Infrastructure," *Proceedings of 1st DARPA Information Survivability Conference and Exposition (DISCEX 2000)*, vol 2, January 2000, pp. 69–83, `http:/ /projects.anr.mcnc.org/JiNao/jouy_reviewed.ps`.

[JPD] J.P. Davis, "The Experience of Bad Behavior in Online Social Spaces: A Survey of Online Users," Microsoft Research, Social Computing Group, `http://research.microsoft.com /scg/papers/Bad%20Behavior%20Survey.pdf`.

[JWS03] C. Jin, H. Wang, and K.G. Shin, "Hop-Count Filtering: An Effective Defense Against Spoofed DDoS Traffic," *Proceedings of the 10th ACM Conference on Computer and Communication Security*, ACM Press, October 2003, pp 30–41.

[KBE01] A.B. Kulkarni, S.F. Bush, and S.C. Evans, "Detecting Distributed Denial-of-Service Attacks Using Kolmogorov Complexity Metrics," Technical Report 2001CRD176, General Electric Research and Development Center, December 2001.

[KC] K. Coale, "Romanian Cracker Takes Down the Undernet," *Wired News*, 14 Jan 1997, http://www.wired.com/news/technology/0,1282,1446,00.html.

[Ker03] O.S. Kerr, "Cybercrime's Scope: Interpreting "Access" and "Authorization" in Computer Misuse Statutes," *NYU Law Review*, vol. 78, no. 5, November 2003, pp. 1596–1668, http://papers.ssrn.com/sol3/papers.cfm?abstract_id=399740#PaperDownload.

[Kes] G.C. Kessler, "Defenses Against Distributed Denial of Service Attacks," 2000, http://www.garykessler.net/library/ddos.html.

[Kle61] L. Kleinrock, *Information Flow in Large Communications Nets*, RLE Quarterly Progress Reports, July 1961.

[KLS00] S. Kent, C. Lynn, and K. Seo, "Secure Border Gateway Protocol (secure-bgp)," *IEEE Journal on Selected Areas in Communications*, vol. 18, no. 4, April 2000, pp. 582–592.

[KMR02] A.D. Keromytis, V. Misra, and D. Rubenstein, "SOS: Secure Overlay Services," *Proceedings of ACM SIGCOMM 2002*, August 2002, pp. 61–72.

[KP] K. Poulsen, SecurityFocus, "Rise of the Spam Zombies," *The Register*, 27 Apr 2003, http://www.theregister.co.uk/content/55/30414.html.

[Lab04] Kaspersky Labs, "SymbianOS-based Worm Cabir," June 2004, http://www.kaspersky.com/news?id=149499226.

[LC04] B. Laurie and R. Clayton, "Proof-of-Work Proves Not to Work," *Proceedings of the 3rd Annual Workshop on Economics and Information Security (WEIS 2004)*, March 2004, http://www.cl.cam.ac.uk/~rnc1/proofwork.pdf.

[Leb] J. Lebbenga, "European Betting Sites Brace for Attack," *The Register*, 28 Jun 2004, http://www.theregister.co.uk/2004/06/28/betting_sites_attack/print.html.

[Lem] R. Lemos, "Attack on SCO Sites at an End," *CNET News.com*, 12 Dec 2003, http://news.com.com/2100-7355_3-5121828.html?tag=nefd_top.

[Leya] J. Leyden, "Phatbot Arrest Throws Open Trade in Zombie PCS," *The Register*, 12 May 2004, http://www.theregister.co.uk/2004/05/12/phatbot_zombie_trade/.

[Leyb] J. Leyden, "Extortionists Attack ibetx.com," *The Register*, 18 Apr 2004, http://www.theregister.co.uk/2004/04/18/online_bookie_ddos/.

[LF00] H. Lipson and D. Fisher, "Survivability—A New Technical and Business Perspective on Security," *Proceedings of the New Security Paradigms Workshop (NSPW 1999)*, ACM Press, September 2000, pp. 33-39, http://www.cert.org/archive/pdf/busperspec.pdf.

[Lip02] H. Lipson, *Tracking and Tracing Cyber Attacks: Technical Challenges and Global Policy Issues*, Technical Report SR009, Software Engineering Institute, 2002, http://www.cert.org/archive/pdf/02sr009.pdf.

[LMW⁺01] J. Li, J. Mirkovic, M. Wang, P. Reiher, and L. Zhang, "SAVE: Source Address Validity Enforcement Protocol," Proceedings of IEEE INFOCOM 2002, March 2002, vol. 2, pp. 1557–1566.

[LTIG] LURHQ Threat Intelligence Group, "Phatbot Trojan Analysis," 15 Mar 2004, http://www.lurhq.com/phatbot.html.

[MB98] S.D. Mitchell and E.A. Banker, "Private Intrusion Response," *Harvard Journal of Law and Technology*, vol. 11, no. 3, Summer 1998, pp. 700–718, http://jolt.law.harvard.edu/articles/pdf/v11/11HarvJLTech699.pdf.

[MBF⁺02] R. Mahajan, S.M. Bellovin, S. Floyd, J. Ioannidis, V. Paxson, and S. Shenker, "Controlling High Bandwidth Aggregates in the Network," *ACM SIGCOMM Computer Communications Review*, vol. 32, no. 3, July 2002, pp. 62–73.

[McC03] J. McCormick, "2003 CSI/FBI Cybercrime Survey Shows Reduced Losses," *TechRepublic.com*, 23 Jun 2003.

[McH03] J. McHugh, "Locality: A New Paradigm for Thinking About Normal Behavior and Outsider Threat," *Proceedings of the New Security Paradigms Workshop (NSPW 2003)*, ACM Press, August 2003, pp. 3–10.

[Meh03] N. Mehta, "Advances in Elf Runtime Binary Encryption—Shiva," *Proceedings of BlackHat USA*, July 2003, http://www.blackhat.com/presentations/bh-usa-03/bh-us-03-mehta/bh-us-03-mehta.pdf.

[mid] *United States v. Middleton*, 231 F.3d 1207, 1210–11 (9th Cir. 2000), http://www.tomwbell.com/NetLaw/Ch09/USvMiddleton.html.

[Mir03] J. Mirkovic, *D-WARD: Source-End Defense Against Distributed Denial-of-Service Attacks*, PhD thesis, University of California Los Angeles, August 2003, http://lasr.cs.ucla.edu/ddos/dward-thesis.pdf.

[MK03] M, Kotadia, "11,000 IP addresses found on accused hacker's PC," *ZDNet UK*, 8 Oct 2003, http://news.zdnet.co.uk/internet/security/0,39020375,39117005,00.htm.

[MPR02] J. Mirkovic, G. Prier, and P. Reiher, "Attacking DDoS at the Source," *Proceedings of the 10th International Conference on Network Protocols (ICNP 2002)*, November 2002, pp. 312–322.

[MRR03] J. Mirkovic, M. Robinson, P. Reiher, and G. Kuenning, "Forming Alliance for DDoS Defenses, *Proceedings of the New Security Paradigms Workshop (NSPW 2003)*, ACM Press, August 2003, pp. 11–18.

[MS03] D. Moore and C. Shannon, *SCO Offline from Denial of Service Attack*, Technical Report, CAIDA, December 2003, `http://www.caida.org/analysis/security/sco-dos/`.

[MSC+03] W.G. Morein, A. Stavrou, D.L. Cook, A.D. Keromytis, V. Misra, and D. Rubenstein, "Using Graphic Turing Tests to Counter Automated DDoS Attacks Against Web Servers," *Proceedings of the 10th ACM conference on Computer and Communication Security*, ACM Press, October 2003, pp. 8–19.

[MV02] V. Mittal and G. Vigna, "Sensor-Based Intrusion Detection for Intra-Domain Distance-Vector Routing," *Proceedings of the 9th ACM Conference on Computer and Communication Security*, ACM Press, November 2002, pp. 127–137, `http://www.cs.ucsb.edu/vigna/pub/2002_mittal_vigna_ccs02.pdf`.

[MvOV96] A.J. Menezes, P.C. van Oorschot, and S.A. Vanstone, *Handbook of Applied Cryptography*, CRC Press, 1996.

[MVS01] D. Moore, G. Voelker, and S. Savage, "Inferring Internet Denial-of-Service Activity," *Proceedings of the 10th USENIX Security Symposium*, August 2001, pp. 9–22.

[Nag84] J. Nagle, "Congestion Control in IP/TCP," IETF RFC 896, January 1984, `http://www.ietf.org/rfc/rfc0896.txt`.

[Nar] R. Naraine, "Massive DDoS Attack Hit DNS Root Servers," *internetnews.com*, 23 Oct 2002, `http://www.internetnews.com/dev-news/article.php/1486981`.

[Naz03] J. Nazario, *Defense and Detection Strategies against Internet Worms*, Artech House, 2003.

[NIoJa] National Institute of Justice, *Electronic Crime Scene Investigation: A Guide for First Responders*, NCJ 187736, July 2001, `http://www.ncjrs.org/pdffiles1/nij/187736.pdf`.

[NIoJb] National Institute of Justice, *Forensic Examination of Digital Evidence: A Guide for Law Enforcement*, NCJ 199408, April 2004, `http://www.ncjrs.org/pdffiles1/nij/199408.pdf`.

[NIP01] NIPC/MITRE, *find_ddos host scanner*, 2001. Cited in NIPC Advisory on TRI-NOO/Tribal Flood Net/tfn2k.

[O'B] E. O'Brien. "NetBouncer: A Practical Client-Legitimacy-Based DDoS Defense via Ingress Filtering," `http://www.networkassociates.com/us/_tier0/nailabs/_media/documents/netbouncer.pdf`.

[oE] The Council of Europe, *Convention on Cybercrime*, Technical Report.

[oECFL] U.S. Department of Energy Computer Forensic Laboratory, *First Responder's Manual*, `http://www.linuxsecurity.com/resource_files/documentation/firstres.pdf`.

[Oet]   T. Oetiker, *MRTG: Multi-Router Traffic Grapher*, `http://people.ee.ethz.ch/~oetiker` `/webtools/mrtg/`.

[oIC]   Committee on Institutional Cooperation, *ICAMP study reports*, `http://www.cic.uiuc` `.edu/groups/cic/listicampreports.shtml`.

[oJa]   U.S. Department of Justice, *Field guidance on new authorities (redacted), enacted in the 2001 anti-terrorism legislation (USA Patriot Act)*, `http://www.epic.org/privacy/terrorism` `/DOJ_guidance.pdf`.

[oJb]   U.S Department of Justice, *Federal guidelines for searching and seizing computers*, `http:/` `/www.usdoj.gov/criminal/cybercrime/searching.html`.

[Ope]   North American Network Operators, NANOG Website, `http://www.nanog.org/`.

[Pax01] V. Paxson, "An Analysis of Using Reflectors for Distributed Denial-of-Service Attacks," *ACM SIGCOMM Computer Communications Review*, vol. 31, no. 3, July 2001, pp. 38-47.

[pcc97] *Adequacy of Criminal Law and Procedure (Cyber), a "Legal Foundations" study—Report 7 of 12*, Report to the President's Commission on Critical Infrastructure Protection, 1997, `http://www.timeusa.com/CIAO/resource/pccip/lf07.pdf`.

[Per02] C. Perkins, "IP Mobility Support for IPv4," IETF RFC 3344, August 2002, `http://www` `.ietf.org/rfc/rfc3344.txt`.

[PF]   P. Festa, "Hackers Attack NASA, Navy," *CNET News.com*, 4 Mar 1998, `http:/` `/digitalcity.com.com/2100-1001-208692.html?legacy=cnet`.

[PL01] K. Park and H. Lee, "On the Effectiveness of Route-Based Packet Filtering for Distributed DoS Attack Prevention in Power-Law Internets," *Proceedings of ACM SIGCOMM 2001*, August 2001, pp. 15–26.

[PLM⁺03] C. Papadopoulos, R. Lindell, J. Mehringer, A. Hussain, and R. Govindan, "Cossack: Coordinated Suppression of Simultaneous Attacks," *Proceedings of 3rd DARPA Information Survivability Conference and Exposition (DISCEX 2003)*, vol. 2, April 2003, pp. 94–96.

[PN98] T.H. Ptacek and T.N. Newsham, *Insertion, Evasion, and Denial of Service: Eluding Network Intrusion Detection*, Technical Report, Secure Networks, Inc., January 1998.

[Pos80] J. Postel, "User Datagram Protocol," IETF RFC 768, August 1980, `http://www.ietf` `.org/rfc/rfc0768.txt`.

[Pos81] J. Postel, "Internet Control Message Protocol," IETF RFC 792, September 1981, `http:` `//www.ietf.org/rfc/rfc0792.txt`.

[Pro]   The Honeynet Project, "The forensic challenge," `http://www.honeynet.org/challenge/`.

[Pro03] N. Provos, "Improving Host Security with System Call Policies," *Proceedings of the 12th USENIX Security Symposium*, August 2003, pp. 257–272.

[Pro04] N. Provos, "A Virtual Honeypot Framework," *Proceedings of the 13th USENIX Security Symposium*, August 2004, pp. 1–14. A preprint is avaiable as CITI-TR-03-1 at `http://www.citi.umich.edu/techreports/reports/citi-tr-03-1.pdf`.

[Reg] J. Leyden, "UK Teenager Accused of Electronic Sabotage Against us Port," *The Register*, 6 Oct 2003, `http://www.theregister.co.uk/2003/10/06/uk_teenager_accused_of_electronic/`.

[Ric] D. Richman, "Internet Attack Slows Web to a Crawl," *Seattle Post-Intelligencer*, 18 Jan 2000, `http://seattlepi.nwsource.com/local/smrf18.shtml`.

[Rob] P. Roberts, "Al-Jazeera Hobbled by DDoS Attack: News Site Targetted for Second Day," *InfoWorld*, 26 Mar 2003, `http://www.infoworld.com/article/03/03/26/HNjazeera_1.html`.

[rou97] daemon9/route, "LOKI2: (the implementation)," *Phrack Magazine*, vol. 7, no. 51, September 1997.

[sar] Financial Crimes Enforcement Network, "Guidance on Preparing Complete and Sufficient Suspicious Activity Report Narrative," `http://www.irs.gov/pub/irs-tege/itg_sarc_prep.pdf`.

[Ser] Congressional Research Service, *Computer Attack and Cyber Terrorism: Vulnerabilities and Policy Issues for Congress*, `http://fpc.state.gov/documents/organization/26009.pdf`.

[Sha] N. Shachtman, "Porn Purveyors Getting Squeezed," *Wired News*, 10 Jul 2003, `http://www.wired.com/news/print/0,1294,59574,00.html`.

[SKK+97] C. Schuba, I. Krsul, M. Kuhn, G. Spafford, A. Sundaram, and D. Zamboni, "Analysis of a Denial of Service Attack on TCP," *Proceedings of the IEEE Symposium on Security and Privacy*, May 1997, pp. 208–223.

[Sko02] E. Skoudis. *Counter Hack: A Step-by-Step Guide to Computer Attacks and Effective Defenses*, Prentice Hall, 2002.

[SMJ00] M. Smart, R. Malan, and F. Jahanian, "Defeating TCP/IP Stack Fingerprinting," *Proceedings of the 9th USENIX Security Symposium*, August 2000.

[SMS+01] L. Sanchez, W. Milliken, A. Snoeren, F. Tchakountio, C. Jones, S. Kent, C. Partridge, and W. Strayer, "Hardware Support for a Hash-Based IP Traceback," Proceedings of the 2nd DARPA Information Survivability Conference and Exposition (DISCEX 2001), June 2001, pp. 146–152.

[Sou] Sourcefire, *Snort: The Open Source Network Intrusion Detection System*, `http://www.snort.org/`.

[Spa89] E.H. Spafford, "The internet worm program: an analysis," *ACM SIGCOMM Computer Communication Review*, vol. 19, no. 1, January 1989, p.17–57.

[SP98] J.R. Suler and W. Phillips, "The Bad Boys of Cyberspace: Deviant Behavior in Online Multimedia Communities and Strategies for Managing It," 1998, http://www.rider.edu /~suler/psycyber/badboys.html.

[SP01] D. X. Song and A. Perrig, "Advanced and Authenticated Marking Schemes for IP Traceback," *Proceedings of IEEE INFOCOM 2001*, vol. 2, March 2001, pp. 878–886.

[Spi02] L. Spitzner, *Honeypots: Tracking Hackers*, Addison-Wesley, 2002.

[SPS+01] A.C. Snoeren, C. Partridge, L.A. Sanchez, C.E. Jones, F. Tchakountio, S.T. Kent, and W.T. Strayer, "Hash-Based IP Traceback," *Proceedings of ACM SIGCOMM 2001*, August 2001, pp. 3–14.

[SPS+02] A. Snoeren, C. Partridge, L.A. Sanchez, C.E. Jones, F. Tchakountio, B. Schwartz, S.T. Kent, and W.T. Strayer, "Single-Packet IP Traceback," *IEEE/ACM Transactions on Networking*, 2002, pp. 721–734.

[SSSW] S. Shankland, "Computer Security Teams Brace for Attacks," *CNET News.com*, 20 Dec 1999, http://news.com.com/2100-1001-234678.html?legacy=cnet&tag=st.ne.1002.

[Sto89] C. Stoll, *The Cuckoo's Egg: tracking a spy through the maze of computer espionage*, Doubleday, 1989.

[SWKA00] S. Savage, D. Wetherall, A. Karlin, and T. Anderson, "Practical Network Support for IP Traceback," *Proceedings of ACM SIGCOMM 2000*, August 2000, pp. 295–306.

[Tea] Razor Team, *Zombie Zapper*, http://www.bindview.com/Support/RAZOR/Utilities /Unix_Linux/ZombieZapper_for m.cfm.

[Tes] Team Teso, *Burneye2 objobf - x86/Linux Elf Object Obfuscator*, http://teso.scene.at /projects/objobf/.

[Tho] R. Thomas, Team Cymru Web site, http://www.cymru.com/.

[Uni] European Union, *Handbook of Legislative Procedures of Computer and Network Misuse in EU Countries*, http://europa.eu.int/information_society/eeurope/2005/all_about /security/handbook/text_en.htm.

[USC] USC/ISI, DETER Project Web site, http://www.isi.edu/deter .

[vABHL03] L. von Ahn, M. Blum, N. Hopper, and J. Langford, "CAPTCHA: Using Hard AI Problems for Security," *Proceedings of the International Conference on the Theory and Applications of Cryptographic Techniques (EUROCRYPT 2003)*, May 2003, pp. 294–311.

[Val] Valinor, "Definition of IRC Channel Takeover," http://www.valinor.sorcery.net /glossary/channel-takeover.html.

[vLL] R. van Loon and J. Lo, "An IRC Tutorial," http://www.irchelp.org/irchelp /irctutorial.html.

[Wal02] M. Waldvogel, "GOSSIB vs. IP traceback rumors," *Proceedings of 18th Annual Computer Security Applications Conference (ACSAC 2002)*, December 2002, pp. 5–13.

[Wan00] C. Wang, *A Security Architecture for Survivability Mechanisms*, PhD thesis, Department of Computer Science, University of Virginia, October 2000, `citeseer.ist.psu.edu /wang00security.html`.

[Wat99] D.J. Watts, *Small Worlds: The Dynamics of Networks Between Order and Randomness*, Princeton University Press, 1999.

[Wik] Wikipedia, "Internet Trolling," Available at `http://en.wikipedia.org/wiki/Internet_ troll`.

[Wil02] M. Williamson, "Throttling viruses: Restricting Propagation to Defeat Malicious Mobile Code," *Proceedings of 18th Annual Computer Security Applications Conference (ACSAC 2002)*, December 2002, pp. 61–68.

[WLS⁺02] B. White, J. Lepreau, L. Stoller, R. Ricci, S. Guruprasad, M. Newbold, M. Hibler, C. Barb, and A. Joglekar, "An integrated experimental environment for distributed systems and networks," *Proceedings of the 5th Symposium on Operating Systems Design and Implementation (OSDI 2002)*, USENIX Association, December 2002, pp. 255–270.

[WR03] X. Wang and M. K. Reiter, "Defending Against Denial-of-Service Attacks with Puzzle Auctions," *Proceedings of the IEEE Symposium on Security and Privacy*, May 2003, pp. 78–92.

[Wright] G.R. Wright and R.W. Stevens, *TCP/IP Illustrated*, Vol. 2, Addison-Wesley, 1995.

[Wro02] G. Wroblewski, *General Method of Program Code Obfuscation*, PhD Thesis, Wroclaw University of Technology, Institute of Engineering Cybernetics, 2002.

[ws] NIPC Web site, "Former federal Court Systems Administrator Sentenced for Hacking into Government Computer System," `http://www.nipc.gov/pressroom/pressrel/dennis .htm`.

[YPS03] A. Yaar, A. Perrig, and D. Song, "Pi: A Path Identification Mechanism to Defend Against DDoS Attacks," *Proceedings of the IEEE Symposium on Security and Privacy*, May 2003, pp. 93–107.

[YPS04] A. Yaar, A. Perrig, and D. Song, "SIFF: a stateless Internet flow filter to mitigate DDoS flooding attacks," *Proceedings of the IEEE Symposium on Security and Privacy*, May 2004, pp. 130–143.

[Zal] M. Zalewski, "I Don't Think I Really Love You," or Writting [sic] Internet Worms for Fun and Profit, `http://seclists.org/lists/vuln-dev/2000/May/0159.html`.

[ZDn04] Reuters, "Scotland Yard and the Case of the Rent-a-Zombies," *ZDnet.com*, 7 Jul 2004, `http://zdnet.com.com/2100-1105_2-5260154.html`.

[Zor]   M. Zorz, Logerror, "Massive Distributed Denial of Service Attack Hits ClickBank and
        SpamCop.net,"   http://www.ds-osac.org/view.cfm?KEY=7E4452434452
        &type=2B170C1E0A3A0F162820, also available at http://www.ds-osac.org/view.cfm
        ?KEY=7E4452434452&type=2B170C1E0A3A0F162820

[ZPW+02] X. Zhao, D. Pei, L. Wang, D. Massey, A. Mankin, S.F. Wu, and L. Zhang, "Detection
        of Invalid Routing Announcement in the Internet," *Proceedings of International Conference
        on Dependable Systems and Networks (DSN 2002)*, June 2002, pp. 59–68.

Index

Register
Your Book

at www.awprofessional.com/register

You may be eligible to receive:

- Advance notice of forthcoming editions of the book
- Related book recommendations
- Chapter excerpts and supplements of forthcoming titles
- Information about special contests and promotions throughout the year
- Notices and reminders about author appearances, tradeshows, and online chats with special guests

Contact us

If you are interested in writing a book or reviewing manuscripts prior to publication, please write to us at:

Editorial Department
Addison-Wesley Professional
75 Arlington Street, Suite 300
Boston, MA 02116 USA
Email: AWPro@aw.com

Addison-Wesley

Visit us on the Web: http://www.awprofessional.com